*CONTEMPORARY
CONSTITUTIONAL
ISSUES*

other books by the author:

INTERPRETATION OF AMBIGUOUS DOCUMENTS BY
INTERNATIONAL ADMINISTRATIVE TRIBUNALS
(1964)

ALAN H. SCHECHTER Wellesley College

CONTEMPORARY CONSTITUTIONAL ISSUES

McGRAW-HILL BOOK COMPANY New York St. Louis San Francisco Düsseldorf
Johannesburg Kuala Lumpur London Mexico Montreal New Delhi Panama
Rio de Janeiro Singapore Sydney Toronto

For Kate, Andrew, and Stephen

*This book was set in Palatino
by Monotype Composition, Inc.,
and printed and bound
by George Banta Company, Inc.
The designer was Paula Tuerk.
The editors were Robert P. Rainier
and James R. Belser.
Matt Martino supervised production.*

CONTEMPORARY CONSTITUTIONAL ISSUES

CONTENTS

PREFACE

Like many political scientists who teach in the fields of American politics and of constitutional law, I have long wanted to offer my students an approach to contemporary political issues which stressed the interrelationship between the legal process and the political process but which did not confuse the two.

Traditionally, scholars believed that judicial decision making involved a set of activities which was separate and distinct from the way in which policies were shaped within political institutions. Law professors taught the case method, the use of legal argument, the function of precedents, but slighted the political origins of every major constitutional issue, the choice of litigation as a political option, the impact of external events on the courts, the role of judicial behavior, and, ultimately, the sociopolitical consequences of judicial decision making. Political science professors, charged with teaching their students about the nature of American politics, tended to focus on the "political" arenas, Congress, the Presidency, the executive departments, and approached judicial institutions with a marked degree of diffidence.

In the last decade or so, social scientists have begun to ask questions about constitutional issues which could not be answered satisfactorily within the framework of case-by-case legal analysis or within the context of interest-group politics. Both frames of reference have proved too narrow for questions about the role of law in the American political system.

Initially, criticism was directed at the case-method approach to law, partially because the critics were by and large political scientists and not law professors, but more significantly because the case method tended to convey the impression that legal decisions were essentially the outcome of intellectual exercises in syntactical conflict. Critics argued that legal training which focuses heavily on microscopic examination of syntax, terminology, and precedents runs a grave risk of turning those who have been subjected to it into "technicians of the law" rather than broad-gauged lawyers. To put the point in contemporary terms, the case method of analysis is no way to study the ecology of any particular constitutional issue!

Proponents of the case method answered that their critics had set up a straw man and proceeded to demolish him, as critics often do. They argued that the case method of analysis was never intended to be used for teaching a broad, functional view of the role of law in the political system; it was not designed for nor was it appropriate for such a purpose. When the case method was first introduced, according to this viewpoint, it was a great advance in the study of law because it replaced outmoded legalism—the study of constitutions, statutes, and rules of law—with a more realistic, dynamic, and stimulating approach. Ultimately, advocates of the case method believe their approach is important and useful because it adds elements of realism to the professional training of future lawyers, just as hospital work adds to the training of medical students even though experience treating individual patients does little to acquaint the student with fundamental questions about the role of medicine in the nation.

Leaving aside for the moment the question of how well the case-method approach does what its proponents claim it should do, let us focus on the "new vogue" introduced by academic critics of the method. Recent efforts to study the place of law and judicial institutions in the political system tend to be labeled "judicial behavior studies," although the title is somewhat misleading since judicial behaviorism ordinarily encompasses far more than the study of how and why judges act as they do. Judicial behaviorists have marked out a field for inquiry which includes the entire legal system and all its interrelated activities. The language of "systems analysis," as developed in political science by Professor David Easton, among others, figures prominently in such studies.[1] The boundaries of judicial behavior can be described, then, as including the study of "inputs" (e.g., how and why certain issues enter the legal system for resolution), "conversion" (e.g., how and why judicial decisions are reached), "outputs" (e.g., what decisions are reached), "feedback" (e.g., the impact of decisions, compliance problems, and further reconsideration by the decision makers).[2] Essentially, the behaviorist scholars focus on empirical study of what happens in the legal system, broadly defined, and why. The leading behaviorist scholars are not lawyers, and it is inevitable, perhaps, that they have tended to ignore or at least discount the role of traditional jurisprudence, the clash of legal and constitutional arguments that characterizes the adversary process.

It is my belief that the arguments employed by legal counsel in any constitutional case do affect the outcome of the case; otherwise, law schools are wasting their time teaching law students how to think and write logically and persuasively. In my judgment, the behaviorists, while making a valid and valuable point about the limitations of traditional jurisprudence, have overstated their case.

This book attempts to bridge the two worlds described above: It has a behavioristic orientation insofar as it focuses on the political origins of contemporary constitutional issues, on politics and interest-group conflict, on the factors which determine how, why, and in what form issues reach the courts as legal issues, on how and why the Supreme Court reaches, or refuses to reach, certain decisions, on the serious problems of implementation and compliance which invariably follow controversial rulings. It has a narrower orientation insofar as it includes legal arguments, citations to precedents, and other features commonly associated with the case-method approach to the study of constitutional law.

Since there are many casebooks on Supreme Court decisions, and I have deliberately attempted to avoid writing a casebook, this book contains few actual decisions. On the other hand, I have made an effort at one major modification of the case method of analysis: By providing full legal briefs arguing both sides of each constitutional issue discussed, I have attempted to correct what, in my opinion, is a significant flaw of the case-by-case approach to the study of law. Ordinarily, students are not asked to think through the possible arguments on both sides of a con-

---

[1] See David Easton, *The Political System*, Knopf, New York, 1953, and his subsequent work, including *A Systems Analysis of Political Life*, Wiley, New York, 1965.

[2] See Sheldon Goldman and Thomas Jahnige, "Systems Analysis and Judicial Systems: Potential and Limitations," 3 *Polity* 334–359, Spring 1971, for a thoughtful analysis of the literature in this field.

stitutional issue, but rather they are asked to read the text of the relevant decision; then, the teacher and his students attempt to reconstruct the arguments that might have been made and to analyze why some were persuasive and others were not. Not only is the cart put before the horse, but the cart is examined minutely and then an attempt is made to describe the horse on the basis of this examination! I hope that the legal briefs will stimulate the interest, intellectual involvement, and critical judgment of those who read the book.

In sum, this book focuses on a number of important contemporary issues which have recently been or will shortly be considered by the Supreme Court. In instances where the issue has already been the subject of a ruling by the Court, the chapter begins with a political analysis of the issue, followed by briefs for the appellant and appellee, excerpts from the decision, and finally, an analysis of the political repercussions of the decision. No effort has been made to reproduce the briefs actually filed with the Court; instead, all of the major arguments have been presented in a relatively short yet comprehensive form. As will be noted, pages containing the briefs have been divided into two columns, and the arguments on each constitutional point have been printed in parallel fashion.

Several of the chapters in the book concentrate on issues which have not yet reached the Supreme Court. In each of these chapters, the format is similar to the one outlined above, except that I have made up and briefed a hypothetical case and, of course, no decision follows the briefs. All these chapters conclude with an analysis of why the Court has not yet considered the issues involved, what is likely to happen when an actual controversy reaches the Court, and what would be the likely political consequences of judicial resolution, one way or another, of the issues involved.

I believe that analysis of hypothetical cases has several advantages which far outweigh that fact that arguments based on such cases cannot be as precise and comprehensive as arguments raised in actual controversies already decided by the Supreme Court. First, the reader of a hypothetical case is unable to rely, even subconsciously, on the viewpoint of a higher authority; he must decide for himself. Second, he is forced to reject the notion that constitutional law is the study of the history of Supreme Court decisions; instead, he must confront questions of a fundamental nature about the society in which he lives and will be living. Third, he cannot avoid coming to grips with questions about the nature of law and the role of the courts in the American system of government. And, finally, since lawyers are continually engaged in the process of arguing unresolved issues before the courts, exposure to unresolved constitutional questions will enable the reader to form a more realistic impression of the work of those lawyers and judges who are responsible for giving the Constitution its contemporary meaning.

It is with great pleasure and gratitude that I acknowledge the contributions of a large number of people to this volume. I owe much of my early thinking on the interrelationship of law and politics to professors at Amherst College, Yale Law School, and Columbia Graduate School, including, in particular, Professors James Nelson, Louis Pollak, Fred Rodell, David B. Truman, Lawrence Chamberlain, Philip C. Jessup, and Oliver J. Lissitzyn. In recent years I have gained many insights from colleagues and students at Wellesley College.

I would also like to thank the following individuals for their assistance during the years I was engaged in research and writing: Professors C. Herman Pritchett, University of California at Santa Barbara; Stuart A. Scheingold, University of Washington; Martin Shapiro, Harvard University, and the late Robert G. McCloskey and Rocco J. Tresolini, of Harvard University and Lehigh University, respectively, for their critical comments on the manuscript; Wellesley College reference librarians Marion Kanaly, Ellen Simpson, and the late Jeanne Doherty; Mrs. Donald Childs and Mrs. Irene Goddard who typed the manuscript and provided other necessary clerical and administrative help; my research assistant and former student, Miss Marianne Chawluk. In addition, I am grateful to Wellesley College and the National Endowment for the Humanities for their generous support. And, finally, no list of my indebtedness would be complete without mention of the continuous help and encouragement of my wife, Alison.

Alan H. Schechter

LITERACY TESTS AND THE RIGHT TO VOTE
Can the Federal Government Suspend State Voter Registration Laws?

ISSUES RAISED   The Right to Vote / States' Rights / Due Process of Law

I.   The Struggle for Effective Voting Rights Legislation

Prior to Sunday, March 7, 1965, few Americans had heard of the normally peaceful Southern city of Selma, Alabama. There was nothing about Selma to distinguish it from innumerable other delta communities. The heated conflicts of contemporary American politics—the war on poverty, urban redevelopment, the civil rights struggle—must have seemed inconsequential and remote to many of Selma's residents.

By the next day, however, the peace of the Alabama delta had been shattered irretrievably. The merciless glare of nationwide attention had been focused narrowly and sharply on the city of Selma. The events of Sunday, March 7, reported in the eyewitness account reprinted below, set into motion a chain reaction which led barely five months later to congressional approval of one of the boldest attempts to exert federal authority over the states ever passed: the Voting Rights Act of 1965.

Alabama Police Use Gas and Clubs to Rout Negroes[1]
   by Roy Reed
Selma, Ala., March 7—Alabama state troopers and volunteer officers of the Dallas County Sheriff's Office tore through a column of Negro demonstrators with tear gas, nightsticks and whips here today to enforce Gov. George C. Wallace's order against a protest march from Selma to Montgomery.

   At least 17 Negroes were hospitalized with injuries and about 40 more were given emergency treatment for minor injuries and tear gas effects. . . .

   The suppression of the march, which was called to dramatize the Negroes' voter registration drive, was swift and thorough.

   About 525 Negroes had left Browns Chapel and walked six blocks to Broad Street, then across Pettus Bridge and the Alabama River, where a cold wind cut at their faces and whipped their coats. They were young and old and they carried an assortment of packs, bedrolls and lunch sacks.

   The troopers, more than 50 of them, were waiting 300 yards beyond the end of the

[1] *New York Times*, March 8, 1965, p. 1.

bridge. Behind and around the troopers were a few dozen possemen, 15 of them on horses, and perhaps 100 white spectators. The troopers stood shoulder to shoulder in a line across both sides of the divided four-lane highway.

They put on gas masks and held their nightsticks ready as the Negroes approached, marching two abreast, slowly and silently. When the Negroes were 50 feet away, a voice came over an amplifying system commanding them to stop. They stopped.

The leader of the troops, who identified himself as Maj. John Cloud, said: "This is an unlawful assembly. Your march is not conducive to the public safety. You are ordered to disperse and go back to your church or to your homes."

Mr. (Hosea) Williams answered from the head of the column. "May we have a word with the major?" he asked.

"There is no word to be had," the major replied.

The two men went through the same exchange twice more, then the major said: "You have two minutes to turn around and go back to your church."

Several seconds went by silently. The Negroes stood unmoving. The next sound was the major's voice. "Troopers advance," he commanded. The troopers rushed forward, their blue uniforms and white helmets blurring into a flying wedge as they moved. The wedge moved with such force that it seemed almost to pass over the waiting column instead of through it.

The first 10 or 20 Negroes were swept to the ground screaming, arms and legs flying, and packs and bags went skittering across the grassy divider strip and onto the pavement on both sides. Those still on their feet retreated.

The troopers continued pushing, using both the force of their bodies and the prodding of their nightsticks. A cheer went up from the white spectators lining the south side of the highway.

The mounted possemen spurred their horses and rode at a run into the retreating mass. The Negroes cried out as they crowded together for protection, and the whites on the sideline whooped and cheered. The Negroes paused in their retreat for perhaps a minute, still screaming and huddling together. Suddenly there was a report, like a gunshot, and a gray cloud spewed over the troopers and the Negroes.

"Tear gas!" someone yelled. . . .

The Negroes broke and ran. Troopers and possemen, mounted and unmounted, went after them. Several more tear gas bombs were set off. After about 10 minutes, most of the Negroes were rounded up. They began to move toward the city through the smell of the tear gas, coughing and crying as they stumbled onto Pettus Bridge.

Four or five women still lay on the grass strip where the troopers had knocked them down. Two troopers passed among them and ordered them to get up and join the others. The women lay still. The two men then set off another barrage of tear gas and the women struggled to their feet, blinded and gasping, and limped across the road.

The ground floor of the two-story parsonage next to the church was turned into an emergency hospital for an hour and a half. Negroes lay on the floor and chairs, many weeping and moaning. A girl in red slacks was carried from the house screaming. Doctors and nurses threaded feverishly through the crowd administering first aid and daubing a solution of water and baking soda on the eyes of those who had been in the worst of the gas. From the hospital came a report that the victims had suffered fractures of ribs, heads, arms and legs, in addition to cuts and bruises.

Throughout the nation, popular reaction to the confrontation in Selma was intense. But more horrors were yet to follow in the succeeding weeks as the drama unfolded: Rev. James J. Reeb, a white Unitarian minister from Boston, died March 11 of skull fractures inflicted by other white men two days earlier. On March 25, the march from Selma to the state capital at Montgomery was successfully completed under the protection of the Alabama National Guard, which had been ordered into federal service by the President. That night, however, Mrs. Viola Liuzzo, a white civil rights worker from Detroit, was shot from ambush and killed while driving with a Negro on the state highway between Montgomery and Selma.

With each new event, popular indignation mounted, and sympathy marches, demonstrations, and sit-ins took place in every part of the country, extending even into the White House itself, where a group of students sat in the corridors and refused to move until they were carried out bodily by White House security officers. Demands were made for federal troops to protect Selma Negroes and white civil rights workers from further brutality. Clergymen throughout the nation spoke out from their pulpits, criticizing the President for his failure to intervene and Congress for its failure to pass legislation ensuring that every citizen, regardless of race, could exercise the right to vote guaranteed by the Fifteenth Amendment. Selma became the Lexington of the modern era—the battle cry of a nation aroused from its lethargy by the struggle for democratic rights.

It was against this background, on March 15, that President Johnson addressed a joint session of Congress televised to the entire nation and uttered words reminiscent of another president martyred a century earlier:

> I speak tonight for the dignity of man and the destiny of democracy. I urge every member of both parties, Americans of all religions and of all colors, from every section of this country, to join me in that cause. . . .
>
> In our times we have come to live with moments of great crisis. Our lives have been marked with debate about great issues, issues of war and peace, issues of prosperity and depression. But rarely in any time does an issue lay bare the secret heart of America itself. Rarely are we met with a challenge, not to our growth or abundance, or our welfare or our security, but rather to the values and the purposes and the meaning of our beloved nation.
>
> The issue of equal rights for American Negroes is such an issue. And should we defeat every enemy and should we double our wealth and conquer the stars and still be unequal to this issue, then we will have failed as a people and as a nation.
>
> Wednesday, I will send to Congress a law designed to eliminate illegal barriers to the right to vote. . . . This bill will strike down restrictions to voting in all elections— Federal, State, and local—which have been used to deny Negroes the right to vote. This bill will establish a single, uniform standard which cannot be used, however ingenious the effort, to flout our Constitution. It will provide for citizens to be registered by officials of the United States Government if the State officials refuse to register them. It will eliminate tedious, unnecessary lawsuits which delay the right to vote. Finally, this legislation will ensure that properly registered individuals are not prohibited from voting. . . .[2]

While the events in Selma crystallized the issue of voting rights for Negro citizens and provided the impetus for passage of the Voting Rights Act of 1965, they were not, from another vantage point, unique; the struggle did not originate in Selma, just as it did not end with the passage of the act. The decision of civil rights leaders to march from Selma to the state capital, a decision which provoked the excessive violence of the Alabama state troopers and of white segregationists who applauded their methods, stemmed from the fact that millions of black citizens were denied the franchise throughout the Deep South states.

INITIAL EFFORTS BY CONGRESS, 1957–1964

Although the Fifteenth Amendment guaranteeing the right to vote was ratified in 1870, Congress failed to pass meaningful legislation to carry out the purpose of the

[2] 111 *Cong. Rec.* 4924 (daily ed. March 15, 1965).

amendment for nearly ninety years.[3] The Civil Rights Act of 1957 ended this inter-regnum and opened the floodgates to legislation which had long been postponed.[4] In itself, the 1957 act was relatively mild and acceptable to representatives from the Southern states; in retrospect, however, it is quite clear that the act was merely the prelude to increased demands by Negroes and sympathetic whites for legislation which would eliminate discrimination and fulfill the century-old promise of the United States Constitution of equal and not merely second-class citizenship.

Prior to 1957, any individual denied the right to vote could bring a lawsuit in either a federal or state court to test the validity of the denial; if the court found that the local registrar or voting official had in fact discriminated against the plaintiff in violation of his Fifteenth Amendment rights, it would order him to allow the ag-grieved citizen to register and to vote. This seemingly simple method of enforcing the right to vote was, unfortunately, ineffective. Few Negroes could afford the expense of bringing a suit and prosecuting it through the lower courts, which frequently sympathized with the local officials, to the appellate courts. Few individuals wished to expose themselves and their families to the reprisals, the threats of loss of em-ployment or of physical violence, which frequently followed attempts to enforce the right to vote through the courts. In addition, each successfully concluded lawsuit re-sulted in registration of the individual plaintiff only, not in registration of the thou-sands of other citizens who were similarly disfranchised. Finally, the plaintiff could find that he had won only a pyrrhic victory if the registrar disqualified him the next time citizens of the particular state involved were required to register to vote.

The 1957 act empowered the Attorney General to seek an injunction when an in-dividual was deprived of his right to vote in primary or general elections for federal officials; thus, the federal government would pay the expenses of a lawsuit to en-force the individual's rights in federal elections. This provision dealt with the prob-lem of the costs of a lawsuit but not with any of the other problems mentioned above. In addition, the act created a bipartisan Commission on Civil Rights to in-vestigate civil rights violations and to make recommendations to the President and Congress for legislation and changes in existing government policies. The act also established a Civil Rights Division in the Department of Justice and authorized the appointment of an assistant attorney general to head the new division.

The legislative struggle over the bill reveals some of the many problems faced by the Eisenhower administration in trying to get a meaningful measure through Con-gress. As originally proposed by the administration, the bill empowered the Attorney General to seek injunctions against deprivation of any civil right and not just voting rights; court orders would be backed up by fines and jail sentences.

Southern strategists, led by Sen. Richard B. Russell of Georgia, recognized that they did not have enough votes to prevent passage of a bill. Because they feared a filibuster would fail, they decided instead to try to weaken the administration's proposals.

Proponents of the bill also followed a definite strategy. Since the Senate Judiciary Committee had never voluntarily reported a civil rights bill out of committee, the strategists in charge of the bill objected to sending the bill to the Judiciary Com-mittee; instead, they placed it directly on the Senate calendar, where it could be called up for consideration by a majority vote at any time. A point of order raised against this unusual procedure was rejected by majority vote. To prevent the pos-

---

[3] For a short but excellent history of federal involvement in civil rights, see *H.R. Rep. No. 439*, 89th Cong., 1st Sess. 8–16 (1965) and *Sen. Rep. No. 162*, 89th Cong., 1st Sess., pt. 3, 3–16 (1965); see also *Revolution in Civil Rights*, Congressional Quarterly News Service, Washington, 1965.

[4] 71 Stat. 634.

sibility of a filibuster, the Senate eliminated the provision giving the Attorney General the right to seek injunctions against the violation of any civil right and added an amendment guaranteeing the right of a jury trial in criminal contempt proceedings brought following deliberate violation of court orders. Thus the bill as finally enacted, while heralded as a first step, did not represent a significant challenge to traditional patterns of discrimination in the South.

Civil rights advocates were dissatisfied with the 1957 act from the moment the President signed it. Their complaints were confirmed by the Civil Rights Commission when it reported in 1959 that the act had had limited impact. With pressure for stronger legislation mounting, the administration decided to seek a stronger bill.

As in the case of the 1957 bill, a bipartisan majority prevailed over Southern representatives, who opposed all civil rights legislation, and a Northern liberal minority who favored far stronger measures. Once again, Southern strategists outmaneuvered their Northern opponents and persuaded the Senate and House leadership to eliminate what they considered the most obnoxious parts of the proposed legislation. A full-scale filibuster developed in the Senate and, against the advice of Majority Leader Lyndon Johnson and Minority Leader Everett Dirksen, the liberals attempted to invoke cloture to cut it off; the premature attempt to close debate was defeated by a large margin, and for the moment it looked as if further civil rights legislation could not pass in the Senate.

In the meantime, the bill was floundering on the other side of Capitol Hill, where the House Rules Committee refused to release it. A discharge petition was filed to dismiss the Rules Committee from further consideration of the bill. When the number of signatures on the petition rose to 211, just 7 short of the requisite majority, the committee saw the handwriting on the wall and finally acted. The House bill was passed by a lopsided majority shortly thereafter.

Following House passage, the Senate abandoned its own versions of civil rights legislation and referred the House bill to the Senate Judiciary Committee with instructions that it be reported out in five days, thereby frustrating any hope of Committee Chairman James Eastland of Mississippi that he could pigeonhole the measure in committee. However, the committee eliminated several provisions of the bill and attached restrictive amendments to the remaining sections. The amended bill was passed by a vote of seventy-one to eighteen nine days later.

The Civil Rights Act of 1960 authorized the Attorney General, after winning a suit under the 1957 act, to bring a second suit seeking a declaration that there was a "pattern or practice" of discrimination in the area involved in the suit.[5] If a court found that such a pattern existed, it could order local officials to register any Negro who proved to the satisfaction of the court that he was qualified to vote under state law and that he had tried to register and been rejected since the judicial finding. The court was empowered to appoint voting referees to carry out the above provision. Unlike the 1957 act, the 1960 provisions were not limited solely to discrimination in federal elections. Other sections of the act required local officials to preserve voting records and registration papers for all federal elections for twenty-two months and made it a federal crime to cross state lines in order to avoid prosecution for bombing or burning or attempting to bomb or burn any building or vehicle.

President-elect John F. Kennedy came into office on a shoestring, with only 50.09 percent of the two-party popular vote for President or a margin of 120,000 votes out of more than 68 million cast. Thus, although he was publicly committed to the goal of equal rights for all Americans, he had no clear mandate from the people. Without strong popular support, Kennedy feared the disruptive consequences of a bruising

[5] 74 Stat. 86.

battle with Southern Democrats over further legislation in the field of civil rights. Therefore the new administration deliberately chose to postpone a drive for stronger legislation in order not to jeopardize other New Frontier programs. A year later, however, the President did support a constitutional amendment to eliminate the poll tax as a requirement for voting in federal primaries and elections; the poll tax amendment was approved by the requisite two-thirds of both houses of Congress and became the Twenty-fourth Amendment when ratified by three-fourths of the states two years later. In addition, Kennedy supported an unsuccessful effort to prohibit local officials from flunking anyone with a sixth grade education on literacy tests required for registering to vote in federal elections.

Events in late 1962 and throughout 1963 altered the priorities set by the administration and forced the President to come out strongly for new legislation. The year prior to President Kennedy's assassination began and ended with violence. In the fall of 1962, segregationists rioted over the admission of James Meredith to the University of Mississippi and, before peace could be restored by a force of federal marshals and troops estimated at 16,000, two men had been killed and many others injured.

Mass demonstrations in Birmingham, Alabama, in the spring of 1963 were suppressed with fire hoses and police dogs. In June, Medgar Evers, the Mississippi state chairman of the NAACP, was killed by a sniper in front of his home, and Governor George C. Wallace of Alabama stood in the doorway of the University of Alabama to prevent two black students from registering. After President Kennedy federalized the Alabama National Guard, the Governor gave up and allowed the two students to register. The civil rights movement reached a high point in the struggle for equal rights when several hundred thousand Americans from all over the country participated in a march on Washington later that summer. Then, the opening of the school year brought renewed violence to Birmingham: an event which shocked the conscience of Americans even more than the murder of Medgar Evers was the killing of four young Sunday school girls by unidentified bomb throwers.

In June, President Kennedy submitted a broad civil rights program to Congress. While the 1957 and 1960 acts had focused primarily on voting rights, the 1963 proposals ranged far afield; included were requests for legislation to guarantee access to privately owned public accommodations, to allow the government to file suits to desegregate schools, to withhold federal funds when there was evidence that they were being used to further discrimination, to authorize federal assistance to areas desegregating their schools, to extend the life of the Civil Rights Commission for four more years, to establish a Community Relations Service in order to help local communities resolve racial disputes, and to strengthen existing laws in the field of voting rights.

Throughout the rest of 1963 the House debated these proposals. The administration worked closely with the Republican leadership in the House in an effort to build the bipartisan support which would be needed to get new civil rights legislation through Congress. On November 20, the bill was reported out of the House Judiciary Committee. Two days later, President Kennedy was dead.

In his first address to Congress the following week, President Johnson asked Congress to give the civil rights bill the earliest possible consideration. Thus, the new administration, headed by a Texan whom liberals had long regarded as lukewarm on civil rights, put its stamp of approval on the proposed legislation. Seven months later, on July 2, 1964, President Johnson signed the most far-reaching civil rights legislation passed since Reconstruction.

Because of the tremendous scope of the 1964 bill, Southern opposition to the measure was intense. As in the case of the earlier civil rights bills, the Senate was the major stumbling block. In the House, the bipartisan coalition formed in 1963 held firm throughout the debate and no amendments opposed by the leadership were adopted. The Senate leadership was determined not to weaken the House-passed bill in order to avoid a Southern filibuster, even though cloture had never been voted on a civil rights measure. Their first strategic decision was to avoid the Judiciary Committee by placing the bill directly on the Senate calendar rather than following the normal referral procedure; Southern objections to this tactic were defeated by majority vote. Prospects for passage looked dim because Minority Leader Dirksen opposed sections of the bill which attempted to eliminate discrimination both in employment and in access to hotels, restaurants, and other public accommodations. Compromises were hammered out behind the scenes by Dirksen, the Democratic leaders, and the Justice Department in a joint effort to win sufficient support for the bill to invoke cloture. On June 10, after a near-record filibuster of fifty-seven days, the historic cloture vote took place and seventy-one senators voted to shut off the debate.

The voting rights provisions of the Civil Rights Act of 1964 can be summarized as follows: Title I authorized the Attorney General to request that suits seeking to prove the existence of discriminatory patterns be heard by three-judge federal courts rather than by district court judges sitting singly; appeals from decisions of three-judge courts could be made directly to the Supreme Court rather than to the circuit courts. This provision was designed to expedite voting rights suits.

In addition, Title I barred unequal application of requirements for voting, prohibited denial of the right to vote because of inconsequential errors on registration applications, required that all literacy tests be administered in writing, and made a sixth grade education a rebuttable presumption of literacy. Title VIII of the act directed the Census Bureau to gather registration and voting statistics based on race, color, and national origin for elections to the House of Representatives and required such information on a nationwide scale in connection with the 1970 census.[6]

The voting rights provisions of the first three civil rights acts passed in the twentieth century all followed the same basic approach to the problem of discrimination against black citizens: Each of them attempted to use the courts as a major instrument for social change. In the face of massive resistance to voting, however, the courts proved unequal to the task, essentially for the following reasons:

Discrimination was so pervasive that isolated court cases could not halt it.

Judges lacked effective enforcement powers.

Litigation was a long, exhausting, and costly process.

Even when court orders were obeyed, new evasions were thought up faster than decisions could be handed down.

Because the device of senatorial courtesy prevented presidents from appointing judges whose views differed from those of most Southern senators, not all district court judges were sympathetic to federal intervention.

And, most significantly, litigation was essentially a passive process; the courts could react to initiatives but could not organize, staff, and finance voter registration drives, nor could they guarantee that participants in such efforts would be protected against reprisal.

Some progress had been made in registering black voters in the post-1957 period, but the gap between the constitutional promise and the realities of voter discrimination remained great. At the end of 1964, Negroes constituted 36 percent of the vot-

---

[6] 78 Stat. 241.

ing-age population of Mississippi but only 5 percent of the registered voters; in Alabama, 26 percent of the voting-age population was black, but 90 percent of the registered voters were white; in Louisiana, black citizens made up 29 percent of the voting-age population but only 14 percent of the registered voters; in Georgia, the figures were 25 and 17; in South Carolina, 29 and 17; in North Carolina, 22 and 12.[7]

The decision of civil rights leaders to provoke a confrontation in Selma in the spring of 1965 resulted from frustration: frustration over the fact that grand speeches had been given, promises made, laws passed, and expectations raised, yet— where it counted—little had been changed. Selma, the county seat of Dallas County, was chosen because it represented, in microcosm, white intransigence to black voting; at the end of 1964, blacks made up 51 percent of the voting-age population but only 3 percent of the registered voters. Four years of litigation by the Justice Department had resulted in two decisions that widespread voter discrimination existed, but registration during those four years had risen to less than 400 out of 15,000 black citizens of voting age.[8]

A MAJOR NEW APPROACH: THE VOTING RIGHTS ACT OF 1965

The bill sent to Congress by President Johnson following his March 15 speech called for a new and radical approach to the problem of securing the right to vote. Major reliance was no longer to be placed on the courts. Instead, literacy tests and certain other registration requirements were to be suspended and the Attorney General was to be empowered to appoint federal examiners to register prospective voters in place of local registration officials.

As in the case of the earlier measures, the 1965 bill was pushed through Congress by a bipartisan effort. The Senate voted to send the proposals to the Judiciary Committee along with instructions that they be reported out within three weeks. Once the bill reached the Senate floor, however, Southern senators seemed unable to mount a challenge to it comparable to their all-out fight against the comprehensive 1964 act; after a month of debate, a cloture motion was filed and adopted by a roll-call vote of seventy to thirty-one, and final passage followed the next day by the overwhelming margin of seventy-seven to nineteen. Floor debate in the House, which lasted for three days, did not begin until after the Senate had voted its version of the bill. Differences in the House and Senate versions of the bill were worked out in a conference committee and the Voting Rights Act of 1965 was signed by the President on August 6, just 152 days after Alabama state troopers had used tear gas and night-sticks to halt the march from Selma to Montgomery.

In its final form, section 4 of the Voting Rights Act of 1965 suspended the use of literacy tests and other voter qualification devices in federal, state, and local elections in states or political subdivisions of any states in which less than 50 percent of the voting-age population was registered to vote or actually voted in the presidential election of November 1964.[9] The phrase "test or device" was defined to include any requirement that an applicant for registration demonstrate the ability to read, write, understand, or interpret any matter, demonstrate any educational achievement or knowledge of a particular subject, possess good moral character, or prove his qualifications by the voucher of registered voters.

Section 6 authorized the Attorney General to appoint voting examiners to enforce the guarantees of the Fifteenth Amendment; and section 7 empowered examiners to

---

[7] Calculated from Appendix C, *Sen. Rep. No. 162*, 89th Cong., 1st Sess., pt. 3, at 44 (1965).

[8] *Ibid.*, at 7–8, and Appendix D, at 44.

[9] 79 Stat. 437.

draw up lists of applicants who possessed the qualifications required by state laws which were not inconsistent with the Constitution and laws of the United States, to transmit such lists to local election officials, and to issue certificates to individuals found qualified to vote. Section 9 provided for challenges to persons who had been listed by the federal examiners, but it required that all challenges be made within ten days of the publication of the relevant list, that challenges be supported by the affidavits of at least two persons having personal knowledge of the facts on which the challenge was based, and that a copy of the challenge and the affidavits be forwarded to the individual challenged. Challenges were to be heard by hearing officers appointed by the U.S. Civil Service Commission, but appeals from the decision of a hearing officer could be filed before the United States Court of Appeals for the circuit in which the challenged individual resided.

States or political subdivisions covered by section 4 were prohibited by the following section from enacting or administering any voting qualifications or procedures different from those in force on November 1, 1964, unless they received in advance the approval of the Attorney General or won a lawsuit before the United States District Court for the District of Columbia that such qualifications or procedures would not deny the right to vote on account of race or color.

Exemption from the provisions of the act could be won by states or political subdivisions covered under section 4 if they could prove to the satisfaction of the United States District Court for the District of Columbia that no literacy test or other requirement had been used during the five years preceding the filing of the action for the purpose or with the effect of denying the right to vote. The act also provided that the activities of federal examiners were to be terminated whenever the Attorney General or the District Court for the District of Columbia determined that more than 50 percent of the nonwhite persons of voting age in the particular state or subdivision were registered, that all persons listed by examiners had been registered, and that there was no longer reasonable cause to believe that any person would be denied the right to vote in violation of the Fifteenth Amendment.

Furthermore, the act established criminal penalties of up to five years in jail and $5,000 in fines for any person, whether acting under color of law or otherwise, who intimidated, threatened, or coerced any voter or anyone urging any person to vote. Criminal penalties for private individuals interfering with the right to vote were included despite the fact that the Fifteenth Amendment specifically prohibits states and not individuals from denying the right to vote on account of race or color.

It was inevitable that the new law would raise hackles all over the South. From the perspective of many, if not most, Southerners, the South had been singled out in a discriminatory and punitive fashion by Northern politicians who wished to benefit politically by attacking the Southern states. Southerners recognized that the "automatic trigger" which would lead to suspension of literacy tests was a cheap charade, since Congress knew in advance exactly which states would be covered by the requirement of 50 percent registered or voting in the 1964 presidential election. Since they believed voting discrimination was a nationwide phenomenon, they resented the "holier than thou" attitude expressed in the halls of Congress and in the nation's press.

Moreover, the law seemed quite radical: it took away from certain states their historic right to establish requirements for voting. Other states would be allowed to continue administering literacy tests, but the states in question would have to allow illiterates to vote. Proponents of the Voting Rights Act had not even attempted to maintain the principle of state control of registration requirements, a goal they could have achieved by using federal examiners to ensure nondiscriminatory administration of state literacy laws.

And the final, crowning insult was the suspension of the authority of the states in question to pass new voter registration laws. For the first time in history, a state would have to go to Washington, "hat in hand," to ask permission to pass a state law. This seemingly radical revision of the relationship between the states and the federal government appeared to violate the historic constitutional doctrine that the federal government and the state governments are each supreme in the exercise of their own powers.

Faced with an act they judged extremely obnoxious and clearly unconstitutional, elected officials of the affected states decided to exercise their last option by asking the Supreme Court to overthrow the statute. This must have been a desperate decision, given the odds against success: in case after case, for more than a decade, the Warren Court had demonstrated that it sympathized with the plight of black Americans and not with whites who wished to continue the historic pattern of discrimination against Negroes.

Most cases which reach the Supreme Court are heard first in federal district courts or in lower state courts; lower-court decisions are then appealed to federal courts of appeal or to state supreme courts and, finally, to the United States Supreme Court. Under certain rare circumstances, such as in cases involving the states, Article 3 of the Constitution gives the Supreme Court the right to hear the case directly, in exercise of the Court's "original" rather than its "appellate" jurisdiction.

South Carolina brought such a suit to challenge the Voting Rights Act of 1965. Briefs supporting the arguments of the attorney general of South Carolina were submitted by Alabama, Georgia, Louisiana, Mississippi, and Virginia. "Friend of the Court" briefs in support of the position of the United States were submitted by the attorneys general of California, Illinois, and Massachusetts; in addition, seventeen other states supported the arguments raised by the attorney general of Massachusetts. Thus, while the constitutional challenge was nominally between South Carolina and the United States, the underlying reality was that twenty-six states and the federal government were vitally concerned about the outcome. The Court was being asked to resolve a fundamental political question by upholding, reinterpreting, or rejecting an important public policy.

. . . .

II. Legal Arguments in South Carolina v. Katzenbach*

BRIEF FOR PLAINTIFF   *BRIEF FOR DEFENDANT*

1. *Does the Voting Rights Act of 1965 violate South Carolina's right under Article 1, sections 2 and 4 of the Constitution to prescribe lawful voting qualifications for her citizens?*

The authors of the Constitution intended to place control over suffrage and elections in the hands of the states, subject only to certain limitations in the case of national representatives. Thus, Article 1, sections 2 and 4 read:

Congress passed the Voting Rights Act of 1965 in order to make the guarantee of the Fifteenth Amendment effective. Section 1 of that amendment commands the states and the United States not to deny citizens the right to vote on

---

*Author's note: the briefs printed below are original and are not excerpts from the briefs actually filed by South Carolina and the United States; the briefs submitted by the parties and the eight amicus curiae briefs were, however, among the primary sources used.

Since South Carolina brought this case directly to the Supreme Court on the basis of the original jurisdiction of the Court, Article 3, section 2 of the Constitution, the parties before the Court are known as plaintiff and defendant rather than appellant and appellee.

...the electors in each State shall have the qualifications requisite for electors for the most numerous branch of the State legislature.

The times, places, and manner of holding elections for senators and representatives shall be prescribed in each State by the legislature thereof; but the Congress may at any time by law make or alter such regulations....

The Fifteenth Amendment, ratified in 1870, ensured that the right of American citizens to vote would not be denied or abridged by the United States or by any state on account of race, color, or previous servitude, but it did not change fundamentally the prerogative of the states to determine voting qualifications and to regulate their elections. As this Court has ruled:

Beyond doubt the Amendment does not take away from the State governments in a general sense the power of suffrage which has belonged to those governments from the beginning, and without possession of which power the whole fabric upon which the division of State and National authority under the Constitution ... rests would be without support.... In fact, the very command of the Amendment recognizes the possession of the general power by the State, since the Amendment seeks to regulate its exercise.

Guinn v. United States, 238 U.S. 347, 362 (1915).

Thus, the sole effect of the Fifteenth Amendment on the rights of the states to regulate suffrage was that they could no longer grant or withhold the right to vote on the basis of race. Congress, therefore, cannot employ section 2 of the Fifteenth Amendment, which gives it power to enforce the amendment by appropriate legislation, to limit the rights of the states further.

But that is exactly what the Voting Rights Act attempts to do. Section 4 of the act, which gives the Attorney General power to suspend South Carolina's literacy requirement, grants previously unqualified citizens the right to vote in violation of state law and *regardless of race*. Under the act, both white and Negro illiterates now have a right to vote.

Section 5 of the act prohibits South Carolina

account of race, color, or previous condition of servitude; section 2 gives Congress power to enforce the amendment by appropriate legislation. Thus, the act is based on power expressly delegated to the national legislature.

But what is the scope of the power conveyed to Congress by the Fifteenth Amendment? This Court long ago ruled that Congress's power to enact legislation pursuant to a specific and plenary grant such as that contained in the Fifteenth Amendment is very broad and unfettered. As Chief Justice Marshall ruled in *McCulloch v. Maryland*, 4 Wheat. 316, 421 (1819):

Let the end be legitimate, let it be within the scope of the constitution, and all means which are appropriate, which are plainly adapted to that end, which are not prohibited, but consist with the letter and spirit of the constitution, are constitutional.

And, in speaking of the Civil War amendments, including the Fifteenth, this Court ruled:

Whatever legislation is appropriate, that is, is adapted to carry out the objects the amendments have in view, whatever tends to enforce submission to the prohibitions they contain, and to secure to all persons the enjoyment of perfect equality of civil rights, if not prohibited, is brought within the domain of congressional power.

Ex parte Virginia, 100 U.S. 339, 345–46 (1880).

Thus, Congress is not limited solely to those measures which are indispensably necessary to give effect to its express powers. Instead, it has broad discretion in fashioning a remedy, subject only to the caveat that the remedy chosen must be reasonably adapted to the end permitted by the Constitution.

There is no merit to the argument that the power of Congress to enforce the amendment cannot be exercised so as to infringe the powers of the states under Article 1—and their reserved powers under the Tenth Amendment—to fix voting qualifications and to conduct elections. In fact, the very purpose of the Fifteenth Amendment was to limit the powers of the states and to give Congress authority to prevent the states from employing their

from changing any of its current requirements for exercising the franchise without first obtaining the approval of the federal government. Again, race is irrelevant; section 5 applies regardless of whether the proposed change affects Negroes or whites, federal or state elections, registration requirements or election procedures. Section 5 clearly transfers control of suffrage from the states to the federal government, in disregard of Article 1 of the Constitution. Thus, both sections 4 and 5 violate the constitutional rights of the states to regulate their own elections.

powers to circumvent the newly created federal right.

We do not question the right of a state to establish a literacy requirement as a voting prerequisite provided that the test is not discriminatory and is not employed for the purpose of denying the right to vote on account of race. The Voting Rights Act does not abolish all literacy tests per se, but only those tests which are used to achieve discrimination.

Congress was faced with extensive evidence that certain literacy tests had been used unjustifiably to restrict the suffrage and with the fact that many illiterate whites had been registered in the past because of discriminatory application of these tests. Under the circumstances, a remedy based on proper administration of state laws in the future would have continued the effects of past discrimination, since illiterates registered prior to federal intervention would still be entitled to vote. Given the plenary power of Congress under the Fifteenth Amendment, Congress did not have to accept such an inadequate remedy. Certainly, Congress cannot be held to have exceeded its powers under the amendment because the incidental effect of the suspension of a particular test might be the registration of some illiterate citizens.

2. *Does the act violate the due process of law guaranteed by the Fifth Amendment by arbitrarily presuming that South Carolina is guilty of racial discrimination in the application of its voting laws?*

A Congressional "presumption" that two facts are related to one another is constitutionally valid if the presumption is reasonable and not arbitrary and if it is open to proof to the contrary. However, if there is no rational connection between the fact proved and the fact presumed the presumption violates the due-process clause of the Fifth Amendment.

We believe that Congress has overstepped the due-process limitation on its legislative powers by presuming that South Carolina was guilty of racial discrimination because she required voters to be literate and because less than 50 percent of her adult population voted in the presidential election of 1964. First, Congress's express purpose in passing the act was to eliminate racial discrimination in registra-

In passing the Voting Rights Act of 1965, Congress reached the conclusion that literacy tests had been and were currently being applied in a discriminatory fashion in various parts of the country. Such a conclusion is hardly arbitrary and unreasonable in the light of overwhelming evidence that these tests were originally conceived and used in the South to bar black citizens from voting.

For example, Senator Tillman, one of the dominant figures at the South Carolina Constitutional Convention of 1895, described the purpose of the literacy test adopted at that time as follows:

If you put in here that a man must understand, and you vest the right to judge whether he

tion and voting, yet South Carolina's laws would not have been suspended, even if she were guilty of massive discrimination, if at least 51 percent of her citizens had been registered and all of them had voted. On the other hand, South Carolina's laws would have been suspended, even if there had been no discrimination whatever and even if 100 percent of her citizens had been registered, if only 49 percent had gone to the polls in the 1964 election. Thus, the presumption is hardly rational.

Second, the absurdity of the presumption is revealed by the fact that Arkansas and Texas are not reached by it, even though less than 50 percent of their citizens voted in 1964, since neither state has a literacy test. This is true despite the fact that Attorney General Katzenbach testified in congressional hearings on the act that there was evidence of voter discrimination in parts of both of these states but no evidence of such discrimination in South Carolina; in addition, evidence was introduced at the hearings which indicated that discrimination existed in several states which are not covered because more than 50 percent of their citizens voted in 1964.[1] Yet none of these states are presumed guilty.

The arbitrary nature of the 50 percent mark selected by Congress is illustrated by the fact that there are circumstances peculiar to South Carolina—and to some of the other states involved—which reduced her voter participation below the national average of 62 percent in 1964, and that these circumstances are unrelated to racial discrimination.

South Carolina has, in recent history, been a one-party Democratic state; as a result, her officials are chosen in the primary elections and not at the general election, which is the measure of presumptive racial discrimination under the act.

Furthermore, the citizens of South Carolina have lower incomes and fewer years of education than the citizens of most other states. South Carolina adults averaged 8.7 years of education in the last census, in contrast to a

understands in an officer, it is a constitutional act. That officer is responsible to his conscience and his God. . . . There is no particle of fraud or illegality in it. It is just simply showing partiality, perhaps, or discriminating.

Journal of the South Carolina Constitutional Convention of 1895, p. 469.

A spokesman at the Virginia Constitutional Convention of 1901–1902 said: "I do not expect an understanding clause to be administered with any degree of friendship by the white man to the suffrage of the black man. . . ."[1]

These explicit statements—and others like them—testify to the historic policy of the states concerned to maintain white supremacy by denying Negroes the right to vote. The use of the subjective nature of literacy tests to discriminate has been the most durable of various schemes designed to prevent Negro voting, many of which have been outlawed by this Court.

Voluminous evidence was presented to Congress to show that literacy tests were currently being used for discriminatory purposes. Congress was told that in each of the thirty-two suits initiated by the Department of Justice since 1957 the courts found discrimination in the administration of literacy tests. The chairman of the United States Commission on Civil Rights testified before Congress that "literacy tests are the one great universal device used for denying Negroes the right to vote."[2] Thus, it was reasonable for Congress to conclude that certain literacy tests carried substantial danger of racial discrimination.

Congress's power to suspend literacy tests did not have to be dependent on proof that a particular test was actually being used to violate the right to vote. It is a settled principle of constitutional law that Congress may deal with dangers—with tendencies and probabilities—at least where the restriction imposed is not wholly disproportionate to the evil confronting the legislature.

For example, in *North American Co. v. SEC,*

---

[1] *Hearings on H.R. 6400 Before the House Comm. on the Judiciary*, 89th Cong., 1st Sess., ser. 2, at 12, 68–69, 75–76, 89, 112–20, 273–84, 362–64, 368–69, 373, 405, 418–21, 461–62, 508–18, 527–29, 674, 714 (1965).

[1] *Proceedings of the Virginia Constitutional Convention of 1901–1902*, p. 2972.

[2] *Hearings on H.R. 6400 before the House Comm. on the Judiciary*, 89th Cong., 1st Sess., ser. 2, at 266; see also 125–27, 259, 267 (1965).

nationwide average of 10.6 years. South Carolina's median family income was $3,821, nearly $2,000 below the comparable national figure.[2]

Because South Carolina has the second-highest illiteracy rate in the nation, her literacy requirement inevitably disqualifies a larger percentage of her total adult population than would a similar test in other states, regardless of race. Yet the triggering provision of the act ignores differences among states in the relative significance of the general election, the average family income, and the level of literacy of their populations. Thus, a presumption of racial discrimination based on a turnout of less than 50 percent of the adult citizens is clearly arbitrary.

We would argue further that this statutory presumption violates the due-process limitation on the powers of Congress because the presumption is conclusive and South Carolina does not have a fair opportunity to disprove the fact presumed. Congress sought to avoid a finding of unconstitutionality of this irrebuttable presumption by including an escape clause in the act. Under this provision, any state which applies can avoid the act by proving to a United States district court in Washington not that it did not discriminate in registration prior to the November 1964 election but that it has not discriminated for five years prior to coming before the court. Thus, the state is required to do far more than refute the presumption on which her guilt is based.

How can any state carry this burden? Can any state prove that it has been entirely free of discrimination for the preceding five years? Assuming the inevitability of isolated instances of discrimination, how can a state prove that such instances are in fact rare, or that they have occurred despite official efforts to prevent discrimination? The presumption, is, in short, conclusive and irrebuttable and, therefore, violates the due-process clause of the Fifth Amendment.

[2] *Eighteenth Census of the U.S., 1960: Population,* vol. I, 1960, part 42, p. 96; part 1, p. 207; part 42, p. 377; part 1, p. 286.

327 U.S. 686, 710–11 (1946), this Court held that the SEC could require the reorganization of a holding company under the Public Utility Holding Company Act of 1935 even though it had not engaged in any of the evil practices Congress had sought to forestall, since Congress could remove what it "considered to be potential if not actual sources of evil." Similarly, in the National Labor Relations Act, Congress outlawed practices which tend to provoke strikes or tend to lead to labor disputes. Thus, this Court should not rule that the suspension of South Carolina's voting qualification laws is arbitrary, and therefore invalid, merely because there has been no prior showing that these laws have been used to discriminate against black citizens.

Nor is the "triggering mechanism" chosen by Congress to achieve the purpose of the Fifteenth Amendment arbitrary and unreasonable. Congress was faced with the need to provide a swift, efficient, and equitable procedure for suspending those tests which might be used for the purpose of achieving widespread discrimination while not interfering with tests which did not pose an equivalent danger. We would argue that the formula established by the act is appropriately suited to this end.

There were only nine states in which less than half the adult population voted in the presidential election of 1964, and seven of these—Alabama, Alaska, Georgia, Louisiana, Mississippi, South Carolina, and Virginia—maintained literacy tests or similar devices.

Six of the seven states which fall within the formula had long histories of racial discrimination, and all six had used other devices like the white primary to deny the right to vote in the past. Public officials in these states had repeatedly indicated their desire to maintain white supremacy at the polls. In five of these six states the Justice Department had found evidence of discrimination in voting. Under such circumstances, it was certainly reasonable for Congress to infer that low voter participation probably resulted from discriminatory application of literacy tests.

Congress was aware of and rejected the argument now made by South Carolina that the participation of her citizens in the presidential election reflected factors such as their low level of education and income. This argument does not prove that Congress acted arbitrarily. First, Congress was required only to determine whether low participation was evidence of a substantial danger that a literacy test or other device was being used for discriminatory purposes. Second, Congress could properly have concluded that the causes cited by South Carolina for low Negro participation in voting might themselves be related to official policies of racial discrimination.

Inevitably, as with any mechanical formula, some areas which discriminate will escape and others which do not may be included. But the Voting Rights Act is hardly arbitrary because Congress has failed to deal comprehensively with a century-old evil in one act. Congress provided an opportunity for states covered by the act to prove in court that their voter qualification tests were not used in a discriminatory fashion. Given the nature of the evil confronted by Congress, this burden is a reasonable one; the state can produce evidence showing the administration of its voting laws much more easily than the Attorney General. Congress attempted to provide further protection for the states by including a provision requiring the court to ignore isolated incidents of discrimination on account of race if such incidents had been few in number, had been corrected, and seemed unlikely to recur.

In the final analysis, the triggering mechanism, the temporary automatic suspension of literacy tests and devices, and the provision for judicial inquiry into their actual operation at the request of any affected state must be viewed as a single integrated measure for halting the widespread abuse of such tests and devices and enforcing the right to vote. We submit, therefore, that the act sets up a fair and reasonable procedure for determining when a literacy test or similar device should be suspended and when it should be permitted as a legitimate exercise of the power to fix voting qualifications.

3. Is an act which violates the constitutional principle of equality of the states "appropriate" legislation under the Fifteenth Amendment?

The Constitution was ratified by equal sovereign states; from the earliest days of our nation, it was commonly understood that all

South Carolina's argument that the Voting Rights Act unconstitutionally violates her right to equal treatment can be answered summarily.

states, old and new, were equal in political rights, power, and sovereignty. Until now, congressional acts affecting the political rights and sovereignty of the states have applied equally, on a nationwide basis, to all of the members of the Union.

This act, however, violates the fundamental principle of equality of states. It has been written specifically to apply to seven states and portions of two others, just as if these states had actually been named in the statute. The act is written in general terms, but it is clear that this terminology is merely a subterfuge to disguise the fact that certain states have been singled out for punishment under the act.

It is significant that Congress's power to enforce the Fifteenth Amendment is not unlimited; section 2 expressly prohibits the passage of "inappropriate legislation." Any law which violates the equality principle cannot be constitutional since it fails to meet this test.

No state has a right to violate the Fifteenth Amendment or any other provision of the Constitution. Section 2 of the Fifteenth Amendment gives Congress authority to enforce the right to vote "by appropriate legislation" and, as we have argued, Congress has wide discretion in the choice of means to achieve this goal. This Court should determine solely whether there is a rational connection between the means chosen by Congress and the evil which Congress has the power to eliminate.

Regardless of the fact that Congress was aware of which states and political subdivisions would be covered by the act, the triggering mechanism was written to apply objectively, just as in the case of any other legislation requiring classification. We find it incomprehensible that states which have had long histories of discrimination against their black citizens can argue that they are being discriminated against when Congress, after years of frustration and failure, enacts a reasonable law to carry out the clear mandate of the Fifteenth Amendment.

4. *Are the provisions of the act so excessive that they are not reasonably designed to enforce the Fifteenth Amendment?*

The grant of power to Congress contained in the Fifteenth Amendment is narrow and precise. In order for any legislation based on this grant to be constitutional, it must not exceed the limits of the grant and must be reasonably designed to accomplish its purpose. We would argue that entirely apart from consideration of other constitutional provisions violated by the Voting Rights Act, the provisions of this statute are excessive and inappropriate.

The Fifteenth Amendment, like the Fourteenth, is worded negatively; it requires that the right to vote "shall not be denied." Yet the Voting Rights Act affirmatively creates a right to vote for illiterate citizens of some states. The authority granted in the amendment is limited to eliminating racial discrimination in the exercise of the franchise, yet the act prescribes discrimination against illiterates. Even if there were more Negro than white illiterates in a state, the amendment could not be used

The Voting Rights Act was passed in order to eliminate the widespread use of registration procedures and other devices in certain states to deny the fundamental right to vote guaranteed by the Fifteenth Amendment. The urgency of the problem and the inadequacy of earlier attempts to deal with it justified the solution which Congress adopted. Undoubtedly, the remedy chosen is within the broad legislative discretion to select appropriate means to enforce the amendment.

It is, of course, true that some persons unqualified under properly applied state literacy laws may be registered as a result of the act. It is absurd, however, to argue that the act gives illiterates the right to vote. Given the alternatives—widespread deprivation of the right to vote on illegal grounds or the risk that some unqualified persons might be registered—Congress could appropriately choose as it did.

to strike down a lawful classification not based on race.

The Fifteenth Amendment prohibits discrimination by states, not by private citizens acting as individuals. Yet the provisions of sections 11 and 12 of the act provide for criminal punishment for any individual who "shall intimidate, threaten, or coerce . . . any person for voting or attempting to vote. . . ." and for any individual who conspires to violate the provisions of the act or deprives or attempts to deprive any person of rights secured by various sections of the act.[3] This Court has consistently held that congressional authority under the Fifteenth Amendment, like that under the Fourteenth Amendment, is limited to state action and does not include the purely private conduct of private individuals.[4]

The statute is excessive because it goes further than necessary to accomplish its purpose. It completely preempts South Carolina's registration requirements and procedures and prevents her from changing them at will; it substitutes rules not provided by South Carolina law. Under the act, all courts are closed to South Carolina and her citizens for questions arising out of the act save the United States District Court for the District of Columbia.

Finally, the act is excessive because there has not been sufficient time to test recently passed legislation designed to eliminate discrimination in voter registration. Years of congressional inaction and impatience with new but lawful measures cannot justify the drastic provisions of the statute in dispute.

[3] 79 Stat. 443–44.

[4] *James v. Bowman*, 190 U.S. 127 (1903); *Guinn v. United States*, 238 U.S. 347 (1915); *Smith v. Allwright*, 321 U.S. 649 (1944).

It would have been within Congress's power to outlaw permanently all registration tests and devices on the basis of the triggering formula, but Congress chose instead to use the formula solely as the best method available for a virtually automatic suspension effective only for the period necessary to allow a state a full judicial hearing on the question of whether the suspension was justified. Was this unreasonable?

South Carolina argues that sections 11 and 12 of the act violate the amendment because they punish private interference with the right to vote. Since the plaintiff is a state and not an individual, these sections are not properly before this Court and a decision on their constitutionality should not be made at this time. This Court has repeatedly indicated that it will not adjudicate the validity of a statute unless the complainant can show that he is injured by its operation.[3]

Congress's decision to require review of all proposed voting standards and procedures was made on the basis of substantial evidence that local officials had frequently attempted to prevent Negro voting in the past by adopting new discriminatory measures. Given the history of ingenious methods used to evade the constitutional guarantee and the fact that it was impossible to foresee every possible novel measure which might be adopted in the future, Congress was fully warranted in requiring review of all changes in voting rules and regulations in the states covered by the act.

Nor should it be concluded that the act is excessive because insufficient time has elapsed to test adequately the 1957, 1960, and 1964 Civil Rights Acts. In Mississippi, for example, twenty-two lawsuits increased registration from 4.4 percent in 1954 to 6.4 percent ten years later. Twelve suits in Alabama doubled the number of blacks who were registered to vote, but even so less than 20 percent were actually registered. In Louisiana, fourteen lawsuits raised black registration from 31.7 to 31.8 percent.[4]

Thus, it was hardly unreasonable for Congress to conclude that sufficient evidence ex-

[3] *Ashwander v. TVA*, 297 U.S. 288, 346–48 (1936).

[4] *Sen. Rep. No. 162*, 89th Cong., 1st Sess., pt. 3, at 6–9 (1965).

isted to prove that case-by-case enforcement of voting rights under existing legislation was not an effective means of ending discrimination.

5. *Does the Voting Rights Act constitute a bill of attainder prohibited by Article 1, section 9 of the Constitution?*

The authors of the Constitution wisely feared the concentration of executive, legislative, and judicial powers in the hands of one body, where they could be used to endanger the liberties of the people. They specifically prohibited the legislative body from exercising the judicial function by Article 1, section 9. In the words of Mr. Justice Black, "Those who wrote our Constitution . . . intended to safeguard the people of this country from punishment without trial by duly constituted courts."[5]

Congress has, by the Voting Rights Act, violated the separation of powers and legislated a bill of attainder, since the act condemns South Carolina and inflicts punishment without a judicial trial. Congress judged South Carolina guilty of using her literacy requirement to prevent Negroes from voting; yet South Carolina has received no judicial hearing and has had no opportunity to confront her accusers or rebut their evidence. No court has concluded that South Carolina or her citizens have violated the Fifteenth Amendment.

The Attorney General will undoubtedly argue that the act is not punitive, since it attempts to prohibit future discrimination. But, can there be any doubt of the punitive design of this legislation? By the act, South Carolina and her citizens lose their right to be governed by a literate electorate as well as their right to control or improve the regulation of their elections. In any case, the deprivation of constitutional rights because of alleged past actions to prevent future misconduct is clearly punitive.

Nor does the "escape clause"—by which a state can seek a declaratory judgment that it has not discriminated in the past five years— eliminate the punitive nature of the act. Apart from the fact that this "remedy" is inadequate, the possibility of escaping the penalties of the

The bill of attainder clause of the Constitution was not designed to apply to the states, nor has it been so applied by the courts. All the cases condemning a statute as a bill of attainder involve instances in which an individual or group has been punished or deprived of a valuable right. See for example, *United States v. Brown*, 381 U.S. 437 (1965), where a statute denied certain individuals the right to be officers or employees of labor unions; *United States v. Lovett*, 328 U.S. 303 (1946), where a statute withheld an individual's salary; *Ex parte Garland*, 4 Wall. 333 (1866), where a statute denied the right to engage in the practice of a profession.

The Voting Rights Act does not punish or deprive anyone of any rights; no person or group loses life, liberty, property, or position when literacy tests and similar devices are suspended. Nor can a state rationally argue that its citizens have lost certain rights through the dilution of their electorate, since every exercise of power under the Fifteenth Amendment must have an impact on those who have enjoyed the benefit of an unconstitutionally restricted suffrage. "Dilution" in this sense is certainly not a deprivation of rights.

Nor can it be argued that the Voting Rights Act is a bill of attainder on the grounds that it constitutes a legislative trial in violation of the separation of powers. This argument proves too much since, if it were accepted, it would prevent Congress from providing for the regulation of any activity. All regulatory legislation must be based on legislative findings as to facts which reveal a need for the imposition of future restraints. The fact that the act was based on substantial evidence of need does not transform it into a legislative adjudication.

One can always argue that the formula chosen by Congress for the suspension of literacy tests and other voting devices is inexact and that a different formula should have

---

[5] *United States v. Lovett*, 328 U.S. 303, 317–18 (1946).

act cannot lessen the constitutional invalidity of the legislative adjudication. Thus, South Carolina asks the Court to overthrow the challenged provisions of the act on the grounds that Congress has violated the separation of powers and legislated a bill of attainder forbidden by the Constitution.

been chosen. But as long as the legislation is reasonable and rational, it is the proper function of Congress and not of the courts to determine an appropriate formula.

Finally, even if the states *were* entitled to protection against bills of attainder, the Voting Rights Act cannot be placed in this category since it imposes no punishment. Congress explicitly provided an opportunity for every state to seek a judicial determination of the applicability of the regulatory scheme. It is surely no punishment to shift the burden of proof in such a judicial proceeding to the states covered by the act. And, no matter how broad the concept of punishment may be, it surely does not include the burden of bringing a suit to prove that the state's literacy tests and other voting devices have not been used in a discriminatory manner for the preceding five years.

. . . .

III. Decision of the Court and Dissenting Opinion*

Mr. CHIEF JUSTICE WARREN delivered the opinion of the Court.

By leave of the Court . . . South Carolina has filed a bill of complaint, seeking a declaration that selected provisions of the Voting Rights Act of 1965 violate the Federal Constitution, and asking for an injunction against enforcement of these provisions by the Attorney General. Original jurisdiction is founded on the presence of a controversy between a State and a citizen of another State under Art. III, § 2, of the Constitution. . . .

The Voting Rights Act was designed by Congress to banish the blight of racial discrimination in voting, which has infected the electoral process in parts of our country for nearly a century. The Act creates stringent new remedies for voting discrimination where it persists on a pervasive scale. . . . Congress assumed the power to prescribe these remedies from § 2 of the Fifteenth Amendment, which authorizes the National Legislature to effectuate by "appropriate" measures the constitutional prohibition against racial discrimination in voting. We hold that the sections of the Act which are properly before us are an appropriate means for carrying out Congress' constitutional responsibilities and are consonant with all other provisions of the Constitution. We therefore deny South Carolina's request that enforcement of these sections of the Act be enjoined.

I

The constitutional propriety of the Voting Rights Act of 1965 must be judged with reference to the historical experience which it reflects. Before enacting the measure,

*Author's note: printed below is an edited version of the decision of eight members of the Court in *South Carolina v. Katzenbach*, 383 U.S. 301 (1965); Justice Black's opinion, in which he concurs in part and dissents in part, follows. Footnotes have been omitted; bracketed material has been added.

Congress explored with great care the problem of racial discrimination in voting. The House and Senate Committees on the Judiciary each held hearings for nine days and received testimony from a total of 67 witnesses. More than three full days were consumed discussing the bill on the floor of the House, while the debate in the Senate covered 26 days in all. At the close of these deliberations, the verdict of both chambers was overwhelming. The House approved the Act by a vote of 328–74, and the measure passed the Senate by a margin of 79–18.

Two points emerge vividly from the voluminous legislative history of the Act contained in the committee hearings and floor debates. First: Congress felt itself confronted by an insidious and pervasive evil which had been perpetuated in certain parts of our country through unremitting and ingenious defiance of the Constitution. Second: Congress concluded that the unsuccessful remedies which it had prescribed in the past would have to be replaced by sterner and more elaborate measures in order to satisfy the clear commands of the Fifteenth Amendment. . . .

The Fifteenth Amendment to the Constitution was ratified in 1870. Promptly thereafter Congress passed the first Enforcement Act, which made it a crime for public officers and private persons to obstruct exercise of the right to vote. . . . As the years passed and fervor for racial equality waned, enforcement of the laws became spotty and ineffective, and most of their provisions were repealed in 1894. The remnants have had little significance in the recently renewed battle against voting discrimination.

Meanwhile, beginning in 1890, the States of Alabama, Georgia, Louisiana, Mississippi, North Carolina, South Carolina, and Virginia enacted tests still in use which were specifically designed to prevent Negroes from voting. Typically, they made the ability to read and write a registration qualification and also required completion of a registration form. These laws were based on the fact that as of 1890 in each of the named States, more than two-thirds of the adult Negroes were illiterate while less than one-quarter of the adult whites were unable to read or write. At the same time, alternate tests were prescribed in all of the named States to assure that white illiterates would not be deprived of the franchise. These included grandfather clauses, property qualifications, "good character" tests, and the requirement that registrants "understand" or "interpret" certain matter.

The course of subsequent Fifteenth Amendment litigation in this Court demonstrates the variety and persistence of these and similar institutions designed to deprive Negroes of the right to vote. Grandfather clauses were invalidated. . . . Procedural hurdles were struck down. . . . The white primary was outlawed. . . . Racial gerrymandering was forbidden. . . . Finally, discriminatory application of voting tests was condemned. . . .

According to the evidence in recent Justice Department voting suits, the latter stratagem is now the principal method used to bar Negroes from the polls. Discriminatory administration of voting qualifications has been found in all eight Alabama cases, in all nine Louisiana cases, and in all nine Mississippi cases which have gone to final judgment. Moreover, in almost all of these cases, the courts have held that the discrimination was pursuant to a widespread "pattern or practice." White applicants for registration have often been excused altogether from the literacy and understanding tests or have been given easy versions, have received extensive help from voting officials, and have been registered despite serious errors in their answers. Negroes, on the other hand, have typically been required to pass difficult versions of all the tests, without any outside assistance and without the slightest error. The good morals requirement is so vague and subjective that it has constituted an open invitation to abuse at the hands of voting officials. Negroes obliged to obtain vouchers from registered voters have found it virtually impossible to comply in areas where almost no Negroes are on the rolls.

In recent years, Congress has repeatedly tried to cope with the problem by facilitating case-by-case litigation against voting discrimination. . . .

Despite the earnest efforts of the Justice Department and of many federal judges, these new laws have done little to cure the problem of voting discrimination. . . .

The previous legislation has proved ineffective for a number of reasons. Voting suits are unusually onerous to prepare, sometimes requiring as many as 6,000 man-hours spent combing through registration records in preparation for trial. Litigation has been exceedingly slow, in part because of the ample opportunities for delay afforded voting officials and others involved in the proceedings. Even when favorable decisions have finally been obtained, some of the States affected have merely switched to discriminatory devices not covered by the federal decrees or have enacted difficult new tests designed to prolong the existing disparity between white and Negro registration. Alternatively, certain local officials have defied and evaded court orders or have simply closed their registration offices to freeze the voting rolls. The provision of the 1960 law authorizing registration by federal officers has had little impact on local maladministration because of its procedural complexities.

During the hearings and debates on the Act, Selma, Alabama, was repeatedly referred to as the pre-eminent example of the ineffectiveness of existing legislation. In Dallas County, of which Selma is the seat, there were four years of litigation by the Justice Department and two findings by the federal courts of widespread voting discrimination. Yet in those four years, Negro registration rose only from 156 to 383, although there are approximately 15,000 Negroes of voting age in the county. Any possibility that these figures were attributable to political apathy was dispelled by the protest demonstrations in Selma in the early months of 1965. . . .

II

The Voting Rights Act of 1965 reflects Congress' firm intention to rid the country of racial discrimination in voting. The heart of the Act is a complex scheme of stringent remedies aimed at areas where voting discrimination has been most flagrant. Section 4 (a)–(d) lays down a formula defining the States and political subdivisions to which these new remedies apply. The first of the remedies . . . is the suspension of literacy tests and similar voting qualifications for a period of five years from the last occurrence of substantial voting discrimination. Section 5 prescribes a second remedy, the suspension of all new voting regulations pending review by federal authorities to determine whether their use would perpetuate voting discrimination. The third remedy . . . is the assignment of federal examiners . . . by the Attorney General to list qualified applicants who are thereafter entitled to vote in all elections.

Other provisions of the Act prescribe subsidiary cures for persistent voting discrimination. . . .

At the outset, we emphasize that only some of the many portions of the Act are properly before us. . . . Judicial review of . . . sections [not challenged] must await subsequent litigation. In addition, we find that South Carolina's attack on §§ 11 and 12 (a)–(c) is premature. No person has yet been subjected to, or even threatened with, the criminal sanctions which these sections of the Act authorize. . . .

III

These provisions of the Voting Rights Act of 1965 are challenged on the fundamental ground that they exceed the powers of Congress and encroach on an area reserved to the States by the Constitution. South Carolina and certain of the *amici curiae* also attack specific sections of the Act for more particular reasons. They argue that the coverage formula . . . violates the principle of the equality of States, denies due process by employing an invalid presumption and by barring judicial review of administrative findings, constitutes a forbidden bill of attainder, and impairs the separation of powers by adjudicating guilt through legislation. They claim that the review of new voting rules . . . infringes Article III by directing the District Court to issue advisory opinions. They contend . . . that the challenge procedure . . . denies due process on account of its speed. Finally, South Carolina and certain of the *amici curiae* maintain that . . . the Act, abridge[s] due process by limiting litigation to a distant forum.

Some of these contentions may be dismissed at the outset. The word "person" in the context of the Due Process Clause of the Fifth Amendment cannot, by any reasonable mode of interpretation, be expanded to encompass the States of the Union, and to our knowledge this has never been done by any court. . . . Likewise, courts have consistently regarded the Bill of Attainder Clause of Article I and the principle of the separation of powers only as protections for individual persons and private groups, those who are peculiarly vulnerable to non-judicial determinations of guilt. . . . Nor does a State have standing as the parent of its citizens to invoke these constitutional provisions against the Federal Government. . . . The objections to the Act which are raised under these provisions may therefore be considered only as additional aspects of the basic question presented by the case: Has Congress exercised its powers under the Fifteenth Amendment in an appropriate manner with relation to the States?

The ground rules for resolving this question are clear. The language and purposes of the Fifteenth Amendment, the prior decisions construing its several provisions, and the general doctrines of constitutional interpretation, all point to one fundamental principle. As against the reserved powers of the States, Congress may use any rational means to effectuate the constitutional prohibition of racial discrimination in voting. . . .

Section 1 of the Fifteenth Amendment declares that "the right of citizens of the United States to vote shall not be denied or abridged by the United States or by any State on account of race, color, or previous condition of servitude." This declaration . . . has repeatedly been construed, without further legislative specification, to invalidate state voting qualifications or procedures which are discriminatory on their face or in practice. . . . The gist of the matter is that the Fifteenth Amendment supersedes contrary exertions of state power. "When a State exercises power wholly within the domain of state interest, it is insulated from federal judicial review. But such insulation is not carried over when state power is used as an instrument for circumventing a federally protected right." *Gomillion v. Lightfoot,* 364 U.S. 339, at 347.

South Carolina contends that . . . to allow . . . Congress [to exercise the authority of the judiciary to strike down state statutes and procedures] would be to rob the courts of their rightful constitutional role. On the contrary, § 2 of the Fifteenth Amendment expressly declares that "Congress shall have the power to enforce this article by appropriate legislation." By adding this authorization, the Framers indicated that Congress was to be chiefly responsible for implementing the rights created in §1. "It is the power of Congress which has been enlarged. Congress is authorized to *enforce* the prohibitions by appropriate legislation. Some legislation is contemplated to make the (Civil War) amendments fully effective." *Ex parte Virginia,* 100 U.S. 339, 345. Accordingly, in addition to the courts, Congress has full remedial powers to effectuate the constitutional prohibition against racial discrimination in voting.

Congress has repeatedly exercised these powers in the past, and its enactments have repeatedly been upheld. For recent examples, see the Civil Rights Act of 1957 . . . ; and the Civil Rights Act of 1960. . . . On the rare occasions when the Court has found an unconstitutional exercise of these powers, in its opinion Congress had attacked evils not comprehended by the Fifteenth Amendment.

The basic test to be applied in a case involving § 2 of the Fifteenth Amendment is the same as in all cases concerning the express powers of Congress with relation to the reserved powers of the States. Chief Justice Marshall laid down the classic formulation, 50 years before the Fifteenth Amendment was ratified:

> Let the end be legitimate, let it be within the scope of the constitution, and all means which are appropriate, which are plainly adapted to that end, which are not prohibited, but consist with the letter and spirit of the constitution, are constitutional.
>
> *McCulloch v. Maryland*, 4 Wheat. 316, 421.

The Court has subsequently echoed his language in describing each of the Civil War Amendments:

> Whatever legislation is appropriate, that is, adapted to carry out the objects the amendments have in view, whatever tends to enforce submission to the prohibitions they contain, and to secure to all persons the enjoyment of perfect equality of civil rights and the equal protection of the laws against State denial or invasion, if not prohibited, is brought within the domain of congressional power.
>
> *Ex parte Virginia*, 100 U.S., at 345–46.

We therefore reject South Carolina's argument that Congress may appropriately do no more than to forbid violations of the Fifteenth Amendment in general terms— that the task of fashioning specific remedies or of applying them to particular localities must necessarily be left entirely to the courts. Congress is not circumscribed by any such artificial rules under § 2 of the Fifteenth Amendment. In the oft-repeated words of Chief Justice Marshall, referring to another specific legislative authorization in the Constitution, "This power, like all others vested in Congress, is complete in itself, may be exercised to its utmost extent, and acknowledges no limitations, other than are prescribed in the constitution." *Gibbons v. Ogden*, 9 Wheat. 1, 196.

IV

Congress exercised its authority under the Fifteenth Amendment in an inventive manner when it enacted the Voting Rights Act of 1965. First: The measure prescribes remedies for voting discrimination which go into effect without any need for prior adjudication. This was clearly a legitimate response to the problem, for which there is ample precedent under other constitutional provisions. . . . Congress had found that case-by-case litigation was inadequate to combat widespread and persistent discrimination in voting, because of the inordinate amount of time and energy required to overcome the obstructionist tactics invariably encountered in these lawsuits. After enduring nearly a century of systematic resistance to the Fifteenth Amendment, Congress might well decide to shift the advantage of time and inertia from the perpetrators of the evil to its victims. The question remains, of course, whether the specific remedies prescribed in the Act were an appropriate means of combatting the evil, and to this question we shall presently address ourselves.

Second: The Act intentionally confines these remedies to a small number of States and political subdivisions which in most instances were familiar to Congress by name. This, too, was a permissible method of dealing with the problem. . . . In acceptable legislative fashion, Congress chose to limit its attention to the geographic areas where immediate action seemed necessary. . . . The doctrine of the equality of States, invoked by South Carolina, does not bar this approach, for that doctrine applies only to the terms upon which States are admitted to the Union, and not to the remedies for local evils which have subsequently appeared. . . .

Coverage Formula   We now consider the related question of whether the specific States and political subdivisions . . . [covered by] the Act were an appropriate target for the new remedies. South Carolina contends that the coverage formula is awkwardly designed in a number of respects and that it disregards various local conditions which have nothing to do with racial discrimination. These arguments, however, are largely beside the point. Congress began work with reliable evidence of actual voting discrimination in a great majority of the States and political subdivisions affected by the new remedies of the Act. The formula eventually evolved to describe these areas was relevant to the problem of voting discrimination, and Congress was therefore entitled to infer a significant danger of the evil in the few remaining States and political subdivisions covered by . . . the Act. No more was required to justify the application to these areas of Congress' express powers under the Fifteenth Amendment. . . .

To be specific, the new remedies of the Act are imposed on three States—Alabama, Louisiana, and Mississippi—in which federal courts have repeatedly found substantial voting discrimination. . . . [T]he Act also embraces two other States—Georgia and South Carolina—plus large portions of a third State—North Carolina—for which there was more fragmentary evidence of recent voting discrimination mainly adduced by the Justice Department and the Civil Rights Commission. All of these areas were appropriately subjected to the new remedies. In identifying past evils, Congress obviously may avail itself of information from any probative source. . . .

The areas listed above, for which there was evidence of actual voting discrimination, share two characteristics incorporated by Congress into the coverage formula: the use of tests and devices for voter registration, and a voting rate in the 1964 presidential election at least 12 points below the national average. Tests and devices are relevant to voting discrimination because of their long history as a tool for perpetrating the evil; a low voting rate is pertinent for the obvious reason that widespread disenfranchisement must inevitably affect the number of actual voters. Accordingly, the coverage formula is rational in both practice and theory. It was therefore permissible to impose the new remedies on the few remaining States and political subdivisions covered by the formula, at least in the absence of proof that they have been free of substantial voting discrimination in recent years. Congress is clearly not bound by the rules relating to statutory presumptions in criminal cases when it prescribes civil remedies against other organs of government under § 2 of the Fifteenth Amendment. . . .

It is irrelevant that the coverage formula excludes certain localities which do not employ voting tests and devices but for which there is evidence of voting discrimination by other means. . . . Legislation need not deal with all phases of a problem in the same way, so long as the distinctions drawn have some basis in practical experience. . . .

Acknowledging the possibility of overbreadth, the Act provides for termination of special statutory coverage at the behest of States and political subdivisions in which the danger of substantial voting discrimination has not materialized during the preceding five years. Despite South Carolina's argument to the contrary, Congress might appropriately limit litigation under this provision to a single court in the District of Columbia, pursuant to its constitutional power under Art. III, § 1, to "ordain and establish" inferior federal tribunals. . . . We have discovered no suggestion that Congress exceeded constitutional bounds in imposing these limitations on litigation against the Federal Government, and the Act is no less reasonable in this respect.

South Carolina contends that these termination procedures are a nullity because they impose an impossible burden of proof upon States and political subdivisions entitled to relief. As the Attorney General pointed out during hearings on the Act, however, an area need do no more than submit affidavits from voting officials, asserting that they have not been guilty of racial discrimination through the use of tests and devices during the past five years, and then refute whatever evidence to the contrary may be adduced by the Federal Government. [The Act] . . . further assures that an area need not disprove each isolated instance of voting discrimination in order to obtain relief in the termination proceedings. The burden of proof is therefore quite bearable, particularly since the relevant facts relating to the conduct of voting officials are peculiarly within the knowledge of the States and political subdivisions themselves. . . .

Suspension of Tests   We now arrive at consideration of the specific remedies prescribed by the Act for areas included within the coverage formula. South Carolina assails the temporary suspension of existing voting qualifications, reciting the rule laid down by *Lassiter v. Northampton County Bd. of Elections*, 360 U.S. 45, that literacy tests and related devices are not in themselves contrary to the Fifteenth Amendment. In that very case, however, the Court went on to say, "Of course a literacy test, fair on its face, may be employed to perpetuate that discrimination which the Fifteenth Amendment was designed to uproot." *Id.*, at 53. The record shows that in most of the States covered by the Act, including South Carolina, various tests and devices have been instituted with the purpose of disenfranchising Negroes, have been framed in such a way as to facilitate this aim, and have been administered in a discriminatory fashion for many years. Under these circumstances, the Fifteenth Amendment has clearly been violated. . . .

The Act suspends literacy tests and similar devices for a period of five years from the last occurrence of substantial voting discrimination. This was a legitimate response to the problem, for which there is ample precedent in Fifteenth Amendment cases. . . . Underlying the response was the feeling that States and political subdivisions which had been allowing white illiterates to vote for years could not sincerely complain about "dilution" of their electorates through the registration of Negro illiterates. Congress knew that continuance of the tests and devices in use at the present time, no matter how fairly administered in the future, would freeze the effect of past discrimination in favor of unqualified white registrants. Congress permissibly rejected the alternative of requiring a complete re-registration of all voters, believing that this would be too harsh on many whites who had enjoyed the franchise for their entire adult lives.

Review of New Rules   The Act suspends new voting regulations pending scrutiny by federal authorities to determine whether their use would violate the Fifteenth Amendment. This may have been an uncommon exercise of congressional power, as South Carolina contends, but the Court has recognized that exceptional conditions can justify legislative measures not otherwise appropriate. . . . Congress knew that some of the States covered by . . . the Act had resorted to the extraordinary stratagem of contriving new rules of various kinds for the sole purpose of perpetuating voting discrimination in the face of adverse federal court decrees. Congress had reason to suppose that these States might try similar maneuvers in the future in order to evade the remedies for voting discrimination contained in the Act itself. Under the compulsion of these unique circumstances, Congress responded in a permissibly decisive manner. . . .

Congress [has not] authorized the District Court to issue advisory opinions, in violation of the principles of Article III. . . . A State or political subdivision wishing to make use of a recent amendment to its voting laws . . . has a concrete and immediate "controversy" with the Federal Government. . . . An appropriate remedy is a judicial determination that continued suspension of the new rule is unnecessary to vindicate rights guaranteed by the Fifteenth Amendment.

Federal Examiners   The Act authorizes the appointment of federal examiners to list qualified applicants who are thereafter entitled to vote, subject to an expeditious challenge procedure. This was clearly an appropriate response to the problem. . . . In many of the political subdivisions covered by . . . the Act, voting officials have persistently employed a variety of procedural tactics to deny Negroes the franchise, often in direct defiance or evasion of federal decrees. Congress realized that merely to suspend voting rules which have been misused or are subject to misuse might leave this localized evil undisturbed. As for the briskness of the challenge procedure, Congress knew that in some of the areas affected, challenges had been persistently employed to harass registered Negroes. It chose to forestall this abuse. . . .

After enduring nearly a century of widespread resistance to the Fifteenth Amendment, Congress has marshalled an array of potent weapons against the evil, with authority in the Attorney General to employ them effectively. Many of the areas directly affected by this development have indicated their willingness to abide by any restraints legitimately imposed upon them. We here hold that the portions of the Voting Rights Act properly before us are a valid means for carrying out the commands of the Fifteenth Amendment. Hopefully, millions of non-white Americans will now be able to participate for the first time on an equal basis in the government under which they live. We may finally look forward to the day when truly "the right of citizens of the United States to vote shall not be denied or abridged by the United States or by any State on account of race, color, or previous condition of servitude."

The bill of complaint is

Dismissed.

Mr. JUSTICE BLACK, concurring and dissenting.

I agree with substantially all of the Court's opinion sustaining the power of Congress under § 2 of the Fifteenth Amendment to suspend state literacy tests and similar voting qualifications and to authorize the Attorney General to secure the appointment of federal examiners to register qualified voters in various sections of the country. . . .

Though, as I have said, I agree with most of the Court's conclusions, I dissent from its holding that every part of . . . the Act is constitutional. . . . Section 5 . . . provide[s] that a State covered by . . . [the Act] can in no way amend its constitution or laws relating to voting without first trying to persuade the Attorney General of the United States or the Federal District Court for the District of Columbia that the new proposed laws do not have the purpose and will not have the effect of denying the right to vote to citizens on account of their race or color. I think this section is unconstitutional on at least two grounds.

(a) The Constitution gives federal courts jurisdiction over cases and controversies only. If it can be said that any case or controversy arises under this section which gives the District Court for the District of Columbia jurisdiction to approve or reject state laws or constitutional amendments, then the case or controversy must be between a State and the United States Government. But it is hard for me to believe that a justiciable controversy can arise in the constitutional sense from a desire by the United States Government or some of its officials to determine in advance what legislative provisions a State may enact or what constitutional amendments it may adopt. If this dispute between the Federal Government and the States amounts to a case or controversy it is a far cry from the traditional constitutional notion of a case or controversy as a dispute over the meaning of enforceable laws or the manner in which they are applied. . . .

. . . [B]y requiring a State to ask a federal court to approve the validity of a proposed law which has in no way become operative, Congress has asked the State to secure precisely the type of advisory opinion our Constitution forbids. . . . Congress has ample power to protect the rights of citizens to vote without resorting to the unnecessarily circuitous, indirect and unconstitutional route it has adopted in this section.

(b) My second and more basic objection to § 5 is that Congress has here exercised its power under § 2 of the Fifteenth Amendment through the adoption of means that conflict with the most basic principles of the Constitution. As the Court says the limitations of the power granted under § 2 are the same as the limitations imposed on the exercise of any of the powers expressly granted Congress by the Constitution. The classic formulation of these constitutional limitations was stated by Chief Justice Marshall when he said in *McCulloch v. Maryland*, 4 Wheat. 316, 421, "Let the end be legitimate, let it be within the scope of the constitution, and all means which are appropriate, which are plainly adapted to that end, *which are not prohibited, but consist with the letter and spirit of the constitution,* are constitutional." (Emphasis added.) Section 5, by providing that some of the States cannot pass state laws or adopt state constitutional amendments without first being compelled to beg federal authorities to approve their policies, so distorts our constitutional structure of government as to render any distinction drawn in the Constitution between state and federal power almost meaningless. One of the most basic premises upon which our structure of government was founded was that the Federal Government was to have certain specific and limited powers and no others, and all other power was to be reserved either "to the States respectively, or to the people." Certainly if all the provisions of our Constitution which limit the power of the Federal Government and reserve other power to the States are to mean anything, they mean at least that the States have power to pass laws and amend their constitutions without first sending their officials hundreds of miles away to beg federal authorities to approve them. . . . And if one law concerning voting can make the States plead for this approval by a distant federal court or the United States Attorney General, other laws on different subjects can force the States to seek the advance approval not only of the Attorney General but of the President himself or any other chosen members of his staff. It is inconceivable to me that such a radical degradation of state power was intended in any of the provisions of our Constitution or its Amendments. Of course I do not mean to cast any doubt whatever upon the indisputable power of the Federal Government to invalidate a state law once enacted and operative on the ground that it intrudes into the area of supreme federal power. . . .

I see no reason to read into the Constitution meanings it did not have when it was adopted and which have not been put into it since. The proceedings of the original Constitutional Convention show beyond all doubt that the power to veto or negative state laws was denied Congress. On several occasions proposals were submitted to the convention to grant this power to Congress. These proposals were debated extensively and on every occasion when submitted for vote they were overwhelmingly rejected. The refusal to give Congress this extraordinary power to veto state laws was based on the belief that if such power resided in Congress the States would be helpless to function as effective governments. Since that time neither the Fifteenth Amendment nor any other Amendment to the Constitution has given the slightest indication of a purpose to grant Congress the power to veto state laws either by itself or its agents. Nor does any provision in the Constitution endow the federal courts with power to participate with state legislative bodies in determining what state policies shall be enacted into law. The judicial power to invalidate a law in a case or controversy after the law has become effective is a long way from the power to prevent a State from passing a law. I cannot agree with the Court that Congress—denied a power in itself to veto a state law—can delegate this same power to the Attorney General or the District Court for the District of Columbia. . . .

In this and other prior Acts Congress has quite properly vested the Attorney General with extremely broad power to protect voting rights of citizens against discrimination on account of race or color. Section 5 viewed in this context is of very minor importance and in my judgment is likely to serve more as an irritant to the States than as an aid to the enforcement of the Act. I would hold § 5 invalid for the reasons stated above with full confidence that the Attorney General has ample power to give vigorous, expeditious and effective protection to the voting rights of all citizens.

. . . .

IV.   Implementing the Voting Rights Act

The Voting Rights Act of 1965 was passed by Congress and signed by the President in the summer of 1965, but the Attorney General did not move immediately to implement the statute throughout the seven Southern states which had been "convicted" by Congress of using literacy tests and other registration devices to prevent black people from voting. It was almost as if the policymakers in the Department of Justice were so exhausted by the effort to get the bill passed that insufficient energy remained to make the new law meaningful.

To a certain extent, the Department of Justice marked time while the Supreme Court debated the constitutionality of the act. After the unanimous decision of the Court, however, in March 1966, there was no legitimate excuse for further procrastination. Leaders of civil rights groups and their allies in Congress began to get restless.

Faced with increased pressure, the Attorney General began to appoint federal examiners. In the first year and one-half after the passage of the act, 150,000 blacks were listed as eligible to vote by examiners in fifty-eight counties of five Southern states. No examiners were appointed, however, to 185 other counties and parishes covered by the Voting Rights Act. The Justice Department announced that (1) no examiners would be appointed to counties where local registrars were making a good faith effort to comply with the Fifteenth Amendment, and (2) no examiners would be appointed unless there was a real possibility of effective political organization in the period following mass registration of new voters. As Attorney General Katzenbach stated in a letter written November 21, 1965:

My conclusion is that success turns principally on the effectiveness of a local registration drive which, of course, turns on the accomplishment of the local organization. This is true whether or not federal examiners have been appointed for the county.

It has been suggested that this work can be done by the federal government. For a number of reasons, I don't think this is either possible or desirable.

The government has no budgetary approval for such a project. Besides, the only way that political participation can be permanently achieved is through many local organizations doing the routine, the drudgery, the step-by-step creating and developing a viable political organization. It seems to me that even if the federal government undertook to accomplish the actual registration of the mass of unregistered Negroes, when the federal government left, there would be little left for the future.[1]

Thus, the Department of Justice staked out a position contrary to that of the U.S. Commission on Civil Rights, which advocated repeatedly the need for affirmative federal programs to encourage voter registration in the South. By the end of 1967, the government agency responsible for implementing the Voting Rights Act still adhered to its original approach that strong federal registration programs would be counterproductive since they would not, of themselves, bring black people out of the Southern caste system and transform them into active participants in state and local politics. When the question was raised again in March 1968 by the staff director of the U.S. Commission on Civil Rights, the assistant attorney general in charge of the Civil Rights Division of the Department of Justice replied as follows:

My experience would indicate that—at least after the first few months of experience with the Voting Rights Act—the key factor is the mounting of a drive for voter registration. The assignment of examiners may help generate enthusiasm but its major significance is as a means to assure that full opportunities are available for registration where the State fails to meet its responsibilities.[2]

While the controversy over the best strategy to follow to encourage widespread registration *and* political participation embroiled the responsible officials in Washington, federal examiners in the fifty-eight counties chosen by the Attorney General and local registrars in the remaining counties covered by the Voting Rights Act continued to register new voters. Besides the 150,000 black citizens who became eligible to vote as a result of the decisions of federal examiners in the first year and one-half after passage of the act, local registrars in states covered by the act registered an additional 416,000. By 1970, over 900,000 black citizens had been registered to vote under the enforcement provisions of the Voting Rights Act.

Prior to the passage of the act, Florida, Tennessee, and Texas were the only Southern states in which more than 50 percent of the adult black population was registered to vote. By May 1967, however, more than 50 percent was registered in every Southern state. The table on page thirty indicates the scope of registration efforts in the two years following congressional approval of the Voting Rights Act.

Progress was most remarkable in the Deep South, where resistance to civil rights for nonwhites has been strongest. In Mississippi, for example, Negro registration increased from 6.7 to 59.8 percent. In Alabama, registration rose from 19.3 to 51.6 percent. Registration in Georgia nearly doubled, going from 27.4 to 52.6 percent. Louisiana registration went from 31.6 to nearly 60 percent.

BLACK POLITICAL POWER BEGINS TO GROW

The raw figures on voter registration do not tell the full story, however. They do not indicate the significance of effective voting power both for the political system in

---

[1] Quoted in U.S. Commission on Civil Rights, *Political Participation*, U.S. Government Printing Office, 1968, p. 156.

[2] Letter from Stephen J. Pollak to William L. Taylor, March 13, 1968, *ibid.*, p. 155.

VOTING REGISTRATION BY RACE BEFORE AND AFTER
PASSAGE OF THE VOTING RIGHTS ACT OF 1965*

State	Preact Registra- tion	Postact Registra- tion	Preact Percent of Voting Age Population Registered	Percent of Voting Age Population Registered as of May 1967
Alabama:				
Nonwhite	92,737	248,432	19.3	51.6
White	935,695	1,212,317	69.2	89.6
Arkansas:				
Nonwhite	77,714	121,000	40.4	62.8
White	555,944	616,000	65.5	72.4
Florida:				
Nonwhite	240,616	299,033	51.2	63.6
White	1,958,499	2,131,105	74.8	81.4
Georgia:				
Nonwhite	167,663	332,496	27.4	52.6
White	1,124,415	1,443,730	62.6	80.3
Louisiana:				
Nonwhite	164,601	303,148	31.6	58.9
White	1,037,184	1,200,517	80.5	93.1
Mississippi:				
Nonwhite	28,500	263,754	6.7	59.8
White	525,000	665,176	69.9	91.5
North Carolina:				
Nonwhite	258,000	277,404	46.8	51.3
White	1,942,000	1,602,980	96.8	83.0
South Carolina:				
Nonwhite	138,544	190,017	37.3	51.2
White	677,914	731,096	75.7	81.7
Tennessee:				
Nonwhite	218,000	225,000	69.5	71.7
White	1,297,000	1,434,000	72.9	80.6
Texas:				
Nonwhite	2,939,535	400,000 ⎱	53.1	61.6
White		2,600,000 ⎰		53.3
Virginia:				
Nonwhite	144,259	243,000	38.3	55.6
White	1,070,168	1,190,000	61.1	63.4

* U.S. Commission on Civil Rights, *Political Participation*, U.S. Government Printing Office, 1968, pp. 12–13 [Explanatory footnotes have been omitted].

general and for black citizens in particular. A survey by the Southern Regional Council after the 1966 elections found that the growing Negro vote was instrumental in the election of a United States senator from South Carolina, a governor in Arkansas, and at least two members of the House of Representatives.[3]

By the fall of 1967, more than 200 Negroes held elective office throughout the South, an increase of over 100 percent. Twenty nonwhites were elected to state

[3] Southern Regional Council, press release, "What Happened in the South, 1966," December 14, 1966.

legislatures, including the first black representative in the Mississippi legislature in nearly a century. A Negro was elected sheriff of Macon County, Alabama, becoming the first nonwhite sheriff in the Deep South since Reconstruction. By the spring of 1968, the number of Negroes holding state or local government posts throughout the eleven states of the South had increased to over 250.

In Selma, Alabama, the town whose name symbolized white resistance to voting by black citizens, the Voting Rights Act had a major impact. Registration rose from less than 500 to more than 5,000. Negroes ran for mayor and for city council. Four nonwhites joined the city police force. A hard-line segregationist was defeated for reelection to the post of Dallas County sheriff; his successor, a moderate, integrated the sheriff's office by hiring two black deputies.

Holmes County, Mississippi, also reflected the growing power of black voters. Although Negro residents of voting age outnumbered whites by two to one, the voting rolls prior to the act carried the names of 4,800 whites and only 20 blacks. The county was one of the first to receive federal examiners, who proceeded to list 5,844 eligible black voters. In the 1967 general elections, twelve Negroes ran for state and county posts, and two of them were elected, including a candidate for the state legislature.

More important than the election of Negroes to public office, however, have been the subtle side effects of electoral participation. As a result of registration drives by well-known organizations such as the Southern Regional Council, the NAACP, and CORE and by several thousand unsung community groups, political skills began to be developed and self-help efforts flourished. Tenants' unions, credit unions, and farmers' cooperatives were formed to improve economic conditions; other community action organizations focused on private discrimination and on inadequate social services.

For example, in Plaquemine Parish, Louisiana, the fiefdom of archsegregationist Leander Perez, demonstrators who were seeking street lights, street signs, and enclosed sewers were put down by tear gas, cattle prods, and cavalry tactics as recently as 1963. With the power of the ballot, plus increased political skills developed during voter registration drives, the black community obtained the lights, the signs, and chemical treatment of sewage.

In West Feliciana Parish, at the Northern end of the state, startling changes began to take place. The first stirrings began in 1963, when a courageous man named Nathaniel Smith became the third Negro to register in the twentieth century. By November 1967, through the efforts of the West Feliciana Voters' League, three Negroes had been elected to serve on the nine-member county police jury; two Negroes were serving as deputy sheriffs; two were on the school board; three were on the Executive Committee of the Democratic Party. The schools were being integrated and improved and, for the first time, black people were being employed by a big paper plant in the vicinity.

Examples like the above could be multiplied many times throughout the South. Politicians realized they could no longer ignore the needs of black citizens. In fact, the whole tone of politics started to change as white candidates for elective office found it less and less profitable to exploit the race issue.

NEW DEVICES TO MAINTAIN WHITE SUPREMACY

On the other hand, each positive change in the pattern of Southern politics was met by a determined counterattack. Inevitably, individuals who had fought every step of the way to maintain the Southern caste system were not going to desert the field just because the federal government passed a law suspending state voter registration laws in certain Deep South states. Instead, they searched for new methods to achieve an old purpose.

Many devices were developed to limit participation in the political system by large numbers of black citizens.[4] Efforts were made—and are being made—to prevent Negroes from becoming candidates for elective office by abolishing the office, by extending the term of incumbent white officials, by substituting appointment for election, by increasing filing fees, by making the requirements for getting on the ballot more stringent, by withholding necessary information from prospective Negro candidates, by withholding or delaying unnecessarily certification of nominating petitions. In numerous instances, candidates have had to seek help from the courts. Some efforts to obtain judicial relief have been successful, while others have not; all of them, however, have been complex, costly, and time-consuming.

Among the more successful challenges to discriminatory devices enacted to circumvent the impact of the Voting Rights Act of 1965 were four appeals which were decided in one Supreme Court ruling.[5] The Court struck down a Mississippi statute that made it harder for independent candidates to get on the ballot and a second Mississippi statute which substituted appointment of county supervisors in eleven counties for choice of supervisors by general election. Since neither of these statutes appeared to involve a new voting qualification or procedure with respect to voting, Mississippi had not followed the requirement of the Voting Rights Act of 1965 that no new voting laws could be enacted by states whose literacy laws had been suspended without prior approval by the Attorney General or the Federal District Court for the District of Columbia.

By a seven to two vote, the Court ruled that Mississippi could not enact the statutes in question without federal approval. The Voting Rights Act was interpreted to include not only newly enacted restrictions on the right to vote but also laws which diminished the effectiveness of voting. Speaking for the Court, Chief Justice Warren held that "The Voting Rights Act was aimed at the subtle, as well as the obvious, state regulations which have the effect of denying citizens their right to vote because of their race."[6] Justice Black, in dissent, continued to express his belief that Congress lacked authority under the Fifteenth Amendment to make states come to Washington to beg for permission to change their laws.

Negro voters, as well as Negro candidates, have had to fight a wide array of discriminatory practices. Intimidation of politically active blacks has, according to the U.S. Commission on Civil Rights, declined, but it has not ceased. Voters have been excluded from precinct meetings at which party officials are chosen and have otherwise been denied the right to participate freely and fully in the activities of the political party organizations. In addition, the names of registered voters have been omitted from voting lists, insufficient polling places have been provided in various communities with heavy black populations, and election officials have harassed black voters, refused to help illiterate voters, provided erroneous or inadequate instructions to voters, disqualified ballots on technical grounds, discriminated in the availability of absentee ballots and, in a few instances, insisted on segregated voting facilities and voter lists. Furthermore, election officials have been selected in a discriminatory manner, black poll watchers have been excluded and harassed, and ballots have been improperly counted.

Finally, a number of states have tried to limit the impact of increased registration

---

[4] The following information is taken primarily from the authoritative study of the U.S. Commission on Civil Rights, *op. cit.*, pp. 21–151.

[5] *Allen v. State Board of Elections*, 393 U.S. 544 (1969).

[6] *Ibid.*, at 565.

and voting by diluting the black vote. In Mississippi and Alabama, election districts with heavy Negro registration have been combined with other districts to ensure the perpetuation of white majorities. By state law, certain counties have been authorized to hold at-large elections or have been consolidated with other counties.

As has been mentioned, a law permitting Mississippi's Forest and Adams counties to switch to at-large voting for the county board of supervisors was thrown out by the Supreme Court because the state failed to comply with the requirement of the Voting Rights Act of 1965 that changes in voting requirements must first be cleared with federal officials.[7] However, the Court upheld elections conducted under the law on the ground that state officials might not have anticipated that the Court would interpret the "hat in hand" provision of the Voting Rights Act to include acts which diminished the effectiveness of voting rights as well as acts which restricted the right to vote itself.

In addition to consolidating counties and holding at-large elections, Alabama and Mississippi have diluted the black vote by reapportioning legislative districts. The Alabama legislature reapportioned both houses shortly after the Voting Rights Act was passed, but the reapportionment did not go unchallenged. A three-judge federal district court upheld the plan for the state Senate, despite inferences that it had been designed to limit nonwhite voting power, since the plaintiffs were unable to prove successfully that the plan was discriminatory. However, the same court threw out the House plan, since "the legislature intentionally aggregated predominantly Negro counties with predominantly white counties for the sole purpose of preventing the election of Negroes to House membership."[8]

Mississippi enacted a statute in 1966 that changed the state's congressional districts in such a way that the predominantly Negro delta district was divided up among three congressional districts. The maps on the following pages show the state's districts both prior to and after the 1966 reapportionment.

The Mississippi Freedom Democratic Party and several Negro plaintiffs brought a suit in federal district court to have the redistricting statute thrown out on the grounds that it was racially motivated and that it did not follow the boundaries of the economic, geological, and geographic regions of the state. A three-judge district court held, however, that it could consider only whether the statute violated the constitutional requirement that one man's vote be the equal of any other man's vote. Since the new districts contained almost identical populations, the court held that the districting plan did not violate the Constitution. The opinion also stated that the plaintiffs had not proved that the legislature acted for discriminatory purposes nor that the effect of the new districts was to dilute or negate Negro votes.[9]

The plaintiffs appealed to the United States Supreme Court, arguing that the redistricting plan created five congressional districts in which the white vote outnumbers the black vote, despite a 43 percent black population in the state as a whole. The defendants argued that the district court's finding that the statute had no racial purpose or effect should be overturned only if it were clearly erroneous. Without hearing oral argument, the Supreme Court summarily affirmed the district court's opinion. The sole dissenter was Justice William O. Douglas, who stated that the Court should have accepted jurisdiction of the case and put it on the docket for oral argument.[10]

Thus, the Voting Rights Act and the decision of the Supreme Court in *South*

[7] 393 U.S. 544.

[8] *Sims v. Baggett*, 247 F. Supp. 96 (M.D.Ala. 1965).

[9] *Connor v. Johnson*, 265 F. Supp. 492 (1966); 279 F. Supp. 619 (1967).

[10] *Connor v. Johnson*, 386 U.S. 483 (1967).

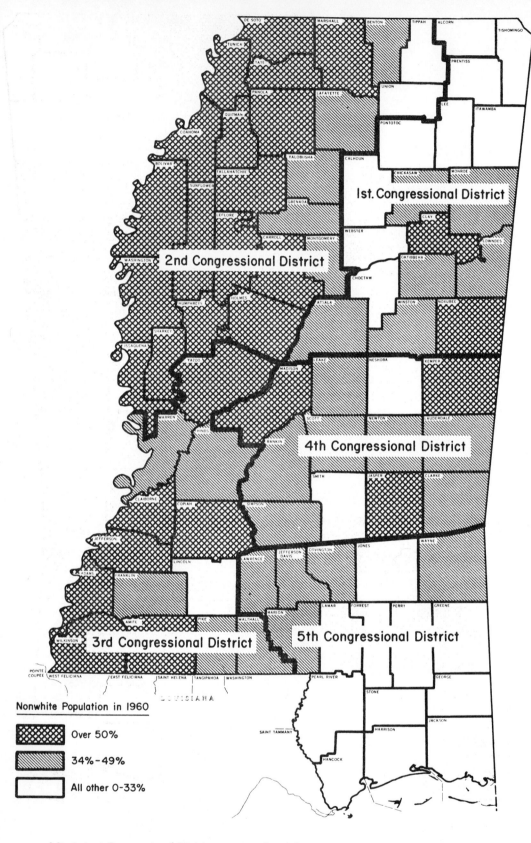

Mississippi Congressional Districts, 1965 and 1966*

*U.S. Commission on Civil Rights, *Political Participation*, U.S. Government Printing Office, 1968, pp. 32–33; counties with a nonwhite population over 50 percent have been marked with diagonal lines.

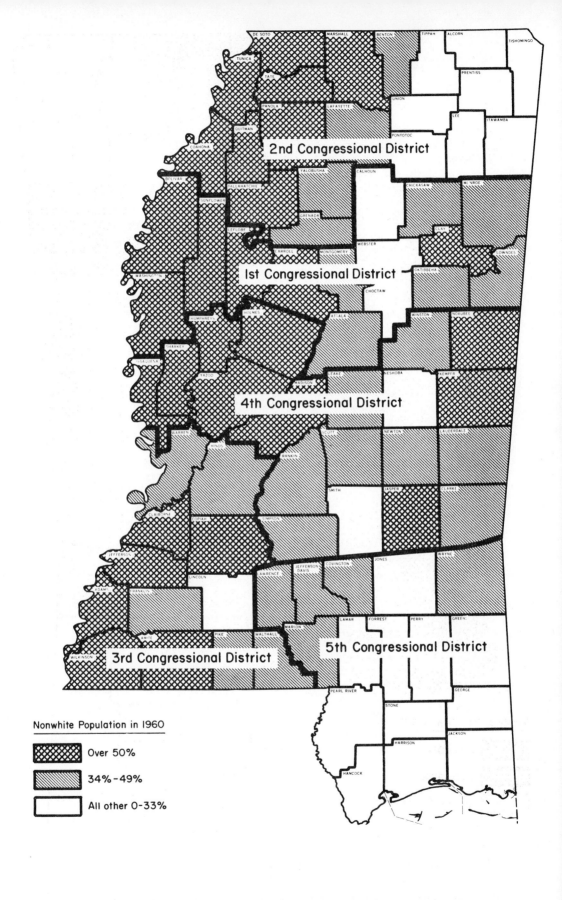

Nonwhite Population in 1960

▨ Over 50%

▧ 34%–49%

☐ All other 0–33%

2nd Congressional District

1st Congressional District

4th Congressional District

3rd Congressional District

5th Congressional District

Carolina v. Katzenbach upholding the constitutionality of the act have not resolved the problem of discriminatory access to the ballot. Vast progress has been made in a few short years, but new methods of resistance have been developed which threaten the gains made under the act. Congress passed the Voting Rights Act, but it has not given the Justice Department sufficient funds or staff to implement it fully. As the U. S. Commission on Civil Rights has stated:

> The gains that have been made have great potential—but they are fragile. If the gains are augmented and strengthened by firm action to deal with the remaining barriers, Negroes may secure enough influence and representation in the political process that the need for Federal intervention will end. If, on the other hand, new barriers are not attacked, the progress made thus far may not be translated into effective political representation, the current Federal presence may be of diminishing effectiveness, and the gains may be destroyed entirely if and when the Federal Government decides to end its intervention and restore to the States control over the registration process and determination of the qualifications of electors.
>
> What kind of action is needed? First, it is necessary to broaden and strengthen enforcement of existing laws. The national political parties must assume responsibility for eliminating present practices of discrimination at the State and local levels and for taking affirmative action to secure participation of Negro citizens in party processes. The Federal Government must assume its share of the responsibility to eliminate illiteracy and provide information and assistance which will enable citizens to exercise fully the rights and duties of citizenship. And action must be taken by the Government to overcome problems of economic dependence, in recognition of the fact that citizens will never be truly free to exercise their political rights if they must fear the economic consequences of their acts.[11]

[11] U.S. Commission on Civil Rights, *op. cit.*, pp. 178–79.

FREE SPEECH IN THE VIETNAM WAR
Are Inflammatory Rites Protected by the Constitution?

ISSUES RAISED   *Freedom of Speech*   /   *Symbolic Speech*   /   *Civil Disobedience*   /   *Due Process of Law*

I. The Domestic Response to Military Involvement in Southeast Asia

In the century since the Civil War, no conflict divided the American people so sharply, nor caused such bitterness and animosity, as the undeclared and seemingly endless war in Vietnam. Opponents of United States participation in the war faced a crisis of conscience of nearly unbearable proportions: they were forced to choose between loyalty to the policy of the government and to the soldiers fighting and dying in support of that policy and their firm belief that what the United States was doing was wrong, immoral, and unlikely to succeed.

Many of these opponents of the war sat silently, observing the ambiguous and distressing events which daily passed before their eyes on television and in the nation's newspapers, cursing Lyndon Baines Johnson, and, subsequently, Richard Milhous Nixon, but remaining mute nonetheless. For others, particularly young men of draft age, silence was equivalent to complicity.

These men—and women—resolved their personal crises of conscience in favor of outright opposition to the war policy of their own government. They hoped, of course, that others could be reached, that opposition to the war would grow, and that the government could be persuaded to alter its established course of action. Among these outspoken opponents were the draft card burners, a small number of individuals who demonstrated by a symbolic and dramatic act their complete alienation from the Vietnam policy of the Johnson administration.

Inevitably, dissent by an active minority aroused the ire of supporters of the American military effort in Southeast Asia. To put the matter as fairly as possible, not all the critics of the war acted out of conscience; some had baser motives. Likewise, not all the supporters of the government formed their judgments on the basis of reasoned analysis of the propriety of United States participation and the effectiveness of the policies followed by the White House and the Defense Department.

Some judged the complex issues posed by the war by applying a simplistic "my country right or wrong" formula, almost as if the Second World War had never occurred and such a response had not been revealed in its true colors by those Germans who shrugged off innumerable acts of inhumanity with the easy statement that only the Pied Piper of National Socialism was responsible for what happened. And, as is the case in every armed conflict, others found it politically advantageous to wrap themselves in the flag and denounce the disloyal and unpatriotic.

PRELUDE TO CIVIL DISOBEDIENCE

Initially, public opposition to United States actions in Vietnam was limited, essentially because American involvement was relatively small and there was little attention given by the nation's press to what was, after all, a brush-fire war half a world away. Through the first half of 1964, the American commitment was no more than 16,000 troops, most of whom served as advisers to South Vietnamese Army units.

Gradually, the war effort of the South Vietnamese deteriorated, in large part because of repeated coups that rocked the government, and American soldiers began to carry on more and more of the fighting. Then, in August, three North Vietnamese PT boats attacked a United States destroyer in the Gulf of Tonkin; first reports stated that the destroyer had been attacked in international waters, but later information raised the possibility that the destroyer had been within the territorial waters of North Vietnam. Acting on the initial intelligence reports, President Johnson ordered a retaliatory bombing raid and asked Congress to pass a resolution pledging full support for any action he might take to protect United States forces in South Vietnam.

Most individuals who were later to become outspoken critics of United States involvement—including national political leaders like Senator William Fulbright, Attorney General Robert F. Kennedy, Senator Eugene McCarthy, and Southern Christian Leadership Conference Chairman Martin Luther King—had either not yet made up their minds or were still unwilling to criticize the President's Vietnam policy publicly. Only Senators Wayne Morse of Oregon and Ernest Gruening of Alaska advocated withdrawal and voted against the Gulf of Tonkin resolution, which passed the House of Representatives 416 to 0 and the Senate 88 to 2.

Shortly after the passage of the resolution, one of the first public demonstrations against the war took place in New York City. About sixty people demonstrated in midtown Manhattan; seventeen individuals, most of whom had long been active in liberal-radical causes, were arrested by the police. A week later, forty more demonstrators were arrested at a second protest meeting.

In the fall of 1964, national attention focused on the presidential election. Lyndon Johnson was reelected at least in part because he advocated a less bellicose and warlike approach to the Vietnam conflict than his opponent, Barry Goldwater. Thus, the administration's policy seemed relatively mild and, as a result, advocates of peace and of negotiations were somewhat subdued in their criticism.

Then, in February 1965, the war took on a new complexion. In response to continued and increasingly heavy attacks by Vietcong guerillas and units of the North Vietnamese Army which had infiltrated into South Vietnam, President Johnson made the hard decision that air strikes against military barracks and staging areas in North Vietnam were necessary. The administration assured the American public that it was not seeking expansion of the war, but that it was determined to back South Vietnam in its fight for independence.

The air attacks caused the enemy to redouble its efforts and, day-by-day, the conflict expanded, with each side blaming the other for escalating the war. By this time, there were 22,000 American troops in Vietnam. Within a month, 3,500 additional marines had landed and been deployed in the area around the city of Danang.

At this juncture, United Nations Secretary General U Thant proposed a preliminary peace conference between the United States, the U.S.S.R., England, France, Communist China, and North and South Vietnam, but President Johnson rejected the proposal on the ground that the United States would not participate in a conference until North Vietnam ceased its aggression against its Southern neighbor.

Domestic criticism of the war escalated step-by-step with the quickening pace of American involvement. At first, criticism was limited mainly to letter writing and to sparsely attended demonstrations. Open letters to the President opposing United States policy and urging negotiations were published as ads in various newspapers. A group called the Women Strike for Peace held a march and vigil outside the United Nations, precipitating further arrests. The World Council of Churches made public a statement that the policy being pursued by the United States was futile. The first major "teach-in" in protest against United States actions was held by students and faculty at the University of Michigan toward the end of March, setting off a wave of similar one-sided rallies at colleges and universities across the country.

The peace movement began to accelerate. Dr. Benjamin Spock, the chairman of the Committee for a Sane Nuclear Policy, led 3,000 marchers from various groups to a rally in front of United Nations headquarters. Over 15,000 people, including many college students, picketed the White House.

On May 6, forty students burned their draft cards at the Oakland, California, draft board. Surprisingly, however, the immediate cause of the protest was not the Vietnam war but the use of 14,000 United States troops to help put down a revolt against the junta then in control of the Dominican Republic. President Johnson stated that he had had to act in order to prevent the possibility of a communist takeover, but the draft card burners and several hundred other demonstrators believed that this was only a self-serving excuse for armed intervention in support of a reactionary government.

Plans for a nationally televised, two-sided "teach-in" were disrupted by the Dominican Republic crisis, and McGeorge Bundy, the Special Assistant to the President for National Security Affairs, was forced at the last moment to cancel his plans to defend America's actions in Vietnam. A substitute did, however, appeal in person to 5,000 students and to 100,000 additional students who watched the presentation on television. Shortly afterward, 10,000 college students attended a "teach-in" on the Berkeley campus and heard Dr. Spock and Senator Gruening criticize the administration's Vietnam policy.

Opposition mounted following an announcement from Washington that the 50,000 United States troops then in Vietnam were no longer acting solely as advisers to the South Vietnamese Army but were engaged as units in defense of major bases and in offensive combat. Secretary of Defense Robert McNamara announced that 21,000 more soldiers would be sent overseas to enable the United States to carry out its redefined mission successfully.

Throughout the spring and early summer of 1965, protests and counterprotests continued unabated. Editorial pages of newspapers were filled with letters attacking or defending the government's policy. The opposition was led by university professors, students, religious leaders, and members of pacifist organizations, but critics of the administration were by no means united. Some spoke out for immediate withdrawal of United States troops; the majority, however, opposed further escalation, sought a bombing halt, and favored more strenuous and realistic efforts to negotiate with the enemy. Another but far smaller group of critics, including many Republican congressmen, argued for more aggressive action in order to force North Vietnam to the negotiating table; a few individuals mentioned the possibility of invading North Vietnam or using nuclear weapons if necessary to win the war.

By midsummer, it was painfully clear that little—if any—meaningful progress was being made in South Vietnam. The North Vietnamese infiltration rate had grown substantially and had offset additional United States troop commitments. Massive bombing of North Vietnamese military and production facilities had not weakened the enemy's war effort. President Johnson decided, therefore, that a sweeping review of existing United States policies was needed.

On July 28, he announced his decision: the American troop commitment would be raised almost immediately to 125,000 and draft calls would be doubled from the June rate of 17,000 to 35,000 monthly. As a result, 400 people wearing black armbands silently picketed the army recruitment and induction center on Whitehall Street in New York City and at least five young men burned their draft cards. About 200 pacifists associated with the Women Strike for Peace and the Vietnam Day Committee attempted to stop a Santa Fe troop train carrying soldiers to an embarkation point in Oakland. The Friends Committee on National Legislation and the Americans for Democratic Action called for an end to the conflict, a cease-fire, and meaningful negotiations by both sides. Leaders of civil rights groups agonized over the question of whether they should speak out on the war, since they knew vocal opposition would weaken their primary cause; nevertheless, the Rev. Martin Luther King of the SCLC concluded that he could no longer remain silent.

CONGRESS RETALIATES AGAINST WAR DISSENTERS

It was in this context, on August 5, 1965, that Congressman L. Mendel Rivers (Dem., S.C.), the chairman of the House Committee on Armed Services, introduced an amendment to the Universal Military Training and Service Act which would make mutilation or destruction of a draft card a felony punishable by up to five years in prison and a fine of up to $10,000. Rivers had often expressed himself in no uncertain terms on the subject of traitors, beatniks, appeasers, pacifists, domestic communists, and their sympathizers, and now he moved to make it clear to the entire nation that Congress opposed the disloyal acts of such dissenters.

In analyzing congressional action on the draft-card-burning amendment, it is important to note the following:

1. Neither the President, the Selective Service System, nor the Defense Department had requested Congress to pass the proposed statute; thus, contrary to most laws passed in recent decades, the draft-card-burning statute was truly a product of congressional initiative.
2. In contrast to most legislation, there were no overt pressures prior to or during congressional consideration of the measure; interest groups which might have been expected to support a legislative prohibition of a supposedly disloyal act, such as the American Legion, were not consulted at the outset, nor were they used by the sponsors of the bill to help develop widespread public demand for action. In this instance, Congress did not "sell out" to special interests, nor did individual legislators "use" interest groups to further their own Machiavellian ends.
3. Individuals and organizations opposed to the Vietnam war did not mount a serious attempt to prevent the passage of the punitive amendment. In part, their failure to make a sustained effort to kill the statute was due to the fact that they had other, more important fish to fry. Additional reasons for the absence of meaningful opposition from groups opposed to the war were:
    a. Most of these organizations were small, relatively new, and inexperienced in legislative infighting. Unlike more traditional, well-established interest groups,

they had had no prior opportunities to work with individual congressmen; thus, they had no long-standing friends in Congress and no legislator owed them any favors.

   b. The nature of the issue was such that opposition groups had two strikes against them from the outset: whenever a legislative proposal is cast in highly charged words like "patriotism" and "disloyalty," few legislators are likely to take the substantial risks involved in speaking out for the minority viewpoint.

   c. Finally, the draft-card-burning amendment passed so quickly that potential opponents had no time to meet, plan a strategy, and get into action.

4. During congressional consideration of the measure, the President, his staff, and other executive department officials maintained a hands-off policy. General Hershey, the director of the Selective Service System, did state after the fact that the bill was unnecessary since draft card burners could already be punished under an administrative regulation requiring registrants to have their draft cards in their possession at all times, but no effort was made to dampen congressional enthusiasm during the time the bill was actually under consideration. In effect, Congress outmaneuvered the President, since the executive branch needed congressional support for the war effort and could hardly speak out against a measure which Congress believed would further that effort. Throughout the entire period of legislative action, the President and Congress functioned according to the original, eighteenth-century concept of separation of powers, not the modified, "corrupted" version which predominates today.

5. As has already been mentioned, the bill passed with remarkable speed: Rivers's proposal was introduced in the House of Representatives on Thursday, August 5, reported out of committee the next day, and passed the following Tuesday, August 10; the bill was introduced in the Senate on the tenth and passed on Friday of that week. Liberals who criticize congressional dalliance over civil rights and social welfare measures should think twice before they conclude that Congress is incapable of acting expeditiously if it wishes to do so!

6. No hearings were held in either house; thus, the need for the legislation in question was never fully demonstrated. By short-cutting the legislative process, Congress did not allow sufficient time either for sober reflection on the strengths and weaknesses of the amendment and of possible alternatives or for the proposal to be debated adequately in the public press. Certainly, the country would not have collapsed if a month or two had been devoted to responsible discussion before the measure was acted upon.

   On the other hand, given the emotional nature of the issue, the potential danger of being labeled "unpatriotic" if one opposed the amendment, and the total absence of individual or organized opposition both in committee and on the floor of Congress, it is entirely possible that delay would not have led to a thorough airing of the pros and cons. In both houses the bill became the pending order of business by the unanimous consent of the members; under this parliamentary procedure, the objection of a single member is sufficient to delay action on a legislative proposal. A few minutes after the bill was brought up in the House of Representatives, it was passed 393 to 1; in the Senate, there was no demand for a roll-call vote and the bill passed by voice vote.

7. Another unfortunate by-product of the failure to hold hearings was that no effort was made to explore the constitutional question of whether a statutory prohibition of destruction of draft cards violated free expression rights protected by the First Amendment. No representative or senator argued against the amendment on the ground that it curtailed freedom of speech and, even more surpris-

ingly, not a single congressman urged delay in order to allow time for committee counsel and legal scholars to explore the potential First Amendment issue. Congress wanted to act, not think.

As a result, no attempt was made to study the limits of the First Amendment in wartime. No attempt was made to relate the draft-card-burning amendment either to (a) past legislative proscriptions of verbal or written ideas, of symbolic expression, of advocacy of unlawful action, or to (b), Supreme Court rulings on the constitutionality of these proscriptions. Thus, unless they were constitutional law experts themselves, congressmen had no way of knowing that certain forms of symbolic expression, such as carrying a red flag in a parade or picketing with signs, had long since been interpreted to be within the scope of the First Amendment.

Without background studies or personal expertise, congressmen had no way of knowing how the Supreme Court had interpreted the First Amendment in past wars or how the Court might interpret the right of free expression in the Vietnam war. Such studies would have revealed, at the least, that in the period since the First World War the Supreme Court had developed and applied various tests for determining whether particular efforts to communicate were protected by the First Amendment. The first of these tests, the so-called "clear and present danger" test, was based on the concept that free expression could be curtailed only under exceptional circumstances, when there was a clear and immediate danger that the expression would lead to unlawful activity. This test, like the ones which followed it, recognized, however, that the scope of the First Amendment varied with the circumstances: speech which might be lawful in certain contexts might be subject to legislative proscription in, for example, wartime. Thus, even the liberal "clear and present danger" test was based on an interpretation of the First Amendment which slighted the literal command of the amendment that "Congress shall make no law . . . abridging the freedom of speech. . . ."

Subsequent tests, such as the "bad tendency" test developed and applied during the 1920s and 1930s, supported legislative prohibition of speech which threatened public order even if there were no possibility that the specific expression would lead immediately to unlawful action. This test was abandoned during the 1940s as too restrictive of free expression, but it was replaced by a "middle-ground" test during the red scares of the following decade. Under the "gravity of the evil" test, the two earlier tests were combined in rough fashion: courts were to relate the gravity of the evil proscribed by statute to the likelihood that the evil would occur. If the danger to the political system were great enough, expression could be suppressed, even if there was little chance that the expression would lead to unlawful action within a reasonable time period.

Examination of historic free speech cases would have made congressmen aware that (a) the Court had refused to give symbolic speech the same degree of protection given "pure" speech, and (b) the Court had been reluctant to interpret the First Amendment liberally in wartime or during the existence of a popularly perceived threat to the political system. With such information at hand, Congress could have carried out its responsibility of making an intelligent judgment on the constitutionality of the proposed legislation; instead, Congress passed the buck to the courts.

8. Furthermore, the shortcomings in the legislative record of the amendment were bound to cause trouble later on, when the courts would be faced with the responsibility of ruling on the constitutionality of Congress's action. The courts frequently use legislative history in order to clarify the meaning of a statute; where ambiguity exists, the record gives some indication of the purpose of a particular piece of legislation. On the other hand, it is not the proper function of

the judiciary to examine legislative motives. Inevitably, the line between motivation and purpose is hard to draw. Lawyers challenging a statute are not hesitant to argue that the legislative record reveals that Congress acted to achieve an illicit purpose; lawyers responding to such an argument invariably urge that the purpose of the statute is clear in the words of the statute and that their opponents are merely trying to trick the courts into ruling on Congress's motives in passing the questioned legislation.

9. Like the act of burning a draft card, the legislative prohibition was itself essentially symbolic, since the new punishment for burning a card was the same as the old punishment for not having a draft card in one's possession at all times. The only new element added by the amendment was the clear statement by Congress at a particular point in time that it regarded a particular form of dissent as disloyal. Because the obvious purpose of draft card burners was to attract as much attention as possible to their view that the war was wrong, the bill may actually have been counterproductive; undoubtedly, the new law added an element of martyrdom to the act of burning a draft card and caused the press to give far more publicity to the demonstrations at which cards were destroyed. Thus, from the outset, it was questionable whether the amendment would discourage individuals from committing the act which it prohibited.

Because virtually no discussion took place during Senate action on the draft-card-burning amendment, the formal legislative record of what transpired in the Senate has been omitted. Senator Thurmond (Rep., S.C.) needed only seven sentences to introduce the bill on August 10. The bill was sent to the Committee on Armed Services, but no report of discussion within the committee was ever issued; whatever discussion took place must have been monosyllabic in nature, since the bill reached the committee on August 11 and the report of the committee recommending passage reached the Senate the next day. This two-page-long recommendation explained the amendment but did not include any justification other than a sentence stating that destruction of draft cards was a potential threat to Congress's power to raise and support armies.[1]

The single page of the Congressional Record of August 13 devoted to a verbatim account of action on the floor of the Senate shows that Senator Thurmond was more prolix during the "debate"; he spoke eleven sentences in support of the bill and then sat down. No senator had anything to add, pro or con, and the amendment was immediately adopted.[2]

On the other hand, the formal legislative record of what took place in the House of Representatives between August 6 and August 10, 1965, is highly informative. Since this legislative history played an important part in subsequent judicial determination of whether the draft-card-burning amendment violated the constitutional guarantee of free speech, it is presented in detail below, starting with the discussion which took place in the House Committee on Armed Services the day after the bill was introduced:

FULL COMMITTEE CONSIDERATION OF H.R. 10306, TO AMEND THE UNIVERSAL MILITARY TRAINING AND SERVICE ACT OF 1951, AS AMENDED

The CHAIRMAN [Hon. L. Mendel Rivers]. The committee will come to order.... I think it would be appropriate at this time to take up H.R. 10306, a bill that I have introduced.

---

[1] *Sen. Rep. No. 589,* 89th Cong., 1st Sess. (1965).
[2] 111 *Cong. Rec.* 19669 (1965).

This bill has been introduced as a result of a speech on the floor of the House by the distinguished chairman of the Un-American Activities Committee, Mr. Willis. . . .

Among other things, Mr. Willis said on the floor of the House they were burning draft cards and otherwise mutilating them. After the speech, Mr. Blandford and I got together and he and I contacted Selective Service and the Department of Justice.

Mr. Blandford prepared this bill which I introduced. We feel it is necessary to strengthen the Universal Military Training and Service Act.

Here is what it says. Section 12 (b) is amended to read as follows:

Who forges, alters, knowingly destroys, knowingly mutilates, or in any manner changes any such certificate or any notation duly and validly inscribed thereon; or . . .

Mr. Blandford will explain to you why we did not put the word "maliciously" in there. Mr. Blandford has persuaded me that maliciously does not mean the same thing that it did when I went to law school.

Mr. BLANDFORD. Since we are dealing with a criminal statute, I would like to make it very clear for the record exactly what we have in mind when we change this law.

Today, the law states among other things:

(b) *Any person . . . (3) who forges, alters, or in any manner, changes any such certificate or any notation duly and validly inscribed thereon; or . . . shall, upon conviction, be fined not to exceed $10,000 or be imprisoned for not more than five years, or both.*

The existing law prohibits forging, or altering a draft card. It does not prohibit the destruction of a draft card. This matter has been informally discussed with the Selective Service and with the Department of Justice. If we use the words "knowingly destroys," or "knowingly mutilates" as opposed to "willfully," it is easier to convict an individual who puts his card into a fire purposely at a mass demonstration, or destroys his draft card in the presence of others. If he knowingly does this, he would be subject to a criminal prosecution by the Department of Justice.

Now, this is the answer, of course, to this attempted mass destruction of draft cards. These bums that are going around the country burning draft cards while people are dying in South Vietnam have brought about this type of action on the part of the chairman.

Mr. Willis disclosed this in a speech on the floor. The word "knowingly" is put in here purposely. It is not an oversight. It is easier to establish that a person does something knowingly than it is to establish he does it willfully. This is to be construed as a criminal statute obviously, and it is for that reason the word "knowingly" is put here. We obviously do not intend to have anyone prosecuted who puts his shirt in the washing machine with his draft card in it and unknowingly mutilates it. I am sure it has happened. This is a short bill. It has not been cleared by the department. It is impossible to conceive of anyone objecting to it. I can think of some who might, but I cannot think of any departments of the Government objecting to it.

The bill was introduced yesterday, and it is presented to the committee today while there is a quorum present.

The CHAIRMAN. There is a quorum present.

Mr. PIKE. I do not think there is.

The CHAIRMAN. The last I saw there was one present. . . .

The CHAIRMAN. Is there objection to our reporting this?

Mr. BLANDFORD. I suggest a rollcall because of the penalty provision.

The CHAIRMAN. I think it would be better.

Mr. EVANS. Before you call the roll, I would like the record to show my feelings in this regard to the addition of the words "knowingly destroys and knowingly mutilates."

We have not had hearings, Mr. Chairman. I suggest the possibility we are acting in haste.

Two circumstances occur to me which could apply and be a crime if this were to become law, where someone with recent contact with his draft office might be angry and knowingly destroy or knowingly mutilate his card and thus become subject to the penalties of the act, or someone might mistakenly destroy a card feeling it was obsolete, or no longer in effect. He also would be included within the language suggested.

I realize a great deal of difficulty could occur if this were to grow in number and become a national problem. I appreciate that. I do think it might be wiser if we had hearings on the bill before it was considered.

Mr. BLANDFORD. If I may respond to that, this language "knowingly" was suggested informally by the Department of Justice. There obviously is no intent, since prosecution would be up to either the Selective Service or the Department of Justice, that in the event a person knowingly destroyed it, perhaps in a fit of temper in front of a draft board member, whether or not they would want to prosecute would be dependent entirely upon the extent of the way he lost his temper.

The purpose here is quite clear. It is aimed at the type of destruction that is not in the best interests of the Nation. It does not quite constitute treasonable action, but it is the type of action that brings great discredit upon the United States and I am sure that in the prosecution of this law, just as in the whole penalty provision before you, as it is administered there are many violations that are never prosecuted. There have been very, very few prosecutions.

The CHAIRMAN. We cannot do any post facto legislating. We can stop it for the future.

Mr. Evans has a right to make his remarks.

Mr. HÉBERT. I, too, share the concern you have and the gentleman's concern also. This is a time that demands dramatic, definitive, positive action on the part of Congress if we are going to stop these sort of things.

This morning again on television was a picture of the stopping of a troop train in Santa Fe by a bunch of pickets. This is an atrocious thing. If we let these things get away and do not do something positively, and dramatically, it will be bad. This should be brought up on the unanimous consent on Monday.

The CHAIRMAN. Call the roll.

Mr. BATES. I want to reiterate what has been said here today. . . . I think we weaken our case when we do not have testimony on these bills.

I am going to vote for it, and I am in favor of it, but I wish it was brought up in the usual way.

Mr. LEGGETT. By passing this bill at this time, are we frustrating the prosecution under the existing act?

Mr. BLANDFORD. There is no other way to prosecute them.

Mr. LEGGETT. I do not think you could destroy a draft card without altering it.

Mr. BLANDFORD. I do not think any definition of criminal law would include destruction as an alteration.

The CHAIRMAN. We just want to make it strong. We do not have any preamble on this.

Mr. HÉBERT. The most important thing is, we take action. That is more important than any other consideration.

The CHAIRMAN. If you are ready to take action, that is all right with me. . . .

Mr. BLANDFORD. Nineteen ayes and one nay on this vote, Mr. Chairman. That is a quorum. I do not have any proxies here.

The CHAIRMAN. The bill is favorably reported and I will discuss it with the Speaker.[3]

---

[3] *Full Committee Consideration of H.R. 10306, to Amend the Universal Military Training and Service Act of 1951, Before the House Committee on Armed Services*, 89th Cong., 1st Sess. (1965).

Chairman Rivers submitted the following report to the House to help illuminate consideration of the proposed amendment:

PROHIBITION OF DESTRUCTION OR MUTILATION OF DRAFT CARDS

The Committee on Armed Services, to whom was referred the bill (H.R. 10306) to amend the Universal Military Training and Service Act of 1951, as amended, having considered the same, report favorably thereon without amendment and recommend that the bill do pass.

Purpose of the Bill   The purpose of the proposed legislation is to provide a clear statutory prohibition against a person knowingly destroying or knowingly mutilating a draft registration card.

Explanation of the Bill   Section 12(b)(3) of the Universal Military Training and Service Act of 1951, as amended, provides that a person who forges, alters, or in any manner changes his draft registration card, or any notation duly and validly inscribed thereon, will be subject to a fine of $10,000 or imprisonment of not more than 5 years. H.R. 10306 would amend this provision to make it apply also to those persons who knowingly destroy or knowingly mutilate a draft registration card.

The House Committee on Armed Services is fully aware of, and shares in, the deep concern expressed throughout the Nation over the increasing incidences in which individuals and large groups of individuals openly defy and encourage others to defy the authority of their Government by destroying or mutilating their draft cards.

While the present provisions of the Criminal Code with respect to the destruction of Government property may appear broad enough to cover all acts having to do with the mistreatment of draft cards in the possession of individuals, the committee feels that in the present critical situation of the country, the acts of destroying or mutilating these cards are offenses which pose such a grave threat to the security of the Nation that no question whatsoever should be left as to the intention of the Congress that such wanton and irresponsible acts should be punished.

To this end, H.R. 10306 makes specific that knowingly mutilating or knowingly destroying a draft card constitutes a violation of the Universal Military Training and Service Act and is punishable thereunder; and that a person who does so destroy or mutilate a draft card will be subject to a fine of not more than $10,000 or imprisonment of not more than 5 years. . . . [The remainder of the report states that the committee vote on giving the bill a favorable report was 19 to 1, indicates that the legislation would not require the expenditure of federal funds, and shows the precise changes in existing law made by the amendment.][4]

Floor action took place the next day, August 10. It should be noted that the discussion was perfunctory at best: Chairman Rivers and Congressman William Bray (Rep., Ind.) were the only two congressmen to speak in favor of the bill; no one spoke in opposition.

Mr. RIVERS of South Carolina. Mr. Speaker, I ask unanimous consent. . . . [for immediate consideration of H.R. 10306.]

The SPEAKER. Is there objection to the request of the gentleman from South Carolina?

There was no objection.

The Clerk read the bill. . . .

Mr. GROSS. . . . I believe we should have an explanation of the bill. . . .

Mr. RIVERS of South Carolina. Mr. Speaker, the bill, H.R. 10306, amends the Universal Military Training and Service Act to establish a clear statutory provision against

[4] H.R. Rep. No. 747 to accompany H.R. 10306, 89th Cong., 1st Sess. (1965). (Brackets added.)

a person knowingly destroying or knowingly mutilating a draft card. Existing law provides a penalty for anyone forging or altering a draft card, but there is no specific prohibition against destroying or mutilating a draft card.

The purpose of the bill is clear. It merely amends the draft law by adding the words "knowingly destroys and knowingly mutilates" draft cards. A person who is convicted would be subject to a fine up to $10,000 or imprisonment up to 5 years. It is a straight-forward clear answer to those who would make a mockery of our efforts in South Vietnam by engaging in the mass destruction of draft cards.

We do not want to make it illegal to mutilate or destroy a card per se, because sometimes this can happen by accident. But if it can be proved that a person knowingly destroyed or mutilated his draft card, then under the committee proposal he can be sent to prison, where he belongs. This is the least we can do for our men in South Vietnam fighting to preserve freedom, while a vocal minority in this country thumb their noses at their own Government.

Mr. GROSS. Mr. Speaker, the gentleman from South Carolina in his usual lucid manner has convinced me that this is a very good bill. . . .

Mr. BRAY. . . . Mr. Speaker, the bill that we have before us today is simple and easy to understand. H.R. 10306 is an amendment to our selective service law providing that it is illegal to knowingly mutilate or destroy a draft card. It is already illegal to alter, forge, or change such a card.

The need of this legislation is clear. Beatniks and so-called "campus-cults" have been publicly burning their draft cards to demonstrate their contempt for the United States and our resistance to Communist takeovers. Such actions have been suggested and led by college professors—professors supported by taxpayers' money.

At Rutgers University, Prof. Eugene Genovese, who prides himself on being a Marxist, publicly said that he "welcomed a Communist Vietcong victory." The board of governors refused to dismiss him.

Just yesterday such a mob attacking the United States and praising the Vietcong attempted to march on the Capitol but were prevented by the police from forcibly moving into our Chambers. They were led by a Yale University professor. They were generally a filthy, sleazy beatnik gang; but the question which they pose to America is quite serious.

These so-called "student" mobs at home and abroad make demands and threats; they hurl rocks and ink bottles at American buildings; they publicly mutilate or burn their draft cards; they even desecrate the American flag. Chanting and screaming vile epithets, these mobs of so-called "students" and Communist "stooges" attempt to create fear and destroy self-confidence in our country and its citizens and to downgrade the United States in the eyes of the world.

Such organized "student" groups in the United States have sent congratulations and money to Ho Chi Minh and have made anonymous and insulting calls to families of our servicemen killed in Vietnam.

This proposed legislation to make it illegal to knowingly destroy or mutilate a draft card is only one step in bringing some legal control over those who would destroy American freedom. This legislation, if passed, will be of some assistance to our country if the officers and courts charged with the enforcement of the law will have the energy, courage, and guts to make use of it.

The growing disrespect for our law and institutions in America holds a real threat to our country and to our freedom. Just 5 short years ago no one would have believed that disrespect for our country could have grown to the proportions that it has today.

Disrespect for our American heritage and anti-American demonstrations are all a part of the cold war in some way directed by those who would destroy us. The Communist world is aware that it cannot destroy the effectiveness of the United States by the use of its economic and military strength, because we are far stronger in these fields than it is and we outdistance it more every year.

Then how is the Communist victory to be brought about? The Communists are planning to use the "Judas goats" to lead those who are free to defect from freedom. So-called "students" and Communist stooges here and abroad, by demonstrations of anti-American feeling, by belittling, and by vilification are to downgrade the United States in the eyes of the world and shake the confidence and faith of our citizens in our democratic way of life. They hope to attain victory over freedom by subversion within the United States and by erosion of our national pride and confidence in the greatness of America and our national heritage.

One of America's greatest sources of strength in discouraging these demonstrations is to pause and consider the greatness of America—to appreciate what our country has done for the benefit of mankind. Let us have a rebirth of patriotism. Let us be proud, possessed not of an arrogant pride, but a humble pride in our greatness, in our heritage.

Aside from becoming the strongest country economically and militarily during the last quarter century, this country, without any desire to gain a square foot of territory, has been the principal force in overthrowing the armed might of Hitler and Japan. The strength of the United States saved both Europe and Asia from the despotic rule of tyrants. We asked nothing in return. We asked no gain for this victory brought about by American dollars, American production, and American youth. The people of the United States have unselfishly contributed more to the feeding, care, welfare, and rehabilitation of the world than has all the rest of the world combined. All of this has been done without any thought of gain except the reward of the deed itself.

The United States, without hope of personal gain, blocked the Communist takeover of South Korea and today is assuming the major role of blocking Communist slavery in southeast Asia. Yet there are today those in America who are weak at heart, those of little faith in the greatness of America and freedom, those who are naive and refuse to face up to the realities of Communist aggression. There are those who in various degrees and for various reasons ask our Government to yield more and more to Communist aggression.

Our Government, through fear of the public opinion at home and abroad of our enemies, is failing to adequately enforce our laws on subversion and anti-governmental attacks. That is exactly as our enemies have planned it. In the exercise of our great ideals of fairness and tolerance, we seem to forget that it is axiomatic that a government must protect its citizenry against illegal acts and against mob violence. When decent, productive people are forced to support and coddle criminals and other dregs and drones of society, chaos, degradation, and ruin are inevitable.

Tolerance ceases to be a virtue when it condones evil. Governmental tolerance ceases to be a virtue when it allows mob violence on the law-abiding members of its society—when it winks at unlawful disrespect to its institutions and the flag. This is true whether this tolerance is the result of apathy, a maudlin sympathy, or a fear of the opinions of enemies.

When the mob once learns that its actions will lead to granting of its demands and its actions are condoned, there is a multiplication both of its demonstrations, riots, and wanton destruction, and of its demands.

If these "revolutionaries" are permitted to deface and destroy their draft cards, our entire Selective Service System is dealt a serious blow.

Mr. Speaker, I strongly urge all my fellow Members to support this legislation.

The SPEAKER. . . . The question is on passage of the bill. . . . The question was taken; and there were—yeas 393, nays 1, not voting 40. . . .[5]

THE NEW LAW IS CHALLENGED

President Johnson signed the draft-card-burning amendment on August 31, amid growing indications that the increase in draft calls, the commitment of additional soldiers to Vietnam, and the attempt to punish dissenters were fanning the flames of discontent. Plans for a nationwide protest against the draft and the war on the weekend of October 15 to 17 were announced by the National Coordinating Com-

[5] 111 *Cong. Rec.* 19871–72 (1965). (Brackets added.)

mittee to End the War in Vietnam. Students for a Democratic Society began an organized campaign against the draft.

Over 70,000 people participated in marches, rallies, and sit-ins in sixty cities across the nation on the target date set by the leaders of the planned demonstration. Approximately 10,000 marched in New York and nearly that many participated in a Berkeley rally. The majority of demonstrators were of college age and belonged to various peace, religious, political, and antiwar organizations. Most of the marches were relatively peaceful, except for isolated incidents stemming from the activities of counterdemonstrators and hecklers.

On October 15, pacifist David J. Miller, a twenty-two-year-old graduate of a Jesuit college and writer for the socially oriented *Catholic Worker,* became the first individual to violate the new law during an antiwar rally outside the Whitehall Street induction center in New York City. Miller was arrested by the FBI.

As a result of the weekend confrontations, Attorney General Nicholas Katzenbach held a news conference in Washington to announce that there were some communists in the antidraft movement and that the Justice Department was beginning an investigation of groups behind the movement. The Internal Security Subcommittee of the Senate Judiciary Committee, headed by Vietnam war advocate Tom Dodd of Connecticut, put this point even more strongly in a report issued during the weekend. Senator Dodd stated that his probe of the antiwar movement convinced him that it was controlled by communists and extremists openly sympathetic to the Vietcong. Many other congressmen denounced the antidraft campaign and called for strong government action to stamp it out.

In addition, the demonstrations provoked Americans who believed that public criticism was disloyal and was prolonging the war, encouraging the enemy, and lowering the morale of United States troops. In the weeks following the nationwide protest, campus groups, veterans' organizations, unions, civic clubs, and other groups sponsored rallies and parades and collected blood for combat troops to demonstrate their loyalty to the men in uniform and their support for United States involvement in the war.

Despite these numerous expressions of support, more draft cards were burned and several young men refused to report for induction into the armed services. Twenty-five men picketed the federal courthouse in Manhattan in support of Miller and distributed a leaflet stating that they had all burned or destroyed their draft cards. In the Midwest, two University of Iowa students were arrested after destroying their draft cards.

Pacifists Thomas C. Cornell, a thirty-one-year-old New York City schoolteacher, Marc P. Edelman, a nineteen-year-old cabinetmaker, Roy Lisker, a twenty-seven-year-old writer and teacher, James E. Wilson, a twenty-one-year-old employee of the *Catholic Worker,* and David McReynolds, a thirty-six-year-old official of the War Resisters League, burned their cards at a rally in New York's Union Square attended by the press, the FBI, and approximately 1,500 demonstrators. The first four were indicted, but McReynolds was not, apparently because he was too old for the draft. One man reached the breaking point as a result of his anguish over the war: Norman R. Morrison, a thirty-one-year-old Quaker official, burned himself to death in front of the Pentagon in Washington.

During the Thanksgiving weekend, 20,000 opponents of the war joined in a non-violent march on Washington, picketed the White House, and rallied at the Washington monument to hear appeals for a cease-fire and negotiations. The dissension that existed within the hydra-headed peace movement was brought out sharply, since—in contrast to the October demonstrations—few calls for immediate withdrawal of United States troops were made. In addition, individuals and organizations opposed to draft card burning and other equally or more extreme forms of protest participated in the Thanksgiving weekend march.

By the end of 1965, six men had been arrested and indicted for violating the draft-card-burning statute. Close to 200,000 United States soldiers were now stationed in Vietnam, with more arriving daily.

On February 11, David Miller became the first individual to be convicted under the August 1965 statute.[6] The American Civil Liberties Union, which defended Miller, was unable to convince Federal District Court Judge Harold Tyler, Jr., that the defendant's act was an integral part of free speech. Instead, Judge Tyler accepted the government's argument that the law had nothing to do with free speech. Miller decided to appeal the decision against him.

Eight more individuals burned their draft cards in late March. Four of these men, including pacifist David Paul O'Brien, the defendant in the case which finally reached the Supreme Court, destroyed their cards during an antiwar demonstration on the steps of the South Boston Courthouse. Like David Miller, O'Brien was indicted, tried, and convicted; he, too, decided to appeal.[7]

As spring wore on, draft card burning became passé as a form of protest. Many opponents of the war realized that potential war critics were being repulsed by an act which appeared to be unnecessarily hostile and extreme. Thus, awareness was growing within the peace camp that burning a draft card had undesirable political consequences. Other opponents focused their efforts on sit-ins at draft boards, on refusal to report for induction, on campus discussions of the inequities of the Selective Service System.

General Hershey became the focal point for a new round of criticism when he came out in support of reclassification and induction of students who participated in sit-ins at draft boards rather than for trying them in the courts for trespassing on government property. Hershey's view that the draft could and should be used to punish dissenters was guaranteed to make opponents of the draft—and others, of course—see red. With renewed fervor, and with renewed conviction that their cause was just, critics of the war began a crusade for General Hershey's hide.

In addition, colleges were plagued by sit-ins against cooperating with the draft, against releasing class ranking, against administering deferment tests. Furthermore, a great debate on the Selective Service System in general and college deferments in particular got under way in Congress, with various national leaders defending the existing system or advocating universal service, an end to college deferments, a lottery-based selection process, or the end of the draft and creation of a volunteer army in its place. Draft card burning was simply no longer at the center of the stage; its day had come and gone.

On October 13, almost a year to the day after he burned his draft card on Whitehall Street, David Miller lost his appeal. The Court of Appeals for the Second Circuit, whose jurisdiction covers Connecticut, New York, and Vermont, ruled unanimously that the law was constitutional and did not violate Miller's right of free speech.[8] As the fall progressed, the trials of many of the men who destroyed their cards in the last months of 1965 and the early months of 1966 came to a conclusion; all the defendants were convicted, despite pleas that the law was unconstitutional. In November, the Court of Appeals for the Eighth Circuit, which covers Arkansas, Iowa, Minnesota, Missouri, Nebraska, and North and South Dakota, joined the Second Circuit in upholding the constitutionality of the law.

[6] *United States v. Miller*, 249 F. Supp. 59 (S.D.N.Y. 1966).

[7] *United States v. O'Brien*, Crim. No. 91 (D. Mass., June 1, 1966).

[8] 367 F.2d 72 (1966).

By the end of 1966, sixteen men had been convicted under the ban and two of these convictions had been upheld on appeal. The Justice Department had not sought indictments against a small number of violators on the ground that they were ineligible for the draft because of age or physical condition, although the law itself made no such distinction. David Miller and the American Civil Liberties Union decided to exhaust their last remaining option by asking the Supreme Court for a final determination.

The door was slammed in their faces on February 13, 1967, when the Supreme Court refused to review the decision of the lower courts.[9] According to the rules of the Court, four justices must favor a petition for certiorari for a case to be heard; in this instance, only Justice William O. Douglas wished to hear the appeal. The refusal of the Supreme Court to accept the case left Miller's conviction standing but did not, of course, represent a judgment on the merits of his argument that the law was not constitutional.

With all possible channels now blocked, further efforts to have the draft-card-burning amendment declared unconstitutional seemed hopeless. But then, barely two months later, new life was breathed into the legal conflict. The Court of Appeals for the First Circuit, whose jurisdiction covers Massachusetts, Maine, New Hampshire, Puerto Rico, and the Virgin Islands, ruled unanimously in *O'Brien v. United States* that the ritual of burning a draft card was a symbolic act protected by the First Amendment guarantee of free speech.[10] While the court upheld O'Brien's primary contention, it, nevertheless, sustained his conviction on another ground. *The New York Times*, in a switch from its earlier editorial policy that draft card burners should be punished, praised the decision of the First Circuit.

Since the ruling in the *O'Brien* case was directly contrary to the verdicts previously announced by the Second and Eighth Circuits as well as a number of district courts, the government decided to appeal the decision to the Supreme Court; O'Brien cross-appealed, arguing that the court of appeals ruled correctly on the constitutionality of the law but made a mistake when it sustained his conviction on an alternate ground.

The Supreme Court was faced with an obvious but unpleasant dilemma. It had just turned down an opportunity to rule on the constitutional question involved in the destruction of a draft card as a means of symbolic protest. If it remained adamant, Congress, the public, and the lower courts would not know whether or not the law violated the Constitution. In effect, the decision of the First Circuit forced the Supreme Court, against its will, to hear the *O'Brien* case and to rule on the validity of the draft-card-burning amendment.

. . . .

II.   Legal Arguments in United States v. O'Brien*

STATEMENT OF THE CASE:

On March 31, 1966, David Paul O'Brien and three other men burned their draft cards on the steps of the South Boston Courthouse. In anticipation of the burning a sizeable crowd had gathered. Newspaper reporters were present, as well as several agents of the Federal Bureau of Investigation. The crowd was restless and hostile,

[9] 386 U.S. 911 (1967).

[10] 376 F.2d 538 (1967).

*Author's note: the statement of the case and the briefs printed below are original; arguments used in the briefs were drawn primarily from the briefs actually filed in the *O'Brien* case and from decisions of lower federal courts in other draft-card-burning cases.

and the FBI men found it necessary to conduct the draft card burners into the court-house to protect them from personal injury.

O'Brien was warned of his right to counsel and his right to remain silent and was then interviewed by two FBI agents. In response to their queries, he stated that he had burned his draft card because of his beliefs, knowing that he was committing an act prohibited by federal law. The agents then photographed the charred remnants of the card.

O'Brien was indicted and brought to trial on a charge of having violated section 12 (b) (3) of the Universal Military Training and Service Act, as amended by Congress in August 1965. Prior to the trial, counsel for O'Brien filed a motion with the federal district court to dismiss the indictment on the ground that the 1965 amendment prohibiting mutilation or destruction of a registration certificate was unconstitutional. The pretrial motion was denied.

At the trial, the defendant stated his reasons to the jury as follows:

> I am a pacifist and as such I cannot kill, and I would not cooperate.
> I later began to feel that there is necessity, not only to personally not kill, but to try to urge others to take this action, to urge other people to refuse to cooperate with murder.
> So I decided to publicly burn my draft card, hopefully so that other people would reevaluate their positions with Selective Service, with the armed forces, and reevaluate their place in the culture of today, to hopefully consider my position.
> And I don't contest the fact that I did burn my draft card, because I did.
> It is something that I felt I had to do, because I think we are basically living in a culture today, a society that is basically violent, it is basically a plagued society, plagued not only by wars, but by the basic inability on the part of people to look at other people as human beings, the inability to feel that we can live and love one another, and I think we can. . . .
> So in this sense I think we are all on trial today. We all have to decide one way or the other what we want to do, whether we are going to accept death or whether we will fight to sustain life.

O'Brien was convicted, but his constitutional claim was sustained on appeal to the First Circuit Court of Appeals. The opinion of the appellate court noted that at the time Congress adopted the 1965 amendment, a regulation of the Selective Service System required all registrants to keep their registration certificates on their persons at all times. Knowing violation of the regulation was a criminal act. Thus, the court concluded that the 1965 amendment to the Universal Military Training and Service Act, which provided for an identical punishment, served no separate or valid function. The court concluded that, in the light of the existing administrative regulations, the decision by Congress to single out persons engaged in protest against government policy violated the First Amendment. The law was thus struck down as an unconstitutional abridgment of freedom of expression.

Although the court held the amendment unconstitutional, it did not overrule O'Brien's conviction. Despite the fact that the indictment had not charged the defendant with violating the nonpossession regulation, the court stated, nevertheless, that the evidence at trial had clearly established that O'Brien had knowingly violated the administrative regulation. Thus, O'Brien's conviction was affirmed.

The government appealed to the Supreme Court, arguing that the court of appeals had erred in holding the statute unconstitutional. O'Brien also appealed, arguing that the appeals court erred in sustaining his conviction on the basis of a crime of which he was neither charged nor tried. The Supreme Court granted both requests for writs of certiorari.

BRIEF FOR APPELLANT

BRIEF FOR APPELLEE

1. Is a statutory prohibition of destruction or mutilation of a draft card an abridgment of the First Amendment guarantee of freedom of speech?

As counsel for the United States, we would like to stress at the outset of our brief that Congress has the authority to classify and conscript manpower for military service; to that end, it may establish a system of registration, provide penalties for violation of the requirements of the system, and may require the active cooperation of citizens in the process of selecting men for service. The power to raise and support armies is not simply an implied or inherent power of government, it is a power expressly granted to Congress in Article 1 of the Constitution.

In carrying out the responsibilities placed on it by the Constitution, Congress has passed the Universal Military Training and Service Act and various amendments, including the 1965 amendment to section 12 (b) (3) of the act specifically prohibiting the knowing destruction or mutilation of any registration certificate issued by the Selective Service System.[1] We believe that this amendment is an appropriate exercise of Congress's power under the Constitution and we hope to convince the Court that the First Circuit Court of Appeals erred in sustaining the appellee's contention that the amendment violated his rights under the First Amendment.

Section 12 (b) (3) of the Universal Military Training and Service Act, like the other provisions of section 12 (b), is directed only at specific conduct—conduct which Congress could reasonably have concluded would seriously impair the safety of the nation and the operation of the Selective Service System if allowed to go unchecked.

The Court can and should take judicial cognizance of the fact that at the time Congress passed the draft-card-burning amendment, the United States was already heavily committed to the cause of freedom in South Vietnam. Congress had voted large sums of money to prosecute the war effort and the President had sent thousands of American

It is our belief that the court of appeals did not err in holding the draft-card-burning amendment unconstitutional on the ground that the act in question was entitled to protection under the First Amendment. The government does not deny that symbolic action may be protected speech, but it asserts that burning a draft card does not fall within the category of acts which are protected by the Constitution and that, anyway, Congress is entitled to pass legislation which does not interfere unduly with freedom of expression. We hope to convince the Court that both of these arguments are incorrect.

Since the government's brief defines the limits of acts which qualify for First Amendment protection in a circumscribed and incorrect fashion in order to exclude the act of which appellee is accused, it is necessary to examine the cases in which this Court has given judicial recognition to symbolic speech.

It is clear from past decisions of the Supreme Court that the First Amendment guarantees include appropriate types of action and are not confined solely to verbal expression. Thus, as the Court said in *NAACP v. Button*, 371 U.S. 415, at 429 (1963), "... [A]bstract discussion is not the only species of communication which the Constitution protects." Justice Sobeloff of the Fourth Circuit Court of Appeals has summarized the relevant decisions of the Supreme Court as follows: "The First Amendment affords protection not merely to voicing of abstract opinions on public issues, but protects implementing conduct which is in nature of advocacy."[1] Appellee's action in burning his draft card at a peaceable demonstration against the war in Vietnam to symbolize his opposition was "implementing conduct ... in nature of advocacy" and certainly was no more than the appropriate symbolic expression of his point of view.

---

[1] 79 Stat 586 (1965).

[1] *NLRB v. International Longshoremen's Association*, 332 F.2d 992, at 993 (4th Cir. 1964).

soldiers to Asia to help the South Vietnamese armed forces. Although, of course, it was impossible in the summer of 1965 to predict the future course of the expanding conflict in Vietnam and the scope of American involvement in the war, prudent representatives could well have decided that the United States should, at any rate, prepare itself for an all-out national effort. Thus, the amendment was a responsible exercise of Congress's legislative judgment.

Since draft card burning involves conduct—a specific act—it is not entitled to the same kind of protection under the First Amendment as pure speech. As the Court said recently in *Cox v. Louisiana,* 379 U.S. 536, at 555 (1965):

> We emphatically reject the notion . . . that the First and Fourteenth Amendments afford the same kind of freedom to those who would communicate ideas by conduct such as patrolling, marching, and picketing on streets and highways, as these amendments afford to those who communicate ideas by pure speech. . . .

The appellee urges, however, that the conduct involved in burning a draft card is a special kind of conduct, that it is a substitute for speech and therefore qualifies for First Amendment protection as "symbolic speech." It is clear, nevertheless, that not all conduct can qualify for protection against legislative proscription simply by calling the act in question "symbolic speech." Otherwise, many traditionally illegal expressions of protest could be made with impunity.

For example, political assassination is a gesture of protest, but few—if any—people would argue that assassins are protected against prosecution by the First Amendment guarantee of freedom of expression. Defacers of public property can hardly argue convincingly that they are protected against prosecution by the First Amendment. Dumping garbage in front of a city hall would not qualify for protection on the ground that it constitutes "symbolic speech."[2] In a recent New York case, a man who deliberately violated an ordinance against clotheslines in front and side yards abutting public streets to protest against high property taxes was unable to

The doctrine that certain acts are protected under the First Amendment was first notably expressed by Chief Justice Hughes in *Stromberg v. Califor013na,* 283 U.S. 359 (1931). Speaking for the Court, Justice Hughes held California's red flag law unconstitutional on the ground that peaceful display of a red flag as a symbol of opposition to organized government was protected by the guarantee of freedom of speech.

Nine years later, the Court employed the precedent of the red flag case in ruling that peaceful picketing was protected by the First Amendment. The opinion of the Court stated that "The carrying of signs and banners, no less than the raising of a flag, is a natural and appropriate means of conveying information of matters of public concern."[2] And the following year, in *Milk Wagon Drivers Union v. Meadowmoor Dairies,* 312 U.S. 275, at 293 (1941), Justice Frankfurter wrote that "Peaceful picketing is the workingman's means of communication."

It was not until two years later, in 1943, that the concept of symbolic speech was employed for the first time by the Court. In the famous case of *West Virginia Board of Education v. Barnette,* 319 U.S. 624 (1943), the Court held that a compulsory flag salute violated the First Amendment rights of school children who were Jehovah's Witnesses, since it forced them to express by word and sign beliefs contrary to their own. Justice Jackson stated, in his opinion for the Court:

> There is no doubt that . . . the flag salute is a form of utterance. Symbolism is a primitive but effective way of communicating ideas. The use of an emblem or flag to symbolize some system, idea, institution or personality, is a shortcut from mind to mind. . . .
>
> 319 U.S. 624, at 632–33.

In recent years, the Court has extended First Amendment protection to civil rights demonstrators on the ground that peaceful sit-ins, stand-ins, and protest marches are all acts of communication comparable to verbal

---

[2] *United States v. Miller,* 367 F.2d 72, at 79 (2d Cir. 1966), *cert. denied,* 386 U.S. 911 (1967).

[2] *Carlson v. California,* 310 U.S. 106, at 112–13 (1940); see also *Thornhill v. Alabama,* 310 U.S. 88 (1940), decided the same day.

void his conviction on First Amendment grounds.[3]

Thus, not all acts which are labeled "symbolic speech" are entitled to constitutional protection. The decisive question in this case is whether the act of burning a draft card fits into the limited class of actions which this Court has held to be so analogous to speech as to be entitled to the protection accorded pure speech.

It is our belief that draft card burning clearly falls outside the narrow category which this Court has defined as protected "symbolic speech." Past precedents reveal that conduct has been treated as analogous to speech only (1) where the conduct in question is an inextricable part of oral expression, or (2) where no reasonably effective alternative method of communication was available.

Let us look at point (1) first. Conduct is inextricably tied to speech when it is a natural extension of speech or when the conduct is the equivalent of, or a traditionally recognized substitute for, a particular verbal statement.

Thus, in the famous flag salute case, *West Virginia Board of Education v. Barnette*, 319 U.S. 624 (1943), the Court ruled that a municipal ordinance requiring public school children to recite the Pledge of Allegiance and salute the flag violated the First Amendment since the ordinance compelled public expression of beliefs to which the defendants did not subscribe. Speaking of the flag salute requirement, the Court held that it also violated the amendment, since "... [I]n connection with the pledges, the flag salute is a form of utterance..." which the state cannot demand of its citizens.[4] The Court gave the defendants' refusal to salute the flag the same constitutional protection it gave their refusal to recite the Pledge of Allegiance, because it recognized that the pledge was rendered devoid of much of its meaning when not accompanied by the ceremonial gesture of the salute. The salute was, as a form of expression, inextricably entwined with the pledge. Neither could be imposed on unwilling citizens by governmental authority.

expression. For example, in *Brown v. Louisiana*, 383 U.S. 131 (1966), the Court reversed by a five-to-four vote the convictions of five Negro men on breach of the peace charges for staging a silent stand-in against segregation in a public library; Justice Fortas's opinion stated that the breach of the peace statute "... [C]annot constitutionally be applied to punish petitioners' actions in the circumstances of this case..." since they were "engaged in lawful, constitutionally protected exercise of their fundamental rights."[3] Moreover, a clear majority of the Court has held that demonstrations for civil rights in the streets are protected by the First Amendment, even though such demonstrations involve the communication of ideas "... [B]y conduct such as patrolling, marching and picketing."[4]

In short, it is our contention that the First Amendment includes within its scope all methods of communication of ideas by conduct which are rational, appropriate, and nonviolent. Or, as was stated by Justice Frankfurter in *Milk Wagon Drivers Union v. Meadowmoor Dairies*:

> It must never be forgotten, however, that the Bill of Rights was the child of the Enlightenment. Back of the guaranty of free speech lay faith in the power of an appeal to reason by all the peaceful means for gaining access to the mind. It was in order to avert force and explosions due to restrictions upon rational modes of communications that the guaranty of free speech was given so generous a scope. But utterance in a context of violence can lose its significance as an appeal to reason and become part of an instrument of force. Such utterance was not meant to be sheltered by the Constitution.
>
> 312 U.S. 275, at 293.

Certainly, the burning of a draft card at a peaceable demonstration against government policy is a "peaceful means for gaining access to the mind" and a prohibition of such conduct is a restriction on a rational mode of communication.

We believe that the government's attempt to define symbolic speech in such a way as to

---

[3] *People v. Stover*, 12 N.Y.2d 462 (1963), *appeal dismissed*, 375 U.S. 42.

[4] 319 U.S. 624, at 632 (1943).

[3] 383 U.S. 131, at 142–43.

[4] *Cox v. Louisiana*, 379 U.S. 536, at 555 (1965).

Under a similar rationale, the Court has upheld the right of citizens to display a red flag or red banner or to carry signs on a picket line during a labor dispute.[5] Both of these acts have been deemed the equivalent of speech, since they convey in generally understood terms opposition to a particular government or to a particular employer.

The Court has, in addition, upheld the right of citizens to stand-in silently and peaceably in order to protest segregation in a public library. Such silent protest was held to be a substitute for actual speech in *Brown v. Louisiana*, 383 U.S. 131 (1966). We submit that burning a draft card, even if carried out in a peaceable fashion, is not directly analogous to displaying a flag or conveying opposition to segregation by a silent stand-in. As Justice Jackson said in *West Virginia Board of Education v. Barnette*, 319 U.S. 624, at 632:

> The use of an emblem or flag to symbolize some system, idea, institution, or personality, is a short cut from mind to mind.... Associated with many of these symbols are appropriate gestures of acceptance or respect; a salute, a bowed or bared head, a bended knee....

The precedents also suggest that this Court will not hold that conduct, as opposed to pure speech, qualifies for protection under the First Amendment as "symbolic speech" unless there is no reasonably effective alternative means of communicating the viewpoint expressed. If the prohibition of certain peaceable conduct results in foreclosing an important—and possibly the sole—method for achieving widespread publicity for a minority viewpoint, greater freedom to express ideas through action should be permitted; otherwise, not all ideas would have a meaningful chance to compete effectively in the marketplace, and our society would be diminished thereby.

This principle has been espoused in various cases: in *NAACP v. Button*, 371 U.S. 415 (1963), the Court ruled that the litigative activities carried on by the NAACP in seeking

separate draft card burning from display of a red flag, saluting a flag, picketing, marching, parading, or conducting a civil rights stand-in or sit-in is ludicrous and blatantly incorrect.

The government suggests that only acts which are inextricably tied to speech qualify for protection. Thus, the peaceable display of a red flag cannot be prohibited by law since such display conveys, in generally understood terms, opposition to an existing government. Isn't this argument equally applicable to the deliberate burning of a draft card at a peaceable rally? Doesn't draft card burning, under such circumstances, convey in generally understood terms opposition to the government and to a policy of the government? Is a civil rights sit-in or the display of a red flag any more the equivalent of pure speech than the act of appellee in burning his draft card? Was the act of Miss Stromberg in displaying a red flag or the act of the five Negro stand-ins who invaded the white sanctuary of the public library of Clinton, Louisiana, any more "inextricably" tied to purely verbal expression than the ritual performed by David Paul O'Brien?

Counsel for the government suggest further that symbolic acts do not qualify for First Amendment protection if there are alternative means to convey effectively the ideas in question. This, too, is arrant nonsense.

First of all, it is a perversion of the First Amendment to suggest that the government can prohibit certain methods of expressing opinion simply because other methods for expressing the same opinion exist. If it were otherwise, why was the state of California unable to punish Miss Stromberg for displaying a red flag or the state of Louisiana unable to punish the men who demonstrated against segregation in a public library?

Secondly, the past decisions of this Court do not support the government's contention that First Amendment protection is given to symbolic speech only when no equally effective alternative ways of expressing dissent are available: O'Brien could have mounted a soapbox, written letters to newspapers and to congressmen, distributed literature, etc., but so could Miss Stromberg, the labor union picketers in *Thornhill v. Alabama*, and the Negro demonstrators in *Brown v. Louisiana*.

---

[5] *Stromberg v. California*, 283 U.S. 359 (1931); *Thornhill v. Alabama*, 310 U.S. 88 (1940).

to achieve political rights for Negroes were protected by the First Amendment; in *Martin v. Struthers*, 319 U.S. 141, at 146 (1943), Justice Black stated that "Door-to-door distribution of circulars is essential to the poorly financed causes of little people"; and in *Milk Wagon Drivers Union v. Meadowmoor Dairies*, 312 U.S. 287, at 293 (1941), Justice Frankfurter wrote for the majority that "Peaceful picketing is the workingman's means of communication."

In contrast to the above examples, draft card burning cannot be characterized as a method for expressing views which could not otherwise be conveyed to a large audience. It is quite clear that opponents of the draft and of American participation in the Vietnam war have available many legitimate ways of expressing their opposition to government policy. The mass communication media have given extensive coverage to the words and actions of dissenters. Dissenters have held innumerable public meetings and peaceable demonstrations, have participated in innumerable debates and discussions on college campuses, have distributed millions of pieces of antiwar literature.

Admittedly, draft card burning dramatizes their protest. But acts which are legitimately subject to restraint are not rendered immune from regulation simply because they dramatize a particular viewpoint. And we stress that this is especially true when the views in question can be expressed effectively in ways which do not interfere unnecessarily with the orderly functioning of government.

For example, this Court has held that individuals who fail to go to court to seek suspension of an injunction against a demonstration may not carry out their plans, even though a demonstration in the face of a judicial order heightens the drama of their protest.[6] In *Kovacs v. Cooper*, 336 U.S. 77, at 89 (1949), the Court ruled that the use of sound trucks to publicize views is not protected by the First Amendment from reasonable regulation, since other "easy means of publicity are open." Finally, in *Schneider v. State*, 308 U.S. 147, at 160–61 (1939), the Court said:

[6] *Walker v. City of Birmingham*, 388 U.S. 307 (1967).

Thirdly, and most importantly, American citizens have a constitutional right—within limits which we will define shortly—to express their views as effectively as possible. Counsel for the government try to frighten the Court by suggesting that our position is that any act that can be labeled an expression of dissent—whether it be political assassination, defacing public buildings, or throwing garbage in front of city hall—is entitled to constitutional protection. We make no such argument.

There are obviously limits to the expressions of opinion which are protected by the First Amendment, but we believe that as long as an individual remains within these limits he is entitled to be as convincing as possible. If a particular expression of opinion fits within the limits, it is irrelevant whether the individual or individuals involved choose to express themselves in a dramatic or in a boring fashion.

As this Court has said, a speaker has the right to choose the place where he can be most effective as long as his expression of opinion meets the proper constitutional test and he does not violate reasonable limitations imposed by the need for traffic safety.[5] Similarly, a speaker can choose, within the above limits, the time when he can be most effective and the manner in which he can be most effective.[6] Thus, we ask the Court to reject appellant's argument that the symbolic act of burning a draft card can be excluded from the category of symbolic acts which qualify for protection under the First Amendment because there are other means available for expressing opposition to the draft and the war in Vietnam.

If the members of this Court decide that the act of burning a draft card, like the acts of carrying a red flag, of picketing, of parading, and of sitting in, is a symbolic communication of ideas protected by the First Amendment, they will then have to decide whether First Amendment rights can be suspended in

[5] *Martin v. Struthers*, 319 U.S. 141, at 150 (1943); *Schneider v. State*, 308 U.S. 147, at 163 (1939).

[6] *Mills v. Alabama*, 384 U.S. 214 (1966); *Saia v. New York*, 334 U.S. 358 (1948); *Kovacs v. Cooper*, 336 U.S. 77 (1949).

... [A] person could not exercise this liberty [of free speech] by taking his stand in the middle of a crowded street, contrary to traffic regulations, and maintain his position to the stoppage of all traffic; a group of distributors could not insist upon a constitutional right to form a cordon across the street and allow no pedestrian to pass who did not accept a tendered leaflet; nor does the guarantee of freedom of speech or of the press deprive a municipality of power to enact regulations against throwing literature broadcast in the streets. Prohibition of such conduct would not abridge the constitutional liberty since such activity bears no necessary relationship to the freedom to speak, write, print or distribute information or opinion.

We believe, therefore, that draft card burning does not meet the criteria which the Court has set up for determining the types of conduct that qualify for First Amendment protection on the ground that they are equivalent to pure speech. If the Court agrees with this position, it must hold that the court of appeals erred in ruling unconstitutional a statute designed to carry out Congress's obligation to raise and support armies.

On the other hand, even if the judgment of the majority is that the act of burning a draft card is equivalent to speech, there is still no need for the Court to uphold the verdict of the court of appeals. Ever since Justice Holmes's classic statement in *Schenck v. United States*, 249 U.S. 47, at 52 (1919), that "The most stringent protection of free speech would not protect a man in falsely shouting fire in a theatre and causing a panic," it has been perfectly clear that the First Amendment does not raise an insurmountable bar against reasonable and appropriate regulation. Prior decisions of this Court show that the constitutionality of a regulation depends upon whether the public purpose served by the regulation outweighs any possible limitation of freedom of speech. Or, as stated in *American Communication Association v. Douds*, 339 U.S. 382, at 399 (1945):

When particular conduct is regulated in the interest of public order, and the regulation results in an indirect, conditional, partial abridgment of speech, the duty of the courts is to

this instance. The Court will have to decide what is the proper test for determining whether section 12 (b) (3) is an unconstitutional abridgment of the rights of the appellee.

We believe that the constitutionality of the statute should be judged by application of the "clear and present danger" test enunciated by Justice Holmes in his classic decision in *Schenck v. United States*, 249 U.S. 47, at 52 (1919):

The question in every case is whether the words used are used in such circumstances and are of such a nature to create a clear and present danger that they will bring about the substantive evils that Congress has a right to prevent.

Assuming, for the purpose of argument, that the statute is not designed to curb free speech but to facilitate the operation of the Selective Service System, it is by no means true that the symbolic burning of draft cards constitutes a "clear and present" danger to the functioning of the system.

The burning of a draft card by its bearer makes it unavailable for identification purposes or for facilitating communication between the registrant and his local draft board. Since these benefits are primarily for the registrant rather than for the government, presumably there is no reason why he cannot choose to waive them.

The utility of a draft card in case of national emergency is dubious, to say the least; certainly, First Amendment rights should not be curtailed on the basis of an argument which is so hypothetical and improbable. The utility of a draft card in case draft records are lost or misplaced is also an empty assertion, since it is common knowledge that the Selective Service System maintains extensive files on all registrants both in Washington and at the offices of local draft boards.

Our argument that the destruction of a draft card does not meaningfully interfere with the operation of the Selective Service System is buttressed by the fact that neither the system—nor the President, the Secretary of Defense, or any other official of the executive branch of the government—requested

determine which of these two conflicting interests demands the greater protection under the particular circumstances presented.[7]

We believe that if these principles are applied, the validity of the amendment in question is clear. As we have already shown, section 12 (b) (3) involves the most minimal and incidental limitation of freedom of expression consonant with the need for government to carry out a necessary and legitimate purpose. This is not a case of government suppression of all dissent or even of suppression of purely verbal dissent.

On the other side of the coin, however, is the fact that the issuance and possession of draft cards facilitates the proper functioning of the Selective Service System. Draft cards provide a speedy means of identification in case of national emergency; they provide a record of registration and classification—a record which may be extremely useful if a file is lost or misplaced either in the office of a local draft board or in Washington; they inform registrants of their obligations, including prompt notification to local draft boards of changes in physical, occupational, marital, and family status; they facilitate communication between registrants and local draft boards by providing registrants with individual numbers and listing the number and address of each registrant's draft board. Thus, draft cards unquestionably are useful tools in the administration of the Universal Military Training and Service Act.

Admittedly, the destruction of a single draft card would hardly jeopardize the functioning of the Selective Service System; Congress reasonably inferred, however, that—in the absence of regulation—draft card burning might become widespread, with serious consequences for the operation of the Selective Service System. Thus, as the Second Circuit Court of Appeals said in *United States v. Miller*, 367 F.2d 72, at 81 (1966), *cert. denied*, 386 U.S. 911, in a decision which upheld the

Congress to pass the legislation in question. In fact, the director of the system, General Lewis Hershey, evidently said in a speech reported on page five of the *Philadelphia Evening Bulletin* of October 29, 1965, that the draft-card-burning law was unnecessary.

Thus, there is no clear and present danger that the burning of a draft card may prevent the effective operation of the Selective Service System, or—more broadly—that it may adversely affect the military power of the nation. Under this standard, the statute is unconstitutional.

While we believe that the "clear and present danger" test should be applied to the statute and to the act of the appellee, we recognize that the Court may choose to follow the argument of the government that the proper test to use is the ad hoc balancing test. Application of this test requires the Court to balance the interest of our society in freedom of expression against the magnitude of the public interests served by the statute in question and the extent to which the statute actually serves to protect those interests.[7]

We think that even under the balancing test the draft-card-burning amendment is unconstitutional. Assuming, *arguendo*, that there is ample magnitude to the public interest served by the proper functioning of the Selective Service System, it is still true, as we have already shown, that the amendment prohibiting draft card destruction bears no substantial relation to the achievement of this purpose. Section 12 (b) (3) of the Universal Military Training and Service Act costs our society far more, by limiting free expression, than it contributes, since it does not, in fact, add anything to the process of selecting manpower for military service.

Furthermore, an examination of the legislative history of the amendment shows beyond doubt that the purpose of section 12 (b) (3) was to limit dissent and not to further the operation of the draft laws. Counsel for the appellant attempt to suggest that the court of appeals came to this conclusion improperly, since it examined the motives of Congress in

[7] See also *Communist Party v. Subversive Activities Control Board*, 367 U.S. 1, at 91 (1961), *Konigsberg v. State Bar of California*, 366 U.S. 36, at 49–51 (1961), *Barenblatt v. United States*, 360 U.S. 109, at 126 (1959), *NAACP v. Alabama*, 357 U.S. 449, at 461 (1958).

[7] *Communist Party v. Subversive Activities Control Board*, 367 U.S. 1, at 93 (1961).

constitutionality of the draft-card-burning amendment:

> Proper functioning of the system depends upon the aggregated consequences of individual acts; in raising an army no less than in regulating commerce, cf. *Wickard v. Filburn*, 317 U.S. 111, 127–28 . . . , the seriousness of an individual's acts must often be assessed not only in isolation but under the assumption that they may be multiplied manifold.

The court of appeals recognized the above facts but felt that the Selective Service System was adequately protected by the administrative regulation that registrants must carry their draft cards at all times. Since the penalty for violation of the amendment was the same as the penalty for violation of the administrative regulation, the court concluded that the amendment served no additional purpose and must, therefore, have been enacted to inhibit dissent rather than to facilitate the operation of the Selective Service System.

We believe that the conclusions of the court of appeals err in several ways: (1) an administrative regulation is not equivalent to a statutory prohibition; (2) it is a fundamental principle of constitutional law that courts of law avoid inquiries into the motives of legislators; (3) even if such an inquiry is conducted, the legislative history of the amendment does not justify a conclusion that Congress passed the prohibition in order to suppress free expression.

First, an administrative regulation is in no way comparable to a statutory pronouncement on the same subject. Administrative rules do not give a clear and explicit picture of the legislative will; in the minds of most citizens, administrative rules are not as significant as legislative acts; administrative rules may be revoked or altered at the discretion of the responsible officials, whereas statutes cannot be modified by administrators.

Congress obviously felt that a statutory prohibition would have a greater deterrent effect than the existing administrative regulation, which required possession of a draft card but did not explicitly forbid mutilation or destruction. And, further, there is no constitutional rule that requires Congress to rely upon

clear violation of the principle of judicial self-restraint.

This argument misconstrues what the court of appeals did: it did not examine the motives of individual legislators but rather the purpose of the statute as revealed by the formal legislative record—the committee reports and the explanatory statements made on the floor of Congress by the sponsors of the measure. Precedents of this Court show that such an examination is entirely appropriate.

In *Grosjean v. American Press Co.*, for example, the Supreme Court unanimously overthrew a Louisiana tax on newspaper advertising on the ground that the tax violated the guarantee of freedom of the press.[8] The tax, while neutral on its face, had been deliberately designed to punish large city newspapers which had criticized Senator Huey Long and his associates.

Justice Sutherland wrote that the tax was unconstitutional because it was passed ". . . [W]ith the plain purpose of penalizing the publishers . . ." and ". . . [B]ecause in the light of its history and its present setting it is seen to be a deliberate and calculated device in the guise of a tax. . . ."[9] And in *Gomillion v. Lightfoot*, 364 U.S. 339 (1960), the Court held an Alabama reapportionment statute unlawful since its purpose was the attainment of an unconstitutional end.

The distinction between the word "motive" and the word "purpose" was pointed out by Judge Soper, in *NAACP v. Patty*, as follows:

> While it is well settled that a court may not inquire into the legislative motive . . . it is equally well settled that a court may inquire into the legislative purpose. . . . Legislative motive—good or bad—is irrelevant to the process of judicial review; but legislative purpose is of primary importance in determining the propriety of legislative action, since the purpose itself must be within the legislative competence, and the methods used must be reasonably likely to accomplish that purpose. Because of this necessity, a study of legislative purpose is of the highest relevance when a claim of unconstitutionality is put forward. Usually a court looks into the legislative history to clear up some statutory ambiguity . . .

[8] 297 U.S. 233 (1936).
[9] *Id.* at 251.

administrative regulations to accomplish its legislative purpose, nor should Congress be barred from legislating simply because the legislation in question may partially supersede an existing administrative regulation.

Secondly, the court of appeals violated a cardinal principle of adjudication by construing the motives of Congress in passing the draft-card-burning amendment. As this Court said in *Barenblatt v. United States,* 360 U.S. 109, at 132 (1959): ". . . [S]o long as Congress acts in pursuance of its constitutional power, the Judiciary lacks authority to intervene on the basis of the motives which spurred the exercise of that power." This view of the judicial function was also expressed in *Sonzinsky v. United States,* 300 U.S. 506, at 513–14 (1937), as follows: ". . . [I]nquiry into the hidden motives which may move Congress to exercise a power constitutionally conferred upon it is beyond the competency of the courts."

There are rare exceptions to this principle of judicial restraint, such as in the case of *Kennedy v. Mendoza-Martinez,* 372 U.S. 144 (1963). In that instance, the Court was unable to determine from the face of the statute in question whether the act was regulatory or penal in nature; to answer the question, the Court proceeded to examine, among other things, the motives of Congress in passing the legislation. Even in an inquiry of this nature, however, the Court has stated clearly that a holding of unconstitutionality would result only if the clearest proof of congressional motive could be established.

There is no need to abandon the principle of restraint in this instance. Since the amendment is clear, does not limit protected methods of protest, and is a reasonable exercise of an express power of Congress, there is no necessity for judicial scrutiny of congressional motives. The court of appeals' judgment that the amendment is unconstitutional should be reversed since it is based on such a scrutiny.

Thirdly, even if the Court should decide that there is sufficient reason in this instance to abandon the rule of judicial restraint, there is insufficient evidence to justify the conclusion of the court of appeals that Congress acted out of illicit motives. The most that the

but such ambiguity is not the *sine qua* for a judicial inquiry into legislative history. See the decision in *Lane v. Wilson,* 307 U.S. 268 . . . in which the Supreme Court showed that the state statute before the court was merely an attempt to avoid a previous decision in which the "grandfather" clause of an earlier statute had been held void.

> 159 F. Supp. 503, at 515 (E.D. Va. 1958);
> *rev'd on other grounds, sub nom. Harrison v.*
> *NAACP,* 360 U.S. 167 (1959).

And, as Justice Douglas said in his concurring opinion in *NAACP v. Button,* 371 U.S. 415, at 445–46 (1963):

> The Virginia Act . . . reflects a legislative purpose to penalize the N.A.A.C.P. because it promotes the desegregation of the races.
> . . . Judge Soper, writing for the Court in *N.A.A.C.P. v. Patty* . . . did not indulge in guesswork. He reviewed the various steps taken by Virginia to resist our *Brown* decision. . . . [T]hey make clear the purpose of the present law—as clear a purpose to evade our prior decision as was the legislation in *Lane v. Wilson.* . . .

Since the court of appeals attempted to ascertain the intentions and purpose of Congress as a whole in enacting the draft-card-burning amendment rather than to investigate the motives of individual congressmen, it did not err in scrutinizing the history of the legislation in question.

Nor did the court of appeals err in holding that the purpose of the amendment was to suppress dissent. The only legislative purpose expressed unequivocally in the committee reports and the statements by the amendment's sponsors was to make draft card burning "insulting and unpatriotic." The government attempts to cloud this point by suggesting that several purposes can be discovered by an examination of the legislative history, some of which, according to appellant's brief, are less constitutionally justifiable than others. The failure of Congress to hold hearings or even to consult the Selective Service System or the Defense Department before passing legislation which neither agency had requested, when considered in conjunction with the fact that only eight days elapsed between the introduc-

legislative history shows is that one senator and two representatives defended the amendment in part on the basis of the need for patriotism and loyalty during the war crisis; certainly, these few statements do not constitute clear proof that the entire Congress— nor even the three speakers, for that matter— acted because of a desire to suppress freedom of expression.

The report of the Senate Armed Services Committee to its parent body stated that the purpose of the amendment was to prevent conduct which "If allowed to continue unchecked . . . represents a potential threat to the exercise of the power to raise and support armies."[8] The report of the House Armed Services Committee did express the "deep concern" of the committee that draft card burning constituted open defiance of the government, but it also expressed the view that "in the present critical situation of the country, the acts of destroying or mutilating these cards are offenses which pose . . . a grave threat to the security of the Nation. . . ."[9] Thus, instead of proving that Congress's underlying motive was to suspend freedom of speech, the reports indicate that Congress enacted the amendment to carry out its responsibilities under the Constitution.

Since there was next to no debate on the amendment, and no opposition expressed on the floor of either house, it is impossible to prove that Congress acted from unconstitutional motives. The floor debates reveal that Senator Thurmond and Congressmen Rivers and Bray were incensed that draft card burners were going unpunished while American soldiers were giving their lives for their country in Vietnam; Representative Bray also stated his own conclusion that the burnings seriously damaged the Selective Service System.

The most that one can concede to appellee's argument that the legislative history reveals that Congress acted out of unconstitutional motives is that the three congressmen who did speak out had several motives—one

tion of the bill and its passage by both houses, throws serious doubt on the premise that Congress's purpose was other than to punish dissent.

The government suggests further that the legislative history is so brief that this Court cannot meaningfully decide what was Congress's purpose. But this is bad logic. The brevity of the record, plus the fact that every one of the three congressmen who spoke out repeated the same sanctimonious and unconstitutional purpose, make the intentions of Congress stand out far more sharply than if there had been a lengthier and more detailed history marked by less unanimous statements of purpose.

For example, Rep. L. Mendel Rivers (Dem., S.C.), the chairman of the House Committee on Armed Services, said on the floor of the House:

> The purpose of the bill is clear. . . . It is a straightforward clear answer to those who would make a mockery of our efforts in South Vietnam by engaging in the mass destruction of draft cards.
> . . . [I]f it can be proved that a person knowingly destroyed . . . his draft card . . . he can be sent to prison, where he belongs. This is the least we can do for our men in South Vietnam fighting to preserve freedom, while a vocal minority in this country thumb their noses at their own government.[10]

Rep. William G. Bray (Rep., Ind.) was even more eloquent:

> The need of this legislation is clear. Beatniks and so-called "campus-cults" have been publicly burning their draft cards to demonstrate their contempt for the United States and our resistance to Communist takeovers. Such actions have been suggested and led by college professors—professors supported by taxpayers' money. . . .
> These so-called "student" mobs at home and abroad make demands and threats; they hurl rocks and ink bottles at American buildings; they publicly mutilate or burn their draft

[8] *Sen. Rep. No. 589*, 89th Cong., 1st Sess., at 2.

[9] *House Rep. No. 747*, 89th Cong., 1st Sess., at 1–2.

[10] 111 *Cong. Rec.* 19871 (1965).

of which was clearly constitutional and one perhaps less so—for their support of the amendment. Since the amendment passed the House by 393 to 1 and the Senate by voice vote, it would be an exercise in imagination for this Court to rule that Congress's motives can be established with any clarity and, secondly, that judicial investigation of those motives reveals unambiguously that Congress enacted the amendment to limit free speech.

Thus, even if the Court does decide that inquiry into Congress's hidden purposes is justifiable in this instance, it should conclude that the holding of the court of appeals is incorrect and must be reversed.

cards; they even desecrate the American flag. Chanting and screaming vile epithets, these mobs of so-called "students" and Communist "stooges" attempt to create fear and destroy self-confidence in our country and its citizens and to downgrade the United States in the eyes of the world.

Such organized "student" groups in the United States have sent congratulations and money to Ho Chi Minh and have made anonymous and insulting calls to families of our servicemen killed in Vietnam.

This proposed legislation to make it illegal to knowingly destroy or mutilate a draft card is only one step in bringing some legal control over those who would destroy American freedom. This legislation, if passed, will be of some assistance to our country if the officers and courts charged with the enforcement of the law will have the energy, courage, and guts to make use of it.[11]

In the Senate, Sen. Strom Thurmond (Rep., S.C.) spoke as follows:

Recent incidents of mass destruction of draft cards constitute open defiance of the war-making powers of the Government and have demonstrated an urgent need for this legislation. . . .

Such conduct as public burnings of draft cards and public pleas for persons to refuse to register for their draft should not and must not be tolerated by a society whose sons, brothers, and husbands are giving their lives in defense of freedom and countrymen against Communist aggression.[12]

As the court of appeals correctly determined, the legislative history reveals a deliberate attempt by Congress to suppress political dissent. The court of appeals saw through Congress's clumsy effort to disguise its real purpose by superficially dressing the amendment up in innocuous language and refused to give it credence. We ask this Court to uphold the decision that the draft-card-burning amendment is an unconstitutional abridgment of freedom of expression.

[11] *Id.* at 19871–72.
[12] *Id.* at 19669.

2. *If the statute prohibiting draft card burning is unconstitutional, did the court of appeals err in sustaining appellee's conviction?*

Although the court of appeals ruled that section 12 (b) (3) was unconstitutional, it nevertheless affirmed O'Brien's conviction on the ground that he had violated the administrative regulation requiring registrants to carry their draft cards at all times. If the Supreme Court upholds our contention that the amendment is constitutional, this aspect of the ruling of the court of appeals will, of course, be irrelevant.

On the other hand, if the decision on constitutionality goes against the government, we believe that the subsidiary ruling of the lower court should be affirmed. While the reasons given by the court of appeals for sustaining O'Brien's conviction are, we admit, incorrect, we think that the holding can be justified on other grounds.

Although O'Brien was not specifically indicted and tried for violating the nonpossession regulation, the court of appeals affirmed his conviction on the ground that violation of the regulation was a "lesser included offense." But, as this Court has said:

> The basic principles controlling whether or not a lesser-included offense charge should be given in a particular case have been settled by this Court. Rule 31 (c) of the Federal Rules of Criminal Procedure provides, in relevant part, that the "defendant may be found guilty of an offense necessarily included in the offense charged.... [T]he lesser offense must be included within but not, on the facts of the case, be completely encompassed by the greater. A lesser-included offense instruction is only proper where the charged greater offense requires the jury to find a disputed factual element which is not required for conviction of the lesser-included offense...."
>
> *Sansone v. United States*, 380 U.S. 343, at 349–50 (1965).

The crime of nonpossession is not a lesser offense than the crime of draft card burning, since the punishment for the commission of either offense is identical; furthermore, since the same evidence that proved knowing destruction also proved nonpossession, there was

As the government explicitly states in its brief, the court of appeals incorrectly applied the lesser-included-offense doctrine in holding appellee guilty of violating the nonpossession regulation. According to Rule 31 (c) of the Federal Rules of Criminal Procedure and the decision of the Court in *Sansone v. United States*, 380 U.S. 343, at 349–50 (1965), it is clear that a defendant can be convicted for committing a crime not specifically included in the indictment against him on the ground that the offense is necessarily included in the offense charged *only if* (1) it is a lesser offense and (2) some disputed factual element required for conviction for the greater offense is not required to prove that the defendant is guilty of the lesser offense.

Even though counsel for the government concede that the court of appeals improperly convicted our client, they argue, nonetheless, that this Court can sustain the conviction on an alternative theory. In effect, the government is arguing that a defendant can be convicted of an offense for which he has not been indicted, regardless of whether the lesser-included-offense doctrine is applicable. As counsel for the government well know, such a conviction would violate the due process of law guaranteed by the Fifth Amendment and would, in addition, contradict many decisions of this Court.

The government attempts to sustain its position by several incorrect arguments. First, counsel for the appellant try to cloud the entire issue of the sufficiency of the indictment by suggesting that it can fairly be read to include the charge of nonpossession. But if the government had wished to indict O'Brien for nonpossession as well as for burning his draft card, it could easily have sought a two-count indictment, as it did in *United States v. Smith*, for example. In that case, the second count of the indictment read as follows:

> On or about the 22nd day of October, 1965, at Iowa City . . . Iowa, Stephen Lynn Smith . . . did fail to have in his personal possession the registration certificate issued to him by the Selective Service System of the United States

no disputed factual element at O'Brien's trial for draft card destruction which was unnecessary for conviction for violating the administrative regulation.

Despite the fact that the theory used by the court of appeals to sustain O'Brien's conviction was inapplicable to this case, we believe that the conclusion of the court of appeals is correct and should be sustained.

First, the indictment on which appellee was tried may—without distortion—fairly be read to include the charge of nonpossession. The indictment charged that O'Brien "... [W]illfully and knowingly did mutilate, destroy, and change by burning a certificate issued ... pursuant to and prescribed by the provisions of the Universal Military Training and Service Act, as amended, and the rules and regulations promulgated thereunder...."[10] The requirement of possession would, of course, be included in such rules. Simply because the indictment focused on the method chosen by O'Brien to divest himself of the offending document rather than on the consequences of his conduct does not mean that it must be construed to exclude such a charge.

Secondly, it is clear that when the jury convicted the appellee of knowing destruction, it necessarily had to rule on all the facts which would have sustained a charge of nonpossession. While it is true that the trial judge told the jury that "... [T]he crime charged is the burning of a draft card" and that "... [W]e are not concerned here with anything other than this statute which prohibits the burning or mutilating of a draft card...,"[11] it is equally true that the jury could not have reached its verdict of guilty without also concluding that appellee intentionally committed an act which would make further possession of his draft card impossible.

Finally, there is no merit to appellee's contention that the decision of the court of appeals violates the due process of law guaranteed him by the Fifth Amendment because he was not specifically indicted and tried for the offense of which he has been convicted. As has been stated, the facts—which proved nonpossession as well as

[10] Record at 3.
[11] Record at 34.

of America in violation of Title 50 App., Section 460 United States Code, and the regulations promulgated pursuant thereto.

> 249 F. Supp. 515, at 520 (S.D. Iowa 1966),
> aff'd. 368 F.2d 529 (8th Cir.).

The difference in the indictment in the *Smith* case demonstrates that O'Brien was indicted for destroying his draft card, and not for nonpossession.

Counsel's argument that the reference in the indictment to the rules and regulations promulgated under the Universal Military Training and Service Act alluded to the regulation prohibiting nonpossession and was, therefore, sufficient to sustain a conviction for nonpossession flies in the face of the rule that mere quotation of statutory language does not constitute a proper indictment. As Chief Justice John Marshall said in *The Schooner Hoppet v. United States*:

> It is not controverted that in all proceedings in courts of common law, the allegation that the act charged was committed in violation of law, or of the provisions of a particular statute will not justify condemnation, unless, independent of this allegation, a case be stated which shows that the law has been violated. The reference to the statute may direct the attention of the court, and of the accused, to the particular statute by which the prosecution is to be sustained, but forms no part of the description of the offense.
>
> 7 Cranch 389, at 393 (1813); see *Russell v. United States*, 369 U.S. 749 (1962), for a recent reaffirmation of these principles.

In the absence of explicit reference to the nonpossession regulation and of the allegations that would have to be made in an indictment charging nonpossession, the indictment was not sufficient to sustain a conviction for nonpossession and appellee's conviction should, therefore, be reversed and the indictment dismissed.

The government argues, however, that regardless of the sufficiency of the indictment, the jury must necessarily have found O'Brien guilty of violating the nonpossession regulation when it judged him guilty of burning his draft card. The language of section 12 (b) (3)

burning—were not in contention in the trial court. Because all the relevant facts were conceded, there is no reason to suggest that O'Brien would have followed a different strategy if the indictment had expressly charged him with violating the administrative regulation.

Thus, if the Court should find that the court of appeals was correct in ruling that the amendment against draft card burning was unconstitutional, it should nevertheless affirm appellee's conviction for nonpossession of his draft card.

requires a jury to convict any person "who forges, alters, knowingly destroys, knowingly mutilates, or in any manner changes any such certificate . . ." but the language of the nonpossession regulation requires in addition that the accused must be an individual who is required by law to register with the Selective Service System and that the card in question must be the card belonging to the accused.

Thus, a nonregistrant who burns someone else's draft card violates section 12 (b) (3) but not the administrative regulation; similarly, a registrant who burns someone else's card violates section 12 (b) (3) but not the regulation. Or, a registrant who burns the blank corners of his own card, but not the part containing registration details, also violates the amendment, but not the regulation. In sum, a jury verdict that a defendant is guilty of burning a draft card, or even *his* draft card, is not necessarily also a verdict that he violated the prohibition against nonpossession.

But even if the Court should find that the jury verdict that O'Brien burned his draft card also included a finding of fact on every question that would be raised under a charge of nonpossession, it is still true, nonetheless, that no man can be convicted without a proper indictment. This Court has always rejected the argument that the validity of a conviction can be determined by the sufficiency of the proof of an illegal act regardless of the sufficiency of the indictment—and it should do so in the present case.

Chief Justice Marshall considered this precise question in *The Schooner Hoppet v. United States*, and he concluded:

> The rule that a man shall not be charged with one crime and convicted of another, may sometimes cover real guilt, but its observance is essential to the preservation of innocence. It is only a modification of this rule, that the accusation on which the prosecution is founded, should state the crime which is to be proved, and state such a crime as will justify the judgment to be pronounced.
>
> 7 Cranch 389, at 394–95.

Procedural due process, guaranteed by the Fifth Amendment, requires that every defendant be given fair notice of the charge against him, in order to enable him to prepare the best defense possible. Since "... [C]onviction upon a charge not made would be a sheer denial of due process," to quote *DeJonge v. Oregon*, 299 U.S. 353, at 362 (1937), appellee's conviction must be reversed. The integrity of our system of justice demands no less.

. . . .

III.   Decision of the Court, Concurring, and Dissenting Opinions*

Mr. CHIEF JUSTICE WARREN delivered the opinion of the Court.

On the morning of March 31, 1966, David Paul O'Brien and three companions burned their Selective Service registration certificates on the steps of the South Boston Courthouse. A sizeable crowd, including several agents of the Federal Bureau of Investigation, witnessed the event. Immediately after the burning, members of the crowd began attacking O'Brien and his companions. An FBI agent ushered O'Brien to safety inside the courthouse. After he was advised of his right to counsel and to silence, O'Brien stated to FBI agents that he had burned his registration certificate because of his beliefs, knowing that he was violating Federal law. He produced the charred remains of the certificate, which, with his consent, were photographed.

For this act, O'Brien was indicted, tried, convicted, and sentenced in the United States District Court for the district of Massachusetts.[1] He did not contest the fact that he had burned the certificate. He stated in argument to the jury that he burned the certificate publicly to influence others to adopt his antiwar beliefs, as he put it, "so that other people would reevaluate their positions with Selective Service, with the armed forces, and reevaluate their place in the culture of today, to hopefully consider my position."

The indictment upon which he was tried charged that he "willfully and knowingly did mutilate, destroy, and change by burning ... [his] Registration Certificate (Selective Service System Form No. 2); in violation of Title 50, App., United States Code, Section 462 (b)." Section 462 (b) is part of the Universal Military Training and Service Act of 1948. Section 462 (b) (3), one of six numbered subdivisions of §462 (b), was amended by Congress in 1965, 79 Stat. 586 (adding the words italicized below), so that at the time O'Brien burned his certificate an offense was committed by any person,

who forges, alters, *knowingly destroys, knowingly mutilates,* or in any manner changes any such certificate. . . . (Italics supplied.)

In the District Court, O'Brien argued that the 1965 Amendment prohibiting the knowing destruction or mutilation of certificates was unconstitutional because it

* Author's note: the text of the Court's decision in *United States v. O'Brien*, 391 U.S. 367 (1968), and the concurring and dissenting opinions of Justices Harlan and Douglas, have been reproduced in full; footnotes have been edited and renumbered.

[1] He was sentenced under the Youth Correction Act, 18 U.S.C. § 5010 (b), to the custody of the Attorney General for a maximum period of six years for supervision and treatment.

was enacted to abridge free speech, and because it served no legitimate legislative purpose. The District Court rejected these arguments, holding that the statute on its face did not abridge First Amendment rights, that the court was not competent to inquire into the motives of Congress in enacting the 1965 Amendment, and that the Amendment was a reasonable exercise of the power of Congress to raise armies.

On appeal, the Court of Appeals for the First Circuit held the 1965 Amendment unconstitutional as a law abridging freedom of speech. At the time the Amendment was enacted, a regulation of the Selective Service System required registrants to keep their registration certificates in their "personal possession at all times," 32 CFR § 1617.1 (1962). Wilful violations of regulations promulgated pursuant to the Universal Military Training and Service Act were made criminal by statute, 50 U.S.C. App. § 462 (b) (6). The Court of Appeals, therefore, was of the opinion that conduct punishable under the 1965 Amendment was already punishable under the nonpossession regulation, and consequently that the Amendment served no valid purpose; further, that in light of the prior regulation, the Amendment must have been "directed at public as distinguished from private destruction." On this basis, the Court concluded that the 1965 Amendment ran afoul of the First Amendment by singling out persons engaged in protests for special treatment. The Court ruled, however, that O'Brien's conviction should be affirmed under the statutory provision, 50 U.S.C. App. § 462 (b) (6), which in its view made violation of the nonpossession regulation a crime, because it regarded such violation to be a lesser included offense of the crime defined by the 1965 Amendment.

The Government petitioned for certiorari, in No. 232, arguing that the Court of Appeals erred in holding the statute unconstitutional, and that its decision conflicted with decisions by the Court of Appeals for the Second[2] and Eighth Circuits[3] upholding the 1965 Amendment against identical constitutional challenges. O'Brien cross-petitioned for certiorari, in No. 233, arguing that the Court of Appeals erred in sustaining his conviction on the basis of a crime of which he was neither charged nor tried. We granted the Government's petition to resolve the conflict in the circuits, and we also granted O'Brien's cross-petition. We hold that the 1965 Amendment is constitutional both as enacted and as applied. We therefore vacate the judgment of the Court of Appeals and reinstate the judgment and sentence of the District Court without reaching the issue raised by O'Brien in No. 233.

I

When a male reaches the age of 18, he is required by the Universal Military Training and Service Act to register with a local draft board. He is assigned a Selective Service number, and within five days he is issued a registration certificate (SSS Form No. 2). Subsequently, and based on a questionnaire completed by the registrant, he is assigned a classification denoting his eligibility for induction, and "[a]s soon as practicable" thereafter he is issued a Notice of Classification (SSS Form No. 110). This initial classification is not necessarily permanent, and if in the interim before induction the registrant's status changes in some relevant way, he may be reclassified. After such a reclassification, the local board "as soon as practicable" issues to the registrant a new Notice of Classification.

---

[2] *United States v. Miller*, 367 F.2d 72 (C.A.2d Cir. 1966), *cert. denied*, 386 U.S. 911 (1967).

[3] *Smith v. United States*, 368 F.2d 529 (C.A. 8th Cir. 1966).

Both the registration and classification certificates are small white cards, approximately 2 by 3 inches. The registration certificate specifies the name of the registrant, the date of registration, and the number and address of the local board with which he is registered. Also inscribed upon it are the date and place of the registrant's birth, his residence at registration, his physical description, his signature, and his Selective Service number. The Selective Service number itself indicates his State of registration, his local board, his year of birth, and his chronological position in the local board's classification record.

The classification certificate shows the registrant's name, Selective Service number, signature, and eligibility classification. It specifies whether he was so classified by his local board, an appeal board, or the President. It contains the address of his local board and the date the certificate was mailed.

Both the registration and classification certificates bear notices that the registrant must notify his local board in writing of every change in address, physical condition, and occupational, marital, family, dependency, and military status, and of any other fact which might change his classification. Both also contain a notice that the registrant's Selective Service number should appear on all communications to his local board.

Congress demonstrated its concern that certificates issued by the Selective Service System might be abused well before the 1965 Amendment here challenged. The 1948 Act, 62 Stat. 604, itself prohibited many different abuses involving "any registration certificate, . . . or any other certificate issued pursuant to or prescribed by the provisions of this title, or rules or regulations promulgated hereunder. . . ." 62 Stat. 622 (1948). Under § 12 (b) (1)–(5) of the 1948 Act, it was unlawful (1) to transfer a certificate to aid a person in making false identification; (2) to possess a certificate not duly issued with the intent of using it for false identification; (3) to forge, alter, "or in any manner" change a certificate or any notation validly inscribed thereon; (4) to photograph or make an imitation of a certificate for the purpose of false identification; and (5) to possess a counterfeited or altered certificate. 62 Stat. 622 (1948). In addition, as previously mentioned, regulations of the Selective Service System required registrants to keep both their registration and classification certificates in their personal possession at all times. 32 CFR § 1617.1 (1962) (Registration Certificates); 32 CFR § 1623.5 (1962) (Classification Certificates). And § 12 (b) (6) of the Act, 62 Stat. 622–623 (1948), made knowing violation of any provision of the Act or rules and regulations promulgated pursuant thereto a felony.

By the 1965 Amendment, Congress added to § 12 (b) (3) of the 1948 Act the provision here at issue, subjecting to criminal liability not only one who "forges, alters, or in any manner changes" but also one who "knowingly destroys, [or] knowingly mutilates" a certificate. We note at the outset that the 1965 Amendment plainly does not abridge free speech on its face, and we do not understand O'Brien to argue otherwise. Amended § 12 (b) (3) on its face deals with conduct having no connection with speech. It prohibits the knowing destruction of certificates issued by the Selective Service System, and there is nothing necessarily expressive about such conduct. The Amendment does not distinguish between public and private destruction, and it does not punish only destruction engaged in for the purpose of expressing views. Compare *Stromberg v. California*, 283 U.S. 359 (1931). A law prohibiting destruction of Selective Service certificates no more abridges free speech on its face than a motor vehicle law prohibiting the destruction of drivers' licenses, or a tax law prohibiting the destruction of books and records.

O'Brien nonetheless argues that the 1965 Amendment is unconstitutional in its application to him, and is unconstitutional as enacted because what he calls the "purpose" of Congress was "to suppress freedom of speech." We consider these arguments separately.

II

O'Brien first argues that the 1965 Amendment is unconstitutional as applied to him because his act of burning his registration certificate was protected "symbolic speech" within the First Amendment. His argument is that the freedom of expression which the First Amendment guarantees includes all modes of "communication of ideas by conduct," and that his conduct is within this definition because he did it in "demonstration against the war and against the draft."

We cannot accept the view that an apparently limitless variety of conduct can be labelled "speech" whenever the person engaging in the conduct intends thereby to express an idea. However, even on the assumption that the alleged communicative element in O'Brien's conduct is sufficient to bring into play the First Amendment, it does not necessarily follow that the destruction of a registration certificate is constitutionally protected activity. This Court has held that when "speech" and "nonspeech" elements are combined in the same course of conduct, a sufficiently important governmental interest in regulating the nonspeech element can justify incidental limitations on First Amendment freedoms. To characterize the quality of the governmental interest which must appear, the Court has employed a variety of descriptive terms: compelling;[4] substantial;[5] subordinating;[6] paramount;[7] cogent;[8] strong.[9] Whatever imprecision inheres in these terms, we think it clear that a government regulation is sufficiently justified if it is within the constitutional power of the government; if it furthers an important or substantial governmental interest; if the governmental interest is unrelated to the suppression of free expression; and if the incidental restriction on alleged First Amendment freedom is no greater than is essential to the furtherance of that interest. We find that the 1965 Amendment to § 462 (b) (3) of the Universal Military Training and Service Act meets all of these requirements, and consequently that O'Brien can be constitutionally convicted for violating it.

The constitutional power of Congress to raise and support armies and to make all laws necessary and proper to that end is broad and sweeping. *Lichter v. United States,* 334 U.S. 742, 755–758 (1948); *Selective Draft Law Cases,* 245 U.S. 366 (1918); see also *Ex parte Quirin,* 317 U.S. 1, 25–26 (1942). The power of Congress to classify and conscript manpower for military service is "beyond question." *Lichter v. United States, supra,* at 756; *Selective Draft Law Cases, supra.* Pursuant to this power, Congress may establish a system of registration for individuals liable for training and service, and may require such individuals within reason to cooperate in the registration system. The issuance of certificates indicating the registration and eligibility classification of individuals is a legitimate and sub-

---

[4] *NAACP v. Button,* 371 U.S. 415, 438 (1963); see also *Sherbert v. Verner,* 374 U.S. 398, 403 (1963).

[5] *NAACP v. Button,* 371 U.S. 415, 444 (1963); *NAACP v. Alabama ex rel. Patterson,* 357 U.S. 449, 464 (1958).

[6] *Bates v. Little Rock,* 361 U.S. 516, 524 (1960).

[7] *Thomas v. Collins,* 323 U.S. 516, 530 (1945); see also *Sherbert v. Verner,* 374 U.S. 398, 406 (1963).

[8] *Bates v. Little Rock,* 361 U.S. 516, 524 (1960).

[9] *Sherbert v. Verner,* 374 U.S. 398, 408 (1963).

stantial administrative aid in the functioning of this system. And legislation to insure the continuing availability of issued certificates serves a legitimate and substantial purpose in the system's administration.

O'Brien's argument to the contrary is necessarily premised upon his unrealistic characterization of Selective Service certificates. He essentially adopts the position that such certificates are so many pieces of paper designed to notify registrants of their registration or classification, to be retained or tossed in the wastebasket according to the convenience or taste of the registrant. Once the registrant has received notification, according to this view, there is no reason for him to retain the certificates. O'Brien notes that most of the information on a registration certificate serves no notification purpose at all; the registrant hardly needs to be told his address and physical characteristics. We agree that the registration certificate contains much information of which the registrant needs no notification. This circumstance, however, leads not to the conclusion that the certificate serves no purpose but that, like the classification certificate, it serves purposes in addition to initial notification. Many of these purposes would be defeated by the certificates' destruction or mutilation. Among these are:

1. The registration certificate serves as proof that the individual described thereon has registered for the draft. The classification certificate shows the eligibility classification of a named but undescribed individual. Voluntarily displaying the two certificates is an easy and painless way for a young man to dispel a question as to whether he might be delinquent in his Selective Service obligations. Correspondingly, the availability of the certificates for such display relieves the Selective Service System of the administrative burden it would otherwise have in verifying the registration and classification of all suspected delinquents. Further, since both certificates are in the nature of "receipts" attesting that the registrant has done what the law requires, it is in the interest of the just and efficient administration of the system that they be continually available, in the event, for example, of a mix-up in the registrant's file. Additionally, in a time of national crisis, reasonable availability to each registrant of the two small cards assures a rapid and uncomplicated means for determining his fitness for immediate induction, no matter how distant in our mobile society he may be from his local board.

2. The information supplied on the certificates facilitates communication between registrants and local boards, simplifying the system and benefiting all concerned. To begin with, each certificate bears the address of the registrant's local board, an item unlikely to be committed to memory. Further, each card bears the registrant's Selective Service number, and a registrant who has his number readily available so that he can communicate it to his local board when he supplies or requests information can make simpler the board's task in locating his file. Finally, a registrant's inquiry, particularly through a local board other than his own, concerning his eligibility status is frequently answerable simply on the basis of his classification certificate; whereas, if the certificate were not reasonably available and the registrant were uncertain of his classification, the task of answering his question would be considerably complicated.

3. Both certificates carry continual reminders that the registrant must notify his local board of any change of address, and other specified changes in his status. The smooth functioning of the system requires that local boards be continually aware of the status and whereabouts of registrants, and the destruction of certificates deprives the system of a potentially useful notice device.

4. The regulatory scheme involving Selective Service certificates includes clearly valid prohibitions against the alteration, forgery or similar deceptive misuse of certificates. The destruction or mutilation of certificates obviously increases the difficulty of detecting and tracing abuses such as these. Further, a mutilated certificate might itself be used for deceptive purposes.

The many functions performed by Selective Service certificates establish beyond doubt that Congress has a legitimate and substantial interest in preventing their wanton and unrestrained destruction and assuring their continuing availability by punishing people who knowingly and wilfully destroy or mutilate them. And we are unpersuaded that the pre-existence of the nonpossession regulations in any way negates this interest.

In the absence of a question as to multiple punishment, it has never been suggested that there is anything improper in Congress providing alternative statutory avenues of prosecution to assure the effective protection of one and the same interest. Compare the majority and dissenting opinions in *Gore v. United States*, 357 U.S. 386 (1958). Here, the pre-existing avenue of prosecution was not even statutory. Regulations may be modified or revoked from time to time by administrative discretion. Certainly, the Congress may change or supplement a regulation.

Equally important, a comparison of the regulations with the 1965 Amendment indicates that they protect overlapping but not identical governmental interests, and that they reach somewhat different classes of wrongdoers. The gravamen of the offense defined by the statute is the deliberate rendering of certificates unavailable for the various purposes which they may serve. Whether registrants keep their certificates in their personal possession at all times, as required by the regulations, is of no particular concern under the 1965 Amendment, as long as they do not mutilate or destroy the certificates so as to render them unavailable. Although as we note below we are not concerned here with the nonpossession regulations, it is not inappropriate to observe that the essential elements of nonpossession are not identical with those of mutilation or destruction. Finally, the 1965 Amendment, like § 12 (b) which it amended, is concerned with abuses involving *any* issued Selective Service certificates, not only with the registrant's own certificates. The knowing destruction or mutilation of someone else's certificates would therefore violate the statute but not the nonpossession regulations.

We think it apparent that the continuing availability to each registrant of his Selective Service certificates substantially furthers the smooth and proper functioning of the system that Congress has established to raise armies. We think it also apparent that the Nation has a vital interest in having a system for raising armies that functions with maximum efficiency and is capable of easily and quickly responding to continually changing circumstances. For these reasons, the Government has a substantial interest in assuring the continuing availability of issued Selective Service certificates.

It is equally clear that the 1965 Amendment specifically protects this substantial governmental interest. We perceive no alternative means that would more precisely and narrowly assure the continuing availability of issued Selective Service certificates than a law which prohibits their wilful mutilation or destruction. Compare *Sherbert v. Verner*, 374 U.S. 398, 407–408 (1963), and the cases cited therein. The 1965 Amendment prohibits such conduct and does nothing more. In other words, both the governmental interest and the operation of the 1965 Amendment are limited to the noncommunicative aspect of O'Brien's conduct. The governmental interest and the scope of the 1965 Amendment are limited to preventing a harm to the smooth and efficient functioning of the Selective Service System. When

O'Brien deliberately rendered unavailable his registration certificate, he wilfully frustrated this governmental interest. For this noncommunicative impact of his conduct, and for nothing else, he was convicted.

The case at bar is therefore unlike one where the alleged governmental interest in regulating conduct arises in some measure because the communication allegedly integral to the conduct is itself thought to be harmful. In *Stromberg v. California*, 283 U.S. 359 (1931), for example, this Court struck down a statutory phrase which punished people who expressed their "opposition to organized government" by displaying "any flag, badge, banner, or device." Since the statute there was aimed at suppressing communication it could not be sustained as a regulation of non-communicative conduct. See also, *NLRB v. Fruit & Vegetable Packers Union*, 377 U.S. 58, 79 (concurring opinion) (1964).

In conclusion, we find that because of the Government's substantial interest in assuring the continuing availability of issued Selective Service certificates, because amended 462 (b) is an appropriately narrow means of protecting this interest and condemns only the independent noncommunicative impact of conduct within its reach, and because the noncommunicative impact of O'Brien's act of burning his registration certificate frustrated the Government's interest, a sufficient governmental interest has been shown to justify O'Brien's conviction.

III

O'Brien finally argues that the 1965 Amendment is unconstitutional as enacted because what he calls the "purpose" of Congress was "to suppress freedom of speech." We reject this argument because under settled principles the purpose of Congress, as O'Brien uses that term, is not a basis for declaring this legislation unconstitutional.

It is a familiar principle of constitutional law that this Court will not strike down an otherwise constitutional statute on the basis of an alleged illicit legislative motive. As the Court long ago stated:

> The decisions of this court from the beginning lend no support whatever to the assumption that the judiciary may restrain the exercise of lawful power on the assumption that a wrongful purpose or motive has caused the power to be exerted.
>
> *McCray v. United States*, 195 U.S. 27, 56 (1904).

This fundamental principle of constitutional adjudication was reaffirmed and the many cases were collected by Mr. Justice Brandeis for the Court in *Arizona v. California*, 283 U.S. 423, 455 (1931).

Inquiries into congressional motives or purposes are a hazardous matter. When the issue is simply the interpretation of legislation, the Court will look to statements by legislators for guidance as to the purpose of the legislature,[10] because

---

[10] The Court may make the same assumption in a very limited and well-defined class of cases where the very nature of the constitutional question requires an inquiry into legislative purpose. The principal class of cases is readily apparent—those in which statutes have been challenged as bills of attainder. This Court's decisions have defined a bill of attainder as a legislative Act which inflicts punishment on named individuals or members of an easily ascertainable group without a judicial trial. In determining whether a particular statute is a bill of attainder, the analysis necessarily requires an inquiry into whether the three definitional elements—specificity in identification,

the benefit to sound decision-making in this circumstance is thought sufficient to risk the possibility of misreading Congress' purpose. It is entirely a different matter when we are asked to void a statute that is, under well-settled criteria, constitutional on its face, on the basis of what fewer than a handful of Congressmen said about it. What motivates one legislator to make a speech about a statute is not necessarily what motivates scores of others to enact it, and the stakes are sufficiently high for us to eschew guesswork. We decline to void essentially on the ground that it is unwise legislation which Congress had the undoubted power to enact and which could be reenacted in its exact form if the same or another legislator made a "wiser" speech about it.

O'Brien's position, and to some extent that of the court below, rests upon a misunderstanding of *Grosjean v. American Press Co.,* 297 U.S. 233 (1936), and *Gomillion v. Lightfoot,* 364 U.S. 339 (1960). These cases stand not for the proposition that legislative motive is a proper basis for declaring a statute unconstitutional, but that the inevitable effect of a statute on its face may render it unconstitutional. Thus, in *Grosjean* the Court, having concluded that the right of publications to be free from certain kinds of taxes was a freedom of the press protected by the First Amendment, struck down a statute which on its face did nothing other than impose just such a tax. Similarly, in *Gomillion,* the Court sustained a complaint which, if true, established that the "inevitable effect," 364 U.S., at 341, of the redrawing of municipal boundaries was to deprive the petitioners of their right to vote for no reason other than that they were Negro. In these cases, the purpose of the legislation was irrelevant, because the inevitable effect—"necessary scope and operation," *McCray v. United States,* 195 U.S. 27, 59 (1904)—abridged constitutional rights. The statute attacked in the instant case has no such inevitable unconstitutional effect, since the destruction of Selective Service certificates is in no respect inevitably or necessarily expressive. Accordingly, the statute itself is constitutional.

We think it not amiss, in passing, to comment upon O'Brien's legislative purpose argument. There was little floor debate on this legislation in either House. Only Senator Thurmond commented on its substantive features in the Senate. 111 CONG. REC. 19746, 20433. After his brief statement, and without any additional substantive comments, the bill, H. R. 10306, passed the Senate. 111 CONG. REC. 20434. In the House debate only two Congressmen addressed themselves to the Amendment—Congressmen Rivers and Bray. 111 CONG. REC. 19871, 19872. The bill was passed after their statements without any further debate by a vote of 393 to 1. It is principally on the basis of the statements by these three Congressmen that O'Brien makes his congressional "purpose" argument. We note that if we were to examine legislative purpose in the instant case, we would be obliged to consider not only these statements but also the more authoritative reports of the Senate and House Armed Services Committees. The portions of those reports explaining the purpose of the Amendment are reproduced in the Appendix in their

---

punishment and lack of a judicial trial—are contained in the statute. The inquiry into whether the challenged statute contains the necessary element of punishment has on occasion led the Court to examine the legislative motive in enacting the statute. See, e.g., *United States v. Lovett,* 328 U.S. 303 (1946). Two other decisions not involving a bill-of-attainder analysis contain an inquiry into legislative purpose or motive of the type that O'Brien suggests we engage in in this case. *Kennedy v. Mendoza-Martinez,* 372 U.S. 144, 169–184 (1963); *Trop v. Dulles,* 356 U.S. 86, 95–97 (1958). The inquiry into legislative purpose or motive in *Kennedy* and *Trop,* however, was for the same limited purpose as in the bill-of-attainder decisions—i.e., to determine whether the statutes under review were punitive in nature. We face no such inquiry in this case. The 1965 Amendment to 462 (b) was clearly penal in nature, designed to impose criminal punishment on designated acts.

entirety.* While both reports make clear a concern with the "defiant" destruction of so-called "draft cards" and with "open" encouragement to others to destroy their cards, both reports also indicate that this concern stemmed from an apprehension that unrestrained destruction of cards would disrupt the smooth functioning of the Selective Service System.

IV

Since the 1965 Amendment to § 12 (b) (3) of the Universal Military Training and Service Act is constitutional as enacted and as applied, the Court of Appeals should have affirmed the judgment of conviction entered by the District Court. Accordingly, we vacate the judgment of the Court of Appeals, and reinstate the judgment and sentence of the District Court. This disposition makes unnecessary consideration of O'Brien's claim that the Court of Appeals erred in affirming his conviction on the basis of the nonpossession regulation.

It is so ordered.

Mr. *JUSTICE MARSHALL took no part in the consideration or decision of these cases.*

Mr. *JUSTICE HARLAN, concurring.*

The crux of the Court's opinion, which I join, is of course its general statement, *ante,* p. 9, that:

> a government regulation is sufficiently justified if it is within the constitutional power of the government; if it furthers an important or substantial governmental interest; if the governmental interest is unrelated to the suppression of free expression; and if the incidental restriction on alleged First Amendment freedom is no greater than is essential to the furtherance of that interest.

I wish to make explicit my understanding that this passage does not foreclose consideration of First Amendment claims in those rare instances when an "incidental" restriction upon expression, imposed by a regulation which furthers an "important or substantial" governmental interest and satisfies the Court's other criteria, in practice has the effect of entirely preventing a "speaker" from reaching a significant audience with whom he could not otherwise lawfully communicate. This is not such a case, since O'Brien manifestly could have conveyed his message in many ways other than by burning his draft card.

Mr. *JUSTICE DOUGLAS, dissenting.*

The Court states that the constitutional power of Congress to raise and support armies is "broad and sweeping" and that Congress' power "to classify and conscript manpower for military service is 'beyond question.'" This is undoubtedly true in times when, by declaration of Congress, the Nation is in a state of war. The underlying and basic problem in this case, however, is whether conscription is permissible in the absence of a declaration of war.[1] That question has not been

---

*Author's note: Since the reports of the Senate and House Armed Services Committees have been discussed on pages forty-three and forty-six, the Appendix of the Court has been omitted.

[1] Neither of the decisions cited by the majority for the proposition that Congress' power to conscript men into the armed services is " 'beyond question' " concerns peacetime conscription. As I have shown in my dissenting opinion in *Holmes v. United States, post,* p. 936, the *Selective Draft Law Cases,* 245 U.S. 366, decided in 1918, upheld the constitutionality of a conscription act passed by Congress more than a month after war had been declared on the German Empire and which

briefed nor was it presented in oral argument; but it is, I submit, a question upon which the litigants and the country are entitled to a ruling. I have discussed in *Holmes v. United States, post,* p. 936, the nature of the legal issue and it will be seen from my dissenting opinion in that case that this Court has never ruled on the question. It is time that we made a ruling. This case should be put down for reargument and heard with *Holmes v. United States* and with *Hart v. United States, post,* p. 956, in which the Court today denies certiorari.[2]

The rule that this Court will not consider issues not raised by the parties is not inflexible and yields in "exceptional cases" (*Duignan v. United States,* 274 U.S. 195, 200) to the need correctly to decide the case before the court. E. g. *Erie R. Co. v. Tompkins,* 304 U.S. 64; *Terminiello v. Chicago,* 337 U.S. 1.

In such a case it is not unusual to ask for reargument (*Sherman v. United States,* 356 U.S. 369, 379, n. 2, Frankfurter, J., concurring) even on a constitutional question not raised by the parties. In *Abel v. United States,* 362 U.S. 217, the petitioner had conceded that an administrative deportation arrest warrant would be valid for its limited purpose even though not supported by a sworn affidavit stating probable cause; but the Court ordered reargument on the question whether the warrant had been validly issued in petitioner's case. 362 U.S., at 219, n. 1; U.S. Sup. Ct. Journal, October Term, 1958, p. 193. In *Lustig v. United States,* 338 U.S. 74, the petitioner argued that an exclusionary rule should apply to the fruit of an unreasonable search by state officials solely because they acted in concert with federal officers (see *Weeks v. United States,* 232 U.S. 383; *Byars v. United States,* 273 U.S. 28). The Court ordered reargument on the question raised in a then pending case, *Wolf v. Colorado,* 338 U.S. 25: applicability of the Fourth Amendment to the States. Journal, October Term, 1947, p. 298. In *Donaldson v. Read Magazine,* 333 U.S. 178, the only issue presented, according to both parties, was whether the record contained sufficient evidence of fraud to uphold an order of the Postmaster General. Reargument was ordered on the constitutional issue of abridgment of First Amendment freedoms. 333 U.S., at 181–182; Journal, October Term, 1947, p. 70. Finally, in *Musser v. Utah,* 333 U.S. 95, 96, reargument was ordered on the question of unconstitutional vagueness of a criminal statute, an issue not raised by the parties but suggested at oral argument by Justice Jackson. Journal, October Term, 1947, p. 87.

These precedents demonstrate the appropriateness of restoring the instant case to the calendar for reargument on the question of the constitutionality of a peacetime draft and having it heard with *Holmes v. United States* and *Hart v. United States.*

. . . .

IV. Aftermath of Congress's Pyrrhic Victory

The seven-to-one decision of the Supreme Court in *United States v. O'Brien* signaled that Congress had won a victory, but was it a meaningful victory or a hollow one? If one regards passage of the draft-card-burning statute at face value,

---

was then being enforced in time of war. *Lichter v. United States,* 334 U.S. 742, concerned the constitutionality of the Renegotiation Act, another wartime measure, enacted by Congress over the period of 1942–1945 (*id.,* at 745, n. 1) and applied in that case to excessive war profits made in 1942–1943 (*id.,* at 753). War had been declared, of course, in 1941 (55 Stat. 795). The Court referred to Congress' power to raise armies in discussing the "background" (334 U.S. at 753) of the Renegotiation Act, which it upheld as a valid exercise of the War Power.

[2] Today the Court also denies stays in *Shiffman v. Selective Service Board No. 3,* and *Zigmond v. Selective Service Board No. 16,* where punitive delinquency regulations are invoked against registrants, decisions that present a related question.

as an attempt by Congress to grapple with a serious national problem rather than as an attempt to punish individual dissenters for holding and expressing certain opinions, the answer is clearly that the victory was pyrrhic in nature. The statute did not prove to be a bulwark against a rising tide of civil disobedience; instead, it turned out to be a matchstick, fragile and unable to fill the breach. Similarly, the Court's decision seemed somehow vaguely disturbing. While Chief Justice Warren's words were facile, they did not chart with any clarity the relationship between freedom of expression and communicative acts. Let us look first at the more general problem of political efforts to limit and channel dissent from the Vietnam policies of Presidents Johnson and Nixon and then at the part played by the Supreme Court in the war crisis.

THE ANTIWAR MOVEMENT: CIVIL DISOBEDIENCE AND CREATIVE POLITICS

Ultimately, the draft-card-burning amendment raises fundamental questions about the nature and function of law. Is the primary purpose of law punitive? Is the primary purpose to establish norms of accepted or expected behavior? These purposes are not invariably complementary; in particular instances, they can actually conflict.

Civil obedience occurs when the vast majority of citizens have internalized a norm of behavior. Law enforcement can be effective as a social agency only when it deals with a relatively small number of individuals who do not accept and practice the general norm but who can be convinced because of fear of punishment or, if not convinced, can be isolated physically from society. Civil disobedience, unlike common lawlessness, stands these principles on their head!

The goal of civil disobedience is to destroy widespread acceptance of a public norm by encouraging more and more people to view the norm as unacceptable. Since the goal is not to escape law enforcement efforts but to flout them publicly, individuals who practice civil disobedience cannot be convinced to accept the norm because of fear of punishment. Physical isolation of the disobedient can be effective as a deterrent only if the dissenters are small in number and unsuccessful in their major purpose. But what if there are many dissenters and for every one arrested a new one springs up to take his or her place? What if arrest, prosecution, and jailing create martyrs and thereby add to the flames of discontent and the number of citizens willing to break the law? Civil disobedience ordinarily is far more dangerous to social stability than common lawlessness, because political dissenters who follow illegal tactics are following what they perceive as moral imperatives that supersede political loyalties. In the face of widespread illegal dissent based on fundamental moral principles, criminal laws appear to be relatively ineffective at best and sources of more and more extreme behavior at worst.

As will be recalled, President Johnson and the Selective Service System were not eager for a draft-card-burning law. Congress thrust the law on a reluctant Chief Executive. Johnson's war policy included minimizing the war by paying for it via federal deficits rather than increased taxes and by playing down American involvement to the greatest extent possible in a society with open communications media. It is probable that the decision to minimize the scope of the Vietnam conflict in the eyes of the American people was not a conscious policy choice at first, but one which gradually emerged from successive events. This policy, whether conscious or not, inevitably narrowed the options available to the government. In particular, it became more and more difficult for the government to communicate that America itself was in serious danger and that all Americans should rally as they had in the Second World War. Furthermore, the policy of minimizing itself sowed the seeds of discontent, because it suggested that the United States was engaged in something underhanded.

As open discontent mounted in 1966 and 1967, the administration was faced with a set of extremely unpleasant choices: the most unpleasant, from a personal standpoint, was an admission that the government's top leaders had been wrong in prosecuting the war; the second choice was to stop minimizing the war and call for all-out loyalty and unity for a maximum effort; the third was to continue in the existing approach, minimizing internal unrest by ignoring it as much as possible, all the while hoping for the enemy to collapse. Whether or not the administration believed in the wisdom of its course of action or was unwilling to face the consequences of admitting that a major policy error had been made, the first course was rejected. The second also seemed extremely risky, given the government's existing policy toward the war, the level of discontent in the country, the possibility that a mailed fist approach to dissent would polarize the country and destroy whatever semblance of unity existed. Furthermore, the second alternative might easily go amok and lead to a witch-hunt which would make the worst excesses of the McCarthy period of the 1950s seem like child's play. Under the circumstances, the third approach appeared to be the least inflexible and the least dangerous.

Thus, the government chose not to prosecute draft card burners forcefully. The amendment was to be minimized for fear that the more one punished dissenters and thereby gave them access to communications media, the more one would encourage dissent. Enforcement of the law might lead to more rather than less lawlessness. In some quarters, the government's failure to prosecute vigorously was taken as a sign of gutlessness; in others, where retribution against dissenters was considered less significant than the possible consequences for the system as a whole, it was viewed as a sign of intelligence.

Paradoxically, by the time of the *O'Brien* decision, draft card burning had almost ceased. Dissenters were turning to other ways of expressing their views on the war. Two reasons for this shift can be isolated. First, the purpose of symbolic dissent was to encourage others to join the antiwar effort, to destroy the norm of support for the government's war policy, and it became clear that many citizens who might otherwise be sympathetic were being repelled by an act that seemed arbitrary, irrational, and excessive. Thus, many dissenters turned to less provocative tactics such as mass demonstrations, peaceful vigils, solemn assemblies, mass collections of draft cards at church services. These efforts did swell the ranks of war dissenters by encouraging citizens who viewed civil disobedience as wrong to oppose the war, and they led ultimately to the decision of President Johnson not to run for reelection.

Secondly, draft card burning died down after a short time because it was no longer new, original, and newsworthy. When it became commonplace, it lost its ability to attract attention from the media and the public. Thus, while certain members of the peace movement concluded that draft card burning was a destructive tactic politically, others concluded that it was not dramatic enough. More and more extreme acts were needed to communicate to each citizen the need for taking a moral stance opposed to the war. Thus, for example, the notorious "Catonsville Nine," led by Fathers Daniel and Philip Berrigan, did get tremendous attention from the media both when they poured blood on draft records in Catonsville, Maryland, and when they were tried for committing this unlawful act.

Which was the more creative approach to the political question of how to destroy widespread public acceptance of the government's policy: the use of tactics which would not be startling but would not be viewed as breaking the accepted rules of American politics, or the use of clear-cut, extremist methods which deliberately went beyond these bounds? Would either of these approaches have succeeded by itself? And, even more fundamentally, was the antiwar effort a success? Clearly, any assessment of the antiwar movement depends to a great extent on the perspective of the analyst.

The movement to end the war did have certain partial successes but it was, in the final analysis, a failure. Dissenters failed to convince the country, the President, or Congress that the war should be ended. In this author's view, the politics of dissent as followed by those who worked within the limits of generally accepted rules of behavior were more responsible for the partial successes which were achieved than the politics of extremism. Lyndon Johnson was not driven from office by the extremist dissenters but by recognition on his part that millions of citizens would vote against him in 1968 because of his role in the war. The supporters of Senator Eugene McCarthy, although they failed in their primary objective, did give a clear indication of the strength of antiwar feeling in the American population and, thereby, they succeeded in limiting President Nixon's options. Any student of Nixon's record prior to the 1968 election would conclude that Nixon's basic instincts would not have been to wind down the war, yet that is what he did. Public reaction to Nixon's brief invasion of Cambodia in June 1970 told him what he seemed to have forgotten momentarily: that his options were narrowly circumscribed unless he was willing to face tearing the United States apart internally. Congressional opposition to enlarging the war was partially a response to awareness by many representatives and senators of the breadth of public dissatisfaction and partially a cause of such dissatisfaction, since opposition by respected lawmakers, unlike opposition by extremists, legitimized opposition to the war by law-abiding citizens.

And what, ultimately, of the draft-card-burning amendment? It failed to achieve the purpose of its authors, both narrowly in terms of punishment and broadly in terms of encouraging loyalty to particular policies. The law attacked a symptom, not a disease. The debate in Congress was shoddy, to say the least: instead of a great debate on the nature and scope of legitimate dissent and the definition of loyalty to the United States, a debate which would have helped to educate and inform the country, Congress responded hastily and thoughtlessly to clichés. Because of the way in which the law was passed, and the level of "debate," students, adults, war critics, and war supporters who expected serious discussion could not help but feel that Congress was adding to public distrust of American institutions and, therefore, of the wisdom of the policies which emerged from those institutions. It was not one of Congress's finest hours.

THE SUPREME COURT AND THE VIETNAM WAR

The Supreme Court did not accept the *O'Brien* case eagerly, but only because of the errant decision of the First Circuit Court of Appeals. The seven-to-one decision indicated that the nation's highest bench would look critically on attempts to reach the public by communicative acts rather than pure speech. Yet the Court as an institution proved unable or unwilling to consider far broader and more fundamental legal questions about the government's war policy than the relatively narrow question of whether draft card burning was protected by the First Amendment. Let us look first at the Court's handling of the issue of symbolic speech.

If the Supreme Court had never held in the 1930s and early 1940s that carrying a red flag in a parade or picket signs in a labor dispute were constitutionally protected means of expression, it would have been able to avoid the dilemma of being forced to articulate what communicative acts are akin to verbal expression and what are not. The Court could have ruled originally that freedom of speech means freedom of verbal speech, no more and no less. Instead, the 1930s Court chose a more liberal path. As Justice Frankfurter said, "Peaceful picketing is the workingman's means of communication."[1] Thus, some communicative acts were to be protected, but not others. But how could the line be drawn in an intellectually responsible and persuasive fashion?

Is a nonviolent communicative act performed in a nonviolent setting for the benefit of news media any different than verbal expression in the same setting? Could O'Brien have been punished if he had held his draft card aloft and denounced it and the government which issued it, rather than destroying it? The only significant difference between these two forms of expression is that one is more newsworthy and more likely to arouse the ire of the majority of citizens than the other. Why is a man exercising his constitutional right of free expression when he carries a Vietcong flag in a nonviolent demonstration, or holds an American flag aloft and denounces it and his country, but not when he defaces that flag to indicate his contempt? Clearly, the communicative act of that individual, misguided or not, is the "common man's means of communication" in an era of mass communication to the same extent that picketing is the "workingman's means of communication."

The opinion of the Court in *United States v. O'Brien* states: "We cannot accept the view that an apparently limitless variety of conduct can be labelled 'speech' whenever the person engaging in the conduct intends thereby to express an idea."[2] This, certainly, is overkill: the statement does not distinguish legitimate communicative acts from illegitimate ones. Violent communicative acts, or inherently criminal ones, such as assassination, sabotage, invasion, and destruction of public buildings are not akin to protected speech and can be differentiated from flag waving, picketing, flag denunciation, nonviolent flag destruction, or draft card mutilation.

Chief Justice Warren attempts to refine the vague statement quoted above later in the same paragraph, when he adds:

> . . . [A] government regulation [of a communicative act] is sufficiently justified if it is within the constitutional power of the government; if it furthers an important or substantial governmental interest; if the governmental interest is unrelated to the suppression of free expression; and if the incidental restriction on First Amendment freedom is no greater than is essential to the furtherance of that interest.[3]

But this definition is not very satisfying, since the criteria suggested are by no means clear. Undoubtedly, many people would say that draft card burning as a form of expression does not easily fall either within or outside the definition adopted by the Court. One cannot help but be troubled further by the fact that derogatory, contemptuous words spoken while a dissenter holds a draft card or flag aloft are to be judged by an entirely different definition, a definition which gives far greater weight to freedom of expression.

Thus, the Court's distinction of pure speech and communicative conduct in *United States v. O'Brien* is not strong analytically. The criteria chosen for separat-

---

[1] *Milk Wagon Drivers Union v. Meadowmoor Dairies*, 312 U.S. 275, 293 (1941).

[2] 391 U.S. 367, 376 (1967).

[3] *Ibid.*, at 377. (Brackets added.)

ing protected and nonprotected communicative acts seem far from compelling. Hopefully a more precise and intellectually respectable method for determining what communicative acts deserve First Amendment protection and what do not will emerge in future cases.[4]

While the Court was willing to investigate the twilight zone between protected and nonprotected symbolic speech in the *O'Brien* case, and, for example, to broaden Congress's definition of what constituted a conscientious objector to military service, it should be noted that the Court avoided war-related issues of far greater significance. As pointed out by Justice Douglas in his dissent in *O'Brien*, for example, "The underlying and basic problem in this case, however, is whether conscription is permissible in the absence of a declaration of war. . . . [I]t is, I submit, a question upon which the litigants and the country are entitled to a ruling."[5] Only Justice Douglas believed it was appropriate for the Court to come to grips with this intense political question.

Similarly, the Supreme Court avoided ruling one way or another on the vital question of the constitutionality of United States participation in the Vietnam conflict without a declaration of war. Strong arguments can be made on both sides of this question, but it is clear that the justices did not believe the Supreme Court was the appropriate forum for resolving a constitutional conflict of this significance while the war was in progress. On these fundamental questions the Court chose, wisely or not, to follow a policy of silence rather than one of outright support or opposition to the elected branches of government. No analyst can assess that position without judging the wisdom of the view that responsibility for decisions of war and peace belongs with the political rather than legal institutions of our society, without weighing the limits of effective judicial power, and without coming to terms with the historic and yet recurring question: what should be the proper role of the judiciary in the American system of government?

[4] For more detailed criticism of the decision of the Court in *United States v. O'Brien*, see Alfange, "Free Speech and Symbolic Conduct: the Draft-Card Burning Case," 1968 *Sup. Ct. Rev.* 1; Velvel, "Freedom of Speech and the Draft Card Burning Cases," 16 *Kan. L. Rev.* 149 (1968).

[5] 391 U.S. 367, 389 (1967).

CONFESSIONS, SELF=INCRIMINATION, AND THE RIGHT TO COUNSEL

What Are the Limits on Police Interrogation of Suspects?

ISSUES RAISED   Protection of Society Against Criminals   /   What Is a Voluntary Confession?   /   Protection Against Self-incrimination   /   The Right to Counsel   /   Due Process of Law

I.   The Revolution in Criminal Procedure

In the decade from 1960 to 1969, the Supreme Court, under the leadership of Chief Justice Earl Warren, rewrote the constitutional protections afforded individuals accused of crimes. Most of the important decisions of the Court in the field of criminal procedure defined and expanded the rights of those who ran afoul of the law and limited the powers of the police and prosecutorial authorities.

For example, an illustrative list of practices which were commonplace prior to the innovative decisions of the Warren Court would include at least the following:

States could deny criminal defendants a trial by jury; the federal government could not.

States could require defendants to incriminate themselves; the federal government could not.

States could try a defendant twice for the same crime; the federal government could not put a man in jeopardy twice.

States were free to refuse to provide counsel for indigent defendants; the federal government had no such option.

State and local police could use evidence of guilt obtained by unlawful and unconstitutional searches to help secure convictions; the federal government could not use tainted evidence in court.

State and local police could refuse to let a suspect see his lawyer and could use confessions secured after such a refusal; federal officials could use confessions obtained during a period of unlawful detention as long as the confessions were given voluntarily.

State and local police were under no obligation to inform arrested suspects of their constitutional rights; federal officers did provide such information.

PROCEDURAL RIGHTS IN THE POLITICAL PROCESS

Before the Supreme Court chose to intervene in the field of criminal procedure, the rights of individuals accused of crimes were not of widespread public interest.

Most Americans assumed, without question, that the procedural guarantees of the Bill of Rights would be available to them if they were ever accused of breaking a law; only experts in the field of law realized that this convenient assumption was simply incorrect. Lawyers and others with specialized knowledge of law knew that the procedural rights spelled out in amendments four through eight of the Constitution would protect citizens from the federal government but not the state governments. States were entitled to establish their own procedures, subject to the Fourteenth Amendment requirement that no state deprive any citizen of life, liberty, or property without due process of law.

Given the ignorance and disinterest of the general public, political candidates seeking vote-getting issues ignored the complex policy questions which existed in the criminal justice process. They recognized, correctly, that there was not much mileage to be gained from taking up these particular questions of individual rights and public order. Thus, the silence of officeholders and candidates reinforced the general public's lack of concern.

This is not to say, of course, that the interest of the general public was never aroused. It is true, however, that the public tended to focus on the gaudy aspects of sensational crimes, not on the policy and legal issues raised by questions of procedural rights.

Although the general public was ordinarily indifferent, criminal procedure as a public policy issue—or, to put it more accurately, a set of closely related policy issues—was of enduring interest to legislators, lawyers, judges, policemen, prosecutors, and, naturally, criminal defendants themselves. Even in the period prior to the intervention of the Warren Court, the rights of those accused of crimes were not simply legal questions, and it would be a mistake to assume that developments in the field of criminal procedure were made in an apolitical process.

Instead, the rights of the accused were political issues—and often intense political issues—in the sense that legislators had to pass laws, individuals and interest groups attempted to influence those laws, administrators had to implement laws, judges had to make legal decisions, which in turn led to demands for new laws and further questions of administration and implementation. In other words, the policy questions involved were handled in a political process, in a highly political manner, but the range of participants was limited to those closely involved with lawmaking and law enforcement.

Because the experts who participated in refining the rights accorded the accused were primarily legislators, judges, and prosecutors—and particularly legislators, judges, and prosecutors at the state level, since the states have the primary responsibility for maintaining law and order in the American federal system— there were few meaningful external pressures for adding to the rights of the accused, for eliminating gross differences in the treatment of suspects in different jurisdictions, for doing away with unequal justice for the rich and for the poor, or even for making the existing rights of those suspected of crimes meaningful rather than merely hypothetical rights.

The fact that laws regulating the treatment of criminal suspects from arrest to final disposition of a case were passed at both the state and federal levels in an atmosphere relatively free from extragovernmental political pressures can be explained simply: (1) the most prestigious and powerful interest groups were disinterested in this area of public policy; they had other legislative fish to fry; (2) for obvious reasons, there were no organizations of criminal defendants, both convicted and acquitted, to press for procedural rights.

The failure of our representative institutions to reform practices which weakened the quality of American democracy—practices which, among others, seemed to violate the philosophy of equal justice for rich and for poor, of protection of one's home from illegal search and seizure, of protection against self-incrimination, of right to counsel, of fair trial—has been well put by former Senator Kenneth Keating, a progressive Republican from New York who has served on the bench of the highest court of that state and was appointed Ambassador to India in 1969:

> I think it is probably fair to say that indigent persons generally, but especially those who are alleged to be not among the law-abiding, are at the tender mercies of all the rest of us, especially those who sit in the Halls of Congress. We are all aware of the weighty influence wielded, for example, by the organized *medical* profession and the organized *bar* upon legislation in Congress. It has become commonplace to speak of the "A.M.A. Lobby" or, in the education field, the "N.E.A. Lobby." But there is no lobby of the A.C.D.A., The American Criminal Defendants' Association. . . .
>
> Fortunately, there *are* groups such as the American Civil Liberties Union and the NAACP which take a strong interest in the administration of the criminal law as it affects the disadvantaged defendant. But their voice in the legislative process is diluted by the fact that the clientele group for which they purport to speak normally exercises little political power, and, in fact, those in the group who have been convicted of felony have been by law politically sterilized. . . .[1]

Like state legislators, most state court judges were not willing to challenge the existing status quo. One at least plausible explanation for their reluctance to innovate is that state court judges frequently tend to be quite sensitive to local politics and to the values which predominate among local political leaders. The recruitment pattern for state judges is strikingly similar throughout the country: most judges have been active in local or state politics before assuming a judicial post, have served in city councils or in state legislatures, or have gained recognition as district attorneys or employees of the state attorney general. Many men serve in several of these capacities prior to appointment to the bench; even in those states where some judgeships are filled by election rather than appointment, the career backgrounds of members of the judiciary usually fit this pattern.

Thus, at the state level in particular, the law and politics of criminal justice evolved quite slowly during the half-century prior to the massive intervention of the Warren Court. In addition, due to decisions of the federal courts and in part to acts of Congress, men accused of federal crimes became entitled to more extensive and meaningful procedural protections than suspects in most states. If an individual was arrested and tried for committing an act which was both a federal and state crime, such as kidnapping, the rights he received throughout the accusatory proceeding against him depended on the seemingly irrelevant fact of whether state or federal officers had made the arrest. Furthermore, states themselves varied remarkably in the rights they accorded men accused of identical crimes; one state might provide an indigent accused with counsel at trial while its neighbor denied this fundamental procedural protection.

This idiosyncratic and inherently unstable situation satisfied the goals and values of most of the men who participated in policy formation in the area of criminal procedure, since it essentially left the definition of procedural rights to state officials. The absence of effective pressures to face head-on the lack of uniformity in procedural rights merely postponed, for a time, what was probably an inevitable confrontation. Throughout the decades in question, the nation was going

---

[1] Speech at the Annual Banquet of the Harvard Legal Aid Bureau, February 18, 1965, at 18–20; see also Archibald Cox, *The Warren Court*, Harvard University Press, Boston, 1968, p. 87.

through a tortured reexamination of the social and economic inequalities which were part of the American way of life in the nineteenth and early twentieth centuries. Labor and minority groups found their voice in the words of Franklin Roosevelt, and particularly in his frequently repeated statements that the New Deal would establish social and economic justice in the United States. Thus, at the federal level at least, reform was in the air.

THE LEGAL DEBATE: WHAT DOES "DUE PROCESS" MEAN?

One further point needs to be made: even before the advent of the Warren Court, the opportunity for judicially inspired reform of federal and state criminal procedures existed. Since the Supreme Court had power to interpret the Constitution and to accept cases in which defendants claimed that particular procedures had violated their rights under the federal Constitution, no new institutions of government or constitutional amendments were needed.

Furthermore, the opportunity for Court-imposed reform was at least as great in the area of state criminal procedure as in any other policy area, due to the extreme ambiguity of the Fourteenth Amendment requirement that "No State shall make or enforce any law which shall ... deprive any person of life, liberty, or property, without due process of law. . . ."

But what, in heaven's name, is due process of law? Is it simply that states must stick within the procedures which they have established, even if those procedures are semibarbaric? Is it that states must apply the same procedures that the federal government must apply as a result of the more specific requirements of the Bill of Rights? Or, that states must apply some, but not all, of the protections provided individuals accused of federal crimes?

Clearly, the phrase "due process of law" is not self-explanatory. It cannot be applied literally, since it is literally meaningless on its face. There is no such thing as a strict or a liberal interpretation of the phrase, since all interpretations of it are, per se, liberal, regardless of their substance.

The phrase could be applied historically, assuming that it might conceivably be possible to discover exactly what the authors of the Fourteenth Amendment meant when they used the phrase. This would, of course, require the courts to apply mid-nineteenth-century standards to twentieth-century situations, many of which could not have been conceived of in 1868, when the amendment was ratified. Such an approach would make of the Constitution a fixed, immutable contract, not a living document, intended, as Chief Justice John Marshall stated, to endure for the ages.

These same questions were faced by the Court in the late 1930s and 1940s. In 1937, for example, the Court had to decide whether the Fourteenth Amendment prevented a state from trying a man twice for murder. The defense argued that since the Fifth Amendment specifically protected suspects from double jeopardy at the hands of the federal government, the Fourteenth's due process clause must be construed to provide equivalent protection.

In a landmark decision, the Court rejected this contention. On the more general question of what constitutes due process, Justice Cardozo ruled for the majority:

> There emerges the perception of a rationalizing principle which gives to discrete instances a proper order and coherence. The right to trial by jury and the immunity from prosecution except as the result of an indictment may have value and importance. Even so, they are not of the very essence of a scheme of ordered liberty. To abolish

them is not to violate a "principle of justice so rooted in the traditions and conscience of our people as to be ranked as fundamental. . . ."

We reach a different plane of social and moral values when we pass to the privileges and immunities that have been taken over from the earlier articles of the federal Bill of Rights [First Amendment] and brought within the Fourteenth Amendment by a process of absorption. These in their origin were effective against the federal government alone. If the Fourteenth Amendment has absorbed them, the process of absorption has had its source in the belief that neither liberty nor justice would exist if they were sacrificed.[2]

Thus, some federal procedural rights were to be accorded state criminal suspects because of the due process requirement and some were not. The nine justices of the Supreme Court would decide which federal rights were necessary to "the very essence of a scheme of ordered liberty" and which were not. If it were not for the fact that—according to the textbooks—the Supreme Court makes "legal decisions," a cynic might conclude that such a definition of due process requires the justices to express policy preferences.

Subsequently, the Court rejected the notion that due process of law protected those accused of state crimes from self-incrimination. The reason: the federal protection against self-incrimination was "not of the very essence of a scheme of ordered liberty." Justice Black, in dissent, expressed a different philosophy of due process:

My study of the historical events that culminated in the Fourteenth Amendment, and the expressions of those who sponsored and favored, as well as those who opposed its submission and passage, persuades me that one of the chief objects that the provisions of the Amendment's first section, separately, and as a whole, were intended to accomplish, was to make the Bill of Rights applicable to the states. . . .

. . . [T]he "natural law" formula . . . should be abandoned as an incongruous excrescence on our Constitution. I believe that formula to be itself a violation of our Constitution, in that it subtly conveys to courts, at the expense of legislatures, ultimate power over public policies in fields where no specific provision of the Constitution limits legislative power. . . .

. . . I fear to see the consequences of the Court's practice of substituting its own concepts of decency and fundamental justice for the language of the Bill of Rights as its point of departure in interpreting and enforcing that Bill of Rights.[3]

Thus, by the time the Warren Court came into being, the outlines of the jurisprudential conflict over the meaning of Fourteenth Amendment due process were already well established. Both philosophies—the relativistic Cardozo position, which was persuasive to Justices Felix Frankfurter and John Marshall Harlan, and the absolutist interpretation of Justice Black—could be used to justify judicial decisions changing the status quo; it should be stressed that a third philosophical position—that the federal courts have no right whatsoever to overrule a state's own definition of due process—received no support even from the most conservative and restrained members of the Supreme Court. By the logic of the Cardozo principle, the Court had elbow room to incorporate selectively—if it wished—Bill of Rights protections into the Fourteenth Amendment, merely by changing its concept of which rights were "so rooted in the traditions and conscience of our people as to be ranked as

[2] *Palko v. Connecticut*, 302 U.S. 319, at 325–26 (1937). (Brackets added.)

[3] *Adamson v. California*, 332 U.S. 46, at 71–72, 75, 89 (1947).

fundamental. . . ." By the logic of the Black position, incorporation could be achieved in one fell swoop.

As it turned out, Justice Black lost the jurisprudential battle but won the war: the Court has followed the theory of selective incorporation, but in the decade of the 1960s it expanded its concept of what constitutes fundamental principles of justice to include nearly all the protections provided in the Bill of Rights. The important point to be made here, however, is not what the Court has done but that the Warren Court inherited (1) institutional power to receive controversies over procedural rights, (2) a method of decision making via reinterpretation of the Constitution, (3) an ambiguous constitutional provision, (4) two philosophies of due process, either of which could be used to justify judicial attempts to enlarge the rights of the criminally accused. In effect, all that was needed was judicial commitment to step into the vacuum left by popular indifference and the failure of representative institutions to act.

EMERGENCE OF AN ACTIVIST MAJORITY

Under Chief Justice Warren, a majority willing to exploit the power of the Court in order to require the states to apply more rigorous and uniform federal standards in the handling of the criminally accused and to require both the states and the federal government to move toward the elimination of unequal justice for the poor and the ignorant gradually coalesced.

How can this phenomenon be explained? Certainly, changes in personnel played a part: Justices Earl Warren and William Brennan replaced two more cautious members of the Court in 1953 and 1956; the leading advocate of judicial restraint throughout the 1950s, Felix Frankfurter, left the Court in 1962 and was succeeded by Justice Arthur Goldberg, who served for three years; Goldberg, in turn, was replaced by another activist liberal, Justice Abe Fortas; finally, Thurgood Marshall, who had spent more than twenty-five years as counsel for the NAACP, was appointed to replace a somewhat more conservative justice in 1967.

But personnel changes explain only so much; the fact that the membership of the Court changed does not explain *why* the new members, plus Justices Black and Douglas, chose to move in the direction of massive reform. Some social scientists have attempted to explain judicial behavior on the basis of the social origins and career experiences of judges, but the symmetry of this simple explanation has frequently been distorted by judges who refuse to conform. Admittedly, the judicial opinions of Justices Goldberg, Fortas, and Marshall seem to be the logical outcomes of their earlier experiences. However, the relationship is far murkier for the remaining members of the activist majority on the Warren Court:

1. Justice Black, although an ardent New Dealer as a Senator, had been born, raised, and educated in Alabama, had practiced law in Birmingham, had spent three years as a police judge and prosecuting attorney, and had belonged to the Ku Klux Klan from 1923 to 1925. Like Justice Frankfurter and Justice Douglas, Black was appointed to the Court by President Roosevelt essentially because he believed in judicial restraint toward federal and state efforts to deal with the economic crisis of the Depression. Frankfurter continued to apply this same philosophy to many of the civil liberties and civil rights issues which increasingly dominated the work of the Court in the 1940s and 1950s, but Black and Douglas, after some hesitation in the early 1940s, switched to an activist position. For example, in *Minersville School District v. Gobitis*, 310 U.S. 586 (1940), the Court held that the First Amendment did not prevent a state from requiring

public school children who were Jehovah's Witnesses to salute the flag and recite the pledge of allegiance. Justice Frankfurter, speaking for the Court, agreed that the law was stupid, since one could hardly expect to instill patriotism in children by forcing them to violate their religious beliefs, but he felt that the Court was powerless to act. Justices Black and Douglas agreed. Three years later, in *West Virginia Board of Education v. Barnette*, 319 U.S. 624 (1943), the Court abandoned the Frankfurter position and held that compulsory flag salute laws do violate the First Amendment. Black and Douglas were again in the majority.

2. Justice Brennan's background included eighteen years of law practice in New Jersey, followed by seven years as a state judge. Although he acquired a reputation as a progressive judge during his years of service on the New Jersey Supreme Court, there was little in his professional background which would have led an onlooker to conclude, at the time of his appointment to the Supreme Court by President Eisenhower, that he would become a leading spokesman for racial equality and for the rights of the criminally accused.

3. Finally, we come to the Chief Justice, Earl Warren. Warren's views were undoubtedly shaped by his long political career in a state heavily influenced by the progressive movement, with its concern for the "common man." Nevertheless, Warren spent a quarter of a century as a prosecuting attorney before becoming governor of California; as State Attorney General in the early 1940s, he had a hand in the seemingly necessary but nonetheless nefarious exclusion of Japanese Americans from the West Coast. Few people, least of all Dwight Eisenhower, foresaw the metamorphosis that would take place when Earl Warren donned the robes of the Chief Justice.

To sum up: the explanatory power of the argument that judicial behavior can be explained on the basis of preappointment background appears somewhat limited. Ultimately, one must conclude that research methods have not been devised—and perhaps cannot be—which will answer with satisfactory rigor the question of why Supreme Court judges behave in particular ways. Possibly the most straightforward answer—although it is vaguely dissatisfying because it sounds more like a resigned rationalization than a meaningful explanation of behavior—is that the Warren Court overthrew the status quo in the field of criminal procedure because a majority became committed to a particular judicial and political philosophy.

It would indeed be a formidable task to discuss in detail the repercussions throughout the political system to each of the important decisions of the Warren Court in the field of criminal procedure prior to 1966, when the Court handed down its verdict in *Miranda v. Arizona*. The problem of collecting comprehensive data might well prove insurmountable; furthermore, even easily available data would fill at least one entire book. Since the Court proceeded in eclectic fashion, feeling its way along by a process that could well be called "creeping innovation," the problems of legal and political analysis are far more complex than they would have been if the Court had abandoned case-by-case decision making in favor of a more sweeping approach.

Fortunately, such detailed analysis is unnecessary to make the simple point that Supreme Court decisions rarely, if ever, constitute final, conclusive resolutions of important constitutional issues. Selected illustrations will demonstrate equally well the political environment within which the Court operated and the political response —the attempts to enforce Supreme Court decisions, to counteract them, to ignore them, to subvert them, to push one step further—to the efforts of the Court to forge new constitutional principles in the field of criminal procedure.

ILLUSTRATION NO. 1: THE PROMPT-ARRAIGNMENT RULE

Mallory v. United States, 354 U.S. 449 (1957). Held, nine to zero: Confessions secured by federal officials during a period of unlawful detention prior to arraignment are inadmissible as evidence at a subsequent trial. This decision sought to enforce the requirement of the Federal Rules of Criminal Procedure that suspects be arraigned promptly before a federal commissioner or other judicial officer, at which time they are charged with a crime and informed of their constitutional rights; it sought to prevent federal law enforcement officers and the Washington, D.C., police from arresting individuals without probable cause, in violation of the Fourth Amendment, and attempting to obtain the requisite probable cause from the suspect's own lips during interrogation in the station house.

The decision strengthened individual rights at the expense of public order. The Court thus indicated a preference for one set of values over another: punishing the guilty was to be less important than protecting the innocent and maintaining the integrity of the legal system. Proof of guilt in a factual sense would continue to be necessary for a criminal conviction, but it would not be sufficient; at least in the area of police activity covered by the prompt-arraignment rule, criminal convictions were to be based on "legal guilt," on proof obtained by legal methods, and not just on "factual guilt."

The Justice Department and the District of Columbia Police Department, whose custodial interrogation practices were directly challenged by the holding in *Mallory v. United States*, were extremely critical of the decision. They believed interrogations would not be productive unless the police possessed considerable discretion as to when an arrested suspect should be formally charged with commission of a crime. State attorneys general and state and local prosecutors and police officers also criticized the verdict, since they feared that the Court might decide in a future case to require them to abide by a similar prompt-arraignment rule.

Many members of the House and Senate Judiciary Committees sympathized with this viewpoint, and hearings were held on bills designed to reverse the *McNabb-Mallory* rule, as it was called. Late in the summer of 1958, just as the off-year congressional election campaigns were getting underway, the House and the Senate passed the proposed legislation; a conference committee resolved differences in the bills passed by each house, but the measure died when the Senate refused to accept the committee's report. Similar legislation passed the House of Representatives in 1959 and again in 1961, but the Senate refused to take further action.

In the early 1960s crime in the District of Columbia grew by leaps and bounds. While numerous observers denied that the prompt-arraignment rule had anything to do with the crime rate, their arguments fell on deaf ears. A bill similar to one rejected in 1963 was introduced and passed by the House early in 1965, despite the opposition of the administration, the Department of Justice, the Budget Bureau, and the District of Columbia Commissioners.

Although Senators Robert Kennedy, Joseph Tydings, and Wayne Morse fought to retain the *Mallory* rule, the Senate also acted favorably on legislation suspending the statutory requirement of prompt arraignment. The Senate did, however, insist that police interrogation prior to arraignment be limited to three hours, that the interrogation be recorded, that the suspect be fully informed prior to questioning of his rights to silence and to obtain counsel. Since the House conferees refused to accept these limitations on police power and the senators on the conference committee refused to give the District of Columbia police sweeping authority in the secrecy of station-house detention rooms, the committee remained deadlocked for over a year.

Ultimately, a District of Columbia crime bill containing essentially the House of Representatives' guidelines for police detention and interrogation was reported. Conferees Kennedy and Morse refused to sign the conference report; Senator Tydings signed, but stated that he did so only because the House conferees made agreement on their version the sine qua non of action on all other pending District of Columbia legislation. The bill passed the Senate and the House just two weeks before the 1966 congressional elections.

President Johnson was pressured on both sides. Acting Attorney General Ramsey Clark, several of the District of Columbia Commissioners, the District of Columbia Bar Association, all federal agencies asked to comment on the bill, the ACLU, the District of Columbia Democratic Party organization, and various civil rights groups urged him to veto the bill. On the other side was the Metropolitan Washington Board of Trade, the Southeast Businessmen's Association, and a group called the Federation of Citizens Association. Despite the fact that a veto would lay him open to charges of being soft on crime, the President chose to follow the advice of his administrators. The issue of congressional action to frustrate the intent of the *Mallory* rule by changing the statutory requirement of prompt arraignment became dormant as a result of the Johnson veto, but it is by no means dead.

ILLUSTRATION NO. 2: THE WARRANTLESS-SEARCH RULE

Mapp v. Ohio, 367 U.S. 643 (1961). Held, six to three: Evidence secured by state police officers in violation of the Fourth Amendment's prohibition of unreasonable searches and seizures cannot be admitted at a subsequent trial. In reaching this conclusion, the Court eliminated a gap in the protection afforded those accused of state and federal crimes which had existed since 1914, when the Court first applied the exclusionary rule to federal trials. The majority did not suggest that evidence obtained by breaking into someone's home without a search warrant was any less probative than evidence secured by lawful means, but it concluded that the failure of state legislatures and courts to prohibit the introduction of evidence seized in violation of the Fourth Amendment encouraged the police to short-cut constitutional protections.

Earlier, in 1949, the Court had ruled that the protection against unreasonable searches and seizures was one of the fundamental principles of justice which was included in Fourteenth Amendment due process, but it had refused to apply the federal exclusionary rule to the states. Instead, it had attempted to determine, on a case-by-case basis, whether particular unconstitutional searches and seizures were so noxious and offensive to our fundamental sense of justice as to require that evidence so obtained be suppressed. This relativistic approach proved to have blatant shortcomings: it provided no meaningful guidelines for the police and for state judges; it led to innumerable appeals; it required the Supreme Court, sitting in Washington, to review the facts of a case in detail; it did not succeed in curbing the police and furthering the evenhanded administration of justice. In *Mapp*, the majority moved to eliminate these evils by adopting an absolute rule that *all* unconstitutionally seized evidence must be excluded.

When the Supreme Court reversed its 1949 position and announced its verdict in *Mapp v. Ohio*, policemen and prosecutors in half the states let loose a tirade of abuse directed at the Supreme Court; they felt that the Court was hamstringing the efforts of law enforcement officials by preventing prosecutors from using evidence in court that proved beyond any doubt the guilt of criminal defendants.

Unfortunately for those law enforcement officials whose job was complicated by the *Mapp* ruling, they were outflanked and outgunned from the start: they found it hard to work up much enthusiasm in Congress or among the public at large to change the ruling by political action. For one thing, the proponents of reversing the decision had unclean hands; they were arguing, in effect, that arbitrary and unconstitutional intrusions by the police were necessary and justifiable. For another, Washington, D.C., police and federal agents were disinterested, since they had lived with an exclusionary rule for half a century. For a third, many states also were disinterested, since they had already adopted a similar rule on their own. As Justice Clark said in his decision for the Court:

> While in 1949, prior to the *Wolf* case [the case applying the search-and-seizure protection to the states], almost two-thirds of the States were opposed to the use of the exclusionary rule, now, despite the *Wolf* case, more than half of those since passing upon it, by their own legislative or judicial decision, have wholly or partly adopted or adhered to the *Weeks* rule [the exclusionary rule].... Significantly, among those now following the rule is California which, according to its highest court, was "compelled to reach that conclusion because other remedies have completely failed to secure compliance with the constitutional provisions...." The experience of California that such other remedies have been worthless and futile is buttressed by the experience of other States.[4]

Thus, opposition to the *Mapp* rule never got far beyond the stage of verbal criticism of the Court. The opposing forces did not organize effectively and did not exert meaningful pressure on Congress. Within a year or two, outspoken opposition gradually vanished, as police officers found they could still conduct searches and could still use the evidence obtained as long as they followed the requirements of the Fourth Amendment. All that was left was the growing burden of resentment at the Court for criticizing the police and making their work more difficult.

ILLUSTRATION NO. 3: THE RIGHT-TO-COUNSEL RULE

Gideon v. Wainwright, 372 U.S. 335 (1963). Held, nine to zero: Any indigent accused by a state of committing a felony has a right to court-appointed defense counsel. Thus, the Supreme Court eliminated another gap in the protections afforded individuals accused of state versus federal crimes, a gap which had existed since 1938, when the Court ruled that the Sixth Amendment right to counsel required the federal government to make counsel available to indigents accused of federal crimes.

Earlier, the Court had held in the famous Scottsboro Boys case, *Powell v. Alabama*, 287 U.S. 45 (1932), that the Fourteenth Amendment due process clause required the states to make counsel available to indigents in all capital cases, not on the grounds that the Fourteenth Amendment incorporated the requirements of the Sixth Amendment, but on the grounds that defendants facing the possibility of a death sentence could not receive a fair trial without legal assistance. In subsequent cases, however, the Court refused to extend this doctrine to noncapital crimes. Instead, it ruled that indigents charged with noncapital crimes in state courts have a constitutional right to be represented by counsel only if all the facts in the case demonstrate that denial of counsel constitutes a denial of fundamental fairness.

This relativistic approach suffered from the same blatant shortcomings as the "special circumstances" rule applied to the admissibility of illegally seized evidence in the years prior to *Mapp v. Ohio*. Imagine the quandary facing a trial judge who has to determine before a trial begins whether the special circumstances of the par-

---

[4] 367 U.S. 643, at 651–52 (1961). (Brackets added.)

ticular case are such that denial of a request for counsel will lead an appeals court to reverse a conviction and remand the case for a new trial. Imagine the quandary facing the Supreme Court, which had to determine in each case whether an accused—in the light of the complexity of the charges against him—was so ignorant, uneducated, or incompetent to defend himself that denial of his request for counsel resulted in a conviction devoid of fundamental fairness.

In *Gideon v. Wainwright*, the members of the Court finally threw up their hands in frustration and ruled that *all* indigents, regardless of whether they have been accused of federal or state crimes, have a right to court-appointed counsel.

Unlike the *Mapp* and *Mallory* decisions, the *Gideon* opinion was greeted with public acclaim. The American Bar Association announced that the decision was consistent with its recommended standards for the protection of indigents and that, therefore, the decision was a great advance in the administration of criminal justice. State and city policemen were somewhat disinterested, even to some extent in states which denied counsel to indigents in noncapital cases, since for once the police were not the focal point of criticism by the Court. Finally, by the time *Gideon v. Wainwright* was handed down, most states were already requiring that all indigents have access to counsel. In fact, twenty-two states had taken the somewhat unusual step of filing amicus curiae briefs in support of Gideon when his appeal reached the Supreme Court; only two states, Alabama and North Carolina, filed briefs in support of the position of the Attorney General of Florida that the right to counsel was not a fundamental requisite of equal justice under law and that a Supreme Court decision requiring the states to provide counsel for the indigent accused would be an unjustified interference with states' rights.

Thus, criticism of the *Gideon* innovation did not lead to substantial efforts to counteract the decision. On the other hand, the *Gideon* holding did have remarkable political consequences of an entirely different sort. At the time of the decision, many states were not adequately prepared to furnish legal assistance to indigents at the trial stage of criminal proceedings. Laws had to be passed, administrative agencies established, lawyers and other personnel hired, offices rented, procedures developed. In the two years following the ruling, no less than twenty-three states took specific actions to improve or to expand the legal services available to poor people accused of felonies.

Although the *Gideon* decision was not addressed to the federal government, it did, nevertheless, have an indirect impact on the provision of legal counsel in federal criminal trials. Prior to 1964, the federal government relied on the willingness of lawyers to defend indigents without compensation. Many of the lawyers appointed by the courts as defense counsel were either recent law school graduates or lawyers experienced in specialized fields unrelated to trial work or to criminal practice. In addition to losing time and income, these appointed counsel frequently had to pay investigative expenses and other costs out of their own pockets. Inevitably, many cases were poorly prepared and many defendants received only cursory attention from their appointed counsel.

For more than twenty years, legislation to remedy the weaknesses of the existing system of unpaid counsel for indigents had been proposed in Congress and supported by various United States attorneys general, but to no avail. On several occasions, remedial legislation had passed the Senate, but the Judiciary Committee of the House of Representatives had refused to take action.

On March 8, 1963, another effort was made. Acting on the recommendations of the Attorney General's Committee on Poverty and the Administration of Federal Criminal Justice, President Kennedy asked Congress to pass legislation providing compensation for counsel and for investigative, expert, and other services necessary for an adequate defense. Ten days later, on March 18, the Supreme Court announced its decision in *Gideon v. Wainwright*.

While it cannot, of course, be proved that the decision of the Court caused Congress to enact the Criminal Justice Act of 1964 a year and a half later, the fact remains that the unanimous holding in *Gideon* was one of the variables to which the members of Congress were exposed. Is it merely coincidence that Congress finally took positive steps to eradicate obvious shortcomings in the administration of justice the same year the Supreme Court focused public attention dramatically on the constitutional question of right to counsel at trial?

ILLUSTRATION NO. 4: EXTENSION OF THE RIGHT-TO-COUNSEL RULE

Escobedo v. Illinois, 378 U.S. 478 (1964). Held, five to four: Where an arrested suspect (a) requests a lawyer; (b) his lawyer is in the police station asking to see the suspect; (c) the investigation is no longer a general inquiry into an unsolved crime but has focused on a particular suspect; (d) the police have not effectively informed him of his absolute right to remain silent; and (e) the purpose of the interrogation is to elicit a confession, the individual has an absolute right to see his lawyer. Therefore, any incriminating statements or confessions made to police interrogators following denial of this right are inadmissible at a subsequent trial.

The decision in *Escobedo* was messy, since the Court limited the right to counsel in the station house to situations in which a suspect is aware of his rights, wishes to exercise them, already has a lawyer, and the lawyer has sufficient warning and diligence to get down to the station before incriminating statements are made to the police. Clearly, suspects who are ignorant of their rights or who do not have a lawyer are at least equally in need of assistance during efforts by the police to elicit a confession. The Court refused, however, to go beyond the specific facts of the *Escobedo* case and to rule on the broad constitutional question of the ultimate scope of the right to counsel during secret interrogation in the police station. It preferred to wait for a case in which this issue was presented squarely.

Prior to *Escobedo*, the Court had held that station-house confessions were admissible if given voluntarily, but that involuntary confessions violated both the Fifth Amendment protection against self-incrimination and the due process of law guaranteed by the Fourteenth Amendment. Under this rule, the Supreme Court had to determine, in each case, whether a confession had been secured by physical or psychological coercion, by trickery, by false promises, by leading the suspect; it had to compare the suspect's intelligence level and emotional state to data on what happened at the interrogation in order to conclude whether his will had been overborne. This highly relativistic judgment invariably had to be made on the basis of sharply conflicting testimony as to what actually happened during the secret, incommunicado interrogation of the accused.

In a way then, *Escobedo*, like *Mallory*, *Mapp*, and *Gideon*, was an admission of failure on the part of the Supreme Court. In sum, the majority was saying that the Court did not have the resources or the data to rule meaningfully on whether any particular station-house confession secured during secret interrogation after the police had denied a request for counsel was given voluntarily. It was saying that the only way to eliminate the possibility of involuntary statements was to require the police to fulfill a request by a suspect to see his lawyer and that this could be achieved only by declaring that confessions made following denial of such a request were no longer admissible in evidence.

It should be noted that the five-member majority emphasized the fact that all six of the men who had interrogated Escobedo paid no attention whatever to Illinois statutes entitling a prisoner to consult with his attorney if he so desires at any point after being taken into custody. The Supreme Court of Illinois had deplored the illegal conduct of the police but had refused to hold that a confession obtained following police violation of a state statute was inadmissible at a subsequent trial. Clearly, the United States Supreme Court felt that such a polite slap on the wrist was inadequate. Once again, as in *Mallory* and *Mapp*, the majority expressed a definite preference for the philosophy that obtaining convictions was less important than maintaining the integrity of the judicial process.

In the weeks following announcement of the *Escobedo* doctrine in June 1964, the Supreme Court again became the focal point of a raging storm. Black clouds hung threateningly over the heads of Justices Warren, Douglas, Black, Brennan, and Goldberg. To many congressmen, newspaper editors, and law enforcement officers, these five were responsible for adding to the crime explosion by making the work of the police and the lower courts increasingly difficult.

The first four of these, joined by Justices Clark and Stewart, had freed Mrs. Mapp even though she was definitely guilty; through a broad interpretation of the Fourteenth Amendment due process clause, they had prevented state and local police from continuing a historic practice of conducting searches without warrants. Now, the hard-core liberals were insisting that the same clause of the Constitution prohibited the use of any confession which is given voluntarily to the police following their refusal to let a suspect speak with his lawyer. Once again, the guilty were to benefit from what appeared to be a technicality.

Opponents of the activists believed the *Escobedo* ruling was an excellent vehicle for stimulating widespread opposition to the Court and for exerting political pressure to reverse the direction in which the Court was going. For one thing, the activists had already made many enemies as a result of other innovative decisions affecting criminal procedures, race relations, free speech, internal subversion, obscenity, school prayers, and reapportionment; the *Escobedo* decision was, therefore, like pouring kerosene on a bed of smoldering coals. For another, the Court had split five to four; thus a strong case could be made that the Court was making policy rather than applying the Constitution. For a third, crime rates had been soaring throughout the 1960s; many people already believed and others could be convinced that the Supreme Court was responsible.

Finally, *Gideon*, *Mallory*, and *Mapp* split the potential opposition, but *Escobedo* united it. *Mallory* was not an attack on the states; *Mapp* and *Gideon* were not attacks on the federal government, nor were they even attacks on all the states since many states had already acted on their own to exclude unconstitutionally seized evidence and to furnish counsel to all indigents accused of felonies. In contrast, the rule that a right to counsel exists in the police station, albeit qualified and limited by the facts of the *Escobedo* case, went far beyond existing practice in nearly every state. Furthermore, since the decision implied that all confessions made during police interrogation were suspect once the accusatory stage of a criminal proceeding has been reached, it was conceivable that a broad interpretation of the *Escobedo* principle might lead the Court to go far beyond existing federal practice by outlawing all confessions made without the advice and continuous presence of defense counsel.

Thus, the implications of the decision were disturbing to police officers and prosecutors at both the state and federal levels. The extent of their concern is revealed by the fact that twenty-seven states seized the opportunity of the first Supreme Court test of the *Escobedo* decision to file an amicus curiae brief supporting the view of the United States, California, New York, and Arizona that no expansion of the holding was warranted; no state came before the Court to present an opposing argument.

Throughout the summer of 1964, the attacks on the Court grew increasingly virulent. Senator Barry Goldwater, the Republican nominee for President, took the Court on head first, calling it the most dangerous branch of government. He made a major campaign issue out of crime in the streets, blaming the administration in general and the Court in particular for the breakdown in law and order. Many citizens opposed to the rulings of the Warren Court devoted their efforts to the election campaign rather than to a direct assault on the decisions via congressional action. The opponents of the Court put all their eggs in one basket and handed it to their champion, Senator Goldwater.

This strategy misfired on Election Day, 1964. Senator Goldwater's overwhelming defeat and President Johnson's capacious coattails changed the balance of power in Congress, causing mass despondency among critics of the Court.

As a result, the Eighty-ninth Congress was not receptive to headstrong attacks on the Supreme Court. In March 1965, the Chief Executive appointed the President's Commission on Law Enforcement and the Administration of Justice and asked it to conduct the first thorough investigation of crime in the United States since 1931. The commission was asked to report within eighteenth months. Inevitably, with liberals dominant in Congress and with a presidential commission doing a lengthy examination of the causes of crime and possible remedies, opponents of the *Escobedo* holding and other decisions in the field of criminal procedure were left cooling their heels.

Meanwhile, across First Street from the Capitol, in the chambers of the Supreme Court, time was not standing still. The questions raised but left unanswered by the narrow holding in *Escobedo v. Illinois* reached the Court in the early spring of 1966. Oral arguments were heard at the end of February and on June 13, two years after the *Escobedo* ruling, the Court decided the instant case, *Miranda v. Arizona.*

. . . .

II. Legal Arguments in Miranda v. Arizona*

STATEMENT OF THE CASE:

Ernesto A. Miranda, a twenty-three-year-old truck driver, was arrested on March 13, 1963, at his home in Phoenix, Arizona, and taken to the police station, where he was put in a lineup consisting of four men. Miranda was identified by an eighteen-year-old girl as the man who had kidnapped and raped her ten days earlier. A second woman claimed Miranda had robbed her on November 27, 1962.

Miranda was then taken to an interrogation room and questioned about both crimes. As was brought out later at the trial, Miranda was not advised of his right to consult an attorney. One of his two interrogators testified that the accused had not been warned that anything he said could be used against him; the other, however, contradicted this testimony and stated that both he and his partner had told Miranda that anything he said could be used against him and that he was not required to tell them anything. Miranda confessed orally to the crimes and subsequently signed a written confession, which is reprinted in full below:

*Author's note: the statement of the case and the briefs printed below are original and are not excerpts from the briefs actually filed in *Miranda v. Arizona, California v. Stewart, Westover v. United States,* and *Vignera v. New York;* these briefs were, however, among the sources used by the author.

STATE'S EXHIBIT 1

CITY OF PHOENIX, ARIZONA
POLICE DEPARTMENT

Form 2000-66-D   Witness/Suspect
Rev. Nov. 59   Statement
SUBJECT: Rape D.R. 63-08380
STATEMENT OF: Ernest Arthur Miranda
TAKEN BY: C. Cooley #413—W. Young #182
DATE: 3-13-63   Time: 1:30 P.M.
PLACE TAKEN: Interr Rm #2

I, Ernest A. Miranda, do hereby swear that I make this statement voluntarily and of my own free will, with no threats, coercion, or promises of immunity, and with full knowledge of my legal rights, understanding any statement I make may be used against me.

I, Ernest A. Miranda, am 23 years of age and have completed the 8th grade in school.

E.A.M. Seen a girl walking up street stopped a little ahead of her got out of car walked towards her grabbed her by the arm and asked to get in the car. Got in car without force tied hands & ankles. Drove away for a few miles. Stopped asked to take clothes off. Did not, asked me to take her back home. I started to take clothes off her without any force and with cooperation. Asked her to lay down and she did could not get penis into vagina got about 1/2 (half) inch in. Told her to get clothes back on. Drove her home. I couldn't say I was sorry for what I had done. But asked her to say a prayer for me. E.A.M.

I have read and understand the foregoing statement and hereby swear to its truthfulness.

/s/ Ernest A. Miranda

WITNESS /s/   Carroll Cooley
                        Wilfred M. Young #182

Prior to the opening of Miranda's trial in the Superior Court of Maricopa County, Judge Warren L. McCarthy requested Dr. James M. Kilgore, Jr., a psychiatrist, to examine the defendant and determine whether he was aware of the charges against him and capable of cooperating in his own defense as well as aware at the time the crimes were committed of the nature of his acts and their wrongful character. Excerpts from the psychiatrist's report follow:

...Mr. Mirande is age 23 and he has a common-law wife, age 30. They have been living together since August 1961. His wife has two children by her first husband, a son, 11, and a daughter, 10. Mr. Mirande and his wife have a daughter, 9 1/2 months of age. He has worked as a truck driver and also as a worker in a warehouse. Mr. Mirande's father is age 55 and works as a painter in Mesa. He stated that he did not get along with his father during his adolescent years and was frequently beaten up by his father when he got into trouble. Mr. Mirande's mother died in 1946 at the age of 34 when Mr. Mirande was six years of age. He was reared by his step-mother, age unknown. He stated with reference to her, "I never could get adjusted to her." Mr. Mirande completed half of the ninth grade at the age of 15. Mr. Mirande was first placed on probation at the age of 14 after having stolen a car. Three months later he was sent to Fort Grant for a period of six months. Shortly after returning he was sentenced for a year on an attempted rape and assault charge. . . .

In 1957 at the age of 17 Mr. Mirande was picked up in Los Angeles for being a peeping tom and charged with lack of supervision and was placed on probation. He was also arrested twice in L.A. on suspicion of armed robbery. He was in the Army from April, 1958, to July, 1959. He was placed in the brig for being a peeping tom and given an undesirable discharge. In December, 1959, he was sentenced to the Federal Penitentiary for transporting a stolen automobile across state lines.

Mr. Mirande is a 23-year-old Mexican man who is alert and oriented as to time, place, and person. His general knowledge and information is estimated to be within normal limits as is his intelligence. He is emotionally bland, showing little if any affect. He is shy, somewhat withdrawn. He tends to be somewhat hypoactive. The patient's responses to proverbs are autistic and somewhat bizarre; for example, to the proverb "a rolling stone gathers no moss," the patient interpreted this to mean "If you don't have sex with a woman, she can't get pregnant." To the proverb "a stitch in time saves nine," Mr. Mirande's response is "If you try to shut something in, you keep it from going out." To the proverb "people in glass houses shouldn't throw stones," Mr. Mirande states "A person with one woman shouldn't go to another woman." Mr. Mirande states that he is not particularly concerned about himself at this point or the trouble that he is in except in that it might interfere with his looking after his wife and child.

It is my diagnostic impression that Mr. Mirande has an emotional illness. I would classify him as a schizophrenic reaction, chronic, undifferentiated type.

It is my opinion that Mr. Mirande is aware of the charges that have been brought against him and is able to cooperate with his attorney in his own defense. Although Mr. Mirande has an emotional illness, I feel that at the time the acts were committed that he was aware of the nature and quality of the acts and that he was further aware that what he did was wrong.

Initially, the two offenses of which Miranda stood accused were consolidated in the trial court, with Dr. Kilgore's sanity examination covering both. Subsequently, they were separated and two separate trials were held. At the trial on the rape-kidnapping charge, Miranda's oral and written confessions were admitted into evidence by Judge McCarthy over the objection of the defendant's lawyer; the prosecutor made full use of the confessions in his summation to the jury. Miranda was convicted and sentenced to twenty to thirty years in prison. He was also convicted on the robbery charge and given a sentence of twenty to twenty-five years.

Faced with the prospect of spending many years in jail, Miranda decided—with the advice of his lawyer—to appeal his conviction for rape and kidnapping. The Supreme Court of Arizona upheld the verdict of the trial court and a petition for a writ of certiorari was filed with the United States Supreme Court in July 1965. The writ was granted the following November and the case was placed on the Supreme Court docket for argument.

BRIEF FOR APPELLANT   *BRIEF FOR APPELLEE*

1. *Does an arrested person have a constitutional right to counsel when interrogated by the police?*

The right of an accused person to legal counsel is—as many past decisions of this Court indicate—a developing and not static constitutional protection. In the years since 1932, the Supreme Court has repeatedly attempted to

Miranda v. Arizona and the three other cases which are currently before the Court involve use at a criminal defendant's trial of incriminatory statements made in response to police questioning shortly after arrest. Such state-

follow a functional rather than formalistic approach to the right to counsel. The Court has tried to avoid distinctions which in one breath upheld the right but in the next rendered it devoid of substance.

As counsel for Miranda, we would not have urged him to appeal his conviction to the Supreme Court if we did not believe that the Court was ready to rule that no confession secured after the accusatory stage of a criminal prosecution has been reached will be admitted into evidence at a subsequent trial unless the accused has had an effective opportunity to exercise or waive his constitutional right to counsel.

We believe that the above rule follows inevitably from the decision of the Court in *Escobedo v. Illinois,* 378 U.S. 478 (1963), that a confession made after an investigation has focused on an individual and the accusatory stage of criminal proceedings has been reached will not be admitted if (1) the suspect has asked to consult his lawyer, and (2) the lawyer has arrived at the police station and repeatedly asked to see his client. Certainly, the right to counsel during police interrogation cannot be made to turn on whether or not a suspect is smart enough to know his constitutional rights or to hire a diligent lawyer prior to his arrest.

In order to understand fully the *Escobedo* ruling and why we feel it should be generalized to apply to all station-house interrogations once the accusatory stage of a criminal prosecution has been reached, it is necessary to review the development of the right to counsel.

The Constitution is silent on the question of whether individuals tried by the states have a right to counsel; it does provide, in the Sixth Amendment that "In all criminal prosecutions, the accused shall . . . have the assistance of counsel for his defence." However, since the Bill of Rights was written to protect citizens against possible tyranny by the federal government, the word "all" has commonly been interpreted to mean all criminal prosecutions by the federal government and not prosecutions for state as well as federal crimes. Whatever right to counsel exists in state criminal prosecutions is the result of judicial interpretation of the provision of the Fourteenth Amendment that "No state shall . . . deprive

ments have always been accepted into evidence by state and federal courts provided they were made voluntarily and were not the result of coercion.

Now, however, counsel for Miranda asks the Court to throw this time-tested practice into the discard and to substitute in its place a rule that the Constitution requires the police to inform suspects that they have the right to remain silent, that anything they say may be used against them, that they have the right to be advised by legal counsel and to have legal counsel provided for them if they are indigent. In the absence of such a warning, according to this argument, even voluntary confessions shall no longer be admissible in evidence.

It is our firm belief that the federal Constitution lays no such obligation on the police, that this Court has never declared the existence of such an obligation or the requirement that confessions secured without prior warning must be excluded from evidence, and that there is no good reason why the Court should now, for the first time, bring into existence a rule so fraught with danger to the maintenance of law and order in the United States.

The appellant leans heavily on the history of the Sixth Amendment and on the five to four decision of this Court in *Escobedo v. Illinois,* 378 U.S. 478 (1963), to imply that a ruling that the Sixth Amendment requires a general right to counsel in the station house prior to the institution of formal criminal proceedings is inevitable. We do not believe that either the history of the amendment or the *Escobedo* decision supports such a conclusion.

Escobedo v. Illinois was the first decision of this Court to hold that the right to counsel extended to the station house; the decision was narrowly circumscribed, however. The majority did not rule that all criminal suspects have a right to counsel prior to interrogation by police officers. Instead, it held that in the light of the specific facts of the case—particularly that Danny Escobedo had repeatedly asked to see his lawyer prior to confessing and that the police had deliberately prevented the lawyer from seeing his client—the incriminatory statements could not be admitted into evidence at the subsequent trial. The holding of the Court is reprinted below:

any person of life, liberty, or property without due process of law."

The seminal case is *Powell v. Alabama*, 287 U.S. 45 (1932). In this famous case, the state appointed counsel to defend six indigent Negroes accused of rape, but counsel permitted the defendants to be summarily tried and performed only a nominal function. The Supreme Court held that the defendants had not been accorded the right to counsel in a substantial sense and that defendants charged with serious crimes must have sufficient time before trial to consult with counsel to prepare their defense. The right to counsel was held to be one of those fundamental principles of liberty and justice which lie at the base of all our civil and political institutions. The Court went on to rule that a person charged with a crime "requires the guiding hand of counsel at every step in the proceedings against him" and that, in capital cases,

> ... [W]here the defendant was unable to employ counsel, and is incapable adequately of making his own defense because of ignorance, feeble-mindedness, illiteracy, or the like, it is the duty of the court, whether requested or not, to assign counsel for him as a necessary requisite of due process of law; and that duty is not discharged by an assignment at such a time or under such circumstances as to preclude the giving of effective aid in the preparation and trial of the case.
>
> 287 U.S. 45, at 69.

Just as in the *Powell* case, Ernesto Miranda did not have counsel at the time he needed it most; counsel did not enter the case until it was too late for him to give "effective aid in the preparation and trial of the case."

The *Powell* decision required the state to make counsel available in capital cases, but it did not resolve whether the Fourteenth Amendment due process clause required the state to appoint counsel in *every* criminal prosecution of an indigent accused and did not specify what was meant by "every step in the proceedings." Six years later, in a federal prosecution for counterfeiting, *Johnson v. Zerbst*, 304 U.S. 458 (1938), the Court ruled that the Sixth Amendment did require that all individuals accused of federal crimes—regard-

We hold, therefore, that where, as here, the investigation is no longer a general inquiry into an unsolved crime but has begun to focus on a particular suspect, the suspect has been taken into police custody, the police carry out a process of interrogations that lends itself to eliciting incriminating statements, the suspect has requested and been denied counsel, and the police have not effectively warned him of his absolute constitutional right to remain silent, the accused has been denied "the assistance of counsel" in violation of the Sixth Amendment to the Constitution as "made obligatory upon the states by the Fourteenth Amendment," *Gideon v. Wainright*, 372 U.S. at 342, and that no statement elicited by the police during the interrogation may be used against him at a criminal trial.

378 U.S. 478, at 490–91.

In *Escobedo*, the Court consciously avoided ruling on the broad question of whether police failure to inform a suspect of his right to remain silent and his right to counsel would, in the absence of any other indications of unfairness or coercion, invalidate the use of any subsequent incriminatory statements. The dissenting justices in *Escobedo*, in their distress at the decision of the majority to create even a limited Sixth Amendment right prior to the institution of formal judicial proceedings, forecast that—like the camel who gets his nose under the tent during a sandstorm—the Court would not be satisfied for long with its narrow verdict. If such is the case, then that is the end of the present controversy.

We choose to believe, however, that the majority meant what it said when it indicated that the unique circumstances of the case accounted for the holding that a Sixth Amendment right had been violated even though the defendant had not yet been formally charged. Since factual situations comparable to *Escobedo* are quite rare, there is no reason for that case to be deemed a precedent for the formulation of a sweeping rule that the right to counsel comes into existence at the moment of arrest.

Because the appellant's case is built on the proposition that the broad rule which would lead to the suppression of his own confession is made inevitable by the decision of the Court in *Escobedo*, it is understandable why his

less of the gravity of the crimes of which they stood accused—must have the assistance of counsel unless they waive this right.

When the question of whether the Fourteenth Amendment due process clause similarly required the availability of counsel in all state criminal prosecutions was ultimately raised, in *Betts v. Brady*, 316 U.S. 455 (1942), the Court refused to analogize from the *Johnson* precedent and ruled instead that counsel need not be available for every state criminal proceeding. Justices Black, Douglas, and Murphy dissented on the ground that the requirements of the Sixth Amendment were applicable to state criminal proceedings.

The Court did not, however, go to the opposite extreme and rule that the state was *never* under an obligation to make legal counsel available to indigent defendants in noncapital cases. During the period from 1942 until *Betts* was overruled in 1963, the Court straddled the fence on the question of right to counsel during a state criminal trial and reversed convictions secured without defense counsel only if the circumstances of the case indicated that "fundamental fairness" would be denied if the conviction were allowed to stand. Among the criteria used to determine whether "fundamental fairness" had been denied were the age, education, and intelligence of the accused and, in general, his capacity to defend himself.

By attempting to avoid making the right to counsel at trial absolute, the Court backed itself into an inequitable and intolerable corner: a well-off defendant could, of course, always hire legal assistance; an indigent defendant's right to government-provided counsel depended on several variables, including whether he was accused of a federal crime, the gravity of the crime, his supposed ability to defend himself without legal advice against skilled prosecutors. Criminal convictions secured without defense counsel were—inevitably—uncertain. The Court had read the Fourteenth Amendment due process clause in a fashion which saved the states from the economic burden of supplying counsel for all criminally accused indigents, but it had, as a result, opened what turned out to be a can of worms.

The approach to the right to counsel during trial followed in *Betts v. Brady* naturally pre-

counsel has chosen to slur over the precise limits which the Court spelled out in delineating its *Escobedo* doctrine.

Another indication that the Court should not lightly be persuaded by appellant's argument that the rule he seeks is all but announced by *Escobedo v. Illinois* is the deliberate refusal of the Court in that case to reverse two prior decisions in which confessions had been accepted into evidence despite the fact that they had been given after requests to see a lawyer had been denied by the police.

In *Crooker v. California*, 357 U.S. 433 (1958), and *Cicenia v. La Gay*, 357 U.S. 504 (1958), the Court had ruled that the admissibility of confessions made after a denial of a request for counsel depended on whether the denial caused the confession to be involuntary, in violation of the right against compulsory self-incrimination. The dissenters in both cases had argued that any accused person who requests a lawyer should have one as a matter of constitutional right.

The failure of the Court to overrule *Crooker* and *Cicenia* suggests that the *Escobedo* decision is not only not a persuasive precedent for the concept that every arrested suspect must be told by the police prior to interrogation that he has a right to counsel, it is not even a conclusive precedent for the view that every denial of a station-house request to contact a lawyer is an infringement of a constitutional right.

Nor should the Court be overly swayed by appellant's one-sided presentation of the history of the Sixth Amendment right to counsel and the Fifth Amendment protection against self-incrimination, both of which are applicable to the states via the due process clause of the Fourteenth Amendment. Appellant's counsel would have us believe that because the Court has gradually expanded the right to counsel after formal judicial proceedings against a suspect have been initiated, it therefore follows logically that the same process of expansion must be applied to station-house interrogation. Apart from *Escobedo v. Illinois*, however, there are no decisions of this Court which suggest that the Sixth Amendment guarantee of the assistance of counsel becomes operative prior to the appearance of a suspect

cluded an absolute right to counsel during police interrogations. This is not to say, however, that no right existed in the station house. Again, the Court followed the "specialized circumstances" approach, and ruled that a station-house confession could not be admitted into evidence at a subsequent trial if the confession were secured by what amounted to a denial of "fundamental fairness."

In *Crooker v. California*, 357 U.S. 433 (1958), for example, the suspect asked for a lawyer during police interrogation and confessed after the police refused his request. The Court upheld the admission of the confession into evidence and stated that the sole issue was whether the denial of the request caused the confession to be involuntary; in order to answer this question the Court applied the "special circumstances" test, and concluded that Crooker was able to take care of himself without counsel at the interrogation stage in the proceedings against him. The opinion stated that refusal of a request for counsel during any part of pretrial proceedings was a denial of due process only if the accused is "... [S]o prejudiced thereby as to infect his subsequent trial with an absence of fundamental fairness."[1]

Justice Douglas, joined by Chief Justice Warren and Justices Black and Brennan, dissented from this position. They argued that any accused person who wants a lawyer should have one at any time after his arrest in order to avoid police use of the third degree, to eliminate disagreement on what actually happened in the interrogation room, and to protect the accused during the crucial pretrial period. The dissenters argued that "the pretrial period is so full of hazards for the accused that if unaided by competent legal advice, he may lose any legitimate defense he may have long before he is arraigned and put on trial."[2] They also argued that people accused of crimes need legal advice right after arrest probably more than at any other time.

Cicenia v. Gay, 357 U.S. 504 (1958), decided the same day, involved similar issues. In the *Cicenia* case, however, the defendant's family had hired a lawyer, but the police re-

before a judicial officer, and there are many decisions which indicate that the constitutional right which must be protected at this time is the Fifth Amendment privilege against compulsory self-incrimination.

It is quite clear, of course, why counsel for appellant slights the Fifth Amendment question and urges instead that the right to counsel should be made operative in the police station; since Miranda confessed within a short time, without coercion or threats of any kind, his counsel would have a difficult time winning a reversal of the conviction on the grounds that the police had violated Fifth Amendment rights.

We hope it is clear that appellee does not suggest for even an instant that the Court misinterpreted the Sixth Amendment in expanding the right to counsel at trial. *Gideon v. Wainwright*, 372 U.S. 335 (1963), in which the Court ruled that all persons accused of serious crimes must have counsel available to them, was the inevitable and beneficial outcome of deliberate efforts by the justices of this Court, extending over several decades, to define as precisely as possible the content of rights included in the ambiguous phrase "due process of law." As a result of experience with more limited concepts of the right to counsel at trial, the Court gradually came to the conclusion that the "fundamental fairness" which was required by the due process clause could not be assured criminal defendants by any halfway measures.

Because the Court was correct in concluding in the *Gideon* case that counsel must be made available to an indigent defendant at his trial does not, however, suggest that the ruling sought by counsel for Miranda would be equally correct. We believe that the commands of the due process clause can be met without a requirement that legal assistance be equally available at both stages of a criminal proceeding, because there is a significant difference in an arrested person's need for counsel during questioning by the police and at a subsequent trial.

During a trial, the average layman is relatively helpless without the aid of a skilled criminal lawyer. The typical defendant does not know the law, cannot prepare his defense adequately, and—once he reaches court—can-

---

[1] 357 U.S. 433, at 439.
[2] *Ibid.*, at 445–46.

fused to let the defendant see the lawyer or his family until after he had confessed. The majority rejected the view "... [T]hat any state denial of a defendant's request to confer with counsel during police questioning violates due process, irrespective of the particular circumstances involved."[3] The same dissenters with the exception of Justice Brennan, who did not participate in the decision, stated their belief that *Cicenia* was "... [T]he occasion to bring our decision into tune with the constitutional requirement for fair criminal proceedings against the citizen."[4]

While the Court's approach to the right to counsel during interrogation by state and local police was consistent with its approach to the right to counsel at trial on noncapital state criminal charges, its approach to interrogations by federal agents differed sharply. Under the *McNabb-Mallory* rule, a suspect arrested by federal officers must be brought promptly before the nearest available commissioner, whose duty it is to inform him of his right to remain silent and his right to counsel; if the accused is indigent and requests counsel, the commissioner is empowered to provide him with the requested assistance.[5] Failure to bring an arrested person before a commissioner without unnecessary delay results in the inadmissibility of any confession secured during police interrogation.

The Court has refused to hold that the "prompt arraignment" rule is a rule of constitutional dimension, required by the Sixth Amendment, and has insisted instead that the source of the rule is the Federal Rules of Criminal Procedure, as passed by Congress and interpreted by the Court. Nevertheless, the *McNabb-Mallory* rule recognizes the need for counsel during interrogation and goes far to provide protection against police overbearing

---

[3] 357 U.S. 504, at 509.

[4] *Ibid.*, at 512. In a subsequent case, *Peck v. Pate*, 367 U.S. 433, at 448 (1961), Justice Douglas said in a concurring opinion that "I would hold that any confession obtained by police while the defendant is under detention is inadmissible unless there is prompt arraignment and unless the accused is informed of his right to silence and accorded an opportunity to consult counsel."

[5] *McNabb v. United States*, 318 U.S. 332 (1943); *Mallory v. United States*, 354 U.S. 449 (1957).

not compete successfully with trained prosecutors. There is serious question whether verdicts arrived at in such a process are, in fact, just.

In contrast, police questioning does not focus on the intricacies of the law or on legal maneuvering but on questions of fact. The police are interested in discovering whether or not the individual being questioned was at a certain place, conspired with other individuals, committed a certain act, etc. Since the questions are specific and primarily factual in nature, it is highly unlikely that the "fundamental fairness" required by due process of law will be denied if counsel is not made available at this stage of the proceedings.

Our belief that the Constitution does not require the availability or the presence of counsel in the station house is made stronger by our conviction—to be argued in depth at a later point in our brief—that such a rule would hamstring the police in the performance of their lawful duty to protect society. In contrast, as has already been noted above, society suffers no deleterious consequences from the presence of defense counsel in the courtroom during the trial stage of a criminal proceeding.

We are not unaware, of course, that due process is occasionally violated during police interrogations; because human beings administer the law, mistakes and errors are inevitable and injustices do occur. It serves the purposes of counsel for the appellant to paint a picture of innocent, naive, and defenseless citizens caught in webs spun by the minions of the law and tricked into making incriminatory statements by these conscienceless public officials. If this characterization were correct, perhaps an arbitrary rule that no confession will be admissible unless defense counsel is present at the time of the taking of the confession would be a requisite of due process of law.

The members of this Court are too familiar with the American legal system to accept the blatant stereotype drawn by counsel for the appellant. The vast majority of policemen would not consider using trumped-up evidence or tricking a suspect into making an incriminatory statement. For every instance of police deprivation of individual rights reported in

for those accused of federal crimes. No such protection now exists for suspects arrested by state or local police.

Much has been written about *Gideon v. Wainwright*, 372 U.S. 335 (1963), and little need be said here. The *Gideon* decision expressly overruled *Betts v. Brady* and was a triumph for those justices who believed that no person should be tried in a state court without the aid of counsel. All nine justices threw up their hands at the difficult task of assessing, on appeal, the "specialized circumstances" that made counsel necessary in some cases but not in others and refused to continue to second-guess trial-court judges. The Fourteenth Amendment due process clause was interpreted to require an absolute rather than a relative right to counsel at trial. The decision thus erased the distinction which the Court had drawn between the right to counsel in federal and state criminal trials.

While the *Gideon* decision resolved the question of the right to counsel in state criminal proceedings, it did not, of course, rule on the related problem of the right to counsel during police interrogations. However, the *Crooker* and *Cicenia* decisions had been based on the "specialized circumstances" approach of *Betts v. Brady. Gideon v. Wainwright*, therefore, undermined a basic premise of these two decisions.

The same year as it decided the *Gideon* case, the Court ruled in *White v. Maryland*, 373 U.S. 59 (1963), that a guilty plea entered without the advice of counsel at a preliminary hearing before a judge was inadmissible at a subsequent trial. White had been aided by counsel at every stage after the preliminary hearing, but the Court held, nevertheless, that an accused is entitled to counsel at the stage when he can plead guilty, since that stage is critical for his defense. The Court had previously held repeatedly—under its power to regulate federal criminal practice—that suspects are entitled to counsel at all federal arraignments. Thus, *White v. Maryland* extended an absolute right to counsel from trial to pretrial judicial proceedings.

In *Massiah v. United States*, 377 U.S. 201 (1964), the Court held that confessions made without the protection of counsel after a suspect has been indicted for a crime cannot

the press, there are literally thousands of unreported examples of unstinting efforts to uncover the truth and to clear suspects who, at first glance, appear guilty. Naturally, the press focuses on the cases of official misconduct and tends to ignore the less newsworthy but more noteworthy examples of dedication to duty.

One of the primary obligations of our judicial system is to deal firmly and courageously with the exceptions to the general rule. The courts must be careful, however, not to prohibit, limit, or unduly hamper the use of investigative techniques which—in their legitimate use—play a vital role in the maintenance of law and order solely because a few individuals abuse their trust and use the techniques to achieve an unconstitutional result.

The courts have long recognized and, we hope, will continue to recognize what medical students learn early in their careers: that even the most salutary medicine will do a patient more harm than good if administered in excessive doses. We believe that the broad and inflexible constitutional rule sought by counsel for Miranda would be such an "excessive dose." It would hamper rather than strengthen the administration of justice at a time when alarming increases in the commission of crimes threaten the very foundations of public order.

As Justice Goldberg, the author of *Escobedo v. Illinois*, said in a subsequent case, the Court vindicates individual rights and strengthens the administration of justice by promoting respect for law and order when it invalidates unconstitutional acts of public officers. He went on to say, however, that:

> This court is equally concerned to uphold the actions of law enforcement officers consistently following the proper constitutional course. This is no less important to the administration of justice than the invalidation of convictions because of disregard of individual rights or official overreaching. In our view the officers in this case did what the Constitution requires. . . . It is vital that having done so their actions should be sustained under a system of justice responsive both to the needs of individual liberty and to the rights of the community.
>
> *United States v. Ventresca*, 380 U.S. 102, at 111–12 (1965).

The two officers who questioned Ernesto Miranda also acted within historic constitu-

be used at trial, thereby expanding the right to counsel to nonjudicial pretrial proceedings.

After the *Massiah* decision, the major remaining question was whether a ruling that the right to counsel attaches with the indictment stage of a criminal proceeding but not prior to indictment was rational. *Escobedo v. Illinois*, 378 U.S. 478 (1964), put this question to rest, at least in instances where the arrested individual requests legal assistance. The Court held that "It would exalt form over substance to make the right to counsel, under these circumstances [the specific circumstances of the *Escobedo* case], depend on whether at the time of the interrogation, the authorities had secured a formal indictment."[6] The Court followed the New York rule in *People v. Donovan*, 13 N.Y.2d 148 (1963), that a confession prior to indictment after an attorney had been requested, had arrived, and had been denied access to his client could not be used in a subsequent criminal trial. The *Cicenia* and *Crooker* decisions were not overruled but were put aside with the comment that ". . . they are not to be regarded as controlling."[7]

The Court attempted to limit the significance of the *Escobedo* ruling by concluding that:

> We hold only that when the process shifts from investigatory to accusatory—when its focus is on the accused and its purpose is to elicit a confession—our adversary system begins to operate, and, under the circumstances here, the accused must be permitted to consult with his lawyer.
>
> 378 U.S. 478, at 492.

Miranda v. Arizona must be viewed in the context of the *Escobedo* opinion and the cases which led up to that decision. The facts of the *Miranda* case are well within the bounds of the circumstances which led the Court to rule the confession inadmissible in *Escobedo v. Illinois*. As in *Escobedo*, the investigation was no longer a general inquiry into an unsolved crime; it had focused on a particular suspect. Miranda had been arrested, placed in a lineup,

tional standards: they did not coerce him physically or psychologically, nor did they otherwise treat him unfairly. The appellant's confession was not secured by official overbearing but was made voluntarily. It is equally vital, therefore, that the actions of the police officers in this case be sustained.

The appellant contends that the *Escobedo* decision supersedes or—at the least—supplements the Court's historic approach to incustody interrogation by requiring that confessions not only be voluntary but that they be taken only after the suspect has full knowledge of his right to counsel and to silence. In the period since *Escobedo* was decided, the lower courts have divided on this point.

We believe that those courts which have ruled that *Escobedo* did not enunciate a general rule requiring warning have interpreted that decision correctly.

Nor is it inconsequential that four members of the Supreme Court dissented even from the limited application of the Sixth Amendment read into the Constitution by the majority in *Escobedo v. Illinois*. Justice Stewart recognized the right of a defendant not to be questioned in the absence of counsel after indictment, but he insisted that Sixth Amendment rights become operative only with the institution of formal judicial proceedings such as indictment or arraignment.

Justice White, in an opinion joined by Justices Clark and Stewart, wrote that the opinion of the majority was an unnecessary and erroneous abandonment of the historic test for admissibility of confessions. He concluded that: "Until now there simply has been no right guaranteed by the Federal Constitution to be free from the use at trial of a voluntary admission made prior to indictment."[1] Justice Harlan agreed with White that the rule announced by the majority was ill-conceived and would seriously and unjustifiably fetter legitimate methods of law enforcement.

If the Court decides to limit the Sixth Amendment doctrine announced in *Escobedo* solely to the circumstances of that case, as we believe it should, it ought to rule against Miranda's claim that his Sixth Amendment right was violated. Certainly, the facts of the

---

[6] 378 U.S. 478, at 486. (Brackets added.)

[7] *Ibid.*, at 492.

[1] 378 U.S. 478, at 497.

and identified by two women, one of whom stated he had robbed her and the other that he had kidnapped and raped her. Surely, at this point, the purpose of secret police interrogation was to elicit incriminating statements. The process of investigation was at an end and the process of convicting the accused was well under way; the purpose of the interrogation was to generate an irrefutable record for subsequent use at trial. It is apparent that the critical, accusatory stage of the proceedings against Miranda had been reached, yet at no time was he advised by the police of his right to counsel or his right to remain silent.

As a result, the only grounds for distinguishing *Miranda* from *Escobedo* is the fact that the appellant in the present case had not retained counsel prior to or at the time of his apprehension and did not ask to communicate with counsel during his interrogation. The Arizona Supreme Court seized upon this adventitious distinction and held Miranda's confession admissible since he had not requested legal assistance.

Because the Supreme Court limited the *Escobedo* rule to the facts of that particular case, attempts to apply the rule have led to a large number of conflicting decisions by both state and federal courts and a good deal of honest puzzlement over the scope of *Escobedo*. The decision of the Arizona Supreme Court is typical of those verdicts which hold that station-house confessions are admissible in the absence of a request for counsel.

We believe that it would be an extraordinary step backward for this Court to hold that the right to counsel does not come into existence when the accusatory stage has been reached because the ignorant accused does not know enough to request a lawyer. The proper rule should be that the right to counsel matures at the critical, accusatory stage and does not originate with the accused's assertion of it.

To make the right to counsel dependent on a request is to favor the sophisticated and the financially able over the ignorant and the poor. As the California Supreme Court said in interpreting *Escobedo*:

Finally, we must recognize that the imposition of the requirement for the request would

present case differ remarkable from those which led the Court to formulate its *Escobedo* doctrine. Danny Escobedo had retained a lawyer and repeatedly asked to see him during police interrogation; these requests were all denied and, at one time, Escobedo was even told that his lawyer did not want to see him. This was a barefaced lie, since the lawyer was in the police station, demanding that he be allowed to speak with his client, a right assured by an Illinois statute. Escobedo was interrogated by a skilled and experienced prosecutor, as well as by police officers, and was told in the course of the interrogation that another suspect had accused him of committing the crime in question. At no time was he advised by either the police or the prosecutor of his constitutional rights.

Ernesto Miranda had had considerable previous experience with the police, but Danny Escobedo had no record of prior experience. Miranda did not seek an opportunity to consult with counsel prior to talking to the police, nor did he ask that counsel be provided. The arresting officers did not deny him an opportunity to consult a lawyer; on the other hand, we do not contest that the suspect was not specifically advised of his right to counsel. While the trial court record is unclear as to what warnings were given to Miranda prior to his confession, one of the two investigating officers stated that the suspect had been told of his right to remain silent and that anything he said could be used against him; in addition, Miranda's confession began with a statement that he was confessing voluntarily, that he had full knowledge of his legal rights, and that he knew that anything he said could be used against him.

No trickery was used in the questioning of Miranda, nor were the questions asked him of such a nature as to involve subtle points of law likely to be unknown to the average layman. For the most part, the questions concerned his own actions in early March 1963. Since Miranda confessed within a very short time, there is no suggestion in the record that the police used coercion of any sort to procure the confession.

The Court could rightfully have concluded from the actions of the interrogating officers in *Escobedo v. Illinois* that Danny Escobedo's

discriminate against the defendant who does not know his rights. The defendant who does not ask for counsel is the very defendant who most needs counsel. . . .

People v. Dorado, 62 Cal.2d at
351 (1965).

Wright v. Dickson, 336 F.2d 878, at 882 (9th Cir. 1964), expressly holds that under *Escobedo* it is immaterial whether or not "appellant asked to consult retained counsel or to be provided with the assistance of appointed counsel, nor, indeed, whether he requested counsel at all, except as the latter fact might bear upon waiver." Nor is the question of waiver relevant here. In *Escobedo v. Illinois,* the defendant's request to consult with his lawyer, followed by his confession, complicated the issue of waiver. But where, as here, there is no evidence that the accused knew of his right to the assistance of counsel, his silence cannot be presumed to constitute a knowing or intelligent waiver of his rights.

Indeed, apart from the language of *Escobedo,* prior constitutional principles make it abundantly clear that the right to counsel does not depend on a request. In *Carnley v. Cochran,* 369 U.S. 506, at 513 (1962), the Court cited numerous precedents supporting the view that ". . . [I]t is settled that where the assistance of counsel is a constitutional requisite, the right to be furnished counsel does not depend on a request."

confession was not the product of his free will. It could have come to the conclusion that the only way to ensure that no taint of compulsion attached to a confession such as his was to require the police to allow suspects to consult with retained counsel.

Given the facts of these two cases, it is clear that the *Miranda* case is not covered by the doctrine announced in *Escobedo v. Illinois.* Nor is there any valid reason for expanding the limited right to counsel under narrowly defined circumstances to a general right to counsel for all suspects being interrogated by the police.

2.   *Does station-house interrogation without prior warning of the right to remain silent violate the privilege against compulsory self-incrimination?*

While we do not agree with appellee's argument that station-house interrogations involve primarily the Fifth Amendment and that the Sixth Amendment is relevant only tangentially, we think it necessary to state that all the points we have already raised are equally relevant under the appellant's Fifth Amendment right to avoid self-incrimination, which is applicable to the states as a result of the decision of this Court in *Malloy v. Hogan,* 378 U.S. 1 (1964).

We will not repeat them at this point in our brief, other than to say that the Court has

Our argument would be far weaker if there were, in fact, no way for the courts to protect the rights of individuals who are brought into police stations for questioning. Such is not the case, however. This Court has, in a series of cases extending over several decades, gradually and thoughtfully developed criteria for determining, in each individual case, whether a suspect has been denied his constitutional rights. Since these criteria are adequate to the task and do strike a balance between individual rights and the rights of the community consonant with the due process of law required

recognized that the privilege against self-incrimination goes beyond the well-established rule against coerced confessions and is the "essential mainstay" of our accusatorial system of justice. When Miranda became the accused, he was entitled to rely on that mainstay.

It is no answer to argue that the Fifth Amendment only prohibits compelled self-incrimination at trial; in the *Escobedo* case, the Court made perfectly clear that an accused has an absolute right to remain silent in the police station.[8] If this right is to be made effective, notice of the existence of the right must be conveyed to a suspect once the accusatory stage of the proceedings against him have begun.

Yet it is not clear that the police chose to inform Miranda of his right to remain silent; at the trial, the two investigating officers contradicted each other on this point. Thus it is at least possible that the choice of silence was carefully concealed from the appellant by his station-house interrogators. Since, as Justice Holmes stated, a choice containing concealed alternatives is no choice at all, one can hardly argue that the accused had a free choice to admit, deny, or refuse to answer. The police required Miranda to participate in an interrogation designed to obtain incriminating statements which would be used to convict him at trial. In the absence of evidence that the accused knew he had a right to remain silent, we believe that such a procedure violated the Fifth Amendment.

Even the best of secret interrogations by the police raises questions about the voluntary nature of confessions made in the station house. As has been suggested by Federal District Court Judge Smith in *United States v. Richmond:*

Statements elicited during questioning are bound to be colored to some extent by the purpose of the questioner who inevitably leads the witness in the absence of court control. This coloring is compounded where the statement is not taken down stenographically, but written out as a narrative in language supplied by the questioner. Where the state of mind of the defendant is an issue in the case, as in

[8] 378 U.S. 478, at 485.

by the Fourteenth Amendment, they should not lightly be abandoned.

Although there may be rare instances, *Escobedo v. Illinois* among them, when the particular facts suggest that the Sixth Amendment right to counsel becomes operative in the police station, these instances constitute exceptions to the general rule; ordinarily, the constitutional right which must be safeguarded prior to the appearance of a suspect before a judicial officer is the Fifth Amendment privilege against self-incrimination.

Past decisions of this Court indicate that the admissibility of incriminatory statements made by a suspect after his arrest should be determined by an inquiry into whether the totality of circumstances surrounding his interrogation justifies a conclusion that his statements were obtained by coercion, trickery, or other evidence of unfairness. The critical question should be neither the state of mind of the police—that is, whether, in their thoughts, the proceedings are no longer investigatory but accusatory—nor should it be whether the police committed or omitted any single act, be it a failure to give a warning, denial of access to a suspect, secret interrogation, or failure to make counsel available on request. Instead, it should be whether the official conduct, taken as a whole, did in fact override the suspect's free choice to refuse to be a witness against himself within the meaning of the Fifth Amendment.

For example, Justice Frankfurter expressed this philosophy in *Culombe v. Connecticut,* 367 U.S. 568, at 601, 602 (1961), as follows:

In light of our past opinions and in light of the wide divergence of views which men may reasonably maintain concerning the propriety of various police investigative procedures not involving the employment of obvious brutality, this much seems certain; it is impossible for this Court, in enforcing the Fourteenth Amendment, to attempt precisely to delimit, or to surround with specific, all-inclusive restrictions, the power of interrogation allowed to state law enforcement officers in obtaining confessions. No single litmus-paper test for constitutionally impermissible interrogation has been evolved; neither extensive cross-questioning . . . ; nor undue delay in arraignment . . . ; nor failure to caution a prisoner . . . ; nor refusal to permit

determining the degree of a homicide, this wording of his account of the crime is of vital importance.... Had counsel been available ... he might have advised ... of the danger to one on trial for his life ... of adopting the language of another in a statement signed by him.

> 197 F. Supp. 125, at 129 (D. Conn. 1960);
> *rev'd on other grounds*, 295 F.2d 83
> (2d Cir. 1961); *cert. denied*, 368 U.S.
> 948 (1962).

Ideally, of course, police interrogators should not lead suspects; yet the books on police interrogation in most widespread use throughout the nation cannot help but breed skepticism as to the extent to which this ideal is actually followed. For example, Inbau and Reid's *Criminal Interrogation and Confessions* and Kidd's *Police Interrogation* have been synopsized as follows:

The Inbau and Reid book is a very specific and highly illuminating study of recommended techniques of interrogation. A paraphrase of the authors' advice to the would-be interrogator might read: Impress the accused with your certainty of his guilt, and comment upon his psychological symptoms of guilt, such as the pulsation of a carotid artery, nail biting, dryness of the mouth, etc.; smoking should be discouraged because this is a tension-reliever for the guilty subject trying desperately not to confess; the sympathetic approach—anyone else under such circumstances would have acted the same way, suggests a less repulsive reason for the crime, and, once he confesses, extract the real reason, condemn the victim, the accomplice or anyone else upon whom some degree of moral responsibility might be placed; understanding approach—a gentle pat on the shoulder, a confession is the only decent thing to do, I would tell my own brother to confess; forceful approach—exaggerate the charges against the accused, sweet and sour technique (one policeman is hostile to him while other acts as his friend); interrogation of the recalcitrant witness—at first be gentle and promise him police protection then, if he still refuses to talk, attempt to break the bond of loyalty between him and the accused or even accuse him of the offense and interrogate him as if he were the offender. The book written by Lt. Kidd provides fascinating reading for the novice. The following paraphrased extracts offer examples: The officer should not interrogate in a business office where there might be

communication with friends and legal counsel at stages in the proceeding when the prisoner is still only a suspect....

Each of these factors in company of the surrounding circumstances—the duration and conditions of detention (if the confessor has been detained), the manifest attitude of the police toward him, his physical and mental state, the diverse pressures which sap or sustain his powers of resistance and self-control—is relevant. The ultimate test remains that which has been the only clearly established test in Anglo-American courts for two hundred years; the test of voluntariness. Is the confession the product of an essentially free and unconstrained choice by its maker? If it is, if he has willed to confess, it may be used against him. If it is not, if his will has been overborne and his capacity for self-determination critically impaired, the use of his confession offends due process....

Obviously, such a test cannot be applied in a mechanical fashion; the courts must continue to analyze the facts in each individual case to determine whether a confession should be admitted into evidence. Mere detention and interrogation should not, of course, be sufficient to invalidate incriminatory statements. The Arizona courts did make such an analysis, and concluded that there was no basis for the suggestion that Miranda's Fifth Amendment rights had been violated by the police. We believe that this conclusion is correct and that it should, therefore, be upheld on appeal.

Appellant contends that because the test is imprecise and because judicial evaluation of the circumstances surrounding a confession cannot help but be highly subjective, the test should be replaced with a simple, automatic requirement that all confessions must be preceded by warning. At first glance, this argument seems appealing: judges will be able to escape the onerous task of determining whether station-house confessions have been made voluntarily.

On deeper reflection, however, appellant's point proves specious. A requirement of warning will not simplify the task of determining the admissibility of confessions, nor will it eliminate the need for judicial evaluation of the surrounding circumstances. According to the rule sought by counsel for appellant,

a recording device because he may make some statements which would be embarrassing if played back in court to rebut his testimony; feed upon suspect's likes and dislikes—love of mother, hatred of father, concern for children; never release pressure even when tears begin to flow; don't allow the accused any form of tension release at a critical moment in the questioning, such as a cigarette, a drink of water, or a trip to the washroom; play two co-conspirators against each other (often termed bluffing on a split pair)—claim that one talked and blamed the other, possibly using a false recording to substantiate this claim, continually take one out separately but never question him—the other will believe it necessary to tell his side of the story; aggressive approach—blame accused for crimes he didn't commit, play on the fact that many defendants fear the mental asylum more than jail.[9]

Given the interrogation techniques suggested by Inbau, Reid, Kidd and others, how can it be concluded otherwise than that (1) information obtained under such circumstances may be highly unreliable, and (2) the constitutional rights of the individual to remain silent and to have counsel for his defense are seriously jeopardized when he is under the exclusive control of the police, has not been warned of his rights, and is beyond the reach of counsel and of friends.

We believe that this Court should not continue in its present practice of attempting to determine whether the violation of Fifth Amendment rights by police interrogators is sufficient in any particular case to require reversal because the subsequent trial has been infected with fundamental unfairness; instead, we ask the Court to follow an exclusionary rule comparable to that laid down in *Mapp v. Ohio*, 367 U.S. 643 (1961). Station-house confessions, no matter how relevant and reliable, can never be truly voluntary if the suspect has no knowledge of his right to silence. To encourage the police to enforce the commands of the Constitution and to protect the integrity of our system of justice, all confessions secured without appropriate warnings should be inadmissible as evidence.

suspects in custody must be effectively informed of their Fifth Amendment right when the focus of the investigation switches from investigatory to accusatory and the authorities begin to carry out a process of interrogation that lends itself to eliciting incriminatory statements.

Who is to determine the point in time at which questioning of a suspect switches from investigatory to accusatory? In many criminal investigations, it is impossible to separate, even conceptually, these two stages. Certainly, a judicial decision on this crucial point could not be made objectively and automatically.

Who is to determine whether a warning has been effective? If the admissibility of a confession made after a warning has been given depends on whether a suspect knowingly and intelligently waived his rights, someone will have to determine through a difficult subjective process whether the suspect in question fully understood both the warning given and the significance of his decision.

In order to determine the effectiveness of a waiver, the courts will have to evaluate the age and intelligence of the suspect, his education, his prior experience with the police and the law, his physical and emotional condition at the time of interrogation or, in other words, exactly the same variables which they now evaluate in order to determine the voluntariness of station-house confessions. Thus, we do not believe that the inflexible constitutional rule sought by appellant would in fact make the task of the courts easier or would eliminate the need for difficult subjective judgments. Appellant's panacea proves, on investigation, to be far worse than existing procedures.

[9] Comment, "The Right to Counsel During Police Interrogation," 53 *Cal. L. Rev.* 337, 351–52, n. 75 (1965).

3. What impact will a requirement of warnings prior to interrogation have on law enforcement?

Naturally, the members of this Court are concerned with the impact of their decisions on law enforcement and the protection of law-abiding citizens. We do not believe that a decision giving the Fifth and Sixth Amendments their full meaning will seriously limit the effectiveness of law enforcement officers.

Inescapably, the recognition by this Court that those accused of crimes have certain rights will be met by cries of outrage from many sincere as well as many self-interested citizens. This Court has always refused to take the easy path and withhold constitutional rights because of such pressures.

Moreover, it is important to focus sharply on appellee's claim that a requirement of warning prior to secret police interrogation of a suspect once the accusatory stage of an adversary proceeding has been reached will have an overwhelmingly detrimental effect on law enforcement. Such a sweeping generalization cannot withstand the light of careful examination.

First of all, such a requirement would have absolutely no effect on organized crime. Professional criminals know all too well the rights which society has established in order to ensure that no citizen, whether innocent or guilty, will be convicted of a crime without a meaningful opportunity to prove his innocence. The right to counsel and confession cases which have come before this Court since *Powell v. Alabama* have almost never involved organized criminals; they have involved primarily poor defendants, poorly educated defendants, and, frequently, defendants of limited mental ability. The wealthy, the educated, the middle class are protected by existing constitutional requirements, and those involved in organized crime do not need the protection we seek for men like Ernesto Miranda.

Secondly, a requirement that the police inform suspects of their constitutional rights once the accusatory stage of a criminal prosecution has been reached will not limit the police more than they ought to be limited. Such a rule will not—despite appellee's asser-

Given the present state of knowledge about the consequences for law enforcement of establishing a general right to counsel at the stage of in-custody interrogation, we believe that the lack of concern expressed by counsel for the appellant over the dangers inherent in severely curtailing the powers of the police is appalling. Because of his responsibility to Miranda, counsel for the appellant has searched the available literature to try to prove that a requirement of warnings prior to police questioning would not have a serious impact on the ability of the police to carry out their duties. All he has been able to show for his efforts, however, is that a minority of the experts do not agree with the viewpoint that interrogation of suspects is essential to the protection of society against lawlessness.

We believe that the great majority of people who have studied the available evidence and are experienced in the field of law enforcement have come to the conclusion that police questioning is indispensable. Although authorities for this proposition are too numerous to cite comprehensively we would like to refer the Court to the following illustrative statements:

> Despite modern advances in the technology of crime detection, offenses frequently occur about which things cannot be made to speak. And where there cannot be found innocent human witnesses to such offenses, nothing remains—if police investigation is not to be balked before it has fairly begun—but to seek out possibly guilty witnesses and ask them questions, witnesses, that is, who are suspected of knowing something about the offense precisely because they are suspected of implication in it.
>
> ... [W]hatever its outcome, such questioning is often indispensable to crime detection. Its compelling necessity has been judicially recognized as its sufficient justification, even in a society which, like ours, stands strongly and constitutionally committed to the principle that persons accused of crime cannot be made to convict themselves out of their own mouths.
>
> *Culombe v. Connecticut,* 367 U.S. 568, at 571 (1961).

tion to the contrary—signal the end of confessions or prohibit legitimate police investigations.

The requirement of warning would not prohibit the admission of spontaneous confessions, which are often made by individuals who wish to admit to crimes they have committed. It would not prohibit the admission into evidence of answers given by individuals found in suspicious circumstances to questions about their presence and conduct as long as the accusatory stage has not been reached. Statements made during police investigations would not be inadmissible unless the process had already become essentially an adversary proceeding.

We do not deny that, at first, until guidelines are developed, it may be difficult for the police and the courts to determine when such an interrogation has begun. As the *Escobedo* decision suggests, the key should be that constitutional rights must be protected when an investigation has "focused" on an accused, when the accusatory stage of the proceedings has been reached, when the police are engaged in a process of interrogation for the purpose of obtaining incriminating statements.

Thirdly, and most importantly, it is by no means clear that a reduction in the number of confessions given to the police will have a deleterious effect on law enforcement and the protection of society against crimes. In fact, the experts are in sharp disagreement on the importance of confessions generally in criminal prosecutions. For example, the FBI has long followed a practice similar to the one advocated here, and no one has claimed that the warning provided suspects by FBI agents has hindered federal law enforcement.[10]

During various congressional hearings on the impact of the prompt-arraignment rule, which achieves the same purpose as a requirement of warning once the accusatory stage of a criminal prosecution has been reached, Deputy Attorney General Ramsey Clark and United States Attorney for the District of Columbia David Acheson both testified that the *McNabb-Mallory* rule has had very little

And, in his concurring opinion in *Watts v. Indiana*, 338 U.S. 49, at 58 (1949), Justice Jackson described the problem faced by the police in the three cases then before the Court:

> In each case police were confronted with one or more brutal murders which the authorities were under the highest duty to solve. Each of these murders was unwitnessed, and the only positive knowledge on which a solution could be based was possessed by the killer. In each there was reasonable ground to *suspect* an individual but not enough legal evidence to *charge* him with guilt. In each the police attempted to meet the situation by taking the suspect into custody and interrogating him....
>
> ... [N]o one suggests that any course held promise of solution of these murders other than to take the suspect into custody for questioning. The alternative was to close the books on the crime and forget it, with the suspect at large. This is a grave choice for a society in which two-thirds of the murders already are closed out as insoluble.

Finally, we can but echo the words of Chief Judge Lumbard of the Second Circuit in the recent case of *United States v. Cone*, 354 F.2d 119, at 126–27 (1965):

> The fact is that in many serious crimes—cases of murder, kidnapping, rape, burglary and robbery—the police often have no or few objective clues with which to start an investigation; a considerable percentage of those which are solved are solved in whole or in part through statements voluntarily made to the police by those who are suspects. Moreover, immediate questioning is often instrumental in recovering kidnapped persons or stolen goods as well as in solving the crime. Under these circumstances, the police should not be forced unnecessarily to bear obstructions that irretrievably forfeit the opportunity of securing information under circumstances of spontaneity most favorable to truth-telling and at a time when further information may be necessary to pursue the investigation, to apprehend others, and to prevent other crimes.
>
> Until the need for immediate advice is properly evaluated in light of the probable detrimental effect of such a requirement—an inquiry that cannot adequately be undertaken by courts examining the facts of particular cases—we think it highly undesirable to lay

---

[10] See Hoover, "Civil Liberties and Law Enforcement: The Role of the FBI," 37 *Iowa L. Rev.* 175, at 180–82 (1952).

effect on the releasing of guilty persons. Acheson stated that only about two cases a year were lost because of the requirement of prompt arraignment. Prof. Louis B. Schwartz of the University of Pennsylvania Law School testified at these hearings that very few proper convictions had been lost because of the *Mallory* rule.[11] On the other hand, there was contrary testimony at the hearings—particularly by the Chief of Police of Washington—to the effect that the rule had hampered law enforcement and resulted in freeing guilty persons.

Faced with a welter of contradictory testimony, a majority of the House Committee on the District of Columbia concluded that there was a relationship between the *Mallory* rule and the increase in the District of Columbia crime rate; but a sizable minority stated that there was nothing to connect the increase in the crime rate to the requirement of prompt arraignment.

Judge George Edwards of the Sixth Circuit Court of Appeals sides with those who believe that prompt arraignment does not have a deleterious effect on law enforcement. During Judge Edwards's tenure as Police Commissioner of Detroit, suspects were taken promptly before a judge and "... [T]he town did not fall apart. Murder and pillage did not run rampant."[12] Judge Edwards is convinced that the decision by Detroit to apply federal arraignment standards made law enforcement *more* rather than *less* effective, since many citizens began to believe that all people, regardless of race and color, were receiving equal treatment.

In New York City, the argument over the utility of confessions in law enforcement has waged hot and furious. The police commissioner estimated in September 1965 that confessions had been essential to conviction in half the 1964 homicides which resulted ultimately in a guilty verdict. Manhattan District Attorney Frank Hogan has said that the police are heavily dependent on confessions, and that

down a rule which would deprive the police of the opportunity to question suspects and to use such statements as are found to have been given voluntarily and to have been procured fairly. In our country, a most valuable right of law-abiding citizens who make up the great majority of our people is the right to be protected against law breakers and criminal interference with their liberty and property. This right can be enjoyed only if those who have the responsibility for law enforcement are able to apprehend and prosecute an appreciable percentage of wrongdoers and solve an appreciable percentage of serious offenses. A time such as the present, when there is grave and growing public concern about the increasing ineffectiveness of law enforcement, and when there is growing legislative concern about the proper scope of the rights of persons accused of crime, is not a time for the courts to stifle or preempt the attempts to reach a reasoned compromise by announcing novel doctrines, constitutional or otherwise, or by extending old doctrines, in novel ways, so that law enforcement will be further crippled and made more difficult.

In his opinion, Judge Lumbard cited statistics from two California cities which revealed that between 75 and 90 percent of all persons charged with crimes in 1960 had given confessions or made admissions in less than two hours of station-house questioning. He also cited the conclusion of the New York City Police Commissioner that 50 percent of the murders committed in 1963 and 1964 which had been solved had in fact been solved either in whole or in part by a confession.[2]

As public servants of the people of Arizona, chosen by them to help maintain law and order, we carry an awesome burden. We fear the consequences of a rule by this Court that the Sixth Amendment, as applied to the states through the due process clause of the Fourteenth Amendment, requires that no suspect can be questioned without warning that he has a right to counsel at the interrogation stage of a criminal proceeding. Such a requirement may well put an end to all meaningful questioning since, as Justice Jackson wrote in *Watts v. Indiana*, 338 U.S. 49, at 59, "... the whole

---

[11] *H. R. Rep. No. 176*, 89th Cong., 1st Sess. (1965); see also *Hearings on H. R. 5688 and S. 1526 Before the Senate Committee on the District of Columbia*, 89th Cong., 1st Sess., pts. 1–2 (1965).

[12] *The New York Times*, Dec. 7, 1965, p. 33.

[2] 354 F.2d 119, at 126.

purpose of police interrogation will be lost if a suspect is entitled to have a lawyer during preliminary questioning, since "any lawyer worth his fee will tell him to keep his mouth shut."[13]

In contrast, New York Supreme Court Justice Nathan Sobel has described the view that confessions are vital to law enforcement as "carelessly nurtured nonsense." Judge Sobel studied 1,000 Brooklyn indictments from February to April 1965 and concluded that fewer than 10 percent involved confessions.[14] Brooklyn District Attorney Aaron Koota also has disagreed with his Manhattan counterpart; Koota believes that a person should have a lawyer at the moment he comes into contact with the law.

The above arguments—and many others which could be cited—demonstrate clearly that there is no way to know with any certainty whether judicial recognition of the full meaning of the Sixth Amendment will severely handicap the police; ultimately, the debate comes down to a conflict of opinion. As counsel for the appellant, we are not arguing that the extension of the right to counsel to the interrogation period will have no effect whatever on the efficiency of the law enforcement process. We do assert that whatever unpredictable decline occurs will be more than balanced by the increased integrity of the judicial system and the protection of what are, in fact, the constitutional rights of the individual.

A requirement of warning when station-house interrogation begins would make the Fifth and Sixth Amendment rights effective rather than ephemeral. Public defender systems and other methods for providing counsel for indigent suspects could be expanded to make legal services available at the time they are most needed. Suspects would be able to make a voluntary decision as to whether they wish legal assistance; if they wish, they would be able knowingly and intelligently to waive their right to counsel. Perhaps the optimum procedure would be to take suspects promptly before a magistrate and initiate formal judicial proceedings; such a procedure would

[A]ny lawyer worth his salt will tell the suspect in no uncertain terms to make no statement to the police under any circumstances."

We do not mean to imply that there is no need to inquire further into whether the optimal balance between the protection of individual rights and the legitimate needs of society has been struck at present. Public and private agencies are heavily engaged in research projects designed to analyze and evaluate prearraignment procedures, and it would be a mistake for this Court to jump the gun and issue hard and fast rules before the results of these studies are known. The President's Commission on Law Enforcement and Administration of Justice, the District of Columbia Crime Commission, the American Bar Foundation, and the Georgetown Law Center, among others, are undertaking independent examinations of the significance of station-house questioning in crime detection and law enforcement. The American Law Institute is drafting a code of prearraignment procedure, following a thorough study of the rights accorded suspects prior to the time they are first brought before a judicial officer. In some jurisdictions, experiments in station-house procedure are being undertaken.

These studies and experiments will provide much knowledge which currently does not exist. With systematic data, legislatures and courts will be better able to fashion procedures which maximize both the protection accorded the individual and the needs of society. For this reason, if for no other, we believe that this Court should decide *Miranda v. Arizona* on the basis of established constitutional principles.

We therefore urge the Court: (1) not to preclude responsible legislative action in the future by abandoning at this time its traditional approach to the admissibility of station-house confessions and adopting in its place an inflexible constitutional rule, and (2) to uphold the decision of the Arizona Supreme Court since appellant confessed voluntarily and without coercion of any kind.

---

[13] *The New York Times*, Dec. 2, 1965, p. 1.

[14] *N.Y.L.J.*, Nov. 22, 1965, at 1, 4–5.

bring state practice in line with contemporary federal practice under the *McNabb-Mallory* rule. At any rate, we are convinced that a legal system which makes counsel available to the uninformed indigent only after it is really too late to matter has not meaningfully enforced the command of the Sixth Amendment.

. . . .

III.   Decision of the Court and Dissenting Opinions*

Mr. CHIEF JUSTICE WARREN delivered the opinion of the Court.

The cases before us raise questions which go to the roots of our concepts of American criminal jurisprudence: the restraints society must observe consistent with the Federal Constitution in prosecuting individuals for crime. More specifically, we deal with the admissibility of statements obtained from an individual who is subjected to custodial police interrogation and the necessity for procedures which assure that the individual is accorded his privilege under the Fifth Amendment to the Constitution not to be compelled to incriminate himself.

We dealt with certain phases of this problem recently in *Escobedo v. Illinois*, 378 U.S. 478 (1964). There, as in the four cases before us, law enforcement officials took the defendant into custody and interrogated him in a police station for the purpose of obtaining a confession. The police did not effectively advise him of his right to remain silent or of his right to consult with his attorney. Rather, they confronted him with an alleged accomplice who accused him of having perpetrated a murder. When the defendant denied the accusation and said "I didn't shoot Manuel, you did it," they handcuffed him and took him to an interrogation room. There, while handcuffed and standing, he was questioned for four hours until he confessed. During this interrogation, the police denied his request to speak to his attorney, and they prevented his retained attorney, who had come to the police station, from consulting with him. At his trial, the State, over his objection, introduced the confession against him. We held that the statements thus made were constitutionally inadmissible. . . .

We start here, as we did in *Escobedo*, with the premise that our holding is not an innovation in our jurisprudence but is an application of principles long recognized and applied in other settings. We have undertaken a thorough re-examination of the *Escobedo* decision and the principles it announced, and we reaffirm it. That case was but an explication of basic rights that are enshrined in our Constitution—that "No person . . . shall be compelled in any criminal case to be a witness against himself," and that "the accused shall . . . have the Assistance of Counsel"—rights which were put in jeopardy in that case through official overbearing. These precious rights were fixed in our Constitution only after centuries of persecution and struggle. . . .

Our holding will be spelled out with some specificity in the pages which follow but briefly stated it is this: the prosecution may not use statements . . . stemming

---

*Author's note: printed below is an edited version of the decision of five members of the Court in *Miranda v. Arizona*, 384 U.S. 436 (1966), decided along with *Vignera v. New York*, *Westover v. United States*, and *California v. Stewart*; the dissenting opinions of Justice Clark and Justice Harlan have been included, but Justice White's dissent has been omitted. Footnotes have been edited and renumbered. Material in brackets has been added by the author.

from custodial interrogation of the defendant unless it demonstrates the use of procedural safeguards effective to secure the privilege against self-incrimination. By custodial interrogation, we mean questioning initiated by law enforcement officers after a person has been taken into custody or otherwise deprived of his freedom of action in any significant way. As for the procedural safeguards to be employed, unless other fully effective means are devised to inform accused persons of their right of silence and to assure a continuous opportunity to exercise it, the following measures are required. Prior to any questioning, the person must be warned that he has a right to remain silent, that any statement he does make may be used as evidence against him, and that he has a right to the presence of an attorney, either retained or appointed. The defendant may waive effectuation of these rights, provided the waiver is made voluntarily, knowingly and intelligently. If, however, he indicates in any manner and at any stage of the process that he wishes to consult with an attorney before speaking there can be no questioning. Likewise, if the individual is alone and indicates in any manner that he does not wish to be interrogated, the police may not question him. The mere fact that he may have answered some questions or volunteered some statements on his own does not deprive him of the right to refrain from answering any further inquiries until he has consulted with an attorney and thereafter consents to be questioned.

I

The constitutional issue we decide in each of these cases is the admissibility of statements obtained from a defendant questioned while in custody and deprived of his freedom of action. In each, the defendant was questioned by police officers, detectives, or a prosecuting attorney in a room in which he was cut off from the outside world. In none of these cases was the defendant given a full and effective warning of his rights at the outset of the interrogation process. In all the cases, the questioning elicited oral admissions, and in three of them, signed statements as well which were admitted at their trials. They all thus share salient features—incommunicado interrogation of individuals in a police-dominated atmosphere, resulting in self-incriminating statements without full warnings of constitutional rights.

An understanding of the nature and setting of this in-custody interrogation is essential to our decisions today. The difficulty in depicting what transpires at such interrogations stems from the fact that in this country they have largely taken place incommunicado. From extensive factual studies undertaken in the early 1930's, including the famous Wickersham Report to Congress by a Presidential Commission, it is clear that police violence and the "third degree" flourished at that time. In a series of cases decided by this Court long after these studies, the police resorted to physical brutality—beatings, hanging, whipping—and to sustained and protracted questioning incommunicado in order to extort confessions. The 1961 Commission on Civil Rights found much evidence to indicate that "some policemen still resort to physical force to obtain confessions." . . . [T]he use of physical brutality and violence is not, unfortunately, relegated to the past or to any part of the country. Only recently in Kings County, New York, the police brutally beat, kicked and placed lighted cigarette butts on the back of a potential witness under interrogation for the purpose of securing a statement incriminating a third party. . . . [The opinion next cites four additional cases of police brutality.]

The examples given above are undoubtedly the exception now, but they are sufficiently widespread to be the object of concern. Unless a proper limitation upon custodial interrogation is achieved—such as these decisions will advance—there can be no assurance that practices of this nature will be eradicated in the foreseeable future. . . .

. . . [T]he modern practice of in-custody interrogation is psychologically rather than physically oriented. . . . Interrogation still takes place in privacy. Privacy results in secrecy and this in turn results in a gap in our knowledge as to what in fact goes on in the interrogation rooms. A valuable source of information about present police practices, however, may be found in various police manuals and texts which document procedures employed with success in the past, and which recommend various other effective tactics. These texts are used by law enforcement agencies themselves as guides. . . . [B]y considering these texts and other data, it is possible to describe procedures observed and noted around the country. . . . [The opinion quotes extensively from the leading manuals on interrogation, Inbau and Reid, *Criminal Interrogation and Confessions* (1962), and O'Hara, *Fundamentals of Criminal Investigation* (1959).]

From these representative samples of interrogation techniques, the setting prescribed by the manuals and observed in practice becomes clear. In essence, it is this: To be alone with the subject is essential to prevent distraction and to deprive him of any outside support. The aura of confidence in his guilt undermines his will to resist. He merely confirms the preconceived story the police seek to have him describe. Patience and persistence, at times relentless questioning, are employed. . . . When normal procedures fail to produce the needed result, the police may resort to deceptive stratagems such as giving false legal advice. It is important to keep the subject off balance, for example, by trading on his insecurity about himself or his surroundings. The police then persuade, trick, or cajole him out of exercising his constitutional rights.

Even without employing brutality, the "third degree" or the specific stratagems described above, the very fact of custodial interrogation exacts a heavy toll on individual liberty and trades on the weakness of individuals.[1]

. . . [I]n the cases before us today, given this background, we concern ourselves primarily with this interrogation atmosphere and the evils it can bring. In . . . *Miranda v. Arizona,* the police arrested the defendant and took him to a special interrogation room where they secured a confession. In . . . *Vignera v. New York,* the defendant made oral admissions to the police after interrogation in the afternoon, and then signed an inculpatory statement upon being questioned by an assistant district attorney later the same evening. In . . . *Westover v. United States,* the defendant was handed over to the Federal Bureau of Investigation by local authorities after they had detained and interrogated him for a lengthy period, both at night and the following morning. After some two hours of questioning, the federal officers had obtained signed statements from the defendant. Lastly, in . . . *California v. Stewart,* the local police held the defendant five days in the station and interrogated him on nine separate occasions before they secured his inculpatory statement.

In these cases, we might not find the defendants' statements to have been involuntary in traditional terms. Our concern for adequate safeguards to protect precious Fifth Amendment rights is, of course, not lessened in the slightest. In each of the cases, the defendant was thrust into an unfamiliar atmosphere and run

---

[1] Interrogation procedures may even give rise to a false confession. The most recent conspicuous example occurred in New York, in 1964, when a Negro of limited intelligence confessed to two brutal murders and a rape which he had not committed. When this was discovered, the prosecutor was reported as saying: "Call it what you want—brain-washing, hypnosis, fright. They made him give an untrue confession. The only thing I don't believe is that Whitmore was beaten." *N.Y. Times,* Jan. 28, 1965, p. 1, col. 5. In two other instances, similar events had occurred. . . .

through menacing police interrogation procedures. The potentiality for compulsion is forcefully apparent, for example, in *Miranda*, where the indigent Mexican defendant was a seriously disturbed individual with pronounced sexual fantasies, and in *Stewart*, in which the defendant was an indigent Los Angeles Negro who had dropped out of school in the sixth grade. To be sure, the records do not evince overt physical coercion or patent psychological ploys. The fact remains that in none of these cases did the officers undertake to afford appropriate safeguards at the outset of the interrogation to insure that the statements were truly the product of free choice.

It is obvious that such an interrogation environment is created for no purpose other than to subjugate the individual to the will of his examiner. This atmosphere carries its own badge of intimidation. To be sure, this is not physical intimidation, but it is equally destructive of human dignity.[2] The current practice of incommunicado interrogation is at odds with one of our Nation's most cherished principles —that the individual may not be compelled to incriminate himself. Unless adequate protective devices are employed to dispel the compulsion inherent in custodial surroundings, no statement obtained from the defendant can truly be the product of his free choice.

From the foregoing, we can readily perceive an intimate connection between the privilege against self-incrimination and police custodial questioning. It is fitting to turn to history and precedent underlying the Self-Incrimination Clause and to determine its applicability in this situation.

II

We sometimes forget how long it has taken to establish the privilege against self-incrimination, the sources from which it came and the fervor with which it was defended. . . . [O]ur accusatory system of criminal justice demands that the government seeking to punish an individual produce the evidence against him by its own independent labors, rather than by the cruel, simple expedient of compelling it from his own mouth. . . . In sum, the privilege is fulfilled only when the person is guaranteed the right "to remain silent unless he chooses to speak in the unfettered exercise of his own will." *Malloy v. Hogan*, 378 U.S. 1, 8 (1964).

The question in these cases is whether the privilege is fully applicable during a period of custodial interrogation. In this Court, the privilege has consistently been accorded a liberal construction. . . . We are satisfied that all the principles embodied in the privilege apply to informal compulsion exerted by law-enforcement officers during in-custody questioning. An individual swept from familiar surroundings into police custody, surrounded by antagonistic forces, and subjected to the techniques of persuasion described above cannot be otherwise than under compulsion to speak. As

---

[2] The absurdity of denying that a confession obtained under these circumstances is compelled is aptly portrayed by an example in Professor Sutherland's recent article, "Crime and Confession," 79 *Harv. L. Rev.* 21, 37 (1965):

Suppose a well-to-do testatrix says she intends to will her property to Elizabeth. John and James want her to bequeath it to them instead. They capture the testatrix, put her in a carefully designed room, out of touch with everyone but themselves and their convenient 'witnesses,' keep her secluded there for hours while they make insistent demands, weary her with contradictions and finally induce her to execute the will in their favor. . . . Would any judge of probate accept the will so procured as the 'voluntary' act of the testatrix?

a practical matter, the compulsion to speak in the isolated setting of the police station may well be greater than in courts or other official investigations, where there are often impartial observers to guard against intimidation or trickery. . . .

Because of the adoption by Congress of Rule 5 (a) of the Federal Rules of Criminal Procedure, and this Court's effectuation of that Rule in *McNabb v. United States*, 318 U.S. 332 (1943), and *Mallory v. United States*, 354 U.S. 449 (1957), we have had little occasion in the past quarter century to reach the constitutional issues in dealing with federal interrogations. These supervisory rules, requiring production of an arrested person before a commissioner "without unnecessary delay" and excluding evidence obtained in default of that statutory obligation, were nonetheless responsive to the same considerations of Fifth Amendment policy that unavoidably face us now as to the States. . . .

Our decision in *Malloy v. Hogan*, 378 U.S. 1 (1964), necessitates an examination of the scope of the privilege in state cases as well. In *Malloy*, we squarely held the privilege applicable to the States. . . . Aside from the holding itself, the reasoning in *Malloy* made clear what had already become apparent—that the substantive and procedural safeguards surrounding admissibility of confessions in state cases had become exceedingly exacting, reflecting all the policies embedded in the privilege. . . . The voluntariness doctrine in the state cases, as *Malloy* indicates, encompasses all interrogation practices which are likely to exert such pressure upon an individual as to disable him from making a free and rational choice. The implications of this proposition were elaborated in our decision in *Escobedo v. Illinois*, 378 U.S. 478, decided one week after *Malloy* applied the privilege to the States.

Our holding there stressed the fact that the police had not advised the defendant of his constitutional privilege to remain silent at the outset of the interrogation. . . . This was no isolated factor, but an essential ingredient in our decision. The entire thrust of police interrogation there, as in all the cases today, was to put the defendant in such an emotional state as to impair his capacity for rational judgment. The abdication of the constitutional privilege—the choice on his part to speak to the police—was not made knowingly or competently because of the failure to apprise him of his right; the compelling atmosphere of the in-custody interrogation, and not an independent decision on his part, caused the defendant to speak.

A different phase of the *Escobedo* decision was significant in its attention to the absence of counsel during the questioning. . . . In *Escobedo* . . . the police . . . denied his request for the assistance of counsel. . . . The denial of the defendant's request for his attorney thus undermined his ability to exercise the privilege—to remain silent if he chose or to speak without any intimidation, blatant or subtle. The presence of counsel, in all the cases before us today, would be the adequate protective device necessary to make the process of police interrogation conform to the dictates of the privilege. His presence would insure that statements made in the government-established atmosphere are not the product of compulsion.

It was in this manner that *Escobedo* explicated another facet of the pre-trial privilege, noted in many of the Court's prior decisions: the protection of rights at trial. That counsel is present when statements are taken from an individual during interrogation obviously enhances the integrity of the fact-finding processes in court. The presence of an attorney, and the warnings delivered to the individual, enable the defendant under otherwise compelling circumstances to tell his story without fear, effectively, and in a way that eliminates the evils in the interrogation process. Without the protections flowing from adequate warnings and the rights of counsel, "all the careful safeguards erected around the giving of testimony, whether by an accused or any other witness, would become empty formalities in a procedure where the most compelling possible evidence of guilt, a confession, would have already been obtained at the unsupervised pleasure of the police." *Mapp v. Ohio*, 367 U.S. 643, 685 (1961) (HARLAN, J., dissenting).

III

Today, then, there can be no doubt that the Fifth Amendment privilege is available outside of criminal court proceedings and serves to protect persons in all settings in which their freedom of action is curtailed from being compelled to incriminate themselves. We have concluded that without proper safeguards the process of in-custody interrogation of persons suspected or accused of crime contains inherently compelling pressures which work to undermine the individual's will to resist and to compel him to speak where he would not otherwise do so freely. In order to combat these pressures and to permit a full opportunity to exercise the privilege against self-incrimination, the accused must be adequately and effectively apprised of his rights and the exercise of those rights must be fully honored.

It is impossible for us to foresee the potential alternatives for protecting the privilege which might be devised by Congress or the States in the exercise of their creative rule-making capacities. Therefore we cannot say that the Constitution necessarily requires adherence to any particular solution for the inherent compulsions of the interrogation process as it is presently conducted. Our decision in no way creates a constitutional straitjacket which will handicap sound efforts at reform, nor is it intended to have this effect. We encourage Congress and the States to continue their laudable search for increasingly effective ways of protecting the rights of the individual while promoting efficient enforcement of our criminal laws. However, unless we are shown other procedures which are at least as effective in apprising accused persons of their right to silence and in assuring a continuous opportunity to exercise it, the following safeguards must be observed.

At the outset, if a person in custody is to be subjected to interrogation, he must first be informed in clear and unequivocal terms that he has the right to remain silent. For those unaware of the privilege, the warning is needed simply to make them aware of it—the threshold requirement for an intelligent decision as to its exercise. . . .

The Fifth Amendment privilege is so fundamental to our system of constitutional rule and the expedient of giving an adequate warning as to the availability of the privilege so simple, we will not pause to inquire in individual cases whether the defendant was aware of his rights without a warning being given. Assessments of the knowledge the defendant possessed, based on information as to his age, education, intelligence, or prior contact with authorities can never be more than speculation; a warning is a clear-cut fact. More important whatever the background of the person interrogated, a warning at the time of the interrogation is indispensable to overcome its pressures and to insure that the individual knows he is free to exercise the privilege at that point in time.

The warning of the right to remain silent must be accompanied by the explanation that anything said can and will be used against the individual in court. . . .

The circumstances surrounding in-custody interrogation can operate very quickly to overbear the will of one merely made aware of his privilege by his interrogators. Therefore, the right to have counsel present at the interrogation is indispensable to the protection of the Fifth Amendment privilege under the system we delineate today. Our aim is to assure that the individual's right to choose between silence and speech remains unfettered throughout the interrogation process. . . . Thus, the need for counsel to protect the Fifth Amendment privilege comprehends not merely a right to consult with counsel prior to questioning, but also to have counsel present during any questioning if the defendant so desires.

The presence of counsel at the interrogation may serve several significant subsidiary functions as well. If the accused decides to talk to his interrogators, the assistance of counsel can mitigate the dangers of untrustworthiness. With a lawyer present the likelihood that the police will practice coercion is reduced, and if coercion is nevertheless exercised the lawyer can testify to it in court. The presence of a lawyer can also help to guarantee that the accused gives a fully accurate statement to the police and that the statement is rightly reported by the prosecution at trial. . . .

An individual need not make a pre-interrogation request for a lawyer. . . . No effective waiver of the right to counsel during interrogation can be recognized unless specifically made after the warnings we here delineate have been given. The accused who does not know his rights and therefore does not make a request may be the person who most needs counsel. As the California Supreme Court has aptly put it:

> Finally, we must recognize that the imposition of the requirement for the request would discriminate against the defendant who does not know his rights. The defendant who does not ask for counsel is the very defendant who most needs counsel. We cannot penalize a defendant who, not understanding his constitutional rights, does not make the formal request and by such failure demonstrates his helplessness. To require the request would be to favor the defendant whose sophistication or status has fortuitously prompted him to make it.
>
> *People v. Dorado,* 62 Cal.2d 338, 351.

In *Carnley v. Cochran,* 369 U.S. 506, 513 (1962), we stated: "[I]t is settled that where the assistance of counsel is a constitutional requisite, the right to be furnished counsel does not depend on a request." This proposition applies with equal force in the context of providing counsel to protect an accused's Fifth Amendment privilege in the face of interrogation. . . .

Accordingly we hold that an individual held for interrogation must be clearly informed that he has the right to consult with a lawyer and to have the lawyer with him during interrogation under the system for protecting the privilege we delineate today. . . . No amount of circumstantial evidence that the person may have been aware of this right will suffice to stand in its stead. Only through such a warning is there ascertainable assurance that the accused was aware of this right.

If an individual indicates that he wishes the assistance of counsel before any interrogation occurs, the authorities cannot rationally ignore or deny his request on the basis that the individual does not have or cannot afford a retained attorney. In fact, were we to limit these constitutional rights to those who can retain an attorney, our decisions today would be of little significance. The cases before us as well as the vast majority of confession cases with which we have dealt in the past involve those unable to retain counsel. . . .

In order fully to apprise a person interrogated of the extent of his rights under this system then, it is necessary to warn him not only that he has the right to consult with an attorney, but also that if he is indigent a lawyer will be appointed to represent him. Without this additional warning, the admonition of the right to consult with counsel would often be understood as meaning only that he can consult with a lawyer if he has one or has the funds to obtain one. The warning of a right to counsel would be hollow if not couched in terms that would convey to the indigent—the person most often subjected to interrogation—the knowledge that he too has a right to have counsel present. . . .

If the interrogation continues without the presence of an attorney and a statement is taken, a heavy burden rests on the Government to demonstrate that the defendant knowingly and intelligently waived his privilege against self-incrimination and his right to retained or appointed counsel. . . . Since the State is responsible for establishing the isolated circumstances under which the interrogation takes place and has the only means of making available corroborated evidence of warnings given during incommunicado interrogation, the burden is rightly on its shoulders.

An express statement that the individual is willing to make a statement and does not want an attorney followed closely by a statement could constitute a waiver. But a valid waiver will not be presumed simply from the silence of the accused after warnings are given or simply from the fact that a confession was in fact eventually obtained. . . .

Whatever the testimony of the authorities as to waiver of rights by an accused, the fact of lengthy interrogation or incommunicado incarceration before a statement is made is strong evidence that the accused did not validly waive his rights. In these circumstances the fact that the individual eventually made a statement is consistent with the conclusion that the compelling influence of the interrogation finally forced him to do so. It is inconsistent with any notion of a voluntary relinquishment of the privilege. Moreover, any evidence that the accused was threatened, tricked, or cajoled into a waiver will, of course, show that the defendant did not voluntarily waive his privilege. . . .

Our decision is not intended to hamper the traditional function of police officers in investigating crime. . . . When an individual is in custody on probable cause, the police may, of course, seek out evidence in the field to be used at trial against him. Such investigation may include inquiry of persons not under restraint. General on-the-scene questioning as to facts surrounding a crime or other general questioning of citizens in the fact-finding process is not affected by our holding. It is an act of responsible citizenship for individuals to give whatever information they may have to aid in law enforcement. In such situations the compelling atmosphere inherent in the process of in-custody interrogation is not necessarily present.

In dealing with statements obtained through interrogation, we do not purport to find all confessions inadmissible. Confessions remain a proper element in law enforcement. Any statement given freely and voluntarily without any compelling influences is, of course, admissible in evidence. The fundamental import of the privilege while an individual is in custody is not whether he is allowed to talk to the police without the benefit of warnings and counsel, but whether he can be interrogated. There is no requirement that police stop a person who enters a police station and states that he wishes to confess to a crime, or a person who calls the police to offer a confession or any other statement he desires to make. Volunteered statements of any kind are not barred by the Fifth Amendment and their admissibility is not affected by our holding today.

[In accordance with the principles stated above, the Court here overrules its earlier, conflicting opinions in *Crooker v. California*, 357 U.S. 433 (1958), and *Cicenia v. Lagay*, 357 U.S. 504 (1958).]

IV

A recurrent argument made in these cases is that society's need for interrogation outweighs the privilege. This argument is not unfamiliar to this Court. . . . The whole thrust of our foregoing discussion demonstrates that the Constitution has prescribed the rights of the individual when confronted with the power of government when it provided in the Fifth Amendment that an individual cannot be compelled to be a witness against himself. That right cannot be abridged. . . .

In announcing these principles, we are not unmindful of the burdens which law enforcement officials must bear, often under trying circumstances. We also fully recognize the obligation of all citizens to aid in enforcing the criminal laws. This Court, while protecting individual rights, has always given ample latitude to law enforcement agencies in the legitimate exercise of their duties. The limits we have placed on the interrogation process should not constitute an undue interference with a proper system of law enforcement. As we have noted, our decision does not in any way preclude police from carrying out their traditional investigatory functions. Although confessions may play an important role in some convictions, the cases before us present graphic examples of the overstatement of the "need" for confessions. In each case authorities conducted interrogations ranging up to five days in duration despite the presence, through standard investigating practices, of considerable evidence against each defendant.[3] Further examples are chronicled in our prior cases. . . .

Over the years the Federal Bureau of Investigation has compiled an exemplary record of effective law enforcement while advising any suspect or arrested person, at the outset of an interview, that he is not required to make a statement, that any statement may be used against him in court, that the individual may obtain the services of an attorney of his own choice, and, more recently, that he has a right to free counsel if he is unable to pay. . . .

The practice of the FBI can readily be emulated by state and local enforcement agencies. The argument that the FBI deals with different crimes than are dealt with by state authorities does not mitigate the significance of the FBI experience.[4]

The experience in some other countries also suggests that the danger to law enforcement in curbs on interrogation is overplayed. The English procedure since 1912 under the Judge's Rules is significant. As recently strengthened, the Rules require that a cautionary warning be given an accused by a police officer as soon as he has evidence that affords reasonable grounds for suspicion; they also require that any statement made be given by the accused without questioning by police. The right of the individual to consult with an attorney during this period is expressly recognized.

The safeguards present under Scottish law may be even greater than in England. Scottish judicial decisions bar use in evidence of most confessions obtained through police interrogation. In India, confessions made to police not in the presence of a magistrate have been excluded by rule of evidence since 1872, at a time when it operated under British law. Identical provisions appear in the Evidence Ordinance of Ceylon, enacted in 1895. Similarly, in our country the Uniform Code of Military Justice has long provided that no suspect may be interrogated without first being warned of his right not to make a statement and that any statement he makes may be used against him. Denial of the right to consult counsel during interrogation has also been proscribed by military tribunals. There appears to have been no marked detrimental effect on criminal law enforcement in these jurisdictions as a result of these rules. Conditions of law enforcement in our country are sufficiently similar to permit reference to this experience as assurance that lawlessness will not result from

[3] Miranda, Vignera, and Westover were identified by eyewitnesses. Marked bills from the bank robbed were found in Westover's car. Articles stolen from the victim as well as from several other robbery victims were found in Stewart's home at the outset of the investigation.

[4] Among the crimes within the enforcement jurisdiction of the FBI are kidnapping . . . white slavery . . . bank robbery . . . interstate transportation and sale of stolen property . . . all manner of conspiracies . . . and violations of civil rights.

warning an individual of his rights or allowing him to exercise them. Moreover, it is consistent with our legal system that we give at least as much protection to these rights as is given in the jurisdictions described. We deal in our country with rights grounded in a specific requirement of the Fifth Amendment of the Constitution, whereas other jurisdictions arrived at their conclusions on the basis of principles of justice not so specifically defined.

It is also urged upon us that we withhold decision on this issue until state legislative bodies and advisory groups have had an opportunity to deal with these problems by rule making. We have already pointed out that the Constitution does not require any specific code of procedures for protecting the privilege against self-incrimination during custodial interrogation. Congress and the States are free to develop their own safeguards for the privilege, so long as they are fully as effective as those described above in informing accused persons of their right of silence and in affording a continuous opportunity to exercise it. In any event, however, the issues presented are of constitutional dimensions and must be determined by the courts. . . . Judicial solutions to problems of constitutional dimension have evolved decade by decade. As courts have been presented with the need to enforce constitutional rights, they have found means of doing so. That was our responsibility when *Escobedo* was before us and it is our responsibility today. Where rights secured by the Constitution are involved, there can be no rule making or legislation which would abrogate them.

V

Because of the nature of the problem and because of its recurrent significance in numerous cases, we have to this point discussed the relationship of the Fifth Amendment privilege to police interrogation without specific concentration on the facts of the cases before us. We turn now to these facts to consider the application to these cases of the constitutional principles discussed above. In each instance, we have concluded that statements were obtained from the defendant under circumstances that did not meet constitutional standards for protection of the privilege.

No. 759. Miranda v. Arizona   On March 13, 1963, petitioner, Ernesto Miranda, was arrested at his home and taken in custody to a Phoenix police station. He was there identified by the complaining witness. The police then took him to "Interrogation Room No. 2" of the detective bureau. There he was questioned by two police officers. The officers admitted at trial that Miranda was not advised that he had a right to have an attorney present. Two hours later the officers emerged from the interrogation room with a written confession signed by Miranda. At the top of the statement was a typed paragraph stating that the confession was made voluntarily, without threats or promises of immunity and "with full knowledge of my legal rights, understanding any statement I make may be used against me."

At his trial before a jury, the written confession was admitted into evidence over the objection of defense counsel, and the officers testified to the prior oral confession made by Miranda during the interrogation. Miranda was found guilty of kidnapping and rape. He was sentenced to 20 to 30 years' imprisonment on each count, the sentences to run concurrently. On appeal, the Supreme Court of Arizona held that Miranda's constitutional rights were not violated in obtaining the confession and affirmed the conviction. . . . In reaching its decision, the court emphasized heavily the fact that Miranda did not specifically request counsel.

We reverse. From the testimony of the officers and by the admission of respondent, it is clear that Miranda was not in any way apprised of his right to consult with an attorney and to have one present during the interrogation, nor was his right not to be compelled to incriminate himself effectively protected in any other manner. Without these warnings the statements were inadmissible. The mere fact that he signed a statement which contained a typed-in clause stating that he had "full knowledge" of his "legal rights" does not approach the knowing and intelligent waiver required to relinquish constitutional rights. . . .

[The Court's discussion of the three cases considered along with *Miranda*— *Vignera v. New York, Westover v. United States,* and *California v. Stewart*—has been omitted.]

Mr. JUSTICE CLARK, *dissenting.* . . .

It is with regret that I find it necessary to write in these cases. However, I am unable to join the majority because its opinion goes too far on too little, while my dissenting brethren do not go quite far enough. Nor can I agree with the Court's criticism of the present practices of police and investigatory agencies as to custodial interrogation. The materials it refers to as "police manuals" are, as I read them, merely writings in this field by professors and some police officers. Not one is shown by the record here to be the official manual of any police department, much less in universal use in crime detection. Moreover, the examples of police brutality mentioned by the Court are rare exceptions to the thousands of cases that appear every year in the law reports. The police agencies—all the way from municipal and state forces to the federal bureaus—are responsible for law enforcement and public safety in this country. I am proud of their efforts, which in my view are not fairly characterized by the Court's opinion. . . .

Custodial interrogation has long been recognized as "undoubtedly an essential tool in effective law enforcement. . . ." Recognition of this fact should put us on guard against the promulgation of doctrinaire rules. . . . Indeed, even in *Escobedo* the Court never hinted that an affirmative "waiver" was a prerequisite to questioning; that the burden of proof as to waiver was on the prosecution; that the presence of counsel—absent a waiver—during interrogation was required; that a waiver can be withdrawn at the will of the accused; that counsel must be furnished during an accusatory stage to those unable to pay; nor that admissions and exculpatory statements are "confessions. . . ."

The rule prior to today . . . depended upon "a totality of circumstances evidencing an involuntary . . . admission of guilt. . . ."

I would continue to follow that rule. Under the "totality of circumstances" rule . . . I would consider in each case whether the police officer prior to custodial interrogation added the warning that the suspect might have counsel present at the interrogation and, further, that a court would appoint one at his request if he was too poor to employ counsel. In the absence of warnings, the burden would be on the State to prove that counsel was knowingly and intelligently waived or that in the totality of the circumstances, including the failure to give the necessary warnings, the confession was clearly voluntary.

Rather than employing the arbitrary Fifth Amendment rule which the Court lays down I would follow the more pliable dictates of Due Process Clauses of the Fifth and Fourteenth Amendments which we are accustomed to administering and which we know from our cases are effective instruments in protecting persons in police custody. In this way we would not be acting in the dark. . . . It will be soon enough to go further when we are able to appraise with somewhat better accuracy the effect of such a holding. . . .

Mr. JUSTICE HARLAN, *whom Mr. JUSTICE STEWART and Mr. JUSTICE WHITE join, dissenting.*

I believe the decision of the Court represents poor constitutional law and entails harmful consequences for the country at large. How serious these consequences may prove to be only time can tell. But the basic flaws in the Court's justification seem to me readily apparent now once all sides of the problem are considered.

I. Introduction

At the outset, it is well to note exactly what is required by the Court's new constitutional code of rules for confessions.... [Justice Harlan here repeats the rules spelled out in the opinion of the Court.]

... [T]he thrust of the new rules is to negate all pressures, to reinforce the nervous or ignorant suspect, and ultimately to discourage any confession at all. The aim in short is toward "voluntariness" in a utopian sense, or to view it from a different angle, voluntariness with a vengeance.

To incorporate this notion into the Constitution requires a strained reading of history and precedent and a disregard of the very pragmatic concerns that alone may on occasion justify such strains. I believe that reasoned examination will show that the Due Process Clauses provide an adequate tool for coping with confessions and that, even if the Fifth Amendment privilege against self-incrimination be invoked, its precedents taken as a whole do not sustain the present rules. Viewed as a choice based on pure policy, these new rules prove to be a highly debatable if not one-sided appraisal of the competing interests, imposed over widespread objection, at the very time when judicial restraint is most called for by the circumstances.

II. Constitutional Premises

It is most fitting to begin an inquiry into the constitutional precedents by surveying the limits on confessions the Court has evolved under the Due Process Clause of the Fourteenth Amendment. This is so because these cases show that there exists a workable and effective means of dealing with confessions in a judicial manner; because the cases are the baseline from which the Court now departs and so serve to measure the actual as opposed to the professed distance it travels; and because examination of them helps reveal how the Court has coasted into its present position....

This ... line of decisions, testing admissibility by the Due Process Clause, began in 1936 with *Brown v. Mississippi*, 297 U.S. 278, and must now embrace somewhat more than 30 full opinions of the Court. While the voluntariness rubric was repeated in many instances ... the Court never pinned it down to a single meaning but on the contrary infused it with a number of different values. To travel quickly over the main themes, there was an initial emphasis on reliability ... supplemented by concern over the legality and fairness of the police practices ... in an "accusatorial" system of law enforcement ... and eventually by close attention to the individual's state of mind and capacity for effective choice.... The outcome was a continuing re-evaluation on the facts of each case of *how much* pressure on the suspect was permissible.

Among the criteria often taken into account were threats of imminent danger ... physical deprivations such as lack of sleep or food ... repeated or extended interrogation ... limits on access to counsel or friends ... length and illegality of detention under state law ... and individual weakness or incapacities.... Apart from direct physical coercion, however, no single default or fixed combination of them guaranteed exclusion, and synopses of the cases would serve little use because the overall gauge has been steadily changing, usually in the direction of restricting admissibility. . . .

There are several relevant lessons to be drawn from this constitutional history. The first is that with over 25 years of precedent the Court has developed an elaborate, sophisticated, and sensitive approach to admissibility of confessions. . . .

The second point is that in practice and from time to time in principle, the Court has given ample recognition to society's interest in suspect questioning as an instrument of law enforcement. Cases countenancing quite significant pressures can be cited without difficulty. . . .

I turn now to the Court's asserted reliance on the Fifth Amendment. . . . The Court's opinion in my view reveals no adequate basis for extending the Fifth Amendment's privilege against self-incrimination to the police station. Far more important, it fails to show that the Court's new rules are well supported, let alone compelled, by Fifth Amendment precedents. Instead, the new rules actually derive from quotation and analogy drawn from precedents under the Sixth Amendment, which should properly have no bearing on police interrogation.

The Court's opening contention, that the Fifth Amendment governs police station confessions, is perhaps not an impermissible extension of the law but it has little to commend itself in the present circumstances. Historically, the privilege against self-incrimination did not bear at all on the use of extra-legal confessions. . . . Even those who would readily enlarge the privilege must concede some linguistic difficulties since the Fifth Amendment in terms proscribes only compelling any person "in any criminal case to be a witness against himself. . . ."

The Fifth Amendment . . . has never been thought to forbid *all* pressure to incriminate one's self in the situations covered by it. . . . This is not to say that short of jail or torture any sanction is permissible in any case; policy and history alike may impose sharp limits. . . . However, the Court's unspoken assumption that *any* pressure violates the privilege is not supported by the precedents. . . .

The Court appears similarly wrong in thinking that precise knowledge of one's rights is a settled prerequisite under the Fifth Amendment to the loss of its protections. . . . No Fifth Amendment precedent is cited for the Court's contrary view. There might of course be reasons apart from Fifth Amendment precedent for requiring warning or any other safeguard on questioning but that is a different matter entirely. . . .

A closing word must be said about the Assistance of Counsel Clause of the Sixth Amendment, which is never expressly relied on by the Court but whose judicial precedents turn out to be linchpins of the confession rules announced today. . . . All these cases imparting glosses to the Sixth Amendment concerned counsel at trial or on appeal. While the Court finds no pertinent difference between judicial proceedings and police interrogation, I believe the differences are so vast as to disqualify wholly the Sixth Amendment precedents as suitable analogies in the present cases.[1]

The only attempt in this Court to carry the right to counsel into the station house occurred in *Escobedo*, the Court repeating several times that that stage was no less "critical" than trial itself. . . . This is hardly persuasive when we consider that a grand jury inquiry, the filing of a certiorari petition, and certainly the purchase of narcotics by an undercover agent from a prospective defendant may all be equally "critical" yet provision of counsel and advice on that score have never been thought compelled by the Constitution in such cases. The second reason why this right is so

---

[1] Since the Court conspicuously does not assert that the Sixth Amendment itself warrants its new police-interrogation rules, there is no reason now to draw out the extremely powerful historical and precedential evidence that the Amendment will bear no such meaning. . . .

freely extended for a criminal trial is the severe injustice risked by confronting an untrained defendant with a range of technical points of law, evidence, and tactics familiar to the prosecutor but not to himself. This danger shrinks markedly in the police station where indeed the lawyer in fulfilling his professional responsibilities of necessity may become an obstacle to truthfinding. . . . The Court's summary citation of the Sixth Amendment cases here seems to me best described as "the domino method of constitutional adjudication . . . wherein every explanatory statement in a previous opinion is made the basis for extension to a wholly different situation. . . ."

III. Policy Considerations

Examined as an expression of public policy, the Court's new regime proves so dubious that there can be no due compensation for its weakness in constitutional law. Foregoing discussion has shown, I think, how mistaken is the Court in implying that the Constitution has struck the balance in favor of the approach the Court takes. . . . Rather, precedent reveals that the Fourteenth Amendment in practice has been construed to strike a different balance, that the Fifth Amendment gives the Court little solid support in this context, and that the Sixth Amendment should have no bearing at all. Legal history has been stretched before to satisfy deep needs of society. In this instance, however, the Court has not and cannot make the powerful showing that its new rules are plainly desirable in the context of our society, something which is surely demanded before those rules are engrafted onto the Constitution and imposed on every State and county in the land.

Without at all subscribing to the generally black picture of police conduct painted by the Court, I think it must be frankly recognized at the outset that police questioning allowable under due process precedents may inherently entail some pressure on the suspect and may seek advantage in his ignorance or weaknesses. . . . Until today, the role of the Constitution has been only to sift out *undue* pressure, not to assure spontaneous confessions.

The Court's new rules aim to offset these minor pressures and disadvantages intrinsic to any kind of police interrogation. The rules do not serve due process interests in preventing blatant coercion since . . . they do nothing to contain the policeman who is prepared to lie from the start. . . .

What the Court largely ignores is that its rules impair, if they will not eventually serve wholly to frustrate, an instrument of law enforcement that has long and quite reasonably been thought worth the price paid for it.[2] There can be little doubt that the Court's new code would markedly decrease the number of confessions. To warn the suspect that he may remain silent and remind him that his confession may be used in court are minor obstructions. To require also an express waiver by the suspect and an end to questioning whenever he demurs must heavily handicap questioning. And to suggest or provide counsel for the suspect simply invites the end of the interrogation. . . .

How much harm this decision will inflict on law enforcement cannot fairly be predicted with accuracy. Evidence on the role of confessions is notoriously incomplete . . . and little is added by the Court's reference to the FBI experience and the

---

[2] This need is, of course, what makes so misleading the Court's comparison of a probate judge readily setting aside as involuntary the will of an old lady badgered and beleaguered by the new heirs. . . . With wills, there is no public interest save in a totally free choice; with confessions, the solution of crime is a countervailing gain, however the balance is resolved.

resources believed wasted in interrogation. . . . We do know that some crimes cannot be solved without confessions, that ample expert testimony attests to their importance in crime control, and that the Court is taking a real risk with society's welfare in imposing its new regime on the country. The social costs of crime are too great to call the new rules anything but a hazardous experimentation.

While passing over the costs and risks of its experiment, the Court portrays the evils of normal police questioning in terms which I think are exaggerated. . . . Society has always paid a stiff price for law and order, and peaceful interrogation is not one of the dark moments of the law.

This brief statement of the competing considerations seems to me ample proof that the Court's preference is highly debatable at best and therefore not to be read into the Constitution. However, it may make the analysis more graphic to consider the actual facts of one of the four cases reversed by the Court. *Miranda v. Arizona* serves best, being neither the hardest nor easiest of the four under the Court's standards. . . .

[Justice Harlan here states the facts of the case.]

Miranda's oral and written confessions are now held inadmissible under the Court's new rules. One is entitled to feel astonished that the Constitution can be read to produce this result. These confessions were obtained during brief, daytime questioning conducted by two officers and unmarked by any of the traditional indicia of coercion. They assured a conviction for a brutal and unsettling crime, for which the police had and quite possibly could obtain little evidence other than the victim's identifications, evidence which is frequently unreliable. There was, in sum, a legitimate purpose, no perceptible unfairness, and certainly little risk of injustice in the interrogation. Yet the resulting confessions, and the responsible course of police practice they represent, are to be sacrificed to the Court's own finespun conception of fairness which I seriously doubt is shared by many thinking citizens in this country.

The tenor of judicial opinion also falls well short of supporting the Court's new approach. Although *Escobedo* has widely been interpreted as an open invitation to lower courts to rewrite the law of confessions . . . no decision at all has gone as far as this Court goes today.

It is also instructive to compare the attitude in this case of those responsible for law enforcement with the official views that existed when the Court undertook three major revisions of prosecutorial practice prior to this case. . . . In [the case] which established that appointed counsel must be offered the indigent in federal criminal trials, the Federal Government all but conceded the basic issue, which had in fact been recently fixed as Department of Justice policy. . . . In *Mapp*, which imposed the exclusionary rule on the States for Fourth Amendment violations, more than half of the States had themselves already adopted some such rule. . . . In *Gideon* . . . an *amicus* brief was filed by 22 States and Commonwealths urging that course; only two States beside the respondent came forward to protest. . . . By contrast, in this case new restrictions on police questioning have been opposed by the United States and in an *amicus* brief signed by 27 States and Commonwealths, not including the three other States who are parties. No State in the country has urged this Court to impose the newly announced rules, nor has any State chosen to go nearly so far on its own.

The Court in closing its general discussion invokes the practice in federal and foreign jurisdictions as lending weight to its new curbs on confessions for all the States. A brief résumé will suffice to show that none of these jurisdictions has struck so one-sided a balance as the Court does today. Heaviest reliance is placed on the FBI practice. Differing circumstances may make this comparison quite untrustworthy,[3] but in all events the FBI falls sensibly short of the Court's formalistic rules. For example, there is no indication that FBI agents must obtain an affirmative "waiver" before they pursue their questioning. Nor is it clear that one invoking his right to silence may not be prevailed upon to change his mind. And the warning as to appointed counsel apparently indicates only that one will be assigned by the judge when the suspect appears before him; the thrust of the Court's rules is to induce the suspect to obtain appointed counsel before continuing the interview.... Apparently, American military practice, briefly mentioned by the Court, has these same limits and is still less favorable to the suspect than the FBI warning, making no mention of appointed counsel....

[Justice Harlan's analysis of practices in foreign jurisdictions has been omitted.]

In closing this necessarily truncated discussion of policy considerations attending the new confession rules, some reference must be made to their ironic untimeliness. There is now in progress in this country a massive re-examination of criminal law enforcement procedures on a scale never before witnessed....

It is no secret that concern has been expressed lest long-range and lasting reforms be frustrated by this Court's too rapid departure from existing constitutional standards. Despite the Court's disclaimer, the practical effect of the decision made today must inevitably be to handicap seriously sound efforts at reform, not least by removing options necessary to a just compromise of competing interests. Of course legislative reform is rarely speedy or unanimous, though this Court has been more patient in the past. But the legislative reforms when they came would have the vast advantage of empirical data and comprehensive study, they would allow experimentation and the use of solutions not open to the courts, and they would restore the initiative in criminal law reform to those forums where it truly belongs.

IV. Conclusions

All four of the cases involved here present express claims that confessions were inadmissible, not because of coercion in the traditional due process sense, but solely because of lack of counsel or lack of warnings concerning counsel and silence. For the reason stated in this opinion, I would adhere to the due process test and reject the new requirements inaugurated by the Court....

. . . .

IV.   Aftermath of the Miranda Decision

An analysis of the impact of the *Miranda* decision must be divided into three parts: (1) On an immediate level, what did the new rules for admissibility of confessions mean for Ernesto Miranda and the defendants in the three other cases heard at the same time? (2) More broadly, how has the decision affected station-house procedures, the behavior of interrogating officers, and the effectiveness of law enforcement? (3) What has been the political reaction to the Supreme Court's holding? Each of these questions will be dealt with in turn.

THE ULTIMATE OUTCOME FOR MIRANDA, VIGNERA, STEWART, AND WESTOVER

Following the Supreme Court's decision throwing out the confessions secured by police interrogators in *Miranda* and the three related cases, the prosecutors in each

---

[3] The Court's *obiter dictum* notwithstanding . . . there is some basis for believing that the staple of FBI criminal work differs importantly from much crime within the ken of local police. The skill and resources of the FBI may also be unusual.

of the cases had to decide whether to seek a new trial on the basis of the remaining evidence or to drop the case entirely because of insufficient evidence to convict the accused. As will be recalled, Miranda had not appealed his conviction for robbery, since his confession dealt only with the rape charges against him; thus, the Supreme Court decision did not upset the twenty- to twenty-five-year sentence he received for robbery. The state of Arizona decided to press the rape charge again, this time without the confession. Miranda was convicted and sent back to prison to serve out the same sentence he had originally received.

Roy Allen Stewart was retried in Los Angeles Superior Court in May 1969 on one count of first-degree murder and three counts of robbery. The evidence against Stewart included eyewitness identifications that he had signed and cashed checks stolen from the robbery victims and property stolen from all four victims which was found by the police in Stewart's home. Each of the crimes, including the one which resulted in death, had been perpetrated in virtually identical fashion. The jury brought in a verdict of guilty on all counts and Stewart was sentenced to the state prison for life.

After Stewart's arrest and completion of the investigation, the Los Angeles police closed their files on six other brutal robbery-murders which had been committed in a similar manner in the same area of the city. Stewart's reconviction and the subsequent action of the police received virtually no newspaper coverage or other publicity, although the original arrest, trial, and Supreme Court verdict had made the front pages of the local press.

Finally, Michael Vignera was retried by New York State and sentenced to twenty to thirty years as a third-felony offender, and Carl Calvin Westover was convicted of bank robbery in federal court and sentenced to two consecutive fifteen-year prison terms. Thus, the Supreme Court's decision that confessions given without adequate warning were inadmissible in court did not lead to freedom for any of the original defendants. All were retried, and all were convicted.

THE IMPACT OF THE MIRANDA DECISION ON POLICE BEHAVIOR

As soon as the *Miranda* decision was announced, the political storm broke. Cries of outrage at how the Court was hamstringing law enforcement were answered with equally emotional statements that such views were absolute nonsense. In the meantime, police departments across the nation geared up, with somewhat less than enthusiasm, to meet the new requirements. So-called "Miranda cards" were printed up; policemen were instructed to read the cards to suspects either at the time of arrest or prior to interrogation. Legislatures set out to reorganize and expand public defender and legal aid systems. Experiments in arraignment procedures were instituted, such as the attempt in New York City sponsored by the Vera Institute of Justice to keep certain courts open around the clock in order to minimize the possibility of station-house abuses.

And yet, when all is said and done, it is impossible to make a clear assessment of the impact of the *Miranda* rules. The difficulty in analysis stems from several sources. First and foremost, of course, is the extremely difficult task of observing the policeman in the field. Policemen have enormous discretion and must make many snap judgments while patrolling. Thus, any policeman who wishes to abuse the *Miranda* rules, either consciously or not, can do so with relative impunity. After all, it is frequently hard to determine when the accusatory stage of an investigation into an unsolved crime has been reached. Ultimately, the preinterrogation warnings are only as good as the desire of each police officer to abide by them.

Secondly, the rules represent something of an abstraction. They would offer meaningful protection to the poor and the ignorant if they were enforced, as stated above, and if most criminal cases were ultimately disposed of in court. Yet, as the President's Commission on Law Enforcement and Administration of Justice has indicated, most criminal cases—as many as 90 percent in many jurisdictions—are disposed of without trial, in the administrative process which occurs before formal judicial proceedings begin.[1] Prosecutors, like policemen, have wide discretion; they can choose whether to charge an arrested suspect and frequently they have a range of choices as to what crime or crimes they charge the accused with. The vast majority of criminal cases which are cleared from the books are disposed of via pleas of guilty, many of which are negotiated between the prosecutor and the accused. Inevitably, the poor and the ignorant are at a striking disadvantage in such plea negotiations when compared to the middle-class citizen and the organized criminal, both of whom are far more likely to know and exercise their rights. And, inevitably, the formalistic warnings required by the *Miranda* decision fail to provide much protection under the circumstances described above. The process of plea negotiation frequently benefits an accused, but it unquestionably negates the concept of equal justice under law.

Furthermore, the Court's attempt to provide the poor and the ignorant with knowledge which would enable them to exercise their rights effectively during station-house interrogation does not really get at the roots of the dissatisfaction of America's underprivileged with local law enforcement agencies. What goes on in the police station is only one source, and possibly not a major source, of the hostility which many residents of urban slums feel toward the police. Racial animosities, aggressive police patrol designed to prevent crime in high-crime areas, instances of police corruption and brutality, frequent use of "stop and frisk" techniques in ghetto areas all exacerbate police-community relations and create highly volatile situations.

On balance, and with some trepidation because of the limited nature of the evidence, one can say that the *Miranda* decision has caused more heat than light. There is some data to suggest that the requirement of warnings prior to police interrogation has not seriously hindered the capacity of the police to fight crime. In New Haven, a study of every police interrogation of a criminal suspect over a three-month period showed that in 87 percent of the cases confessions were irrelevant since the suspects' statements were not used at trial. Some of the police interrogators failed to follow the *Miranda* requirements; strangely, one-third of the suspects who were not warned gave statements, but one-half of those warned talked to the police.

A Pittsburgh study revealed that the number of confessions fell by 17 percent after the *Miranda* decision, but the rate of convictions for crime remained constant. Only one of seventy-four suspects who refused to make statements had to be released after arrest because of insufficient evidence. Furthermore, the crime clearance rate, based on the ability of the police and prosecutors to dispose of cases with or without a trial, remained the same. And, perhaps most significantly, a Washington study conducted over an entire year revealed that the rate of statements was the same in 15,000 arrests before and after the *Miranda* decision.[2]

In the years since the decision was handed down, police officers across the nation appear to have adjusted to the new requirements. The vast majority of suspects do receive the benefit of full-scale warnings of their rights prior to undergoing interrogation. On the other hand, the rules have probably had limited impact on the behavior of those policemen who employed excessive interrogation tactics prior to

---

[1] *The Challenge of Crime in a Free Society*, U.S. Government Printing Office, 1967, pp. 130–37.

[2] See, *e.g.*, Richard Harris, *The Fear of Crime*, Praeger, New York, 1969, pp. 80–81.

Miranda, given the wide range of police discretion in handling cases. Finally, the rules have not had much significance for police-community relations, nor have they convinced the urban slum dweller that he has the same rights before the law as other Americans.

THE POLITICAL RESPONSE TO THE DECISION

In order to analyze the political reaction to the *Miranda* decision, it is first necessary to examine a collateral matter: the upsurge in federal attention to the crime problem in the period immediately prior to and after the Supreme Court's ruling. From a descriptive viewpoint, it might suffice to say simply that Congress passed legislation repealing the *Miranda* decision and that such legislation in itself raises complex questions of constitutional law. Analytically, however, it is important to assess *why* and *how* Congress was able to achieve its purpose.

The assertion that most important legislative proposals originate in the executive branch, despite the separation of powers that supposedly characterizes our presidential system of government, has become part of the conventional wisdom about American politics. In this instance, though, the President and his administration opposed legislative interference with the Supreme Court. It will be argued below that Congress succeeded in beating the President at his own game because—as time passed—the President became more and more convinced of the urgency of his own anticrime proposals. Administration strategists perforce were distracted from fighting congressional reaction head-on. Since the President wanted something from Congress, Congress held the whip hand and, ultimately, the President was forced to accept legislative repeal of *Miranda* as the price of passage of his own anticrime program.

The first presidential message to Congress devoted exclusively to the subject of crime was delivered by President Johnson in March 1965, shortly before he appointed the President's Commission on Law Enforcement and Administration of Justice to undertake a thorough investigation of crime in the United States. The President's call for a concerted war on crime by all levels of government represented a historic departure from the belief that crime was essentially a local problem, to be handled primarily by state and local governments.

Unfortunately, the President's rhetoric was not matched by his specific legislative proposals, which were highly tentative. To put it simply, the federal government was not ready for a major attack on crime; before significant new policies could be introduced and passed, the information gap on what needed to be done and how best to do it had to be closed. As a first step, President Johnson asked Congress to authorize the Attorney General to undertake and to publish studies of law enforcement techniques and practices and to award grants for demonstration projects on new methods of law enforcement and control. Congress complied with these requests, passed the Law Enforcement Assistance Act of 1965 in September and appropriated the insignificant sum of 7 million dollars to carry out the purposes of the legislation.

Was President Johnson right in adopting a finger-in-the-dike approach? Should he have pressed harder, despite the lack of information? Would he have gotten more from Congress if he had acted more forcefully? These are all tactical questions to which there is no clear-cut answer, and there probably never will be.

The administration decided not to propose a comprehensive crime bill in 1966 but to wait for the report of the President's commission, due in early 1967. Nonetheless, the President concluded that he could not afford to mark time throughout 1966. In his State of the Union message and in his second annual report to Congress on crime, President Johnson exhorted Congress to face the problem of increasing lawlessness head on. To finance his stepped-up program to combat lawlessness, Johnson asked Congress to double its appropriation for the Law Enforcement Assistance Act of 1965. Congress refused, however, to expand the activities of the Justice Department's Office of Law Enforcement Assistance.

Other presidential requests got a mixed reception: Congress passed a bill providing for civil commitment of drug addicts in place of imprisonment, a bill revising bail procedures in federal courts to allow the release of certain "low-risk" indigent defendants during the pretrial period, and a bill establishing a National Commission on Reform of Federal Criminal Laws to review federal criminal laws and to suggest needed reforms.

On the other hand, Congress rejected: (1) a program to send about 3,000 police officers to institutions of higher learning for a year of intensive professional study, (2) a law to forgive National Defense Education Act loans received by college students who chose careers in law enforcement, (3) a measure to curtail mail-order shipment of firearms, (4) a bill to unify and consolidate federal prison, parole, and probation functions within the Department of Justice, (5) a witness immunity statute to allow the courts to compel witnesses to testify in racketeering cases involving organized crime, (6) a pistol registration law for the District of Columbia to prohibit the sale of guns to persons convicted of crimes of violence, to individuals with backgrounds of mental instability, and to chronic alcoholics.

While congressional committees and individual congressmen were dismantling the President's limited anticrime program, the Supreme Court handed down its decision in *Miranda v. Arizona.* Cynics should note the seeming paradox that many of the representatives who picked the bones of the administration's anticrime proposals clean were among the first to push their plates back, rise to their feet, and alert the general public to the fact that the Supreme Court majority was again coddling criminals, returning murderers to the streets, and frustrating the efforts of the police.

By the outset of 1967, the President's Commission on Law Enforcement and the Administration of Justice had completed its massive study of crime in the United States. Relying on the Commission's data and conclusions and the initial experiences of the federal government in strengthening law enforcement, President Johnson announced to Congress his intention to escalate the government's war on crime. The heart of the President's program was the Safe Streets and Crime Control Act of 1967, which called for an expenditure of 50 million dollars in fiscal year 1968 and approximately 300 million dollars the following year to stimulate state and local efforts.

According to the proposed legislation, the federal money would be administered by an Office of Law Enforcement and Criminal Justice Assistance to be established in the Department of Justice. Communities seeking aid would be entitled to receive (1) 90 percent of the cost of developing plans to improve the police, the courts, and correctional systems; (2) 60 percent of the cost of implementing such plans provided that the community increased its anticrime expenditures by 5 percent, that no more than one-third of the federal funds be used for improving police salaries, and that each community receiving grants have a program for coordinating the efforts of all law enforcement agencies; (3) 50 percent of the cost of construction of new facilities such as crime laboratories, community correction centers, and police academies, (4) 100 percent of the cost of contracts with public agencies and universities to carry out research and education projects.

In addition to the Safe Streets and Crime Control Act of 1967, the President sought congressional approval of a number of other measures, including several which he had proposed the previous year. He asked Congress to pass a gun control bill, to unify federal correctional services within the Justice Department, to pass a witness immunity statute, to establish a Federal Judicial Center which would do research on improving the federal court system, to allow the Bureau of Narcotics and the Food and Drug Administration to expand existing programs for training local police officers in narcotics control, to prohibit all wiretapping and electronic eavesdropping of an interstate nature except in cases involving national security, and to prohibit the distribution of eavesdropping devices in interstate commerce.

Finally, President Johnson proposed a major attack on juvenile delinquency, which had been growing by leaps and bounds—at a far higher rate than crimes by adults—throughout the decade. A Juvenile Delinquency Prevention Act called for expenses of nearly half a billion dollars over four years, in contrast to expenses averaging 8 million dollars during the years from 1961 to 1967. Grants-in-aid were to be given to states and communities to develop coordinated plans, to provide technical assistance to local agencies responsible for diagnostic and rehabilitative treatment, to construct detention and treatment facilities, to finance delinquency prevention projects.

Thus, the Ninetieth Congress was greeted in January and February 1967 with a barrage of administration proposals for new and expanded federal efforts to aid state and local law enforcement agencies. Substantial help was on the way, if only Congress could be persuaded that action was necessary. It should be added parenthetically that (1) the Congress which came into being in January 1967 was—as a result of the fall election—far more conservative than the preceding Congress, (2) the escalating war in South Vietnam was increasingly preoccupying the administration, diverting time and energy from domestic legislative needs, and (3) the fiscal demands of the war were such that the cards were stacked against the proponents of major new domestic expenditures.

Since the Safe Streets and Crime Control Act of 1967 would be sent to the Subcommittee on Criminal Laws and Procedures of the Senate Judiciary Committee, the administration asked Senator John L. McClellan (Dem., Ark.), the chairman of the subcommittee, to manage the bill. Two weeks before introducing the administration's legislation, however, Senator McClellan joined with Senators Sam Ervin, Jr. (Dem., N.C.), Robert Byrd (Dem., W.Va.), and Roman L. Hruska (Rep., Neb.) in cosponsoring a bill to reverse the Supreme Court's decision in *Miranda v. Arizona*.

Then, just as hearings were getting under way, McClellan, Ervin, and Byrd, along with nine other Democrats from the South, Republicans Strom Thurmond (S.C.), Paul Fannin (Ariz.), Wallace Bennett (Utah), and Clifford Hansen (Wy.), and Democrats Carl Hayden (Ariz.) and Tom Dodd (Conn.), introduced a bill under Article 3 of the Constitution to strip the Supreme Court of jurisdiction to review the decisions of both federal and state trial courts on the admissibility of confessions into evidence.

Senator McClellan and his colleagues argued heatedly for eight months before reluctantly sending an anticrime measure on to the full Judiciary Committee. In the process, the conservatively oriented subcommittee rewrote the administration's bill to suit its own views. The subcommittee did approve the 50-million-dollar administration request for law enforcement assistance, but it added 35 million dollars earmarked expressly for prevention and control of riots. The administration had requested legislation to limit police wiretapping to cases involving national security, but the subcommittee changed the wiretapping provision to give policemen authority to use wiretaps and eavesdropping devices in a broad range of criminal investigations.

A number of anti-Supreme Court amendments were added to the administration's bill, including three aimed at Court rulings on the use of confessions at criminal trials: First, the *Miranda* ruling was partially reversed by a provision that confessions were to be admissible in federal courts, even if the suspect has not been warned of his constitutional rights, if the trial judge determines that the confession has been given voluntarily; second, the Supreme Court and all other federal courts were stripped of authority to review any decision by a state trial court judge that a confession was voluntary if that decision has been upheld by the highest court of the state in question; third, the *Mallory* decision was reversed by a provision that delay in arraigning an arrested suspect before a judicial officer could not, of itself, render a confession inadmissible.

Liberal senators on the Judiciary Committee, with the firm backing of the administration, made a determined effort to undo the work of the subcommittee, but to no avail. The full committee was equally divided between those who wanted to untie the hands of the police and those who supported the libertarian decisions of the Supreme Court. As a result, the committee remained deadlocked and no further action was taken in 1967.

In the House of Representatives, consideration of the administration's bill proceeded in a more expeditious fashion. The Judiciary Committee, under the chairmanship of Rep. Emanuel Celler (Dem., N.Y.), was dominated by administration supporters. During the hearings, the objectives of the bill were supported by representatives of the National Association of Counties, the National League of Cities, the National Sheriff's Association, the National Council on Crime and Delinquency, the Americans for Democratic Action, the National Association of Attorneys General, the National Council on Crime, the International Association of Chiefs of Police, the United States Conference of Mayors, the American Legion, and the International Conference of Police Associations. Minor amendments were adopted and the bill was reported in mid-July.

Three weeks later, the House passed the Safe Streets bill by the lopsided vote of 387–23, but only after the entire measure had been virtually rewritten on the floor. The language of the bill was replaced with Republican-backed amendments to take control over the expenditure of funds away from the Attorney General and give it to the states. On the key vote, Republicans and Southern Democrats combined to defeat supporters of the administration. In addition, the House added a proviso that priority in the expenditure of funds was to be given to antiriot programs.

Thus, although the bill was passed overwhelmingly, the vote was by no stretch of the imagination a victory for the administration. The substitution of block grants to the states for federal administration of funds represented a major triumph for the minority party.

The first session of the Ninetieth Congress ended virtually where it had begun. Despite the alarming conclusions of the President's Commission on Law Enforcement and the Administration of Justice that there was a nationwide shortage of more than 50,000 policemen and that police departments around the country were in desperate need of assistance, none of the commission's major proposals was enacted into law. With the exception of several minor and noncontroversial measures, President Johnson's entire anticrime program was bogged down in Congress.

In his State of the Union message the following January, the President stressed that there would be no more vital business before Congress in 1968 than the need to capture the initiative in the battle against crime. He again urged Congress to pass the Safe Streets statute, the Juvenile Delinquency Prevention bill, and other parts of his anticrime program.

The deadlock persisted in the Senate Judiciary Committee as liberals and conservatives continued to disagree as to whether the Supreme Court's decisions in the field of criminal procedure were responsible for the growth in crime throughout the nation. Finally, a bill containing the anti-Supreme Court amendments was reported out of committee after a motion to strike the restrictions failed to carry, by a vote of nine to nine.

Floor debate began with the ultimate outcome in serious doubt, since no one was entirely pleased with the patchwork quilt reported by the Judiciary Committee. The minority leader announced he would attempt to amend the law enforcement assistance provisions to eliminate federal control and replace it with block grants to the states; the administration publicized that it would oppose the broad wiretapping authority provided in the bill; liberals in the Senate stated that they would make a last-ditch effort to delete the restrictions on the Supreme Court; and, finally, a group of conservative senators banded together to fight the limited gun controls which had been approved by the Judiciary Committee.

Southern Democrats and Republicans united to pass a Dirksen-sponsored amendment to transfer 85 percent of the law enforcement planning and assistance grants from direct grants to communities and agencies to block grants to the states. The administration suffered another defeat when it failed by a vote of twenty to sixty to limit the scope of wiretapping authorized by the bill. Efforts by administration loyalists to expand the gun-control provisions also came to naught, as did the attempt by opponents of gun-control legislation to kill a ban on interstate sale of pistols.

Finally, the Senate turned to the guts of the battle between liberals and conservatives, the anti-Supreme Court provisions contained in Title II of the proposed legislation. Seven roll-call votes were taken; the senators who wished to rebuke the Supreme Court won four and lost three. Administration supporters were able to defeat provisions of the bill which restricted the jurisdiction of the Court, but they were unable to muster sufficient support to defeat statutory repeal of specific Supreme Court decisions, including *Miranda v. Arizona.*[3] Title II, section 3501 (a) and (b), as approved by the Senate, reads:

3501. Admissibility of confessions

(a) In any criminal prosecution brought by the United States or by the District of Columbia, a confession, as defined in subsection (e) hereof, shall be admissible in evidence if it is voluntarily given. Before such confession is received in evidence, the trial judge shall, out of the presence of the jury, determine any issue as to voluntariness. If the trial judge determines that the confession was voluntarily made it shall be admitted in evidence and the trial judge shall permit the jury to hear relevant evidence on the issue of voluntariness and shall instruct the jury to give such weight to the confession as the jury feels it deserves under all the circumstances.

(b) The trial judge in determining the issue of voluntariness shall take into consideration all the circumstances surrounding the giving of the confession, including (1) the time elapsing between arrest and arraignment of the defendant making the confession, if it was made after arrest and before arraignment, (2) whether such defendant knew the nature of the offense with which he was charged or of which he was suspected at the time of making the confession, (3) whether or not such defendant was advised or knew that he was not required to make any statement and that any such statement could be used against him, (4) whether or not such defendant had been advised prior to questioning of his right to the assistance of counsel, and (5) whether or not such defendant was without the assistance of counsel when questioned and when giving such confession. The presence or absence of any of the above-mentioned factors to be taken into consideration by the judge need not be conclusive on the issue of voluntariness of the confession.[4]

---

[3] The roll-call vote on the motion to delete the anti-*Miranda* provision was 29 in favor, 55 opposed. For data on the roll-call votes in the Senate, see 114 CONG. REC. 6019ff. (daily ed. May 21, 1968).

[4] 82 Stat. 210.

Thus, the liberal Democrats did succeed in preventing passage of the most extreme anti-Supreme Court proposals, in part because some of their more conservative colleagues were unhappy at the thought of shaking American political institutions to their very roots by employing Congress's constitutional but rarely used power to limit the jurisdiction of the Supreme Court. Nevertheless, following passage of the entire bill, as amended, by a lopsided margin of seventy-two to four, senators who had long sought an opportunity to chastise the Court for failing to mend its ways left the floor triumphant.

Despite all the water which had gone over the dam, however, the administration still was not ready to give in. With the support of the President, liberals in the House decided to try to send the bill to a conference committee in hopes that the restrictive provisions could be modified as the price of House agreement on a final bill.

Then, on June 5, two months after the senseless killing of the Reverend Martin Luther King, Jr., Senator Robert Kennedy also fell victim to an assassin's bullet. The House of Representatives met the next day in an atmosphere of anger and impatience. Representative Celler rose to ask the House to send the crime bill to conference, but his motion was overwhelmingly defeated. Then, the House voted 368 to 17 to accept the Senate bill. Since Senator Kennedy had strongly opposed the restrictive provisions contained in the Senate bill, it would have been far more in keeping with respect for his name for the House to have sent the measure to a conference committee.

The act which emerged from the legislative struggle demonstrated clearly the independence of Congress and President Johnson's limited influence during the final year of his term of office. The act bore little relationship to the administration's original proposals for fighting the increasing breakdown of law and order in the nation.

The President was faced with the unpalatable prospect of signing a bill which was not to his liking or vetoing what would undoubtedly go down in the history books as the most important federal anticrime legislation passed during his presidency. He decided, with evident reluctance, to sign the act because it contained "more good than bad," but he called for immediate repeal of the wiretapping provisions.[5] Furthermore, he announced that he would instruct federal law enforcement officers to continue to warn arrested suspects of their constitutional rights, despite Title II.

With the signing of the Omnibus Crime Control and Safe Streets Act of 1968, the ball bounced from Congress's side of the net to the side occupied by the highest court in the land. The game was, of course, not yet over. The Supreme Court now had an opportunity to respond, either by giving in meekly or ruling that judicial interpretations of the Constitution cannot be overturned by legislative fiat. To confuse the issue, however, the composition of the Court began to change. As of this writing, only Justices Douglas and Brennan of the five-man majority in *Miranda v. Arizona* are still on the bench; White and Stewart continue to oppose them on *Miranda*-type issues. President Nixon's first two appointees, Chief Justice Warren Burger and Justice Harry Blackmun, have lined up with White and Stewart on most constitutional questions involving procedural rights. Thus, it appears that the minority view in *Miranda* may become the dominant view of the Court. If the President's hopes materialize, Congress will not have to face the challenge of adopting a new strategy to continue its battle with the Court.

[5] *The New York Times*, June 20, 1968, p. 23.

FEDERAL OPEN HOUSING LEGISLATION
Can the Federal Government Regulate the Sale of Private Homes?

ISSUES RAISED   Regulation of Interstate Commerce / Congress's Power to Enforce the Thirteenth and Fourteenth Amendments / Private Property and Due Process of Law / Rights Reserved to the States or to the People

I.   The Politics of Open Housing

Throughout the length and breadth of the United States, racial discrimination in the rental and sale of housing is notorious. The U.S. Commission on Civil Rights has stated with a great deal of self-restraint that "Housing . . . seems to be the one commodity in the American market that is not freely available on equal terms to everyone who can afford to pay."[1]

The urban racial ghetto, which is in part the result of housing discrimination, is unquestionably the most explosive issue in American domestic politics today. The brutalizing circumstances of life in the ghetto are catalogued daily in the nation's newspapers and need little repetition. For most black inhabitants of our urban areas, there is no possibility of escape; poverty is an insuperable barrier to the rental or purchase of decent housing. In addition, however, the harsh facts of racial bigotry and fear severely limit the housing available to more affluent black families.

Americans are fond of stressing the virtues of life in the United States, particularly in conversations with citizens of other nations: we stress individual freedom, equal treatment of all citizens by government, opportunity for all to participate, to improve oneself, to share in the rewards of society on the basis of initiative, responsibility, and individual effort. Yet, these political ideals ring hollow to the inhabitants of our urban ghettos. Such ideals are mocked by blatant evidence of discrimination based on race, of poor schools, of unemployment, of slum housing. It is hardly any wonder then that bitterness, alienation, futility, crime, and violence are characteristic of life in the slums of our major cities. As President Johnson said when he asked Congress on April 28, 1966, to pass legislation outlawing discrimination based on race in the sale or rental of housing: "The ghettos of our major cities —North and South, from coast to coast—represent fully as severe a denial of freedom and the fruits of American citizenship as more obvious injustices. As long as

---

[1] U.S. Commission on Civil Rights, *With Liberty and Justice for All*, U.S. Government Printing Office, 1959, p. 180.

the color of a man's skin determines his choice of housing, no investment in the physical rebuilding of our cities will free the men and women living there."[2]

Most Americans are aware of and concerned about the riots, looting, and meaningless violence which have made headlines during the hot summer months in the past few years and will undoubtedly continue to take place in the future. Even a partial listing of some of the cities in which the slums have erupted indicates that the economic, social, and political problems of the ghetto are not a regional but a national dilemma: Atlanta, Boston, Buffalo, Chicago, Cincinnati, Cleveland, Detroit, Los Angeles, Memphis, Milwaukee, Minneapolis, Nashville, New York, Newark, Philadelphia, Rochester, St. Louis, Washington, D.C.

Many political leaders have, quite understandably, reacted to these conclusive proofs that the veneer of civilization is incredibly thin in the slums by calling for harsher laws, longer criminal sentences, and increased police power in order to protect property, punish individuals responsible for disorder, and prevent future outbreaks. Clearly, anarchy must be halted and lawlessness punished. But although it is necessary to treat the symptoms of the cancer that is gnawing away at the vitals of urban America, such palliatives are not and will not be sufficient; the illness is so serious that it cannot be eradicated or even held in check for very long without serious and sustained efforts to attack its causes.

Awareness of the riots which have occurred is commonplace, perhaps because the mass media have communicated the simple and stark message of urban violence clearly and dramatically. On the other hand, no similar effort has gone into reporting the far more complex and difficult data on the scope of urban ghetto problems and their implications for the future. It can probably be said without exaggeration that the future of America's cities is dependent on the fate of America's black population. The following statistics support this generalization: in 1910 over 70 percent of the black population lived in the rural South; today over 70 percent live in the urban centers of the North, Midwest, and West. From 1940 to 1960 the black population outside the eleven states of the Confederacy increased nearly 250 percent, from four million to over nine million. Most of these people moved to the nation's twelve largest metropolitan areas. The black population of Detroit more than tripled; Chicago's black population increased more than 250 percent; Philadelphia's about 200 percent; New York's slightly less than 200 percent; Los Angeles went from 74,000 to 464,000 black residents, a 600 percent increase in twenty years; and the migration has continued in the years since 1960.

In Washington, D.C., and Newark, New Jersey, black residents make up more than 50 percent of the entire population; in Detroit, Cleveland, St. Louis, and Baltimore, more than a third of the population is nonwhite. The elementary schools of Washington, Newark, St. Louis, Baltimore, Philadelphia, Detroit, Cleveland, Chicago, and Atlanta are more than 50 percent black, and a number of other cities are hovering close to the 50 percent mark.

At the same time as black families have been moving in large numbers into the oldest and most dilapidated houses in the commercial nerve centers of the nation, whites have been leaving the cities for newer homes and better schools in the suburbs. Between 1950 and 1960, the twenty-four largest cities in the country lost nearly 1½ million whites to the suburbs and gained more than 2 million blacks. In the decade from 1960 to 1970, 14 million whites moved to suburban homes and apartments. In the early years of the decade, 400,000 blacks moved every year to the central cities and only 52,000 moved to the suburbs; late in the decade, the pattern changed somewhat: 262,000 blacks moved annually to central cities and

2 112 CONG. REC. 9393 (1966).

85,000 moved to the suburbs. However, most of the increase in the black suburban population occurred as a result of spillover from urban ghettos into adjacent inner suburbs whose housing stock varied little from that available within the city itself.[3]

These figures suggest that the National Advisory Commission on Civil Disorders was not incorrect when it concluded in 1968 that America is moving toward two racially separate societies. In the words of former Philadelphia Mayor Richardson Dillworth, the suburbs have become "the white noose around the city."

Within the cities themselves residential segregation is intense. The overwhelming majority of urban blacks and whites live on blocks which contain no members of the other race. This is true throughout the United States regardless of the size of the black population in any particular city and in spite of the fact that many blacks can afford housing outside the slums. While conditions vary somewhat from city to city, the general pattern is for black families to crowd into the oldest, poorest, and most inadequate housing. Overcrowding of rundown facilities fast turns the area into a slum, even if it wasn't one to start with. Population growth resulting from migration and birth causes intense pressures on the boundaries of the ghetto area. For example, the U.S. Commission on Civil Rights concluded in its 1959 report that "If the population density in some of Harlem's worst blocks obtained in the rest of New York City, the entire population of the United States could fit into three of New York's boroughs."[4]

The housing shortage leads to "blockbusting" on adjacent streets: one black family finds an apartment or house on an all-white street, and shortly thereafter all the white residents leave and the street becomes entirely black. This practice is sometimes furthered by unscrupulous real estate agents who can make a quick profit by scaring white residents into selling their homes at prices below the market value; then the agents can turn around and sell such houses to middle-class blacks at inflated prices because of the pent-up demand for housing. The immoral practice of blockbusting inevitably adds to racial ill feeling and increases tensions between whites and blacks.

As increasing overcrowding creates more slums, the exodus to the suburbs of middle- and upper-income whites grows. Retail stores and white collar employers move to the suburbs, thereby shrinking employment opportunities and the municipal tax base just at the moment when the costs of social welfare, education, and police and fire protection skyrocket. For example, the U.S. Commission on Civil Rights has estimated that the substandard 20 percent of our urban centers contains one-third of the urban population, accounts for 45 percent of total city costs, but yields only 6 percent of the real estate revenue.[5] The inability of the cities to meet the needs of the urban poor and to cope with the myriad problems of the slums completes the cycle and sets off a new round of degeneration and decay. Thus, the pathology of urban America in the postwar period is all too plain: the effect of slums, discrimination, and lack of opportunity is more slums and more discrimination; demoralized adults pass negative values on to children raised in living conditions beyond the comprehension of individuals who have never experienced the world of slum tenements.

---

[3] The above information has been compiled from the following sources: U.S. Commission on Civil Rights, *Racial Isolation in the Public Schools*, U.S. Government Printing Office, 1967, pp. 11–13; Karl Taeuber and Alma Taeuber, *Negroes in Cities*, Aldine, Chicago 1965, pp. 11–14; *Hearings on H.R. 14765, The Civil Rights Act of 1966, Before Subcommittee No. 5 of the House Committee on the Judiciary*, 89th Cong., 2d Sess., at 1520–23; David L. Birch, *The Economic Future of Cities and Suburbs*, Committee for Economic Development, New York, 1970.

[4] U.S. Commission on Civil Rights, *With Liberty and Justice for All*, p. 148.

[5] *Ibid.*, p. 152.

Before leaving the discussion of some of the fundamental problems of our metropolitan areas, it is important to stress that housing discrimination is only one small part of the entire complex pattern of disadvantages confronting urban blacks. Poverty, unemployment, lack of job skills, and inadequate education are widespread within the slums. Even if housing discrimination were eliminated, these problems would not be solved.

On the other hand, one must be careful not to jump to the conclusion that because the problems of the ghetto will not be solved by the elimination of discrimination in housing there is no reason to fight such discrimination. At the least, elimination of housing discrimination would:

Provide more and better housing opportunities for the growing number of middle-class black families

Increase incentives to work hard and get ahead

Relieve some of the population pressure on the slums

Provide opportunities for white children to know and understand black children, and vice versa

Eliminate artificial distortions in the housing market and the utility of many of the less admirable practices currently employed by some real estate agents and landlords to keep blacks out

Replace injustice with justice, and bring actual behavior more in line with American political ideals

In contrast, failure to act to reduce discrimination and to improve the conditions of ghetto life is not a rational alternative: the implications of sitting back and ignoring the fact that our central cities are increasingly being occupied by the alienated, poorly educated, underemployed, impatient members of a minority race which has suffered centuries of maltreatment and discrimination at the hands of a seemingly callous white majority are all too clear.

FEDERAL INVOLVEMENT IN HOUSING, 1866–1965

Before the 1930s the federal government did not assume a major role in the field of housing. Housing was considered a private matter, subject to the control of each individual citizen or, at most, subject to limited regulation by local governments. Congress did attempt to change this philosophy somewhat when it passed a law in 1866 granting the newly freed slaves the same basic right as all other citizens "... [T]o inherit, purchase, lease, sell, hold, and convey real and personal property," but this law was insignificant for more than a century, until June 1968.[6] The Fourteenth Amendment, ratified in 1868, prohibited the states from denying due process of law or equal protection of the laws, but it did not change the right of private citizens to discriminate against each other, for whatever reason.

In the first decades of the twentieth century segregated housing was achieved by means of racially exclusive zoning laws and private discriminatory practices. The Supreme Court declared in *Buchanan v. Warley*, 245 U.S. 60 (1917), that racial zoning ordinances violated the clear command of the Fourteenth Amendment, but some communities continued to enforce such ordinances throughout the twenties and thirties. Real estate agents, builders, landlords, and homeowners used various techniques to exclude unwanted minorities, but the most widespread method of preventing certain individuals from buying homes was the use of restrictive covenants

---

[6] 14 Stat. 27.

which bound the buyer not to sell subsequently to a member of the specified minority; for example, a covenant in common use throughout the period reads as follows:

> No part of the land hereby conveyed shall ever be used, or occupied by, or sold, demised, transferred, conveyed unto, or in trust for, leased, or rented or given to Negroes, or any other person or persons of Negro blood or extraction, or to any person of the Semitic race, blood, or origin, which racial description shall be deemed to include Armenians, Jews, Hebrews, Persians and Syrians.[7]

Although restrictive covenants achieved the same purposes as discriminatory zoning ordinances, the courts upheld and enforced them since they were based on private agreements and, therefore, were not considered to violate the state action clause of the Fourteenth Amendment. Prior to the Second World War, owners and developers who used restrictive covenants advertised these discriminatory policies blatantly; at about this time, however, signs and advertisements stating "No Jews or Negroes allowed" or, more politely, "Restricted" began to be replaced by more subtle and covert techniques.

Then, in 1948, the Supreme Court adopted a novel and expansive interpretation of the Fourteenth Amendment in *Shelley v. Kraemer,* 334 U.S. 1 (1948). The Court began by holding that state action was not limited to laws passed by legislatures or policies followed by executive officials but included the decisions of the courts; thus, judicial enforcement of private discrimination made the state a party to the discrimination and thereby violated the Fourteenth Amendment. The Court went to some length to indicate that it was not outlawing private discrimination but simply enforcement of that discrimination by agencies of the state. As a result of this decision racially restrictive covenants are no longer enforceable in the courts. They are still used, however, and to the extent that they discourage homeowners from selling property to blacks and members of other minorities, they perpetuate housing discrimination.

Massive federal involvement in the housing market began in 1934, when the government established the Federal Housing Administration to stimulate the private home building industry and the overall economy. The FHA guaranteed private lenders against default on home mortgages, thereby making mortgage money more available, encouraging builders, and increasing sales. In its first decade, the FHA insured mortgages on 1,200,000 new houses, or more than one-third of the houses built during that period. By 1965, the administration had written 84 billion dollars in mortgage insurance and 17 billion dollars in home improvement loans.

In order to ease the transition of 15 million veterans to civilian life and to overcome the severe housing shortage caused by the decline in home building during the Depression and the war, the Veteran's Administration was authorized in 1944 to guarantee low-interest home financing loans made to veterans by banks and other private lenders. By 1965, the VA had guaranteed 65 billion dollars in mortgage loans to 7 million veterans.

Since the major purpose of the FHA and the VA was to stimulate construction and home ownership, no attempt was made to upset existing discriminatory practices in the private housing market. The FHA, in fact, followed an explicitly discriminatory policy until 1950. For example, the 1938 *F.H.A. Underwriting Manual* declared: "If a neighborhood is to retain stability, it is necessary that properties shall continue

---

[7] Quoted in U.S. Commission on Civil Rights, *Racial Isolation in the Public Schools,* p. 21.

to be occupied by the same social and racial groups."[8] The manual provided builders with a model restrictive covenant and recommended its use; it also advised appraisers to lower property valuations in interracial neighborhoods.

Robert Weaver, the first secretary of the Department of Housing and Urban Development, has argued that the federal government pursued a discriminatory housing policy because of the partnership between FHA and its constituents, the private mortgage lending agencies. In his book, *The Negro Ghetto*, written in 1948, Weaver stated that: "The financial institutions through which the F.H.A. operated, and through which most of its key officials . . . were recruited, were the very financial and real estate interests and institutions which led the campaign to spread racial covenants and residential segregation."[9]

A year and a half after the Supreme Court's decision in *Shelley v. Kraemer*, the FHA and the VA announced that they would no longer protect mortgage loans on property limited by restrictive covenants; no effort was made, however, to undo the damage already done or to prevent home builders from pursuing other discriminatory practices. Thus, from 1934 until further changes were made in 1962, the federal government helped to produce millions of suburban homes, few of which were available to black families.

Other federal programs, while not discriminatory in nature, have also had the effect of separating the races and intensifying concentrations of the poor and nonwhite in the cities. For example, in the years since 1937, over 600,000 low-rent public housing units have been built by local public housing authorities with the assistance of the federal government. Designed to encourage the construction of housing for low-income groups, the public housing program provided $47,000,000 in construction loans and nearly 1½ billion dollars in subsidies to help the local agencies pay their annual mortgage and maintenance expenses in the years 1937 to 1965.[10]

Public housing has been an important source of new housing for black families, as is indicated by the fact that, as of March 1966, 273,000 of the 488,000 rented units were occupied by nonwhites. In metropolitan areas public housing has been built almost exclusively in the central cities, since the consent of the local governing body must be obtained before such housing can be constructed. By 1966 more than 250,000 units had been built by city housing authorities in the twenty-four largest cities in the nation, but because of the veto power of local officials only seventy-six apartments had been built in the suburbs surrounding these major cities.[11]

Finally, the federal government has invested a great deal of time and money since 1949 on urban renewal programs designed to help local renewal agencies clear and redevelop some areas. By 1969, over 2,500 renewal projects in nearly 1,500 communities had been approved and over 8 billion dollars of federal money spent under a formula which allowed the federal government to defray up to two-thirds of the cost of each project.[12]

A major criticism of urban renewal has been the tendency of cities to replace slum housing with shopping centers, high-rent apartments, and expensive town

[8] Quoted in U.S. Commission on Civil Rights, *1961 Housing Report*, U.S. Government Printing Office, p. 16.

[9] Robert Weaver, *The Negro Ghetto*, Harcourt, Brace, New York, 1948, p. 78.

[10] *Housing a Nation*, Congressional Quarterly News Service, Washington, 1966, p. 4.

[11] U.S. Commission on Civil Rights, *Racial Isolation in the Public Schools*, p. 23.

[12] U.S. Bureau of the Census, "Table 1109, Urban Renewal Program—Summary: 1949 to 1969," *Statistical Abstract of the United States, 1970*, U.S. Government Printing Office, p. 691. For a brief but detailed description of urban renewal and related federal programs, see *Housing a Nation*, *supra* n. 10.

houses in order to improve the municipal tax base; thus, urban renewal has frequently been dubbed "Negro removal." Unable to afford housing in the renewal area and unable to find low-rent public housing, many of the people displaced by renewal projects have had no other choice but to move to adjacent areas which were already slums or in the process of becoming slums.

During the 1960 presidential campaign, John F. Kennedy accused the Republican administration of having been lax in its efforts to end discrimination in housing built, purchased, or financed with federal assistance; his position was appealing since tax money raised from all the people was being used primarily for the benefit of some of the people. Kennedy urged President Eisenhower to issue an executive order and end discrimination in publicly assisted housing "by a stroke of the pen." These words undoubtedly came back to haunt him in the following two years, during which time he postponed signing such an order rather than jeopardize his entire legislative program by antagonizing powerful Southern congressmen.

Finally, several weeks after the 1962 elections had been held, President Kennedy issued Executive Order No. 11063 banning discrimination in housing built with federal assistance after November 20, 1962; the order covered federally owned and operated housing, federally subsidized public housing, nonprofit housing constructed with federal loans, housing in urban renewal projects, and private housing insured by the FHA and the VA. In order to avoid being accused of imposing a retroactive reform and to circumvent possible legal complications, Kennedy did not include previously constructed housing which was still receiving the benefits of federal mortgage insurance. Thus, millions of FHA- and VA-insured houses were exempted from the open-housing requirement.

As of 1966, Executive Order No. 11063 covered about 3 percent of the nation's housing supply. HUD projections indicated that this figure would grow at a rate of somewhat less than 1 percent per year due to new construction and other changes in the housing market.[13] Thus even if the executive order were fully obeyed by all those developers and homeowners who pledge not to discriminate upon receiving federal assistance, little progress would be made toward ending housing discrimination based on race.

The executive order could have been extended to cover over 90 percent of all new private housing by including in its reach all federally supervised lenders and not just those who receive the direct benefits of federal mortgage insurance. Because of the limited scope of the order, the mortgage banking industry was most heavily regulated but similar controls could have been extended to savings and loan associations, to commercial banks, and to mutual savings banks, all of which receive the benefits of insurance of deposits by the Federal Savings and Loan Insurance Corporation and the Federal Deposit Insurance Corporation. Of course, the legality of such a move could have been contested in the courts, but it is unlikely that the courts would have held for the plaintiff in such a case. Aside from the question of legality, the main argument against extension of President Kennedy's order in the period from 1962 until Congress passed an open housing law in 1968 was that extension was not warranted given the degree of noncompliance with the existing regulation.

STATE ANTIDISCRIMINATION LAWS

During the years when the federal government, acting through the FHA, was encouraging discrimination against members of minority groups, a number of states

[13] *Hearings on H.R. 14765, The Civil Rights Act of 1966, Before Subcommittee No. 5 of the House Committee on the Judiciary*, 89th Cong., 2d Sess., at 1349–54.

and cities began to pass laws aimed at achieving equality of treatment in the housing market.

One of the earliest antidiscrimination laws, passed in New York in 1939, barred discrimination in public housing. A number of other states adopted similar laws in the following decade, but most of these laws accomplished little, due to the absence of effective enforcement procedures. Laws prohibiting discrimination in publicly assisted housing—including housing built under urban renewal and urban redevelopment programs on land which had been taken over by the state and resold at below market-value to private builders—were passed in New York and several other states starting in 1950.

Then, in 1954, New York City banned discrimination in privately owned rental housing which benefited from FHA and VA mortgage insurance. The following year the New York State legislature enacted a law prohibiting discrimination in new apartment houses and housing projects of ten or more units aided by government mortgage insurance. Shortly thereafter, Massachusetts, New Jersey, Oregon, Washington, and California passed roughly comparable legislation.

In 1957, New York City enacted the first law in the United States prohibiting discrimination in private housing which had not received the benefit of government assistance. Although this ordinance applied only to apartment houses and to houses in developments of ten or more units, it was subsequently amended to include all apartments and houses except units in owner-occupied two-family houses and rooms in private residences. By June 1, 1966, thirty-five cities had followed New York's lead and adopted fair-housing legislation applying to varying segments of the private housing market.

Between 1959 and 1966, seventeen states—containing 98 million people—enacted similar legislation. These statutes vary remarkably in coverage and enforcement procedures; many have been amended to include larger segments of the housing market and to provide for speedier, more effective implementation of public policy. As of 1966, nine of the seventeen states—Alaska, Colorado, Connecticut, Indiana, Massachusetts, Michigan, New Jersey, New York, and Rhode Island—barred discrimination in all residential property offered for sale and in most rental housing.[14] Despite the determined opposition of many individuals and organizations in the real estate industry, the trend has clearly been toward more fair housing laws, fewer exemptions from the laws, and more effective enforcement procedures.

While there has been a great deal of litigation challenging the constitutionality of state and municipal fair housing laws, in only one instance has such a law been declared invalid. The argument that state legislation against discrimination in the sale or rental of private housing violates the due process clause of the Fourteenth Amendment, since it prevents private owners from disposing of their property as they see fit, has been rejected by the highest courts of Massachusetts, Connecticut, California, New York, Colorado, and New Jersey.[15]

Instead, these courts have upheld fair housing statutes as legitimate extensions

[14] For a complete summary of state and municipal fair housing laws as of 1966, see *Hearings on S. 3296, The Civil Rights Act of 1966, Before the Subcommittee on Constitutional Rights of the Senate Committee on the Judiciary*, 89th Cong., 2d Sess., pt. 2, at 1422–27.

[15] The exception was a five to four decision of the Supreme Court of the State of Washington against a state law prohibiting discrimination in publicly aided housing. Only two members of the majority felt that the law violated property rights protected by the Fourteenth Amendment; the other three condemned the law for making an unreasonable and arbitrary distinction between homes receiving government-insured loans and all other housing. Perhaps the law would have been sustained if it had been more comprehensive in its coverage. *O'Meara v. Board Against Discrimination*, 365 P.2d 1 (1961).

of the police power—the power to protect health, safety, and general welfare. For example, the New Jersey Supreme Court has ruled:

> There is no doubt that the right to acquire, own and dispose of real property is within the protective scope of the Fourteenth Amendment... but the private right is not absolute. It is subject to the reasonable exercise of the police power, the reach of which is not capable of precise delineation. Exercise of that power by the state is valid so long as the regulation... bears a reasonable relation to public health, safety, morals or general welfare.
> Discrimination against Negroes in the sale and rental of housing accommodations results in inadequate housing for them and in segregation in housing. They are thus compelled in large numbers to live in circumscribed areas under substandard, unsanitary and crowded living conditions. These conditions in turn produce disease, increased mortality, unstable family life, moral laxity, crime, delinquency, risk of fire, loss of tax revenue and inter-group tensions.... Manifestly, in their totality these conditions reveal an evil which is within the competence of the lawmakers to correct.
>
> *Jones v. Haridor Realty Co.*, 181
> A.2d 481, at 484–85 (1962).

Opponents of legislation against discrimination in housing have been far more successful at the polls than in the courts. In 1963 and 1965, fair housing laws in Berkeley, California; Tacoma and Seattle, Washington; and Akron, Ohio were struck down by popular referenda. Finally, in November 1964, following a bitter campaign, the California electorate voted 4.5 to 2.4 million in favor of a constitutional amendment repealing existing antidiscrimination laws and prohibiting the passage of such laws in the future. Known as Proposition 14, the amendment provided that "Neither the State, nor any of its subdivisions... shall deny, limit or abridge... the right of any person... to sell, lease or rent any part or all of his real property... to such person or persons as he, in his absolute discretion chooses."[16]

Subsequently, Proposition 14 was declared unconstitutional by the California Supreme Court and the decision was upheld by the United States Supreme Court.[17] The majority in both instances refused to accept the argument that Proposition 14 simply returned the state to a position of neutrality in real estate transactions. Instead, both courts ruled that the state had taken affirmative action of a legislative nature designed to make possible discriminatory practices which previously were legally restricted. Since Proposition 14 thereby authorized and encouraged private discrimination, it violated the equal protection clause of the Fourteenth Amendment.

THE FIGHT FOR A FEDERAL OPEN HOUSING LAW: PHASE ONE

In 1957, the first thin crack appeared in the ninety-year-old dam which had been built by Southern congressmen to prevent changes in the civil rights status quo. Once the initial breakthrough occurred, the breach was widened and legislation designed to check discrimination in public facilities—including schools, parks, and hospitals—in voting, employment, and public accommodations was passed in 1960, 1964, and 1965. Then, in 1966, the coalition of northern Democrats and Republicans which had fought to pass the earlier measures fell apart; when the votes were tallied, it was clear that civil rights adherents had suffered their first major legislative defeat in a decade.

---

[16] The full text of Proposition 14 can be found in the decision of the California Supreme Court in *Mulkey v. Reitman*, 413 P.2d 825, at 828 (1966).

[17] *Reitman v. Mulkey*, 387 U.S. 369 (1967).

The source of dissension was the administration's proposal for a federal open housing law, known as Title 4 of the Civil Rights Act of 1966. From the outset it was clear that an open housing proposal would be fought tooth and nail. Among the factors which the administration had to take into account were the following:

Title 4 was unique; Congress and the nation at large had not had any prior opportunity to get used to the idea that the federal government should act against discrimination in privately owned housing.

Unlike voting rights legislation, Title 4 could not be based on any specific, clear-cut constitutional right; equal access to housing is not mentioned in the Constitution.

Title 4 cut into some long-accepted and emotionally strong beliefs about the rights of homeowners; it is hard, for example, to mount a convincing argument against allowing citizens to vote, but it is easy to argue persuasively about the historic freedom of property owners to dispose of property at their own discretion.

As Senator Sam Ervin, Jr., of North Carolina later observed with a good deal of perverse pleasure, for once a so-called "civil rights" bill wouldn't gore only Southern oxen; Title 4 would be opposed by individuals and interest groups in every state.

Organized opposition to voting rights legislation had been relatively puny; in contrast, any attempt to limit the freedom of real estate agents and home builders would run head-on against industries which were well organized, well led, had enormous financial resources to devote to their opposition, and were skilled at political infighting as a result of many past campaigns against public housing proposals.

Knowing that the opposition would be intense under any circumstances, the administration decided to submit an extremely strong bill to Congress, rather than a bill filled with loopholes and exemptions. White House strategists must have been aware that the bill had little chance of passing in its initial form, but they deliberately chose to leave plenty of room for bargaining, compromises, and concessions. As originally proposed, Title 4 made it unlawful for homeowners, landlords, and real estate brokers to discriminate in the sale or rental of housing because of race, color, religion, or national origin; no exemptions were allowed for individuals selling their own homes, renting rooms in their houses to boarders, or renting the other half of an owner-occupied two-family home. Every single rental or sale of residential property would be covered by the act. In addition, Title 4 prohibited real estate advertising that indicated any preference, limitation, or discrimination, and discrimination on the part of institutions engaged in the home financing business.

Enforcement of the act would be by civil suits brought in the courts by aggrieved individuals within six months of the alleged act of discrimination. The federal courts were authorized to appoint attorneys for plaintiffs in such suits, to grant permanent or temporary injunctions and restraining orders, and to award damages of an unspecified amount to successful plantiffs for humiliation and mental pain as well as $500 in punitive damages. In addition, the Attorney General was authorized to bring suits to prevent any person or persons from engaging in a pattern or practice of discrimination.[18]

The administration's strategy was to establish a favorable record for the bill before a subcommittee of the pro-civil rights House Judiciary Committee, chaired by

[18] H.R. 14765, 89th Cong., 2d Sess. (1966).

Congressman Emanuel Celler of New York, and to secure House passage before the bill was brought up in the Senate. On the Senate side, an attempt would be made (1) to avoid sending the bill to the hostile Judiciary Committee of Mississippi Senator James Eastland, (2) to head off a prospective Southern filibuster, and (3) to send the bill directly to the floor for debate and voting.

Unfortunately for these plans, Senate minority leader Everett Dirksen—whose support had been absolutely crucial in the fight for earlier civil rights bills—announced his adamant opposition to Title 4 even before the House hearings could begin. With the prospect for final passage thus dimmed, the House hearings opened on a somber note.

The hearings before the Celler subcommittee went as planned: twenty-one favorable witnesses were received warmly, but the six men allowed to testify against the bill were treated in a polite but detached fashion. The first eight of the ten days used for the hearings were devoted exclusively to testimony by proponents of open housing.

Meanwhile, behind the scenes, the members of the full Judiciary Committee were debating a Republican amendment which would weaken the open housing title but would win support for the bill from the leading Republicans on the Committee and would, hopefully, lead to bipartisan support on the floor. Drafted by Charles Mathias, Jr., of Maryland, the amendment made it unlawful for builders and landlords to discriminate in the rental or sale of housing. The sale of private homes by individuals was exempted, as was the rental of rooms in private homes, the rental of apartments in small, owner-occupied apartment houses, and the rental of rooms in buildings run by religious, charitable, and fraternal organizations.[19]

The Mathias amendment was adopted, despite the fact that it exempted 60 percent of the nation's housing, as the best of a bad bargain. Chairman Celler and ranking Judiciary Committee Republican William McCulloch of Ohio had assessed the situation and concluded that the House might support a limited open housing bill, but that a comprehensive bill had no chance of passage.

The complex maneuvering and jockeying that characterize the legislative process had only just begun, however. The Rules Committee decided to sit on the revised bill rather than send it to the floor of the House. Fortunately for Celler, he was able to use an exceptional procedure in force during the Eighty-ninth Congress to dismiss the Rules Committee from further consideration of the bill after twenty-one days had passed.

The bipartisan support for open housing which had been carefully nurtured within the Judiciary Committee fell apart less than a week after floor debate began, when the influential House Republican Policy Committee announced that it was unalterably opposed to both the original open housing proposal and the Mathias compromise. In response, another weakening amendment was introduced, in hopes that its inclusion would convince some of the reluctant Republican congressmen to change their position. Real estate brokers acting for exempt homeowners were to be allowed to discriminate if they received written instructions to that effect from the prospective seller. Administration supporters did not like being asked to support an anti-civil rights amendment, but most of them chose the pragmatic rather than the philosophical path and the amendment passed by one vote. Shortly thereafter, the bill, as amended, passed the House 259–157. As had been calculated, Republican votes provided the margin of victory.

Throughout June and July the Subcommittee on Constitutional Rights of the

---

[19] For the full text of the Mathias amendment, see *H.R. Rep. No. 1672* to accompany H.R. 14765, 89th Cong., 2d Sess. (1966).

Senate Judiciary Committee held hearings on the administration bill. Chairman Sam Ervin, Jr., of North Carolina, a firm opponent of civil rights measures, led the attack on the open housing proposal and the other sections of the bill. Twenty-nine witnesses, including representatives of seventeen state real estate associations, testified against limiting the freedom of property owners by law, and twenty-two witnesses spoke in favor of a federal antidiscrimination law. Proponents of the bill were treated by Senator Ervin to an unmerciful barrage of hostile and perceptive questions; few were able to give as well as they got. In contrast, opponents were encouraged verbally and used as a foil by the chairman to ensure that his own views were recorded in full.

Thus, neither the Senate nor the House hearings were designed primarily to inform the committee members of the merits and weaknesses of the proposed legislation; instead, the members of both subcommittees used the hearings essentially to "make a record" for positions to which they were already committed.

After the House of Representatives passed the amended Civil Rights Act of 1966, the Subcommittee on Constitutional Rights substituted the House version for the original administration bill and sent it to the full Judiciary Committee, headed by Senator James Eastland of Mississippi. Known as the graveyard for civil rights legislation, the committee had never before voluntarily reported out a civil rights' bill; Chairman Eastland was again prepared to do a requiem.

The administration and its congressional strategists were unwilling, however, to let the bill die in committee, even though there was little chance of getting it out of committee, or of getting it passed, without Senator Dirksen's support. On September 7, Senator Hart of Michigan moved to set aside consideration of a pending bill and to take up the House-passed bill instead; this motion, if it carried, would have had the effect of discharging the Judiciary Committee from further consideration of the measure. In the meantime, President Johnson invited Senator Dirksen to the White House for a conference but was unable to persuade him to change his position. After six days of intermittent debate on the Hart motion, a cloture petition was filed. Successful petitions to close debate—by votes of seventy-one to twenty-nine and seventy to thirty—had preceded passage of both the 1964 and 1965 civil rights acts; this time, however, the necessary two-thirds of those present and voting could not be mustered. The vote was fifty-four in favor, forty-two opposed. Twenty-seven Republicans voted for cloture in 1964 and twenty-three supported cloture in 1965, but only twelve voted to shut off debate on the Hart motion to take up the Civil Rights Act of 1966.

Although he was discouraged by the 1966 setback, President Johnson must have felt that time was on his side. After all, postwar American history had been characterized by gradual efforts to reduce discrimination and to provide better treatment for black citizens. The House had voted for open housing and a majority of the Senate had voted to cut off debate designed to prevent the Senate from acting on the merits of antidiscriminatory legislation. Since the scales would not have to be tipped very far for Congress to reverse its verdict, the President concluded that it was worth continuing the struggle. Legislation might not pass in 1967 or 1968—or even for a decade—but once the novelty and uniqueness of the concept of limiting the power of landlords and homeowners to discriminate on the basis of race in the rental or sale of housing had worn off, open housing might become the law of the land.

THE FIGHT FOR A FEDERAL OPEN HOUSING LAW: PHASE TWO

As a result of the midterm elections, the Ninetieth Congress convened in January 1967 amidst predictions that open housing and other progressive legislative proposals did not stand a ghost of a chance; moderates and conservatives reoccupied many of the seats which had been lost to liberal Democrats swept into office on the President's coattails two years earlier. The predictions proved accurate, but only for the first session of the Ninetieth Congress.

On the opening day of the second session, January 15, 1968, the Senate again focused on open housing and a filibuster began. After five weeks of debate, an attempt to invoke cloture was made, even though supporters of open housing knew the effort was futile without Senator Dirksen's support. The effort failed, even though fifty-five senators voted for cloture. A second effort, made a week later, also failed, this time by a vote of fifty-six in favor of cloture and thirty-seven opposed.

During the crucial week, however, Senator Dirksen began to shift his position. It had become clear that the majority of the Republicans in the Senate now favored some form of open housing, despite the position of the minority leader, and Dirksen announced that he was working out a compromise bill with Attorney General Ramsey Clark and seven proponents of open housing: Democrats Philip Hart and Walter Mondale and Republicans Jacob Javits, Hugh Scott, Charles Percy, Edward Brooke, and Howard Baker, Dirksen's son-in-law.

The 1967–1968 administration bill would have banned discrimination in 97 percent of the nation's housing; the Dirksen compromise bill scaled the ban down to approximately 80 percent, by exempting sales of homes by private owners without the aid of real estate brokers. Paradoxically, the 1966 bill, which had died in the Senate because of Senator Dirksen's adamant opposition, would have covered less than 40 percent of the nation's housing supply.

Obviously, Dirksen's "switch in time" needs explaining. Yet it defies explanation. No prudent man would risk his reputation by attempting an in-depth interpretation of the enigmatic behavior of the late Illinois orator. When pressed for a personal statement on his sudden 180-degree turn, Senator Dirksen stated, somewhat circuitously, that "Time only makes you older and wiser. Time and reality." Faced with the fact that he would be condemned for his inconstancy, Dirksen indicated: "Maybe I can find comfort in the fact that you almost have to be an Atlas to take the slings and arrows." Ultimately, he concluded: "I don't care for a moment whether my influence is involved. The question is what is the right thing to do."[20]

With Everett Dirksen throwing his weight behind open housing, another effort was made to close debate. It failed by four votes. Intensive pressures were put on several wavering senators during the next few days; the leadership announced that the bill would be dropped if cloture could not be achieved on a fourth vote. Faced with this unpleasant fact, five men switched their positions and cloture was finally invoked, sixty-five–thirty-two, with not a single vote to spare. Then, the Dirksen compromise amendment was adopted sixty-one to nineteen. Thirty-seven Democrats and twenty-four Republicans supported the measure. On the opposite side were sixteen Southern Democrats and three Republicans: Thurmond of South Carolina, Tower of Texas, and Williams of Delaware. Ultimately, the majority was able to have its way, but only by perseverance, compromise, persuasion, and the fortuitous switch of one influential senator.

Since the House of Representatives had already passed an open housing measure, albeit a far more limited one, civil rights supporters were cautiously optimistic. They recognized, however, that forty-seven House seats had shifted to Republicans in the 1966 election and that in the switch many supporters of open housing had been defeated. To a great extent, the fate of open housing lay with first-term Republican representatives.

[20] *The New York Times*, Feb. 28, 1968, p. 35.

The House Republican leadership, headed by minority leader Gerald Ford, announced that it would try to send the bill to a conference committee, where the Senate version could be scaled down to resemble the bill passed by the House in 1966. The Democratic leadership, in contrast, stated that it would attempt to force a vote on the Senate bill.

The conservative strategy was to stall the bill in the House Rules Committee until after the Easter recess in hopes that the Poor People's March on Washington, scheduled to begin April 22, would offend many members of the House. On April 4, the Rev. Martin Luther King, Jr., was shot and killed in Memphis, Tennessee. In the following days, the simmering American racial crisis finally reached the boiling point. Rioting broke out in many cities, and troops were needed to preserve order. Front pages of the nation's newspapers contained pictures of armed troops silhouetted against the Capitol.

Within, the Rules Committee debated a motion to send the civil rights bill to conference. Seven members opposed the motion and seven, including four of the five Republicans on the committee, supported it. Pressure on the fifth Republican, John Anderson of Illinois, was enormous. After much thought, Anderson took the bit in his teeth, ignored his future as a congressman, and cast the deciding vote against the motion. The Rules Committee then voted to send the Senate bill to the floor under a closed rule, which would require a vote on the bill without further amendments.

On the floor of the House the next day, debate on the bill was highly emotional. The Republican leadership made a last effort to send the bill to a conference committee. Joined by 89 Southern Democrats, 106 Republicans voted in favor of further delay. When 77 Republicans broke with the party leadership, the motion was defeated 229–195. Once again, Republican support had been crucial in the passage of a civil rights bill.

The Civil Rights Act of 1968, as passed by Congress and signed by the President, makes it unlawful to:

Refuse to sell or rent a dwelling to any person because of race, color, religion, or national origin

Discriminate against any person in the terms, conditions, or privileges of rental or sale

Publish any notices or advertisements which state a discriminatory preference or limitation

Represent to any person that a dwelling is not available for sale or rent when it is in fact available

Induce any person to sell or rent any dwelling by representations regarding the entry or prospective entry into the neighborhood of persons of a particular race, color, religion, or national origin

Deny a bank loan or discriminate in the fixing of the amount, interest rate, or other conditions of a loan because of the race, color, religion, or national origin of the borrower

Deny to any realtor access to or membership in any multiple listing service or otherwise discriminate in the provision of brokerage services[21]

Coverage under the act was staggered in the following fashion: the above prohibitions on discrimination in the rental or sale of dwellings applied immediately to houses and apartments owned by the federal government, to dwellings built since

21 82 Stat. 81.

November 1962 with the aid of federal loans or grants or with the aid of private loans insured by the federal government, and to dwellings built since November 1962 in urban renewal projects which have received federal financial assistance. On January 1, 1969, the prohibitions applied to apartment houses and new single-family houses which had not yet been sold to private owners. Finally, on January 1, 1970, the provisions covered all single-family houses sold or rented by the owner with the assistance of real estate agents. Single-family homes sold directly, without such assistance, were exempted from coverage under the act, as were rooms and apartments in owner-occupied apartment houses containing no more than four families. Religious organizations which operated dwellings for noncommercial purposes also received an exemption in order to allow them to continue to give preference to persons of the same religion.

Authority for administering the act was given to the Secretary of the Department of Housing and Urban Development, who must study the nature and extent of discriminatory practices, publish and disseminate reports, cooperate with private groups and other federal, state, and local government agencies, and conduct whatever educational activities might serve to help accomplish the purposes of the act.

The Secretary must investigate any complaint of housing discrimination within thirty days and, if he decides the complaint has merit, must attempt to correct the discrimination by informal methods of conference, conciliation, and persuasion. Whenever a state or local open housing law provides remedies substantially equivalent to those provided in the 1968 act, the Secretary must notify the appropriate agency and cannot take further steps unless the responsible state or local official fails to take action within thirty days.

In conducting an investigation, the Secretary may administer oaths and issue subpoenas to compel the presence of individuals and the production of relevant records, documents, and any other possible evidence. Any person who willfully fails to attend and testify or to produce records in accordance with a subpoena may be fined up to $1,000 or imprisoned for up to a year, or both.

If conciliation fails, the aggrieved person may bring a lawsuit in federal district court to enforce the statutory rights mentioned in the complaint previously filed with the Secretary. However, no lawsuit may be brought in a federal court if the complainant has access to a state court under the terms of a state or local open housing law as long as the state or local law provides substantially equivalent remedies. If the court finds that discrimination has occurred or is about to occur, it may issue an injunction to prohibit the illegal practice or order whatever affirmative action is appropriate under the circumstances.

In the alternative, an aggrieved person may choose not to file a complaint with the Secretary but to go directly to a federal district court or an appropriate state or local court. A civil action brought to secure the rights granted in the act must be brought within 180 days of the alleged discriminatory practice. The court may issue temporary and permanent injunctions and other orders and may award to a prevailing plantiff actual damages and up to $1,000 in punitive damages as well as court costs and attorney's fees if, in the opinion of the court, the plaintiff is not financially able to pay for his attorney.

Finally, whenever the Attorney General believes that any individual or group is engaged in a pattern or practice of discrimination, or that any group of persons has been denied any of the rights included in the act, providing that such denial raises an issue of general public importance, he may bring a civil action for preventive relief against those responsible for the pattern or practice of discrimination.

While liberals cheered the new law—and were amazed at the fact that it had been passed by Congress—a number of black leaders were less than dazzled. Embittered by the death of the Rev. Martin Luther King and by evidence that open housing might not have passed otherwise, the Rev. Ralph Abernathy, who succeeded Dr. King as head of the Southern Christian Leadership Conference, said: "This is a great stride toward freedom for white America, but it is barely a step forward for black America. New York has had this type of law for ten years and we still have the ghetto." Mississippi NAACP leader Charles Evers stated: "Hundreds of laws are on the books and none of them are being enforced. Until they are ready to enforce the ones already passed, why adopt any more?" And the late Whitney Young, executive director of the National Urban League, added trenchantly, "Those whites who feel they have been purged of national guilt and shame caused by Dr. King's assassination are dead wrong. This law is only one step toward a national resurgence of decency."[22]

Of course, they were right: the barriers to meaningful implementation of the law will ultimately make congressional resistance to passage appear relatively puny. The open housing law cannot eliminate prejudice, prevent clever evasions, or provide black people with the jobs and income without which free access to better housing will be meaningless. The compliance procedure established by the act cannot prevent dissimulation and delay, even where proof of discrimination exists.

If experience under the executive order banning discrimination in federally assisted housing is any indication, complex and time-consuming grievance procedures tend to limit the significance of open housing efforts. State fair housing laws have not been notably successful, for similar reasons. Administrative complexity, bureaucratic indifference, and lengthy court proceedings have all hindered implementation of state laws and municipal ordinances, and there is no reason to assume that experience under the Civil Rights Act of 1968 will be remarkably different.

While implementation of the 1968 law will be a hard and frustrating business, the fact remains, nevertheless, that Congress and the President have stamped housing discrimination as unlawful. For the first time, the federal government is no longer neutral; instead, the Civil Rights Act of 1968 indicates to the nation that discrimination in the rental and sale of housing is morally and legally reprehensible.

THE SUPREME COURT DEVELOPS A NOVEL CONSTITUTIONAL DOCTRINE

Public interest in the open housing issue had barely begun to wane when, a scant two months after passage of the Civil Rights Act, opponents of equal access to privately owned housing received another jolt. The Supreme Court declared, in the precedent-shattering case of *Jones v. Mayer*, 372 U.S. 409 (1968), that Congress had outlawed private discrimination in housing back in 1866.

The suit had resulted from the refusal of the owners of Paddock Woods, a suburban housing development in St. Louis, to sell a home to Mr. and Mrs. Joseph Lee Jones, an interracial couple. With the aid of several lawyers from the National Committee Against Discrimination in Housing, Mr. Jones took his case to the courts, arguing that the owners of Paddock Woods had violated (1) the state action clause of the Fourteenth Amendment, since private subdivisions which provide streets, utilities, and other services normally provided by public authorities assume the characteristics of towns, and (2) an 1866 statute which stated that all citizens "... [S]hall have the same right, in every State and Territory . . . as is enjoyed by white citizens thereof, to inherit, purchase, lease, sell, hold, and convey real and personal property. . . ."[23]

[22] *Boston Globe*, April 11, 1968, p. 8.
[23] 14 Stat. 27.

These arguments were rejected by the district court, and subsequently by the U.S. Court of Appeals for the Eighth Circuit, on the grounds that (1) the action of the private developers was not state action, and (2) the 1866 law, passed by Congress under its power to enforce the Thirteenth Amendment's ban on slavery and involuntary servitude, prohibited only state-imposed limitations on the right to purchase property. In ruling that the 1866 act did not reach private discrimination, the lower courts followed a long-established precedent that the Reconstruction acts, passed to enforce the provisions of the Thirteenth, Fourteenth, and Fifteenth Amendments, prohibited only discriminatory acts by public officials.

A petition for a writ of certiorari was filed with the Supreme Court, even though the appellant's lawyers knew the chances of ultimate victory were slim. In order to sustain their Fourteenth Amendment argument, the Supreme Court would have to stretch the concept of what constituted "state action" to new and dubious limits; to sustain their Thirteenth Amendment argument, the Court would have to repudiate its own past decisions.

In December 1967, the writ was granted. Oral argument was heard during the first week of April, while Congress was debating the Civil Rights Act. The attorneys for the appellant were cheered somewhat by the decision of the Justice Department to file an amicus curiae brief in their behalf and encouraged further when it became known that the Attorney General would personally argue the government's position before the Supreme Court. The significance of the case in the civil rights struggle became even clearer when additional amicus curiae briefs were submitted by the state of California; the Michigan Civil Rights Commission; the Missouri Commission on Human Rights; Kansas City, Missouri; Kansas City, Kansas; the American Civil Liberties Union; the National Committee Against Discrimination in Housing; the American Federation of Teachers; the National Catholic Conference for Interracial Justice; the National Council of Churches of Christ; the American Jewish Committee, etc. Only an unknown organization called the Maryland Petition Committee sought to bolster the arguments of the realty company. Under the circumstances, it was impossible for the justices of the Supreme Court not to be aware of the strong support of public agencies and private interest groups for the appellant and the lack of organized support for the realty company's position.

On June 17, 1968, two months after Congress passed the Civil Rights Act of 1968, the Supreme Court announced that the 1866 act barred all racial discrimination, private as well as public, in the rental or sale of housing, and that the act was a valid exercise of Congress's power to enforce the Thirteenth Amendment. The seven-man majority chose not to decide the appellant's Fourteenth Amendment contention.

Justice Stewart, speaking for the Court, held that the Congress which passed the act wished to eliminate private as well as public barriers to the ownership of property. Justice Harlan, is a dissent joined by Justice White, found persuasive historical data for the position that the act was passed to prevent the southern states from enacting statutes—such as the infamous "Black Codes"—which effectively destroyed the legal rights of the newly freed slaves.

To substantiate his argument, Justice Harlan quoted statements made on the floor of Congress by Senator Trumbull, the author of the 1866 act. Speaking of the coverage of the proposed statute, Senator Trumbull had said:

> It will have no operation in any State where the laws are equal, where all persons have the same civil rights without regard to color or race. It will have no operation in the State of Kentucky when her slave code and all her laws discriminating between persons on account of race or color shall be abolished.

On a subsequent occasion, Senator Trumbull added:

> If an offense is committed against a colored person simply because he is colored, in a State where the law affords him the same protection as if he were white, this act neither has nor was intended to have anything to do with his case, because he has adequate remedies in the State courts. . . .
>
> This bill in no manner interferes with the municipal regulations of any State which protect all men alike in their rights of person and property. It could have no operation in Massachusetts, New York, Illinois, or most of the States of the Union.[24]

Justice Stewart argued that the statutory grant to all citizens of the same right to purchase property as is possessed by white citizens was, on its face, a clear-cut prohibition of private as well as public discrimination. In reply, the dissenting justices noted that the right granted was not unambiguous, since "The 'right' referred to may either by a right to equal status under law, in which case the statute operates only against state-sanctioned discrimination, or it may be an 'absolute' right enforceable against private individuals."[25] Justice Harlan concluded that, to him, the words of the statute actually suggested the former interpretation, not the interpretation accepted by the majority.

Justice Harlan found additional support for his narrow view of the scope of the Civil Rights Act of 1866 in Supreme Court precedents, including the *Civil Rights Cases*, 109 U.S. 3 (1883). In those cases, the Court ruled that Congress had no power under the Thirteenth and Fourteenth Amendments to prohibit discriminatory acts by private owners of inns, public conveyances, and theaters; instead, the Court held that the Civil War amendments authorized Congress solely to remove state-imposed discrimination based on race.

Ironically, Justice John Marshall Harlan, the grandfather of the present Justice Harlan, had written an impassioned dissent in the *Civil Rights Cases*, stating that discrimination practiced by private individuals offering to serve the public for profit was a badge of servitude which Congress could prohibit under its power to enforce the Thirteenth Amendment by appropriate legislation. The majority rejected this position, however, in favor of the concept that discrimination by innkeepers could not be "regarded as imposing any badge of slavery or servitude. . . ." The Court held that "It would be running the slavery argument into the ground to make it apply to every act of discrimination which a person may see fit to make as to the guests he will entertain . . . or admit to his concert or theater, or deal with in other matters of intercourse or business."[26]

In *Jones v. Mayer*, the position taken by the first Justice Harlan eighty-five years earlier was finally vindicated. The majority construed the 1866 act to prohibit private as well as public discrimination and then held that Congress was empowered, under the enforcement clause of the Thirteenth Amendment, to pass laws eliminating all badges or relics of slavery, whether they were imposed by state law or by the acts of private citizens. The Court concluded:

> And when racial discrimination herds men into ghettos and makes their ability to buy property turn on the color of their skin, then it too is a relic of slavery. . . .
>
> At the very least, the freedom that Congress is empowered to secure under the

[24] *Cong. Globe*, 39th Cong., 1st Sess., at 476, 1758, 1761, quoted in 372 U.S. 409, at 459–60.

[25] 372 U.S. 409, at 453.

[26] 109 U.S. 3, at 24–25.

Thirteenth Amendment includes the freedom to buy whatever a white man can buy, the right to live wherever a white man can live. If Congress cannot say that being a free man means at least this much, then the Thirteenth Amendment made a promise the Nation cannot keep. . . .

372 U.S. 409, at 442–43.

Because of its novel and expansive interpretation of the Thirteenth Amendment, *Jones v. Mayer* came as a shock to nearly every lawyer in the country, including to some extent Jones's lawyers themselves. Ever since the *Civil Rights Cases* of 1883, lawyers had taken it for granted that the Thirteenth Amendment could not be used to pass laws striking at private discrimination; as a result, the 1866 law had become virtually a dead letter, and the Supreme Court had never before been asked to rule on whether the law could be used to strike down anything but state-imposed discrimination.

Justices Harlan and White were not impressed with the majority's dazzling performance. Calling the decision "ill-considered and ill-advised," they questioned the wisdom of resurrecting a century-old law and the need for establishing a new and sweeping constitutional doctrine when Congress had just finished work on an open housing statute. They criticized the majority for wiping out the exceptions to open housing which Congress had written into the 1968 law. And, finally, they were critical of their colleagues for their aggressive judicial activism and failure to follow the historic practice of deciding constitutional questions by the narrowest relevant constitutional principle.

By breathing new life into the old law, the Court in effect created an open housing law far broader than the 1968 statute. All housing was covered, not just 80 percent of the nation's housing supply; furthermore, coverage was immediate, not in three separate stages extending to January 1970. The 1968 law exempted sales of private homes by homeowners without the aid of realtors as well as apartment rentals in owner-occupied buildings containing four units or less; the Court decision eliminated both these exceptions.

On the other hand, the remedies available under the old law are far more limited than the remedies written into the new statute. Under the 1866 law, individuals must bring a lawsuit challenging suspected discrimination, and the courts can issue an order barring discrimination. However, the law is vague on whether the courts can go beyond such orders and demand monetary damages from defendants found guilty of discriminating. Under the new statute, responsibility for enforcement rests with HUD and the Department of Justice. Following a complaint of discrimination, HUD must investigate and attempt to redress the complainant's grievance by conciliation. If mediation fails, the complainant may go to court to request relief. Courts are authorized to issue orders barring discrimination and to award actual monetary damages plus up to $1,000 in punitive damages. In addition, the Attorney General is authorized to bring lawsuits to destroy any pattern or practice of discrimination.

Thus, the decision in *Jones v. Mayer* does not undermine the Civil Rights Act of 1968. Nevertheless, the decision does raise several fascinating questions:

1. Are there any limits to the doctrine that Congress can outlaw private discrimination based on race by hanging its statutes on the new constitutional peg which the Supreme Court has fashioned?
2. Can Congress use the "badge of servitude" argument to justify future civil rights legislation, or will the Court find this argument applicable only to statutes passed shortly after the Civil War?

3. If the Thirteenth Amendment is a catch-all for future civil rights legislation, is Congress now the sole judge of the constitutionality of civil rights laws, as long as the legislation in question appears rational and not arbitrary and capricious?
4. If the Court has given Congress sweeping power under the Thirteenth Amendment, has it thereby abandoned its historic function of checking Congress?
5. If Congress does possess new and enlarged power to legislate against private discrimination, what impact will exercise of this power have on the size and power of the federal government, and on the relationship between the states and the federal government?
6. If Congress can get at private discrimination via the Thirteenth Amendment, can it, finally, abandon its traditional reliance on the devious logic that it is regulating interstate commerce when it acts to prohibit private discrimination?
7. Will the Supreme Court itself discontinue the practice of upholding statutes attacking private discrimination by the "back-door" method of the interstate commerce clause?
8. And, finally, what of the constitutionality of the open housing title of the Civil Rights Act of 1968? Clearly, the decision in *Jones v. Mayer* swept the ground from under the feet of individuals who might oppose the law in the courts. Only someone who believes in long-shot chances, or feels that the historic right of property owners to discriminate cannot be given up without a last-ditch effort, would be likely to pursue the issue all the way to the Supreme Court.

When the act is challenged, what reasons will the Supreme Court use to justify its decision? At the time the Civil Rights Act of 1968 was passed, Congress had no idea whatever that it might have power under the Thirteenth Amendment to ban discrimination in private housing. When the members of the Court pulled the dropcloth off their chef d'oeuvre shortly thereafter, congressmen were no less bedazzled than the legal profession and the public generally! Thus, the legislative history of the act reveals no intention whatever to ban housing discrimination in order to enforce the Thirteenth Amendment's prohibition of slavery and involuntary servitude. Therefore, what the Court will choose to do is by no means clear.

. . . .

II. Hypothetical Open Housing Case: Conroy v. Adams*

STATEMENT OF THE CASE:

Walter Adams is married and has two young children. He is an electrical engineer, with an M.A. degree from Ohio State University. His wife, Frances, is also a college graduate and has had ten years' experience as an elementary school teacher. Adams and his wife are Negroes.

On April 5, 1970, Adams was promoted by his employer, a major national corporation, and transferred from the West Coast to a new research facility outside Chicago. Adams immediately wrote to the Village Realty Co., mentioning his employer and his new job and describing his housing needs; by return mail, he received a friendly letter stating that the townspeople were delighted that Mr. Adams's corporation had chosen to build its new research office in their town, that the Village Realty Co. had many listings of the description and in the price category mentioned by Mr. Adams, and that its brokerage services were at his disposal.

---

*Author's note: the following case and briefs are original; among the sources used in writing the briefs were interstate commerce clause precedents and state court decisions interpreting state and local fair housing statutes.

Several months before his scheduled move, Adams flew to Chicago to look for a house. He was greeted courteously at the office of the Village Realty Co., but he quickly became aware of the fact that they had not expected a Negro and that his presence was causing some embarrassment. Determined, nevertheless, to find a home near good schools in a town close to his new job, he brought up the subject of discrimination himself and was relieved to hear that the Village Realty Co. supported the code of ethics which had been adopted by all the realtors in the community.

Among the houses viewed by Adams later that day was one owned by Thomas Conroy, a recently retired sales manager who wanted to move to Florida. The realtor indicated that the house had been on the market for four months, but that no one had yet offered its owner anything near his asking price. Adams decided—on the spot—to make such an offer. The realtor tried to dissuade him but, finding his client adamant, told him that he would transmit the offer to purchase to Conroy and would be in touch with Mr. Adams shortly.

Later that week, Mr. and Mrs. Adams got a letter from the Village Realty Co. stating simply that Conroy had refused Adams's offer to buy his house. Enclosed with the letter—without any comment—was a clipping from the town newspaper which read as follows:

To the Editor:

This week, a Negro offered to buy my house and I refused to sell it to him. All of us know what happens when Negroes move into towns like ours. Property values go down, the streets become dirty, their houses get rundown, property taxes go up, good people no longer want to move here, the quality of our schools will go down. I have lived in this town for the past twenty years and I have a great deal of affection for the town and its people; I don't want to see our town go the way of Chicago, New York, Los Angeles and other cities. Although I am leaving, I feel it my duty to write this letter in the hope that other home owners will give the problem their serious attention.

Sincerely,
Thomas Conroy

Frances Adams was visibly shaken by the clipping, but her husband was just plain mad. He told his wife that he was determined to buy the house, even if he had to go to court to get his rights enforced. The next day, at work, he talked with the company's legal counsel, who gave him the name of a lawyer in Chicago and told him that Conroy probably was violating the Civil Rights Act of 1968.

Adams contacted the recommended attorney and asked his advice. By return mail, he got a letter suggesting that the attorney write to the Village Realty Co. to try to bring about an amicable settlement. If this didn't work, the attorney suggested that Adams ask the federal district court for a restraining order to prevent the sale of the house to another party pending trial of a lawsuit for specific enforcement of Adams's offer to buy the house at the asking price. The attorney added (1) that Title 8 of the Civil Rights Act of 1968 gave the district court jurisdiction over the lawsuit, (2) that the court had power under Section 812 of the act to order specific enforcement and to award a prevailing plaintiff actual damages and $1,000 in punitive damages, (3) that Adams had no possible remedy under state law since Illinois had no fair housing statute, and (4) that Adams could bring suit under the Civil Rights Act of 1866, as had Mr. Joseph Lee Jones of St. Louis in *Jones v. Mayer.* The attorney advised against such a suit, however, since the 1866 act did not explicitly authorize the courts to award punitive damages. Adams wrote back authorizing the attorney to follow the proposed course of action.

When the conciliatory letter produced no action, Adams's attorney asked the federal district court for a restraining order, which was granted on the failure of Conroy to reply to a query from the court asking him to show cause why a restraining order should not be issued. In the meantime, Conroy consulted a lawyer who told him the letter to the newspaper had been a mistake, since it could be used to prove in court that Conroy had discriminated against Adams on the basis of race in violation of the Civil Rights Act of 1968. The lawyer suggested that Conroy avoid trouble by selling his house to Adams, but Conroy refused this advice. Next, the lawyer suggested that the courts might find the new law unconstitutional—although this was a long shot—if Conroy contested the case and was prepared to appeal a contrary decision right up to the Supreme Court should this prove necessary. He added that he believed the Supreme Court was less liberal than when it decided *Jones v. Mayer*, since only four members of the seven-man majority in that case were still on the Court. Conroy decided to proceed on this basis.

The trial court held the law constitutional and found the evidence sufficient to prove that Conroy had violated its requirements. The court of appeals upheld this verdict and Conroy appealed to the Supreme Court to reverse the holding of the lower courts. The Supreme Court decided to review the case in order to rule on whether the provision of the Civil Rights Act of 1968 banning discrimination in the sale through a broker of privately owned single-family homes was constitutional.

BRIEF FOR APPELLANT   *BRIEF FOR APPELLEE*

1. *Is the prohibition of discrimination in the sale of single-family homes a valid exercise of Congress's power to regulate interstate commerce?*

Can the power of Congress to regulate interstate commerce be used to take away the historic right of every individual to choose to whom he will sell or rent his property? Can the federal government use this power to coerce property owners into signing unwanted contracts? If so, then we have indeed gone a long way toward destroying the liberty and freedom which have made this country great as well as the principles of limited government enshrined in our Constitution.

Until the present time, no one has suggested that houses move in interstate commerce. Certainly, there is nothing more local in nature than a residence fixed to the earth on which it sits. Building materials move in commerce and may, therefore, be regulated under the commerce clause; mortgage funds are similarly subject to congressional regulation. But we find it hard to understand the logic by which Congress has arrived at the conclusion that, therefore, the sale or rental of a house can also be regulated under the commerce clause.

Counsel for the appellee relies on testimony by various witnesses at the congressional hearings on Title 8 of the Civil Rights Act of 1968

In order to determine whether the provision of the Civil Rights Act of 1968 banning discrimination in the sale of private homes is constitutional, this Court must first examine the scope of the power to regulate interstate and foreign commerce granted to Congress by Article 1, section 8 of the Constitution. The Court has made such an examination on innumerable occasions and each time has ruled that the controlling principles are those announced by Chief Justice John Marshall in the first important case under the commerce clause to reach the Supreme Court, *Gibbons v. Ogden:*

> It is the power to regulate; that is, to prescribe the rules by which commerce is to be governed. This power, like all others vested in Congress, is complete in itself, may be exercised to its utmost extent, and acknowledges no limitations, other than are prescribed in the Constitution.
>
> 22 U.S. 1, at 196 (1824).

Chief Justice Marshall concluded that Congress was barred from regulating only "commerce which is completely internal, which is

to prove that interstate commerce is burdened by discrimination in the sale or rental of housing. However, the testimony reveals only that the construction industry and the housing market are nationwide and play an important part in the national economy, not that the choice of tenants or buyers by landlords and homeowners curtails interstate commerce.

In the absence of evidence that interstate commerce is adversely affected by the freedom of choice which homeowners have possessed since the day this nation was founded—as well as evidence that the interstate movement of construction materials, credit, and people would be advanced by eliminating this historic freedom—it is clear that Congress acted solely on inference, because of a desire to right what it considered an injustice against Negro citizens. Although congressional power over interstate commerce is plenary, legislation based on this power is unconstitutional if it is manifestly arbitrary and unreasonable.

Of course, it is not the province of this Court to judge the wisdom of the legislation in question. However, the Court cannot shirk its obligation to judge the constitutionality of Title 8 as a regulation of interstate commerce. A ruling that the act cannot be supported under Article 1, section 8 of the Constitution would not be an attempt to second-guess the wisdom of Congress but simply a determination that the national legislature acted arbitrarily in concluding that commerce among the states was hindered by the freedom of choice exercised by homeowners or that commerce would be aided by limiting this basic freedom.

However, even if the Court should reject our contention that Title 8 is unconstitutional for the reasons cited above, it should nevertheless throw out the law as an unconstitutional regulation of intrastate commerce. We do not contend that Congress has no power to regulate local, intrastate commerce as an adjunct to its express power to regulate commerce among the states. However, the nature and extent of Congress's power over local commerce is, of necessity, more limited than its power over interstate commerce. The former is based on implication and judicial interpretation; the latter is an express grant of power contained in the Constitution.

carried on between man and man in a state . . . and which does not extend to or affect other states."[1] There can be no doubt that—under conditions prevailing today—the rental or sale of housing is commerce that "affects other states."

There was ample testimony before Congress during the hearings on the Civil Rights Act of 1968 to allow Congress to draw the conclusion that the housing market is national in character and that the interstate movement of people, commodities, and money is burdened by discrimination in the rental and sale of housing. In many past cases, this Court has ruled that such legislative judgments carry a presumption of constitutionality and should not be overturned by the judiciary unless they are clearly arbitrary and unreasonable. Such is not the case here since Congress thoroughly investigated the interstate nature of the housing market.

For example, Robert Weaver, the Secretary of the Department of Housing and Urban Development, testified before Congress that between 1955 and 1960 more than 14 million Americans moved from one state to another and—as a consequence—purchased or rented housing in their new state. In addition, Secretary Weaver stated that the construction industry is heavily interstate in nature. Thus, in 1963 alone, more than 300,000 tons of lumber, plywood, wallboard, brick, and cement were transported by railroads across state lines for use in the residential construction industry. Furthermore, approximately 40 percent of residential mortgages are held by banking institutions outside the state in which the mortgaged property is located.

Attorney General Nicholas Katzenbach testified that over 27 billion dollars in new private investments went into the housing industry in 1965; this expenditure was considerably more than the 23 billion dollars contributed by American agriculture to the gross national product in the same year. The Attorney General also stated that in 1963 over 40 million tons of lumber and finished wood stock were shipped by various means of transportation, and over 40 percent of this tonnage was shipped at least 500 miles.

[1] 22 U.S. 1, at 194 (1824).

If the distinction between commerce among the states and the purely internal concerns of a state is to be meaningful, Congress's power over intrastate commerce cannot be plenary. During this century, federal control over local commerce has expanded greatly; at no time, though, has the federal government gone to the extreme of regulating the liberty of private homeowners. Thus, this case provides a test of whether any real distinction still exists between federal power over interstate and intrastate commerce. We urge on the Court the view that Title 8 differs remarkably in degree from earlier federal regulations of local activities and that, in substance, it obliterates the constitutional distinction entirely.

The appellee's argument that all that is necessary for the Court to uphold a regulation of intrastate commerce is a finding that a close and substantial relationship exists between the local activity and interstate traffic is, in effect, a recognition that a distinction does exist between congressional power over interstate and intrastate commerce. He relies on a pat formula drawn from the decision of this Court in *United States v. Darby*, 312 U.S. 100 (1941), and *NLRB v. Jones and Laughlin Steel Corp.*, 301 U.S. 1 (1937), two cases contesting the constitutionality of federal efforts to rescue the nation from the 1929 Depression by raising purchasing power and limiting industrial strife. In these instances, there was absolutely no doubt that the health of the nation's economy depended substantially on the power of the federal government to regulate the local activities in question. Such is not the case presently before the Court.

Because it is not self-evident that Title 8 has a close and substantial relationship to interstate commerce, the appellee merely cites his pat formula and then jumps to his conclusion that congressional regulation of the freedom of property owners is justifiable under the commerce clause. We believe that the fundamental responsibility of the Court in this case is to examine precisely whether the relationship between the traditional freedom exercised by property owners and interstate commerce is sufficiently close and substantial to justify Congress's obliteration of the distinction between interstate and intrastate commerce. As Justice Black suggested in his concurring

Numerous other witnesses indicated that the confinement of black families to urban ghettos has a limiting effect on the construction of new homes and apartment buildings and thereby reduces the amount of building material which moves in interstate commerce. The unavailability of suitable housing impedes the interstate movement of Negroes, particularly the job mobility of Negro professionals and skilled workers who may be less likely to accept new jobs or to move if faced with the necessity of living in a "black ghetto." The unavailability of mortgage funds as a result of discrimination also limits construction and job mobility.

Thus, Congress could reasonably have concluded that discrimination in the rental and sale of housing has an adverse effect on interstate commerce. It could reasonably have concluded that the removal of discriminatory barriers would protect interstate commerce and promote its growth. We submit that nothing more is necessary for Congress to act under the plenary powers granted it in Article 1, section 8 of the Constitution.

The appellant argues that houses do not move in commerce and that the rental or sale of a house or apartment is a local, intrastate activity, and thereby beyond the reach of the power to regulate interstate commerce. It has long been settled, however, that the power to promote interstate commerce includes the power to regulate local activities which have a substantial or harmful impact on interstate commerce. Thus, Chief Justice Stone said for a unanimous Court in *United States v. Darby*:

> The power of Congress over interstate commerce is not confined to the regulation of commerce among the states. It extends to those activities intrastate which so affect interstate commerce or the exercise of the power of Congress over it as to make regulation of them appropriate means to the attainment of a legitimate end, the exercise of the granted power of Congress to regulate interstate commerce.
>
> 312 U.S. 100, at 118 (1941).

Similarly, in *NLRB v. Jones and Laughlin Steel Corp.*, the Court ruled that "Although activities may be intrastate in character when

opinion in *Polish Alliance v. Labor Board*, 322 U.S. 643, at 652 (1943):

> The doctrine that Congress may provide for regulation of activities not themselves interstate commerce, but merely "affecting" such commerce, rests on the premise that in certain fact situations the federal government may find that regulation of purely local and intrastate commerce is "necessary and proper" to prevent injury to interstate commerce. . . . In applying this doctrine to particular situations this Court properly has been cautious, and has required clear findings before subjecting local business to paramount federal regulation. . . . It has insisted upon "suitable regard to the principle that whenever the federal power is exerted within what would otherwise be the domain of state power, the justification of the exercise of the federal power must clearly appear. . . ."

If such an examination is made in this case, we are confident that the Court will rule that the Civil Rights Act of 1968 transgresses the vague line between appropriate and unconstitutional regulations of intrastate commerce.

Thorough study of the legislative record prior to the passage of the act reveals many sweeping and undocumented references to the impact of racial discrimination in the rental or sale of housing on interstate commerce. Clearly, an effort was made to convince congressmen that such a relationship existed. Yet Congress did not attempt to pass a law which regulated only those rentals or sales which it could conceivably conclude might affect commerce among the states.

For example, such a law could have regulated the sale of new apartments and homes, under the theory that interstate movement of building materials is affected by discrimination in access to new buildings, sale of apartments and homes which have been advertised in interstate media, sale of apartments and homes by brokers who operate in more than one state, etc. It could have excluded from regulation sales which have only a casual and incidental relationship to interstate commerce, such as locally advertised sales by local brokers of homes whose materials moved in commerce many years ago.

It is our contention that Title 8 is uncon-

separately considered, if they have such a close and substantial relation to interstate commerce that their control is essential or appropriate to protect that commerce from burdens or obstructions, Congress cannot be denied the power to exercise that control."[2] And, in *United States v. Women's Sportswear Manufacturing Association*, the Court succinctly stated: "If it is interstate commerce that feels the pinch, it does not matter how local the operation which applies the squeeze."[3]

In the last thirty years this Court has refused—without exception—to limit the word "commerce" as used in the Constitution to a narrow, technical concept. Instead, the Court has insisted that unitary transactions which take place in more than one state—such as the rental and sale of housing—may be regulated by Congress if they have a substantial or injurious impact on interstate commerce. Earlier cases which attempted to limit the power of Congress by various formulas—including a distinction between commerce and manufacturing, agriculture, or mining, between commerce which moved in interstate commerce and commerce which moved solely intrastate, between interstate movement of goods which are noxious in themselves and goods which are wholesome—have long since been discredited as aberrant departures from the principles first enunciated by John Marshall.

Appellant stresses an argument that has frequently been reiterated before this Court and has frequently been rejected. He argues that the interpretation of the commerce power which has been accepted by the Supreme Court in recent decades violates the Constitution since it effectively transfers all power over intrastate commerce to Congress and thereby undermines the very basis of our federal system. Chief Justice John Marshall confronted a similar contention in *Gibbons v. Ogden* and ruled as follows:

> The wisdom and the discretion of Congress, their identity with the people, and the influence which their constituents possess at

---

[2] 301 U.S. 1, at 37 (1937).
[3] 336 U.S. 460, at 464 (1949).

stitutional as a regulation of interstate commerce because it includes within its scope nearly all rentals and sales, despite the fact that many such transactions do not have a close and substantial effect on commerce among the states. Because Congress was trying to legislate against what it considered to be a moral wrong rather than to regulate interstate commerce, the law suffers from the vice of overgenerality. One can argue that such sweeping legislation should be held constitutional when Congress is acting under one of its express powers; we agree with Justice Black, however, that implied powers should be construed more narrowly—that when Congress is legislating in a field which is ordinarily within the domain of the states, the justification for federal intervention must be clear and the resultant legislation must be drawn sufficiently carefully to avoid overreaching constitutional limitations. In our opinion, neither of these conditions has been observed in the Civil Rights Act of 1968.

If the act had been written to prevent housing discrimination which has a substantial effect on interstate commerce (rather than to prevent freedom of choice by nearly *all* property owners), our client would not be before the Court. The sale of appellant's house had at most a casual and remote relationship to interstate commerce. Since the building materials used in his home were purchased more than twenty years ago, no one can argue reasonably that interstate movement of lumber, shingles, plywood, appliances, etc., is affected by the sale. The house was sold locally, by a real estate firm which operated solely within the borders of one suburban town. Admittedly, the plaintiff was a resident of another state at the time he attempted to buy the house in question; however, the plaintiff did not try to buy any other house in the community and has at no time asserted that he was unable to move to his new job because of the refusal of the appellant to convey title to the property. Thus, it cannot reasonably be asserted that interstate movement of persons was hindered by the appellant's decision not to sell to the plaintiff.

It should be clearly understood that we are not arguing that the law should not be applied to the appellant because the sale of his house

elections are, in this, as in many other instances...the sole restraints on which they have relied, to secure them from...abuse. They are the restraints on which the people must often rely solely, in all representative governments.

22 U.S. 1, at 196–97 (1824).

Appellant contends further that even if the Court abides by an interpretation of the commerce clause that allows Congress to regulate intrastate activities that have a substantial or injurious effect on interstate commerce, the sale of his house is so local and so remote from interstate commerce that it cannot be regulated by Congress. This Court has, in the past, refused to judge the constitutionality of an act of Congress by looking solely at the activities of the individual or enterprise engaged in the litigation and ignoring the fact that the single, local event in question—when added to many others of a similar nature—may impose a burden on interstate commerce. Instead, the Court has insisted that constitutionality must be determined by examination of the aggregate effect of a great number of similar acts and not by the impact of a single act on interstate commerce.

The most dramatic illustration of this point is undoubtedly the decision of the Court in *Wickard v. Filburn*, 317 U.S. 111 (1942), a case involving the constitutionality of congressional regulation of wheat grown by a farmer for consumption on his own farm. Filburn sowed twenty-three acres of wheat in excess of his allotment under the Agricultural Adjustment Act of 1938 and was, as a result, subjected to the penalties provided by the act. He contended that Congress was without power to penalize him for growing wheat on his own farm for his own consumption, since his activities were totally local and had at most an indirect effect on interstate commerce.

The Court rejected this contention and held that the power of Congress was not to be determined by any hard and fast formula but by the actual effects of the activity in question on interstate commerce. It ruled that Congress could even restrict the production of wheat for home consumption under its commerce power since such production would reduce commercial demand for wheat and

was so local and remote from interstate commerce that it cannot be regulated by the federal government. We are arguing that the law itself is unconstitutional because it fails to exclude hundreds of thousands of sales in every state which, like the sale in question, cannot be regulated by the federal government since such regulation is not necessary in order for Congress to exercise effectively its express power over commerce among the states.

Counsel for the appellee argue that the decision of this Court in *Wickard v. Filburn*, 317 U.S. 111 (1942), indicates that even the most local of activities may be regulated by Congress. But, this argument misses the point. The *Wickard* decision was based on the theory that local activities which have only a slight impact on interstate commerce may be regulated if the cumulative effect of many such activities creates a substantial burden on interstate commerce. In that case, wheat grown for home consumption constituted a substantial and varying percentage of total demand for wheat and congressional efforts to stabilize prices and foster sales of a commodity which moved in interstate commerce would have been totally defeated if the growth of wheat for home consumption could not have been regulated under the commerce clause.

The cumulative effect of many housing sales, each of which—like the sale in question in this case—does not hinder commerce among the states, does not amount to a substantial burden on interstate commerce. No mathematician has ever suggested that zero plus zero plus zero ad infinitum equals anything but zero.

Finally, the appellee claims that there is no real difference between the public accommodations provisions of the Civil Rights Act of 1964, upheld in *Heart of Atlanta Motel v. United States*, 379 U.S. 241 (1964) and *Katzenbach v. McClung*, 379 U.S. 294 (1964), and Title 8. He believes that because the Court rejected the argument that hotels and restaurants serving interstate travelers or selling food which has moved in interstate commerce cannot be regulated under Congress's power to control interstate commerce, it must arrive at the same conclusion in *Conroy v. Adams*.

We contend, however, that there are substantial differences between regulation of

thereby defeat Congress's efforts to stimulate trade and increase prices. The Court ruled: ". . . [T]hat appellee's own contribution to the demand for wheat may be trivial is not enough to remove him from the scope of regulation where, as here, his contribution, taken together with that of many others similarly situated, is far from trivial."[4]

In the light of the above, we believe that the appellant's contention that his act of discrimination was so local and remote from interstate commerce that he cannot be regulated by Congress cannot be upheld. If this Court were to accept appellant's thesis, nearly every act of discrimination in the rental or sale of housing would be exempt from regulation and Congress would be impotent to remove the burden on interstate commerce which has resulted from the cumulative impact of many seemingly isolated instances of discrimination.

Title 8 is an attempt by Congress to come to grips with a national commercial problem of the first magnitude. As such, it is comparable to the public accommodations provisions of the Civil Rights Act of 1964, which sought to eliminate the burdens placed on interstate commerce by the refusal of hotels, motels, and restaurants to serve Negro patrons. This Court upheld the act, in a case brought by the owner of a Birmingham, Alabama, restaurant, despite his claim that he served local patrons almost exclusively and that only a small amount of the food he served came from sources outside the state. The Court concluded that Congress ". . . [H]ad a rational basis for finding that racial discrimination in restaurants had a direct and adverse effect on the free flow of interstate commerce" and added, ". . . [T]he power of Congress in this field is broad and sweeping; where it keeps within its sphere and violates no express constitutional limitation it has been the rule of this Court, going back almost to the founding days of the Republic, not to interfere."[5] We submit that the same principles should guide the Court in determining the constitutionality of Title 8 of the Civil Rights Act of 1968.

---

[4] 317 U.S. 111, at 127–28 (1942).

[5] *Katzenbach v. McClung*, 379 U.S. 294, at 304–05 (1964).

hotels and restaurants and regulation of the sale of houses. The hotel or restaurant owner is explicitly engaged in commerce, is licensed by the state to serve the public, and makes his living by such service. The homeowner sells his home relatively infrequently, does not attempt to earn his living by selling his home, and needs no license from the state to offer it for sale. His home is private and personal; a restaurant or hotel is privately owned but can hardly be described as personal. It can fairly be said that the restaurant or hotel owner gives up some of his personal rights when he offers to serve the public for profit.

Hotels on interstate highways serve interstate commerce; restaurants which purchase supplies out of state serve them shortly thereafter. Thus hotels and restaurants carry on activities which are closely related to interstate commerce. In contrast, the sale of many private homes has only the remotest relation to interstate commerce. Congress had sufficient data on the impact of discrimination by hotels and restaurants on Negroes to conclude that interstate commerce was being burdened by such discrimination; as we have argued, Congress had no important data about housing discrimination and, therefore, no reasonable grounds for enacting the challenged legislation under the commerce power.

Finally, and perhaps most importantly, Congress attempted to distinguish between hotels serving interstate travelers and hotels which could not be regulated by the federal government, between restaurants serving interstate travelers and selling food which has moved in interstate commerce and restaurants whose activities were so local that they could not be subjected to federal authority. Thus, Congress itself recognized the limits of its power to regulate intrastate activities in the Civil Rights Act of 1964. As we have argued, those limits have been abandoned in Title 8. For this reason alone, if for no other, appellee's assertion that there is no real difference between the Civil Rights Act of 1964 and the Civil Rights Act of 1968 rings hollow. *Heart of Atlanta Motel v. United States* and *Katzenbach v. McClung* are clearly distinguishable from the case at bar.

The simple truth is that Congress has attempted to end discrimination in the rental or

Finally, appellant claims that the act is not a constitutional use of Congress's power over interstate commerce since the purpose of the act is primarily to legislate against a social problem and only incidentally to regulate commerce. Appellant claims that Congress has acted hypocritically, that the constitutional basis of the act is a subterfuge, and that the interstate commerce clause is simply a convenient peg on which to hang an unconstitutional infringement of the fundamental right of property owners to rent or sell their property as they see fit.

These claims are, however, irrelevant. As the Supreme Court said in *United States v. Darby*, "The motive and purpose of a regulation of interstate commerce are matters for the legislative judgment upon the exercise of which the Constitution places no restriction and over which the courts are given no control."[6] The function of this Court is, simply, to decide whether Congress had a rational basis for its conclusion that interstate commerce was impeded by discrimination in the sale or rental of housing and, if it had such a basis, whether the means chosen to eliminate the impediment are reasonable and appropriate.

Moreover, even if this Court did examine Congress's purpose and did conclude that Congress was, in part, legislating against moral wrongs, such a conclusion would not detract from the overwhelming evidence of the disruptive effect that housing discrimination has on interstate commerce. Congress cannot be precluded from exercising its power over interstate commerce because the particular obstruction in question is also a moral and social wrong.

The use of the commerce power to promote public welfare and public safety is neither novel nor alarming. The Supreme Court has, in many historic cases, supported the power of Congress to pass laws under the commerce clause against the shipment of impure food and drugs, the white slave traffic, lotteries, prostitution, kidnapping, child labor, exploitation of labor, and industrial strife. In upholding the constitutionality of the public accommodations provisions of the Civil Rights Act of

[6] 312 U.S. 100, at 115 (1941).

sale of housing, regardless of whether (1) interstate commerce can reasonably be said to be burdened by housing transactions, and (2) there is any causal connection between a particular discriminatory act and commerce among the states. If Congress has the naked power to totally demolish the line between interstate and intrastate commerce and—even more significantly—the line between intrastate commerce which is validly subject to federal regulation and intrastate commerce which is so local as to be beyond the authority of the federal government, there is no facet of human behavior which is not subject to congressional control. Undoubtedly, the rights of every citizen to liberty and property are imperiled by such transcendent federal power. We ask the Court, therefore, to conclude that Title 8 goes beyond Congress's power to regulate commerce among the states.

1964, the Court specifically ruled that Congress could use the commerce power to end racial discrimination. Thus, the appellant's claim that Congress cannot use the commerce power to forbid discrimination in the rental or sale of housing finds no support in the past decisions of this Court.

2. *Is the open housing title a valid exercise of Congress's power to enforce the Fourteenth Amendment?*

Section 1 of the Fourteenth Amendment reads, in part, "No state shall . . . deny to any person within its jurisdiction the equal protection of the law." The final section of the amendment authorizes Congress to enforce the amendment by appropriate legislation. Certainly, if plain English conveys any meaning whatsoever, Congress's power under section 5 of the amendment is limited to prohibiting denials of equal protection by the states or, at the most extreme, by private individuals acting under color of state law. The argument that somehow the Fourteenth Amendment allows Congress to pass a law depriving private citizens of their right to dispose of property at their own discretion stretches the imagination beyond the breaking point. On many occasions, this Court has interpreted various provisions of the Constitution liberally; at no time, however, has the Court accepted an interpretation which contradicts the plain meaning of a contested provision.

From 1883, when it decided the *Civil Rights Cases*, 109 U.S. 3, until 1966, when it decided *United States v. Guest*, 383 U.S. 745, the Supreme Court consistently held that the Four-

What is the scope of Congress's power under section 5 of the Fourteenth Amendment? Is Congress limited, as appellant argues, to passing laws against state actions which deprive people of equal protection of the law? Or can Congress use its authority "to enforce, by appropriate legislation, the provisions of this article" to pass laws guaranteeing civil and political equality?

Appellant asserts that the meaning of the Fourteenth Amendment has been clear ever since the decision of this Court in the *Civil Rights Cases*, 109 U.S. 3 (1883), that Congress could not guarantee equal access to inns and other places of public amusement and public accommodation under section 5 of the Fourteenth Amendment. The Court generalized that private conduct, no matter how discriminatory or wrongful, was beyond the reach of the Fourteenth Amendment.

We believe that recent decisions of the Supreme Court have undermined the ruling against the Civil Rights Act of 1875 and weakened its utility as a precedent. We ask the Court to hold that Congress has power under section 5 to pass laws punishing indi-

teenth Amendment protects the individual against discriminatory state action, not against wrongs done by individuals. Thus, any laws passed by Congress under its authority to enforce the amendment which are not directed solely at state action are unconstitutional. In the *Civil Rights Cases*, the Court held invalid a law which prohibited discriminatory acts by privately owned inns, carriers, and theaters. The Court held:

> It is State action of a particular nature that is prohibited. Individual invasion of individual rights is not the subject matter of the amendment. It nullifies and makes void all State legislation, and State action, of every kind, which impairs the privileges and immunities of citizens ... or denies to any of them the equal protection of the laws.... The last section of the amendment invests Congress with power ... to adopt appropriate legislation for correcting the effects of such prohibited State laws and State acts....
>
> In fine, the legislation which Congress is authorized to adopt ... is not general legislation on the rights of the citizen, but corrective legislation, that is, such as may be necessary and proper for counteracting such laws as the State may adopt or enforce ... or such acts and proceedings as the State may commit or take, and which, by the amendment, they are prohibited from committing or taking.
>
> 109 U.S. 3, at 11, 13–14 (1883).

In the years since 1883, the Supreme Court has had many opportunities to interpret the scope of the Fourteenth Amendment. Among the more important cases was *Shelley v. Kraemer*, 334 U.S. 1 (1948), which ruled that judicial enforcement of racially restrictive covenants was state action prohibited by the Fourteenth Amendment. In a six to zero opinion, the Court, speaking through Chief Justice Vinson, held "... [T]he action inhibited by the First Section of the Fourteenth Amendment is only such action as may fairly be said to be that of the States. That Amendment erects no shield against merely private conduct, however discriminatory or wrongful."[1] The Court went on to conclude that

viduals for interfering with rights guaranteed by the Fourteenth Amendment and to overrule those aspects of the *Civil Rights Cases* which are inconsistent with such a holding.

Our thesis is as follows: the right to equal protection is a right secured by the Fourteenth Amendment. This right places a constitutional obligation on the states to ensure that equal protection of the law is, in fact, achieved. Congress, under its power to enforce the provisions of the Fourteenth Amendment, can act positively to secure the rights protected by the Amendment and is not limited simply to preventing states from carrying out unconstitutional policies.

The decision of the Court in *United States v. Guest*, 338 U.S. 745 (1966), indicates that at least three of the present justices agree with this interpretation of the scope of Congress's power under section 5, and not with the 1883 ruling in the *Civil Rights Cases*. The *Guest* case grew out of the killing of Colonel Lemuel Penn, a Negro educator from Washington, D.C., as he was driving through Georgia. The individuals charged with the killing were not connected with the state in any way nor did they act "under color of law." The defendants were charged with violating section 241 of Title 18 of the United States Code, which outlaws conspiracies to injure any citizen in the free exercise of his constitutional rights. Since the constitutional rights which had been abridged in this case were Fourteenth Amendment rights to equal use of public facilities, the fundamental question posed was whether Congress could punish denials of equal protection regardless of their relationship to state action.

The district court dismissed the indictment on the ground that the Fourteenth Amendment does not protect an individual against wrongs done by individuals. The Supreme Court did not affirm the dismissal but ruled instead that the indictment was ambiguous on the question of the degree of state involvement in the case and that a trial might disclose proof of state action prohibited by the Fourteenth Amendment.

In two separate concurring opinions, six of the justices went much further and suggested that section 241 could be used to punish private conspiracies. Justice Clark, joined by Justices Black and Fortas, noted that the

---

[1] 334 U.S. 1, at 13 (1948).

racially restrictive agreements do not violate Fourteenth Amendment rights as long as they are implemented by voluntary adherence to their terms and there has been no action by the state.

Other cases considered the right of a political party to exclude Negroes from participating in the choice of party nominees and the right of restaurant owners to refuse service to Negro patrons. In each of these instances the Court held to the view that the Fourteenth Amendment did not of itself reach acts of private racial discrimination. However, the Court gradually broadened the concept of state action to prohibit acts of private discrimination which were linked in even a remote way with the state.

None of these twentieth-century cases, however, considered whether the power of Congress under section 5 of the Fourteenth Amendment was sufficiently broad to justify prohibition of private acts which were not prohibited by the amendment itself. In *United States v. Guest,* the Court faced this question but did not rule on it; the majority opinion adhered to the rule that "It is a commonplace that rights under the Equal Protection Clause arise only when there has been an involvement of the State or of one acting under the color of its authority. The Equal Protection Clause does not add anything to the rights which one citizen has under the Constitution against another."[2] The opinion went on to find sufficient allegation of state involvement in the denial of equal rights by the individuals indicted to reverse the dismissal of the indictment by the district court.

Since the federal law under which the accused were indicted prohibited conspiracies to injure any citizen in the free exercise or enjoyment of any right or privilege secured to him by the Constitution or laws of the United States, the Court ruled:

We emphasize that section 241 by its clear language incorporates no more than the Equal Protection Clause itself; the statute does not purport to give substantive, as opposed to remedial, implementation to any rights secured by that Clause. Since we therefore deal here

Court's interpretation of the indictment avoided any decision on Congress's power to punish private conspiracies which interfere with Fourteenth Amendment rights, and added that ". . . [T]here now can be no doubt that the specific language of section 5 empowers the Congress to pass laws punishing all conspiracies—with or without state action—that interfere with Fourteenth Amendment rights."[7]

Justice Brennan, supported by Justices Warren and Douglas, wrote:

A majority of the members of the court expresses the view today that section 5 empowers Congress to enact laws punishing *all* conspiracies to interfere with the exercise of Fourteenth Amendment rights, whether or not state officers or others acting under the color of state law are implicated in the conspiracy.

and

Viewed in its proper perspective, section 5 appears as a positive grant of legislative power, authorizing Congress to exercise its discretion in fashioning remedies to achieve civil and political equality for all citizens. No one would deny that Congress could enact legislation directing state officials to provide Negroes with equal access to state schools, parks and other facilities owned or operated by the State. Nor could it be denied that Congress has the power to punish state officers who, in excess of their authority and in violation of State law, conspire to threaten, harass and murder Negroes for attempting to use these facilities. And I can find no principle of federalism nor work of the Constitution that denies Congress power to determine that in order adequately to protect the right to equal utilization of state facilities, it is also appropriate to punish other individuals—neither state officers nor acting in concert with state officers—who engage in the same brutal conduct for the same misguided purpose.

383 U.S. 745, at 782, 784 (1966).

Other recent decisions support the thesis that Congress's power under section 5 of the Fourteenth Amendment is not limited to striking down unconstitutional state laws. In *South*

only with the bare terms of the Equal Protection Clause itself, nothing said in this opinion goes to the question of what kinds of other and broader legislation Congress might constitutionally enact under section 5 of the Fourteenth Amendment to implement that Clause or any other provision of the Amendment.

383 U.S. 745, at 754–55 (1966).

Thus, the opinion of the Court in *United States v. Guest* does not support the appellee's contention that Congress can legislate against private activities under the Fourteenth Amendment. Admittedly, six members of the Court indicated in dicta that they believed Congress possessed such broad authority.

As counsel for the appellant, we hope the Court will not use the present case to establish a precedent which will have such destructive consequences for the federal framework of government established by the authors of the Constitution. Nothing is surer than that the states will become mere dependencies of the federal government if the Court rules that the Fourteenth Amendment gives Congress general rather than remedial legislative authority. The following statement by Justice Harlan makes this point eloquently:

> Underlying the cases involving an alleged denial of equal protection by ostensibly private action is a clash of competing constitutional claims of a high order: liberty and equality. Freedom of the individual to choose his associates or his neighbors, to use and dispose of his property as he sees fit, to be arbitrary, capricious, even unjust in his personal relations are things entitled to a large measure of protection from governmental interference. This liberty would be overridden, in the name of equality, if the strictures of the [Fourteenth] Amendment were applied to governmental and private action without distinction. Also inherent in the concept of state action are values of federalism, a recognition that there are areas of private rights upon which federal power should not lay a heavy hand and which should more properly be left to the more precise instruments of local authority.
>
> *Peterson v. Greenville*, 373 U.S. 244,
at 250 (1963). (Brackets added.)

However, even if the Court decides to reject these arguments and to rule that section

Carolina v. Katzenbach, 383 U.S. 301 (1966), for example, the Court upheld a statute suspending state literacy tests and empowering the Attorney General to use federal examiners to register voters, despite the fact that literacy tests are not in themselves unconstitutional. The Court did not rule that Congress only had power to ensure that state literacy tests are applied in a nondiscriminatory fashion. Instead, it held that Congress could use any rational means to enforce the guarantees of the Fourteenth and Fifteenth Amendments.

Although the Supreme Court refused to rule on the provisions of the Voting Rights Act of 1965 punishing private individuals for interfering with the right to vote, on the ground that the issue was not germane to a suit by South Carolina, we believe that these provisions are constitutional, even though they are directed at private discrimination. The Fifteenth Amendment establishes the right to vote and the Fourteenth the right to equal opportunity to exercise the franchise. Practical enjoyment of these constitutional rights requires that both private intimidation and discriminatory state action be prohibited. If Congress's power to enforce the provisions of the Fourteenth and Fifteenth Amendments is limited to proscribing unconstitutional state action, the constitutional rights will survive conceptually but not effectively.

While *United States v. Guest* focuses on equal enjoyment of public facilities and *South Carolina v. Katzenbach* on equal opportunity to vote, we believe there is no reason to draw a distinction between these equal protection rights and the right of Negroes to own, buy, and sell property equally with whites. If Congress can, under its Fourteenth Amendment powers, act to prevent private interference with access to public facilities and to the ballot, it can also remove obstacles to the equal enjoyment of the legal right to own property.

Furthermore, segregated housing means inferior provision of public services, including fire and police protection, education, public welfare, access to the courts, etc. Congress could reasonably have concluded that prohibition of discrimination in the rental and sale of private housing would facilitate the breakup of the ghettos and would help to eliminate unconstitutional inequalities in the provision of

5 allows Congress to regulate private action, we believe, nevertheless, that Title 8 should still be held unconstitutional. Unless the Court is willing to construe section 5 as an unlimited grant of legislative power, a line will have to be drawn somewhere between those private activities which Congress can regulate under the Fourteenth Amendment and those which cannot be regulated.

In *United States v. Guest,* the Court was concerned only with the right to equal utilization of public facilities owned or operated by or on behalf of the state, not with privately owned facilities. In his dictum that section 5 empowers Congress to punish private conspiracies, Justice Brennan emphasized that the right to equal use of public facilities was guaranteed by the amendment. Similarly, the provisions of the Voting Rights Act of 1965 which provide for punishment of private individuals who interfere with equal access to the ballot focus on acts which clearly violate the rights guaranteed by the Fourteenth and Fifteenth amendments. Such acts are definitely criminal and the constitutional question at issue is whether Congress has concurrent jurisdiction with the states to punish them.

In contrast, nothing in the Fourteenth Amendment makes the decision of a homeowner to rent or sell to a person of his own choosing unlawful. Nothing in the Fourteenth Amendment requires the state to outlaw discriminatory acts by private homeowners. Title 8 goes far beyond the dicta in *United States v. Guest,* since it regulates a private activity which has always been held to be outside the scope of the Fourteenth Amendment.

Our contention that Title 8 cannot be supported, even under a novel and broadened view of the power conveyed to Congress by the Fourteenth Amendment, should not be construed to suggest that we do not place any credence in our initial premise. We have made the argument solely because several members of the Court have taken the unusual step of indicating in dicta that they are prepared to accept the view that Congress can prohibit at least certain types of private action under section 5 of the amendment.

As we have stressed, we fully believe that Congress's power is limited to acts designed to prevent the states from denying equal protec-

tion of public services by the state. Since the states are obligated by the Fourteenth Amendment to provide equal access to all public aspects of community life and since private discrimination in housing impedes the carrying out of this obligation, Congress has power under section 5 of the amendment to use any rational means to eliminate the impediment to equal provision of public services.

tion; otherwise, the words of the amendment are meaningless. The decision of the Supreme Court in the *Civil Rights Cases* has been followed for nearly a century and should not be overthrown lightly. The function of this Court is not to amend the Constitution, nor is it to right moral wrongs. If the American people believe that the federal government should have power under the Fourteenth Amendment to pass laws like Title 8 of the Civil Rights Act of 1968, the proper procedure would be a constitutional amendment prohibiting individuals as well as states from depriving other citizens of their right to equal protection.

3. *Is Title 8 a valid exercise of Congress's power to enforce the Thirteenth Amendment?*

One looks in vain throughout the legislative history of the 1968 act for evidence that Congress passed the act in order to enforce the Thirteenth Amendment's ban on slavery and involuntary servitude. The hearings and discussion on the floor of Congress include frequent references to Congress's power to regulate interstate commerce and to enforce the equal protection clause of the Fourteenth Amendment, but they make no mention of the Thirteenth Amendment.

Yet, counsel for the appellee insist that this Court can uphold Title 8 on Thirteenth Amendment grounds. Such a decision would constitute a gross abuse of the Supreme Court's power to rule on the constitutionality of acts of Congress.

Since Congress had no intention whatsoever of enforcing the Thirteenth Amendment, a ruling that Congress did act under that amendment would be a flagrant example of judicial lawmaking. This Court has refrained from assuming legislative powers in the past, and it should continue to do so in order to protect the separation of powers that has contributed so much to the American form of government. It will be time enough to determine the constitutionality of a modern open housing statute under the enforcement clause of the Thirteenth Amendment when and if Congress acts under that amendment.

Contrary to appellee's assertion, *Mapp v.*

Congress did not enact Title 8 under the Thirteenth Amendment for the simple reason that no one in Congress knew that discrimination by private individuals could be reached under that amendment at the time the Civil Rights Act of 1968 was passed. It was not until the decision of the Supreme Court in *Jones v. Mayer*, 392 U.S. 409 (1968), ten weeks after passage of the act, that Congress and the nation knew the Court might uphold open housing legislation enacted pursuant to the enforcement clause of the Thirteenth Amendment. Until the decision in *Jones v. Mayer*, it was widely assumed that Congress's power under the Thirteenth was limited to legislation designed to eliminate state-enforced relics of slavery.

In passing the Civil Rights Act of 1968, Congress attempted to do away with some of the remaining relics or badges of slavery. It used whatever constitutional provisions were available at the time; clearly, the Thirteenth Amendment would have been used as a basis for the act if Congress had known it could be employed in the fight against discrimination by private homeowners. Thus, although the legislative history reveals no specific reliance on the Thirteenth Amendment, Congress clearly acted within the spirit of that amendment when it passed the Civil Rights Act of 1968.

Secondly, we believe that the question of

Ohio, 367 U.S. 643 (1961), does not support the view that the Supreme Court can uphold an act of Congress on the basis of a constitutional provision that was not even considered by Congress at the time the act was passed. *Mapp v. Ohio* is clearly distinguishable.

The *Mapp* case did not involve a decision of a coordinate branch of government but a precedent of the Court itself. The Court decided to reverse the earlier decision, even though counsel for the appellant had not urged reversal. Surely, there is a significant difference between a decision to reverse a judicial precedent and a decision by the Court to take on itself the function of rewriting the constitutional basis of an act of Congress.

It is true that the Court tries to construe statutes so that they can be saved. In this instance, however, there is no question of statutory construction. The statute is clear enough. What the appellee is asking is that this Court should rewrite the constitutional basis on which Title 8 was passed.

whether Congress relied on the Thirteenth Amendment, either explicitly or implicitly, is not particularly important. The sole question should be: is there a constitutional basis for the act? If there is, that is the end of the matter and the Court should go no further. The Court has repeatedly stated that if an act is constitutional, it will not construe the intent of Congress in passing the questioned legislation.

Unless the Court is willing to reverse its decision in *Jones v. Mayer*, the Thirteenth Amendment constitutes a valid basis for any act banning discrimination in the sale or rental of privately owned housing.

The appellant argues that the Court would be usurping the legislative function if it held Title 8 constitutional under the Thirteenth Amendment. Yet it is precisely the function of the judiciary to determine whether a statute meets the demands of the Constitution. Just as the Court, in *Mapp v. Ohio*, 367 U.S. 643 (1961), took on itself the responsibility of reversing *Wolf v. Colorado*, 338 U.S. 25 (1949), even though counsel for the appellant had not urged reversal, so should the Court, in this instance, uphold Title 8 under the Thirteenth Amendment, even though Congress did not explicitly have the Thirteenth Amendment in mind when it passed the Civil Rights Act of 1968.

4. *Does the Civil Rights Act of 1968 violate the Fifth Amendment by depriving appellant of liberty and property without due process of law?*

Title 8 of the Civil Rights Act of 1968 is the most far-reaching and thoroughgoing deprivation of freedom and of property that has ever been passed in the United States. It restricts the historic and fundamental right of homeowners to own, control, and dispose of their property in contravention of the due process of law guarantee of the Fifth Amendment. Unless this Court acts to protect personal liberty and private property by holding the act unconstitutional, the power of Congress to destroy these rights will be virtually absolute and the Fifth Amendment will be meaningless as a check on legislative majorities. The Founding Fathers deliberately inserted the

The appellant argues that even if the Supreme Court should find that Congress had power under the commerce clause or the Fourteenth Amendment to enact Title 8, the right of a property owner to discriminate in the rental or sale of his property is so basic and fundamental that it may not be regulated by government at all. This argument is wholly without foundation. Simply because discrimination in the rental or sale of housing has always existed does not elevate such discrimination to the level of a constitutional right that cannot be abridged.

Unquestionably, Title 8 causes some loss of preexisting freedom, but that is exactly the

Fifth Amendment in the Constitution to prevent the federal government from becoming such an all-powerful leviathan.

As we have argued, Congress has no power under the interstate commerce clause or the Fourteenth Amendment to pass an open housing law. However, even if this Court should rule that the law is not an unconstitutional abuse of these provisions of the Constitution, it should, nevertheless, hold the law invalid, since both provisions are subject to the limitations of the Constitution, including the Fifth Amendment. Certainly, the fundamental rights of the people protected by the Fifth Amendment are not subordinate to Congress's power over commercial matters.

The appellee argues that the due process clause of the Fifth Amendment is nothing more than an admonition to Congress to avoid arbitrary and capricious action when passing laws which curb the cherished freedoms of American citizens. If this argument is carried to its logical conclusion, its import is all too obvious: no rights are safe from legislative curtailment as long as Congress acts according to its established procedures. We ask the Court to reject emphatically such a destructive proposition.

The Fifth Amendment does not draw a line between those regulations of liberty and property which are constitutionally permissible and those which so violate fundamental rights that they constitute a deprivation without due process of law. If the Fifth Amendment is to remain more than a hollow shell, however, a line must be drawn somewhere and must be drawn by the Supreme Court. Since the function of the Court is to decide only the case before it, and not to rule on theoretical problems, appellant asks the Court in the present instance to hold only that Title 8 clearly transgresses the line between permissible and unconstitutional regulations of liberty and property.

For example, in *Griswold v. Connecticut,* 381 U.S. 479 (1965), the Court ruled that a law forbidding the use of contraceptives rather than their manufacture or sale has the maximum destructive impact on the privacy of the marital relationship and is too broad and sweeping to stand the test of constitutionality.

purpose of every regulatory enactment. For example, the freedom of property owners to use their property as they see fit has long been curtailed by zoning ordinances and health and fire laws; nonetheless, the courts have refused to accept the argument that such regulations are unconstitutional because they deprive property owners of liberty and property without due process of law.

In *Heart of Atlanta Motel v. United States,* 379 U.S. 241 (1964), the Supreme Court upheld the power of Congress to require owners of hotels and restaurants to serve Negroes and rejected the contention that the Fifth Amendment due process clause prevented the government from interfering with the freedom of hotel and restaurant owners to choose their own patrons.

In *Jones v. Mayer,* 392 U.S. 409 (1968), the Court went even further: it ruled that Congress had power under the Thirteenth Amendment to prohibit discrimination in the rental and sale of private housing and that Congress had banned such discrimination in the Civil Rights Act of 1866. Thus, the Court has already supported the constitutionality of a federal open housing measure. The majority refused to hold that Congress was forbidden to regulate the sale of housing because such regulation violated private rights which were protected against government action by the due process clause of the Fifth Amendment; two justices dissented from the Court's opinion in *Jones v. Mayer,* but neither suggested that the due process clause established vested rights. The failure of even a single member of the Court to hold that the Fifth Amendment was a bar to open housing legislation suggests that the appellant's present contention has no merit whatsoever.

As this Court has frequently stated, the purpose of the due process clauses of the Fifth and Fourteenth Amendments is to prevent tyranny by precluding arbitrary and capricious government action, not to prevent regulation entirely. In *Nebbia v. New York,* the Court ruled:

The right of a citizen to exercise exclusive dominion over property and freely to contract is always in collision with the right of the state

Justice Goldberg, in a concurring opinion joined by Justices Warren and Brennan, stated:

> This Court has held that the Fifth and Fourteenth Amendments protect certain fundamental personal liberties from abridgement. . . . In determining which rights are fundamental, judges . . . must look to the "traditions and [collective] conscience of our people to determine whether a principle is so rooted [there] as to be ranked as fundamental."
>
> 381 U.S. 479, at 492–93 (1965).

Thus, the Court held that the substance of the law violated the due process clause of the Fourteenth Amendment. Certainly, the historic rights of homeowners are no less fundamental and basic than the right of married couples to use contraceptives. If the Fourteenth Amendment due process clause protects citizens from state-imposed deprivations of liberty, the Fifth Amendment due process clause should be construed to prohibit federal destruction of one of the freedoms which have made this nation great.

Even if the Court should hold that the substance of Title 8 does not violate the Fifth Amendment, we believe that the law does not meet the standards of reasonableness imposed by the requirements of due process. The administrative procedures established by the act are arbitrary and unreasonable and will subject homeowners to harassment and litigation. The sale of houses will be tied up interminably by lawsuits, many of which will be brought by individuals who have no real intention of buying the house in question. While plaintiffs will presumably have to prove discrimination, homeowners will—in actual practice—be presumed guilty if they decide, for any reason whatever, not to sell to a Negro. Homeowners caught in such a bind will be hard put to prove that they have not discriminated, since evidence of their innocent intent will rarely be available. Thus, the problems of evidence will make a mockery of due process at the expense of innocent homeowners. Any law which fails to distinguish between the innocent and the guilty contravenes the guarantee of due process of law and must be judged unconstitutional.

to regulate the use of property and the conduct of business. Private right must yield to public need, subject only to constitutional restriction.

> The Fifth Amendment, in the field of Federal activities, and the Fourteenth, as respects state action, do not preclude governmental regulation for the public welfare. They merely condition the exertion of the admitted power, by securing that the end shall be accomplished by methods consistent with due process. And the guarantee of due process, as has often been held, demands only that the law shall not be unreasonable, arbitrary, or capricious, and that the means selected shall have a real and substantial relation to the object sought to be attained.
>
> 291 U.S. 502, at 510, 524–25 (1934).

Nor can it be argued that Congress acted arbitrarily in deciding that Title 8 was a reasonable and appropriate measure to eliminate the evil which it found to exist. There is nothing novel or capricious about the law. Similar laws are in effect in seventeen states covering over one-half the population. They have been challenged repeatedly, but in all but one instance the courts have held that such laws do not violate the due process clause of the Fourteenth Amendment. The Civil Rights Act of 1968 is no more subject to attack under the due process clause of the Fifth Amendment than are state fair housing laws under the due process clause of the Fourteenth Amendment.

Furthermore, since this Court has already held that discrimination in the sale or rental of privately owned housing violates the Civil Rights Act of 1866, it could hardly rule that the 1968 statute is arbitrary, capricious, and unreasonable.

Nor need much be said in response to appellant's contention that the law is unreasonable since homeowners will be deemed guilty of discriminating if they refuse for any reason to sell their homes to Negroes. As long as the courts sit, it is their responsibility to ensure that no such miscarriage of justice occurs.

Finally, the Supreme Court has frequently dealt with the contention that a particular regulation violates the provision of the Fifth Amendment that private property shall not be taken for public use without just compensation. Clearly, a fair housing regulation is not a

Finally, Title 8 violates the provision of the Fifth Amendment that no private property shall be taken for public use without just compensation. It is incomprehensible to us how the appellee can argue that the act does not constitute a "taking" of private property. The act gives courts power to order the transfer of title to property against the owner's will; such a court order is to be made in furtherance of an express public policy, but the federal government will not pay any compensation to the owner whatever. One can sugarcoat such highhanded action to make it sound palatable, but once the semantics are stripped away, nothing is left but an arrogant taking of private property in contravention of the literal command of the Fifth Amendment.

"taking for public use," just as the regulation against discrimination in hotel and restaurant service was held not to be a "taking" of private property in *Heart of Atlanta Motel v. United States.* The decisions of this Court uniformly support the proposition that the government is not liable if property is injured or destroyed as a result of lawful action unless the government actually takes possession of the property in question. Thus, for example, in *Jacob Ruppert v. Caffey,* 251 U.S. 264 (1920), the closing of a brewery as a result of prohibition did not constitute a "taking" within the meaning of the Fifth Amendment.

We ask the Court to reject the appellant's contention that the right to discriminate in the rental or sale of housing is enshrined in the due process clause of the Fifth Amendment. Such a ruling would contradict important recent precedents, such as the unanimous decision of the Court in the *Heart of Atlanta* case, and would effectively prevent Congress from attempting to eliminate the evils of racial discrimination in the United States.

5. Does the Civil Rights Act of 1968 destroy rights reserved to the states and to the people by the Ninth and Tenth Amendments?

Are the Ninth and Tenth Amendments meaningless verbiage, inserted into the Constitution for no purpose whatsoever? Or do they, in fact, reserve those rights not enumerated in the Constitution to the people? The fundamental goal of the United States Constitution was to set up a national government capable of governing effectively but restrained from exercising arbitrary and unlimited power. Thus, the Ninth and Tenth Amendments are crucial to the survival of constitutional government in the United States and cannot properly be viewed simply as an inconsequential afterthought. We sincerely believe that the failure of the Supreme Court to recognize this important fact in recent years has caused a great deal of mischief and has undermined the form of government envisaged by the authors of the Constitution.

The Constitution nowhere mentions the power of the federal government to limit the rights of property owners. The power claimed

The Ninth and Tenth Amendments reserve to the states and to the people rights not granted to the federal government in the Constitution. Nothing in these two amendments, however, acts as a limit on the powers contained in the Constitution. As has frequently been reiterated by this Court, the Tenth Amendment "states but a truism that all is retained which has not been surrendered."[8] Since Congress had power to enact the challenged statute under the interstate commerce clause and the Thirteenth and Fourteenth Amendments, the act does not invade reserved rights.

Furthermore, the Tenth Amendment does not limit the power of Congress to regulate commerce by appropriate means. As Chief Justice Stone, speaking for the Court, said in the *Darby* case:

From the beginning and for many years the Amendment has been construed as not depriv-

[8] *United States v. Darby,* 312 U.S. 100, at 124 (1941).

by Congress in this case is neither enumerated nor delegated to the federal government. Under common principles of interpretation then, this power is reserved to the people or to the states. The appellee claims that ample power to sustain the law can be found in the interstate commerce clause and the Thirteenth and Fourteenth Amendments, but even a generous reading of these provisions cannot sustain such a tortured interpretation. If the Ninth and Tenth Amendments are to retain some meaning in the future, a line will have to be drawn somewhere between those powers which can legitimately be imputed from the commerce clause, the prohibition of slavery and involuntary servitude, or the equal protection clause and those which are beyond the scope of the federal government as the Constitution presently stands.

ing the national government of authority to resort to all means for the exercise of a granted power which are appropriate and plainly adapted to the permitted end. Whatever doubts may have arisen of the soundness of that conclusion, they have been put at rest. . . .

312 U.S. 100, at 124 (1941).

Appellant's contention that the Ninth and Tenth Amendments bar federal open housing legislation flies in the face of recent decisions of this Court on the subject of discrimination in housing. In *Heart of Atlanta Motel v. United States*, the Court ruled unanimously that these two amendments did not prohibit federal regulation of hotels and motels under the interstate commerce clause. Even more directly, in *Jones v. Mayer*, the Court upheld Congress's power to prevent discrimination in the sale of privately owned homes under the Thirteenth Amendment and ignored the argument that Congress's power under the Thirteenth Amendment was in some sense curtailed by the Ninth and Tenth Amendments.

. . . .

III. The Future of Open Housing

At present, the most thought-provoking question in regard to open housing is not what the Supreme Court will do when confronted with the arguments presented in Part II of this chapter but what impact the Civil Rights Act of 1968, and state and local ordinances, will have on housing discrimination. Few constitutional law experts believe the Supreme Court will interfere with congressional efforts to establish a national policy against discrimination in the sale of private, single-family homes.

After all, the Court supported federal regulation of hotels, motels, restaurants, and other places of public accommodation by a unanimous decision in 1964. There is no more than a minor step between such regulation and prohibition of discrimination by landlords, banks which are in the mortgage and home financing business, and real estate firms. And it is merely another logical if perhaps somewhat less minor step to include sale of single-family dwellings through real estate agents. Such a sale is a business transaction in which a private individual offers some commodity for sale to the general public; it is not comparable to a strictly private "transaction," such as a social evening in a private home.

Furthermore, numerous decisions of the Court since 1937 indicate that Congress's power to regulate localized transactions under its interstate commerce power is virtually unlimited. All the arguments against a broad view of the interstate commerce power, such as the point that regulation of intrastate commerce interferes with rights reserved to the states or to the people or that such regulation deprives individuals of liberty or property without due process of law, have repeatedly been rejected. There is no reason to assume they would be any more persuasive when the Court considers the Civil Rights Act of 1968. In fact, many constitutional law experts believe that the only real limit on Congress's power to regulate the economy for social purposes is political; if Congress is willing to pass a particular piece of legislation under this rubric, that is virtually the end of the matter, since the Supreme Court has shown extreme reluctance to interfere with legislation passed under the commerce clause.

On the other hand, it is by no means clear that the members of the Court would find that Congress has equivalent power under the Thirteenth and Fourteenth Amendments. Apart from *Jones v. Mayer*, there are no important precedents to strengthen a Court ruling based on either or both of these amendments, and there are many historic decisions which would make such a ruling awkward indeed. A few justices have indicated in various cases that they find the devious logic of using the interstate commerce clause to uphold antidiscrimination laws somewhat difficult to swallow and that they would prefer a frontal assault through the equal protection clause of the Fourteenth Amendment, but this view has never appealed to a majority.[1] The easiest path is the one already marked out under the interstate commerce clause, not the unbroken terrain of the post-Civil War amendments.

Assuming that, barring fortuitous developments, the above analysis is correct, what will be the outcome of a Supreme Court decision upholding the Civil Rights Act of 1968? While such a decision will carry moral weight, it will not, of course, put an end to housing discrimination. The camel's nose will be inside the tent, but it will be a long time until the camel is inside and the Arab is out in the sandstorm.

Of course, it goes without saying that poverty, unemployment, and the high cost of private housing which is not substandard in quality are insuperable barriers to tearing down the walls of our urban ghettos. Unless and until these problems are faced and fought, the vast majority of black families will have little real interest in the reduction or elimination of discrimination in the rental or sale of apartments and houses. For these people, other federal and state programs are far more important than the Civil Rights Act of 1968.

But what about the increasing number of middle-class blacks who could afford better housing if it were available? Will the act provide meaningful assistance to them? There are several reasons for feeling that the federal law will have only a limited impact.

First, the law is addressed to private individuals, not to public officials. Experience in the last few decades suggests that public officials, and particularly nonelected officials, are more likely to yield, however unhappily, to antidiscriminatory legislation and court decrees than private citizens. Discrimination in jury selection, in public parks and hospitals, and in civil service systems has not been eliminated, but greater progress has been made in these areas than, for example, in the field of private employment. Similarly, there is evidence to suggest that voting discrimination by registrars and other public officials has to some extent been replaced by intimidation by private citizens. HEW officials have found that school superintendents, principals, and teachers frequently seem more willing to comply with desegregation orders than state governors, school board members, and self-appointed representatives of the public.

Second, discrimination which is blatant and overt is far easier to combat than discrimination which is covert in nature. Local ordinances or policies that blacks must sit in the backs of buses or that blacks cannot be served at white lunch counters cannot be hidden from the eyes of reformers. Furthermore, such regulations are even

---

[1] See, for example, the concurring opinions of Justices Douglas and Goldberg in *Heart of Atlanta Motel v. United States*, 379 U.S. 241 (1964).

more blatant because they apply to blacks as a whole, without distinction, rather than to individual blacks. In contrast, discriminatory refusals to rent or sell dwellings can be and are concealed easily, since each discriminatory act applies solely to an individual and the possibilities for dissimulation and evasion are infinite. Ordinarily, homeseekers have no hard and fast idea why sellers reject their offers to purchase; sellers frequently hold out for more money, decide not to move, sell to a personal acquaintance, or reject individuals for entirely arbitrary but not necessarily discriminatory reasons. Given the range of options open to sellers, blacks whose offers to purchase are rejected will ordinarily find it next to impossible to prove that a seller acted illegally. Only sellers who act in a crude, blatant fashion will face a substantial risk of being caught by the law.

Third, resistance to antidiscriminatory public policies varies with the extent to which each particular policy is viewed by those accustomed to discriminating as undermining fundamental values. Thus efforts to maintain discrimination in jury selection, or in public facilities such as buses, railroad trains, hotels, and restaurants, have proved far more feeble than efforts to resist school integration. The "neighborhood school" has acquired a sanctity in America which goes far beyond its educational value. Similarly, one can expect strong resistance to the movement of black families into white neighborhoods, despite the 1968 federal law, because many whites perceive housing integration as an extreme rather than a minor threat to their way of life. While part of this perceived threat is due to racism, part of it may be rational, particularly for lower-income whites who currently live on the fringes of urban ghettos. For these individuals, the end of housing discrimination does not imply that a few black families will move into white neighborhoods; it implies the expansion of the ghetto, the flight of most whites from their present homes or apartments, and a relatively uncomfortable existence for those whites who choose to remain or are forced for economic reasons to do so.

Fourth, enforcement of antidiscriminatory policies varies with the extent to which individuals subject to discrimination seek implementation of their legal rights. If individuals and interest groups assert themselves aggressively, it will be harder for responsible officials to take refuge in bureaucratic inertia. But, black Americans are not united on the desirability of housing integration. Many feel the game is not worth the candle; many wish to live in predominantly black communities; many have no desire to undergo the pain and humiliation which inevitably accompany leadership of social causes. And, finally, an increasing number of blacks has no interest whatever in integration on the white man's terms. Militants believe that open housing would divide and weaken black communities just when they are coming of age politically, would separate middle-class and poor blacks, and would divert attention from the problems of urban ghettos.

Fifth, and more directly, the Civil Rights Act of 1968 is not a remarkably strong statute, particularly in the light of the above analysis. In order to maintain a semblance of federalism, the act ties the hands of federal officials whenever a complaint comes from a state or city which has a substantially equivalent open housing law. Yet in the judgment of most observers, none of these state and local statutes has had a meaningful impact on housing discrimination. To the extent that the Secretary of the Department of Housing and Urban Development is required to defer to local officials, the federal law does not contribute anything exceptional to the struggle against housing discrimination.

Furthermore, notice what happens when the Secretary's hands are untied: he dare not clench his fists and come out swinging against discriminators. Instead, he must put his manicured hands palms up on the table and start smooth-talking the complainant and the individual accused of discrimination. He can conciliate, persuade, and negotiate, but he has no legal authority to go further if these efforts are unsuccessful. Since "jawboning" rarely works when presidents try to interfere in labor-management negotiations, why should more be expected of it as a tool for implementing an antidiscrimination housing policy?

The Secretary cannot initiate action against discrimination; he must await specific complaints. He cannot stage investigations of real estate practices in various communities and take appropriate action following such an investigation. He cannot issue binding orders against discrimination or levy fines, nor can he use the public press to broadcast the results of his conciliatory efforts unless both parties agree to such publicity. He may or may not have the manpower and the willpower to carry out his assigned functions, depending in part on how tightfisted Congress is with federal tax money.

In sum, the administrative procedures set up for enforcing the act are limited indeed. Under the circumstances, officials charged by the Secretary with carrying out his responsibilities may become frustrated with their impotency, and bureaucratic inertia will supplant the enthusiasm and energy which are essential ingredients of successful regulatory efforts. Lest one be overly pessimistic about the Secretary's powers, it should be added that experience is the real test, not conjecture, that even bad statutes can be made to work by men with unusual capabilities, and that one of the major functions of the Secretary and those to whom he delegates his authority will be to return to Congress with requests for stronger procedures if these prove necessary.

Furthermore, it is not unimportant that black citizens who fear they will become mired in bureaucratic quicksand if they file a complaint with the Department of Housing and Urban Development have the option under the act of going directly to the courts. A threatened lawsuit may lead landlords and homeowners to comply with the public policy established by the Civil Rights Act of 1968 far more expeditiously than the filing of a complaint with HUD. Nevertheless, legal action will be a meaningful method of enforcement only for those hearty individuals who have the patience, determination, and money to become litigants and to prosecute their claims through the courts. Experience in the field of voting rights shows that litigation by individuals may protect the rights of those few people but does little to protect the rights of the vast majority of blacks; it was not until Congress gave up the idea of enforcement of voting rights through the courts in the Voting Rights Act of 1965 that millions of black citizens first became able to register and to vote.

In the Civil Rights Act of 1968 the popularly elected branches of the federal government took hesitant steps toward reducing discrimination in the rental and sale of private housing. By enacting a national public policy, Congress and the President committed the nation to a new morality. Whether that public policy and that moral commitment will be ephemeral or meaningful in the coming decades will depend on political leadership, administrative capability, and the capacity of the general public to live down the racism that has characterized American society by responding positively to efforts to implement the egalitarian ideals spelled out so plainly in the Declaration of Independence.

FEDERAL AID TO PAROCHIAL EDUCATION
Has the Wall Between Church and State Crumbled?

ISSUES RAISED   Government Establishment of Religion   /   Free Exercise of Religion   /   Federal Control of Public Education   /   Federal Control of Private Education

I. Interest-group Politics: The Sensitive Issue of Public Support for Parochial Schools

Locked in between two decaying five-story walk-ups, in the midst of a New York slum, stands Saint Theresa's Roman Catholic Elementary School, with decades of dust and neglect written across its Gothic façade. It was not always this way: a generation ago, the neighboring tenements were tidy, if lower class, the blocks surrounding St. Theresa's were predominantly Irish-American, the problems of the community seemed manageable, and the sisters who taught at St. Theresa's lived lives fulfilled by their service to church and to humanity. The Gothic façade imposed an elegance and an image of solidity on what would otherwise have been an undistinguished area.

Now, all this has changed. Like many other church schools in former immigrant and working-class neighborhoods, St. Theresa's has inherited all the stubborn problems of America's core cities. Immigrants and their children have moved up the socioeconomic ladder and left the community; the blue-collar jobs which provided an entrée for the unskilled have dried up. Blacks and Puerto Ricans have moved into the tenements, so that now the Irish population is in the minority. The tenements themselves are older, owned by absentee landlords, and neglected almost to the point of being uninhabitable. Unemployment, poverty, crime, drug addiction, racial conflict and, above all, hopelessness pervade the area.

St. Theresa's shares the decay which permeates the neighborhood: it is neglected, its physical plant overused and worn out. The sisters find it harder and harder to teach increasingly recalcitrant, turned-off students. Lay teachers tend to grumble about their jobs, working conditions, and meager salaries. The once imposing Gothic façade is now cheap and shabby.

To put it plainly, St. Theresa's is in the midst of a maelstrom, and its chances for survival are slim. Like thousands of parochial schools across the nation, it is failing in its educational purpose and may have to be closed because it can no longer be supported by tuition, Sunday church giving, and other contributions from the local diocese. If the diocese closes the school, 600 students will have to be absorbed by the neighboring public school, which has no room for additional students. An interim decade of crisis would exist until new public facilities could be constructed. In the meantime, the public schools would be faced with double and triple sessions, makeshift facilities, and ruinous overcrowding. The quality of education in the neighborhood, already low, would undoubtedly decline. Ultimately, the public would have to assume the entire burden of construction costs and operating expenses which would follow a decision to cease operations.

It has been estimated that St. Theresa's alone saves the public nearly a million dollars a year, since the average per-pupil expenditure in the public schools of New York City and the surrounding suburbs is at least $1,250. If all the Roman Catholic parochial schools in New York City were to close, the public schools would have to absorb over 400,000 students and the public would have to pay an additional 500 million dollars annually in taxes; more than a billion dollars in capital funds would be needed to provide facilities for the new public school students.

In the nation as a whole, over 2,000 Catholic schools closed or were consolidated in the six years from 1965 to 1971. By the summer of 1971, there were 11,351 Catholic schools in the nation, enrolling 4.3 million students. As a result of the school closings, more than 1 million students were forced to transfer to public schools.

The United States Catholic Conference, a pressure group which speaks for the interests of the Catholic Church, estimates that two million elementary school children—or about half the current parochial school enrollment—will have to transfer to public schools in the next six years *unless* church schools receive millions of dollars of additional income.[1] Whether or not the picture drawn by the USCC is exaggerated, the point remains, nevertheless, that the financial condition of the nation's parochial schools is increasingly desperate. As operating deficits have mounted, pleas for public support have grown in volume.

Frequently, it is difficult to determine why certain social questions become important political issues. Cause-and-effect relationships are obscure and hard to examine. In the case of public aid to parochial education, however, causation appears to be comparatively simple: changing economic and social forces have been making it increasingly difficult for parochial schools to survive on the income received from tuition and other normal sources.

Expenditures on the nation's public elementary and secondary schools have risen dramatically in the postwar period. For example, the cost of public education was approximately two billion dollars in 1940; a quarter of a century later, it had grown to more than 22 billion dollars.[2] At the risk of oversimplification, it is possible to point out what appear to be the major causes of this shift in investment in public education.

1. During the Depression of the 1930s and the Second World War of the 1940s, capital expenses were cut drastically. Only two-thirds as much money was spent

[1] *The New York Times*, June 16, 1969, p. 1, Sept. 4, 1969, p. 48, and July 4, 1971, sec. E, p. 7. While the above pages focus on the plight of Catholic schools rather than of parochial schools in general, this is simply because 87 percent of all nonpublic school students attend Catholic schools. Other reasons are (1) due to numbers and organization, the political strength of Catholics is far more significant than that of other religions which operate sectarian schools, and (2) the consequences for the public at large of closing Catholic schools are obviously far greater than the consequences of closing schools operated by other religions denominations.

[2] *Progress of Public Education in the U.S.A. 1963–1964*, U.S. Department of Health, Education, and Welfare, 1964, p. 16; Eugene Eidenberg and Roy D. Morey, *An Act of Congress*, Norton, New York, 1969, pp. 11–12.

on facilities in 1940 as was spent a decade earlier.[3] Thus, many school physical plants were worn out and in need of massive refurbishing by the 1950s.

2. The school population, which had remained relatively constant for a period of years, suddenly began to grow dramatically as children born during the post-war baby boom entered elementary school. In 1946, 2.2 million students enrolled in the first grade; by 1953, the number had jumped to 3.7 million. In the fifteen years after 1950, the number of high school students went from 6.5 million to double that figure. Total public school enrollment went from 23 million in 1949 to approximately 60 million as the nation entered the decade of the 1970s.[4] Massive expenses for new construction and for swollen operating budgets were the inevitable result of these surges in enrollment.

3. Russia's space successes in the late 1950s made the nation's leaders take stock of the American educational system; major weaknesses were revealed and demands for costly improvements were made more and more insistently.

4. Two major population migrations contributed to the financial problems facing public education. In the 1950s alone, approximately 2.5 million black Americans left the South in hopes of finding a better life in the cities of the North, the Midwest, and the West. At the same time, millions of white Americans moved to the suburbs. The influx of undertrained, underemployed, undereducated, low-income families caused the tax base of the cities to shrink at the same time as the educational needs of the population served by urban school systems grew. Increasing sums were spent on urban education, but public awareness of fiscal disparities which resulted from reliance on the local property tax for financing public education and public willingness to eliminate these inequalities was—and continues to be—slow in coming.

5. Finally, teachers, who had been comparatively well off during the Depression and war years, found themselves increasingly left out of the country's growing affluence. Teachers became more and more militant, and salaries began to go up, causing further expansion of operating budgets.

Parochial schools faced nearly all the above problems as well as several additional ones. Unlike the public schools, the parochial schools could not turn to the taxpayers for increased support. In fact, increased taxation to support public schools simply increased the financial burdens faced by parents who enrolled their children in private schools. Further, each parochial school had to adjust its tuition rates to the incomes of the particular families it served. This imposed a heavy strain on schools in urban areas which educated the children of low-income families.

And finally, Catholic parochial schools were challenged by a changing phenomenon within the church itself: fewer and fewer young people chose to become nuns and priests. Seminaries had to close down or to consolidate. As a result, more and more lay teachers were hired. The economic consequences of this shift from teaching clergy who could be hired for the equivalent of room and board to individuals who needed professional salaries in order to support their families are obvious and require no elaboration. Without question, changing vocational patterns among Catholic youth compounded the financial problems facing church school administrators.

[3] *Statistics of State School Systems, 1963–1964*, U.S. Department of Health, Education, and Welfare, 1964, p. 21.

[4] Statistics on enrollment taken from *Statistics of State School Systems, 1961–1962*, U.S. Department of Health, Education, and Welfare, 1962, p. 42; *Progress of Public Education in the U.S.A., 1963–1964*, *supra* n. 2, p. 10; and *Projections of Educational Statistics to 1975–1976*, U.S. Department of Health, Education, and Welfare, 1964, p. 5.

HISTORY OF THE FEDERAL AID CONTROVERSY

Thus, the 1950s and 1960s were decades of crisis in American public and parochial education. Pressure for federal financing of public elementary and secondary education gradually mounted throughout the period. On the other hand, opposition to changing the traditional pattern of local autonomy and local responsibility for financing education was extremely powerful. The skirmishes which preceded the crucial battle over passage of the Elementary and Secondary Education Act of 1965 reveal both the intensity of feeling which existed on the subject of federal subsidy of education and the interplay of political interests which led finally to the defeat of those individuals and organized interests who opposed changes in the status quo.

Crucial to this history is the role played by organized interests, particularly the National Education Association (NEA) and the National Catholic Welfare Conference, now known as the United States Catholic Conference. By far the largest of the groups favoring federal aid to education, the NEA has over 1 million members and over 8,000 affiliates in every state. Because the NEA includes both teachers and administrators at all educational levels in its membership, it is not a monolith. Instead, it is a loose federation of state and local affiliates which is further split by divisions organized by educational level, by divisions organized on the basis of educational function—e.g., administration, teaching, research—and by divisions organized by academic subject areas.

Nevertheless, despite the virtual autonomy of its constituent units, the NEA does take positions on many national educational issues. Throughout the postwar period, until 1965, the NEA pushed for federal aid to education provided (1) that the aid be granted in a general fashion so that specific resource allocations could be made by state and local authorities, and (2) that no federal aid be given to parochial schools. The NEA believed that federal aid to parochial schools would violate the First Amendment, since such aid would destroy strict separation of church and state. And secondly, the NEA took it as an article of faith that public money should be used for public education and not diverted to private schools.

The other major interest groups in the field of education shared to a great extent the NEA's position on federal aid, although they disagreed with the NEA's views on various other questions. The NEA's chief rival for the loyalty of teachers, the American Federation of Teachers, stood with the NEA on federal aid, as did the National Congress of Parents and Teachers, the Council of Chief State School Officers, the National School Boards Association, the American Association of University Professors, and the American Association of University Women. The NEA derived further support from the National Council of Churches, the American Jewish Congress, the Council of the Churches of Christ, the National Association of Evangelicals, the Baptist Joint Committee on Public Affairs, Protestants and Other Americans United for Separation of Church and State, the American Civil Liberties Union, the AFL-CIO, the National Farmers Union, the Teamsters Union, Americans for Democratic Action, and the American Library Association.

Opposed to the NEA were two types of groups: those that feared the growth of the federal government and those that were opposed to federal aid as long as parochial school students were excluded. In the former category were the United States Chamber of Commerce, the National Association of Manufacturers, the American Farm Bureau Federation, the Southern States Industrial Council, the National Conference of State Taxpayers Association, and the Daughters of the American Revolution. In the latter category were the National Catholic Welfare Conference, the National Catholic Education Association, the Council of Catholic Men, and Citizens for Educational Freedom.

One other pressure group should be mentioned here: the U.S. Office of Education in the Department of Health, Education, and Welfare. Prior to the 1960s, the Office of Education was a sorry excuse for a federal agency; a stepchild of the Interior Department from its creation in 1867 until 1939, the Office of Education had been charged primarily with gathering statistics. It had little money, an insignificant staff, and few meaningful responsibilities. Perhaps its place in the hierarchy of Washington bureaucracies can be described best by saying that the Office of Education did not have enough political muscle to prevent frequent evictions from whatever office space it was able to find. It symbolized the widely shared philosophy that education was a local matter, not a matter of national concern.

In 1939 the Office of Education was transferred to the Federal Security Agency. Then, in 1950, it was given responsibility for administering a program of grants to school districts swollen by the presence of children of military personnel—the so-called "impacted areas program." The next big step in the metamorphosis of the Office of Education was the creation of the Department of Health, Education, and Welfare by President Eisenhower in 1953. The following year the newly upgraded Office of Education was given responsibility for administering grants to stimulate educational research at colleges and universities.

After the launching of Sputnik, Congress passed the National Defense Education Act, and the Office of Education was charged with distributing large sums of money to high schools and colleges in order to increase rapidly the number of scientists, engineers, and foreign-language specialists graduating each year. In little more than twenty years, the Office of Education had grown from a staff of approximately 300 and a budget of 40 million dollars to a staff of 1,400 and a budget of 600 million dollars.

According to Stephen K. Bailey and Edith K. Mosher, authors of the authoritative book *ESEA: The Office of Education Administers a Law*, the postwar period of growth was also one of tremendous strain. Bureaucratic inertia and conflict proliferated within the agency as tradition-minded personnel were confronted with younger, more aggressive individuals. Efforts to develop strong support for federal assistance to elementary and secondary schools never met with success. It was not until the advent of John F. Kennedy's Presidency and the appointment of a strong commissioner, Francis Keppel, Dean of the Harvard Graduate School of Education, that the Office of Education began to kick over the traces and to push vigorously for a national educational policy.[5]

Throughout the 1940s and the 1950s, bills providing general aid to public elementary and secondary education were submitted in each session of Congress. Every attempt to use the federal income tax to provide general support for public education foundered on the shoals of strong congressional opposition.

It would be a mistake, however, to assume that the federal government turned a deaf ear to all the pleas of school administrators during the decades following the war. Higher education received large-scale support, starting with the GI Bill of Rights in 1944. Under this program, eight million World War II veterans received over 14 billion dollars for living expenses, books, and tuition.

Six years later, the National Science Foundation (NSF) was established to promote research and education in the sciences. In its first fifteen years, the NSF spent over half a billion dollars on research fellowships, teacher training institutes, and other

[5] Stephen K. Bailey and Edith K. Mosher, *ESEA: The Office of Education Administers a Law*, Syracuse University Press, Syracuse, N.Y., 1968, pp. 1–71; see also Corinne Silverman, "The Office of Education Library," and Stephen K. Bailey, "The Office of Education and the Education Act of 1965," cases No. 16 and 100 in The Interuniversity Case Program, Bobbs-Merrill, New York, 1966.

activities. In the same year, Congress passed the 1950 Housing Act, which authorized low-interest loans for the construction of college dormitories. Initially, 300 million dollars was appropriated for dormitory loans; subsequently, the loan program has been extended further.

The next big step in federal aid to higher education was the National Defense Education Act (NDEA) of 1958. The NDEA provided 1 billion dollars for science, math, and foreign-language programs; interest in these defense-related areas was stimulated by the award of loans and fellowships, by grants for the purchase of expensive technical equipment, and by the establishment of teacher training institutes. Finally, in 1963 and 1965, Congress authorized the expenditure of several billion additional dollars for college classroom construction, for college libraries, and for student scholarships.

While Congress refused to provide general aid to elementary and secondary schools throughout the period under discussion, it did, however, provide limited and categorical assistance. Thus, the impacted areas program of World War II was extended and made more permanent in 1950, when Congress passed legislation authorizing payment of federal funds to school districts whose tax bases had been affected adversely by major government installations. Included in this aid was money for teachers' salaries, school construction, and building maintenance. The popularity of the impacted areas program is indicated by the fact that Congress spent more than 3 billion dollars on aid to specific school districts in the period from 1950 to 1965.[6]

Secondly, the National Defense Education Act of 1958, mentioned above, provided substantial support for secondary schools as well as for colleges and universities. Under the act, states could receive matching grants for purchasing scientific equipment and remodeling classrooms used in teaching science, mathematics, and foreign languages. Furthermore, funds were authorized for the development of testing, guidance, and counseling programs. Teacher training institutes, already mentioned, were designed to benefit both college and secondary education.

The impacted areas program and the NDEA grant system were both a far cry from general aid to the nation's public schools. Impacted areas money went only to certain specific school districts. NDEA money not only strengthened scientific curricula at the expense of the humanities and the social studies but also tended to go to specific schools. The act strengthened science courses in the superior, primarily suburban, secondary schools. Elementary schools were left out, and rural and urban ghetto high schools received few benefits. Schools which were most in need of large sums of money received what can be best described as marginal assistance.

Why did congressional supporters of federal aid to education succeed in passing categoric aid bills but not proposals for broader and more widespread assistance? The answer can be found in a brief analysis of what happened to the general aid bills submitted in every session of Congress.

The first general aid bill to clear either house of Congress was passed by the Senate in 1948 by a vote of fifty-eight to twenty-two. It is worth noting, even though the point perhaps deserves no more than a footnote, that one of the key figures in the fight *for* passage was "Mr. Republican," Senator Robert A. Taft, the chairman of the Republican Policy Committee in the Senate.

---

[6] Two additional examples of extremely popular specific aid are the school lunch program, established in 1946, and the school milk program, set up in 1954. Congressional support for these programs is overwhelming, as Lyndon Johnson found out when he attempted to reduce the school lunch program in response to congressional budget-cutting demands during the fight over the 1967 income tax surcharge.

In the 1948 elections, both parties endorsed federal aid to education. President Truman pledged support in his State of the Union Message the following January. Once again, a bill passed the Senate, by an even more overwhelming vote than the Taft bill of the year before. An attempt to add an amendment denying assistance to segregated schools was beaten back by a coalition of federal aid supporters and Southern Democrats after it became clear that the bill would have no chance of passage if the amendment were adopted.

In the House of Representatives, hearings were held by a subcommittee of the Education and Labor Committee headed by Graham Barden of North Carolina, a Southern Democrat. The Barden subcommittee reported to the full committee a bill which included a specific prohibition on assistance to private and parochial schools. At this point, the roof fell in.

The chairman of the Education and Labor Committee, a Roman Catholic, vowed that Barden's "anti-Catholic" bill would never clear his committee. Cardinal Spellman joined the fray with a blast of his own, calling the bill "a craven crusade of religious prejudice against Catholic children" and the bill's supporters "new apostles of bigotry." Eleanor Roosevelt replied and the daily newspapers burned with the heated interchange between Mrs. Roosevelt and Cardinal Spellman. With supporters of federal aid unable to compromise the religious conflict, opponents of any aid at all had the upper hand, and the bill was killed in committee.

The election of President Eisenhower consolidated the position of those who favored the American tradition of local financing of education. Unlike Senator Taft, President Eisenhower was opposed to federal aid to all states in the nation. Eisenhower had stated as early as 1949 his belief that such aid would undermine the strength of the country and would "... [B]ecome yet another vehicle by which the believers in paternalism, if not outright socialism, will gain still additional power for the central Government."[7] Thus, throughout the 1950s, traditional Republican fears of federal control caused White House opposition to general aid measures and encouraged the President to approach even categorical aid circumspectly.

School aid legislation did not reach the floor of either house in 1953 or 1954. In 1955, Eisenhower proposed what the Democrats labeled a "banker's bill," a billion-dollar school construction program. Republican and Democratic supporters of federal aid on the House Education and Labor Committee reported out a far stronger bill, but it never got through the labyrinth of the House Rules Committee.

The following year a compromise bill cleared the Rules Committee but was axed on the floor. An antisegregation amendment was proposed by Adam Clayton Powell of New York and added to the bill by Powell's colleagues. The Powell amendment amounted to a kiss of death, since Southern supporters of federal aid refused to go along with a civil-rights-oriented piece of legislation. The events of 1957 amounted to a replay of the previous year: again, school aid reached the floor of the House of Representatives; again, the Powell amendment was voted; again, Southern Democrat and Republican opposition killed the measure.

In 1960, for the first time, legislation passed both houses of Congress. The Powell amendment was added on the floor of the House, but the bill passed nevertheless. Since the Senate and House bills differed, they had to be sent to a conference committee. In the House, the bill went first to the Rules Committee, where it was sidetracked once again. The original House bill had been reported out of the Rules Com-

---

[7] Letter from Columbia University President Dwight D. Eisenhower to the Barden subcommittee of the House Committee on Education and Labor, as quoted in *Congress and the Nation 1945–1964*, Congressional Quarterly News Service, Washington, 1965, p. 1203.

mittee by a seven to five vote; with the Powell amendment attached, however, two of the members reversed themselves, and the final tally was seven to five against sending the bill to a conference committee.

KENNEDY AND JOHNSON: THE STRUGGLE INTENSIFIES

The election of 1960 brought to the presidency a man as devoted to the philosophy of massive federal aid to the nation's schools as President Eisenhower had been opposed to this idea. Aid to education became the key domestic issue of President Kennedy's first year in office.

Before pushing hard for any legislation, however, the new administration chose to take on the powerful House Rules Committee and its chairman, Judge Howard Smith of Virginia, on the ground that a conservative majority on the committee had prevented and would continue to prevent the majority in Congress from enacting liberal legislation. With the assistance and support of Speaker Sam Rayburn, the Rules Committee was "packed" by the addition of three members, bringing the total membership to fifteen. The President's legislative strategists calculated that they now had a one-vote majority in favor of aid to education.

Shortly after the inauguration, the administration, backed by the National Education Association, introduced its major legislative request in the field of education, a 2.5-billion-dollar bill for construction of public schools and teachers' salaries. Aid to private schools was prohibited, even though the President knew the Catholic Church would oppose the exclusion of sectarian schools.

Kennedy was on the horns of a dilemma: he could not gain support from Catholics without including aid to sectarian schools; yet he could not include such assistance, since the major proponent of federal aid, the NEA, was unalterably opposed to aid to parochial schools. Further, Kennedy had campaigned for the presidency in part on the ground that he believed in strict separation of church and state; as the first Catholic President, he could not afford to go back on his commitment to remain neutral on church-state questions. Thus, he was boxed in.

The Kennedy Aid to Education Bill cleared the Senate with little difficulty. In the House, the Education and Labor Committee, now under the chairmanship of Representative Powell, reported out a similar bill. Powell promised to withhold the famous Powell amendment when the bill reached the floor, but Rules Committee Chairman Smith and his colleague Rep. William Colmer of Mississippi feared it would be offered by someone else. They opposed the bill, as did the five Republicans on the committee. Kennedy's majority of eight collapsed when one of the Democrats on the committee, James Delaney, a Catholic from New York, responded to the arguments of church leaders and voted with the opposition. Subsequent Kennedy bills, in 1962 and 1963, shared the fate of the all-important 1961 legislation.

To sum up, federal aid to education was moribund by 1963. The Senate had been responsive, passing bills in 1948, 1949, 1960, and 1961, but the House had failed to act. From 1943 to 1955, seven bills were pigeonholed in the Education and Labor Committee. As the proponents of federal aid gathered strength on this committee, the real fighting ground shifted to the Rules Committee and to the floor of the House itself. Bills were sidetracked by the Rules Committee in 1955, 1960, 1961, 1962, 1963, and 1964; other legislative proposals were killed on the floor of the House in 1956, 1957, and 1961.

Aid to education—or, to be more exact, general aid to education—had foundered on the rocks of race, religion, and traditional federalism. On these issues, congressional attitudes seemed rigid and uncompromising. Opponents of general aid were in the minority, yet they were able to maintain the status quo because of their strength on certain key committees, whose consent had to be obtained before legislation could reach the floor of the House of Representatives, and because of their skill at dividing the proponents of federal aid and playing them off against one another. Advocates of aid recognized that new approaches were clearly necessary, but who would be the first to yield? Under the circumstances, it was not surprising that nearly every academic observer who wrote on the subject of general federal aid to public education in the 1961 through 1963 period predicted that Congress would not pass such legislation in the foreseeable future.[8]

Ironically, just as the books and articles, with their dour predictions, began to appear in print, the situation started to change. While many of the changes were fortuitous, others were brought about by hard work, intensive bargaining, and astute political decision making.

The death of John F. Kennedy on November 22, 1963, shocked the nation and brought an end to a period of intense bickering and political infighting in Congress. The emotional wave which swept the country in the following months made it uncomfortable for congressmen to remain intransigent. Suddenly, legislative proposals which had been stalled for months and years became viable.

Lyndon Johnson became President at a time when the country needed reconciliation and union, not continued political divisiveness. Johnson instinctively seized the reins of power and pressed forward with Kennedy's legislative program. Kennedy's civil rights program, which had been tied in knots for the simple reason that it included the strongest civil rights bill to reach Congress in nearly 100 years, became untied when President Johnson indicated he would push hard for enactment.

While public attention has focused primarily on the public accommodations section of the Civil Rights Act of 1964, another provision of the act played a significant part in the fight for federal aid to education the following year. Title VI of the act prohibited the distribution of federal funds to any state agency which operated in a discriminatory fashion; thus, the old Powell amendment of the 1950s was finally enacted into law.[9]

Suddenly, one of the three factors which had been used by opponents of federal aid to education to divide proponents of such aid was no longer relevant. It was no longer necessary for civil rights activists to fight for an antisegregation rider every time an aid to education bill came before Congress. Southerners could now vote for or against aid to education on its own merits, without reference to the race question.

At the same time as he was pushing forward with the Kennedy legislative program, President Johnson began to put his own stamp on legislation. From 1961 to 1963 Congress had passed a number of antipoverty bills; now, Johnson decided to accelerate government efforts to eliminate poverty. In his first State of the Union address, in January 1964, Johnson committed his administration to a massive war on poverty. His major vehicle was the Economic Opportunity Act, which created the Job Corps, the Neighborhood Youth Corps, and Adult Basic Education programs.[10]

Another major innovation was the decision not to divide responsibility for administering antipoverty programs among various federal agencies but to centralize the effort in a single Office of Economic Opportunity to be located in the Executive

---

[8] See, e.g., Frank Munger and Richard T. Fenno, Jr., *National Politics and Federal Aid to Education*, Syracuse University Press, Syracuse, N.Y., 1961; H. Douglas Price, "Race, Religion, and the Rules Committee: The Kennedy Aid to Education Bills," in Alan F. Westin (ed.), *The Uses of Power*, Harcourt, Brace, New York, 1961; Robert Bendiner, *Obstacle Course on Capitol Hill*, McGraw-Hill, New York, 1964.

[9] 78 Stat. 241, at 252–53.

[10] 78 Stat. 508.

Office of the President. Johnson's basic idea was that only a centralized OEO under his own wing would have sufficient political power to administer its own antipoverty programs and to orchestrate successfully the efforts of federal agencies which were already administering antipoverty programs.

The Johnson administration's emphasis on combating poverty had a notable influence on the struggle for federal aid to education. For the first time, attention began to shift from general aid to all public schools to aid to schools which served the educationally disadvantaged. Clearly, poverty and poor education were intimately related, and progress could not be made in one area without meaningful change in the other as well.

It is hard to pinpoint the origin of the idea that federal aid should be directed at improving the educational opportunities of the economically underprivileged. Like many important political ideas, it appeared to spring up in many places at the same time during 1964. In February 1964, Senator Wayne Morse of Oregon introduced a proposal to add the categories of poverty, welfare, and unemployment to the definition of what constituted "impacted areas." Senator Morse's version of what happened is as follows:

Last year my subcommittee had a brainstorm. We were working on impacted areas legislation. I felt that we needed a new section to this impacted area legislation to provide Federal funds for another type of impact—namely the impact of poverty and deprivation upon youngsters in the low-standard school districts of the country and in rural and urban slums. We talked about it for quite a while as an amendment to the impacted area legislation. Finally we introduced a separate bill.

We didn't think that we had a chance of getting it passed last year, but we felt we could get some hearings. That's how the Morse Bill of last year came into being. Unless you understand this bill and its history, you can't possibly understand Title I of the Perkins-Morse bill [the Elementary and Secondary Education Act of 1965].[11]

In a speech to the American Association of School Administrators a month after passage of the Elementary and Secondary Education Act of 1965, Morse went into somewhat greater detail:

I will never forget those hearings last summer. To my astonishment the Administration, speaking through the mouth of the Commissioner of Education, pleaded against the enactment on the grounds that my bill cost too much and on the grounds that there would be administrative difficulties in working out the formula provided.

Now I conduct my hearings in the form of a seminar, with term papers assigned to the Administration witness. So I told the Commissioner, more in sorrow than in anger, that, in my judgment, he had flunked the course. And I made him my emissary to the Administration to tell it, all the way to the top, that they had failed it, too. But I held out hope. I told the Commissioner that he could repeat the course for make-up credit in this session.

Last fall...the Commissioner came over to me and said, "Senator, the President wants us to tell you that we are for your bill. We are even going to expand it. We don't know by how much, but we are going to expand it."

The rest is history. Instead of my little $218 million a year bill, they took me at my word and increased it fivefold.... When we talked with the HEW people and the Office of Education people about their bill prior to its introduction last January, we had a great deal of fun with them, pointing out how much time and effort they could have saved themselves. But seriously, the key point consisted in finding a formula which

---

[11] *School Management*, June, 1965, p. 87. (Brackets added.)

was (1) objective, (2) verifiable from independent sources without too great an investment in personnel, and (3) most importantly, which was based on forerunner legislation which was known to Congress, so that the strawmen such as the myth of Federal control could be laid to rest. This helped us to build a bridge across the chasm which had swallowed up every Federal aid bill since 1947.[12]

While the role of Senator Morse should not be overlooked, it would be incorrect to suggest that he alone generated the ideas that evolved into the Elementary and Secondary Education Act. After the failures of the Kennedy administration, the National Education Association began to abandon the idea of general aid to all public schools and started to think in terms of a broadened "impacted areas" concept for delivering federal assistance. Furthermore, Commissioner Keppel played a key role, perhaps the single most important one, in working with the inevitably suspicious interest groups, congressmen, and other executive branch officials to resolve the conflicts on which previous legislative proposals had foundered. According to Bailey and Mosher, it was Keppel more than any other single person who created a working partnership between the NEA and the National Catholic Welfare Conference.[13]

Early in 1964, President Johnson announced his strong commitment to improving the quality of education throughout the nation. He charged Commissioner Keppel with finding a way through the maze of interest-group conflicts. Johnson also established a high-level Task Force on Education, headed by John Gardner, then president of the Carnegie Corporation, and instructed it to report back to the White House shortly after the presidential election that fall.

In a series of private, informal meetings with the NEA and the NCWC, Keppel attempted to work out compromises which would be acceptable to both groups. Given the recent history of federal aid proposals, Keppel was able to stress that there would be no massive federal aid to elementary and secondary education unless compromises could be worked out. Each group would have to be realistic if the President's goals were to be achieved.

In the meantime, Keppel met with the Gardner Task Force as an ex officio member, worked with the Office of Education to meet the commitment made to Senator Morse, and maintained contact with the Department of Health, Education, and Welfare, key senators and congressmen, the White House staff, and the President himself. It was Keppel's function to act as a broker between these diverse individuals and interests.

Initially, at least, the NEA and the NCWC were somewhat reluctant to abandon their historic positions; leaders of the two dominant interest groups spent many hours arguing among themselves as to the advisability and necessity for compromise. Then, an event occurred which made both groups rethink their strategy.

The presidential election was an unmitigated disaster for opponents of federal aid to education. Barry Goldwater led the Republican Party to the worst defeat of the century. For the first time, the President and the Northern, liberal Democrats appeared to have a working majority in both houses of Congress; they would be able to act strongly and expeditiously, without having to water down legislative proposals in order to pick up a few essential Republican or Southern Democratic votes.

In the Senate, the Democrats picked up two seats, making their margin sixty-eight to thirty-two. More important, however, were the results in the House of Representa-

---

[12] Comments of Senator Wayne Morse to the American Association of School Administrators, May 13, 1969 (mimeographed). At no place in the official record is there any statement by Commissioner Keppel that the Morse proposals would be too costly.

[13] Bailey and Mosher, *op. cit.*, p. 35.

tives. The Johnson coattails helped 69 Democratic freshmen to be elected; 38 of these replaced Republicans who had accumulated over 400 years of seniority before their 1964 defeat. The new lineup in the House was 295 Democrats and only 140 Republicans on the other side of the aisle. Most of the new Democrats were enthusiastic supporters of the administration's two major goals: eradication of poverty and improvement in educational opportunity throughout the nation. Thus, the Johnson victory broke down the second of the three barriers to federal aid: the strong position of congressmen who feared federal control of education. Now, the major remaining hurdle was the church-state controversy.

The election added at least one other new element to the interest group calculus. Suddenly, federal aid to education looked not only vaguely possible but indeed probable. Within the NEA, it became clear that the Office of Education staff believed the NEA was ideological and rigid. If a bill were to pass after all these years without NEA support, the NEA would be frozen out of the Office of Education. It would also be excluded from the vital decisions that would be made before an education bill went to Congress and then after enactment, when the Office of Education drew up the administrative guidelines for implementing the legislation. Commissioner Keppel and his staff conveyed a similar message to leaders of the NCWC.

Shortly thereafter, it became clear that both groups were willing to move off dead center. The NEA would no longer insist that aid go only to public schools, and the NCWC would not insist on equal treatment for parochial schools in any federal aid program. To put the point in its crudest form, half a loaf seemed better than no loaf at all, particularly when it seemed that one's chances of obtaining even half a loaf were endangered by continued rigidity. Thus, for political reasons, the NEA decided to swallow, at least for the time being, its constitutional objections. NEA leaders rationalized this strategic decision by deciding that they would seek a court test of the meaning of the First Amendment soon after a bill was passed.

Douglass Cater, President Johnson's special assistant charged with maintaining contact with Commissioner Keppel and other individuals and organizations interested in federal aid to education, has described the administration's strategy in the following terms:

> The problem we faced was not one of having to mold public opinion. Public opinion had been generally in favor of such a bill for at least several years. The problem continually facing the bill was the opposition of the two major interest groups: the National Education Association and the National Catholic Welfare Conference. The overwhelming victory of the President and the party in 1964 had the effect, beyond expanding Democratic majorities in the Congress, of forcing the pressure groups to come to terms with each other. Both had to know that a bill was going to be passed; and as a consequence, the legislative goal for both groups was to maximize their gains in the bill while minimizing the gains of the other side . . . with the major difference that now they both accepted the fact that the other side had to be given something.[14]

President Johnson rode herd on his various "agents" throughout the months prior to the inauguration as they pursued the delicate process of negotiations and consensus building. For the first time, prospects for massive federal aid looked good: the race issue was no longer directly relevant; the federal control issue had been reduced to a point of relative insignificance, the church-state conflict was being defused. If effective compromises could be reached, the President would be able to introduce a bill built on consensus rather than divisiveness, the major pro-federal-aid

---

[14] As quoted in Eidenberg and Morey, *op. cit.*, pp. 79–80.

interest groups would work together for passage, and congressmen would be able to vote for federal aid without having to take sides publicly on a highly controversial religious issue.

Throughout the summer of 1964 the Gardner task force, Commissioner Keppel, and the Office of Education analyzed the massive problems facing elementary and secondary education as well as various proposals for aid to educationally disadvantaged children. When the task force submitted its conclusions to President Johnson shortly after the election, Keppel and his staff were already working in high gear: general conclusions were translated into relatively specific legislative proposals without any time lag. By Thanksgiving, the President and his immediate advisors had approved Keppel's suggestions and the Office of Education was asked to draft the proposed legislation. What had formerly been informal consultations with the relevant interest groups began to seem more and more like negotiations as Keppel and the Office of Education sought to explain the administration's plans and to gain support. Cater invited leaders of the NEA and the NCWC to the White House for conferences designed to impress on them the need for compromise. The administration clearly was in command, and arm-twisting was unnecessary; since the President's goal was to draft a bill which gave something to everybody but did not meet the total expectations of any one interest group, what was needed was subtle persuasion.

These efforts paid off handsomely. By the time President Johnson was ready to announce his education proposals, all potential opposition from the NEA and the NCWC had been blunted. On January 12, the President's program was sent to Congress, with appropriate national publicity. Later that day, the NEA held a press conference in Washington and announced its support for the education bill; within a few hours, the chief legislative representative of the NCWC made a public statement which generated further support for the bandwagon which was artfully being constructed by Messrs. Johnson, Keppel, and company.

THE ELEMENTARY AND SECONDARY EDUCATION ACT IS UNVEILED

The bill submitted to Congress contained numerous compromises in addition to the proposed solution of the church-state controversy. The supporters of federal aid had to resolve (1) the questions of who should get aid, how much, and for what purposes; (2) the issue of federal, state, and/or local control of funds and programs; (3) the problem of how to stimulate reform, experimentation, and innovation. All these potential conflicts were resolved in a complex tapestry of five major titles, as summarized and analyzed below:[15]

TITLE I—FINANCIAL ASSISTANCE TO LOCAL SCHOOL DISTRICTS FOR THE EDUCATION OF CHILDREN OF LOW-INCOME FAMILIES

Congress declared it to be the public policy of the United States to provide financial assistance to local educational agencies serving areas with concentrations of children from low-income families in order to expand and improve programs designed to help educationally deprived children. The Commissioner of Education was ordered to make payments to state educational authorities for basic grants to local school boards for a three-year period; the amount to be granted to a local school district was to be determined by multiplying a fixed percentage of the average per-pupil expenditure in the state by the number of children in the district from low-

---

[15] Since the act that emerged from Congress was essentially the same as the administration's bill, the following summary is based on the actual law, as passed by Congress, 79 Stat. 27–58.

income families. The specific percentage to be used and the definition of low-income families were to be determined each year by Congress.

Applications for grants were to be approved by the appropriate state agency upon its determination that (1) the proposed programs had reasonable promise of meeting the special educational needs of deprived children in areas where there were high concentrations of poor families; (2) the local school district had made provision for special educational services and arrangements—including dual enrollment, educational radio and television, and mobile educational services and equipment—for private school students to the extent consistent with the number of educationally deprived children in the district who attended private elementary and secondary schools; (3) the local agency had provided assurance that both control and administration of funds and ownership of property purchased with these funds was in the hands of a public agency. Other provisions of Title I required local school districts to adopt procedures for evaluating the effectiveness of Title I programs, required annual reports to the state agency, required dissemination of significant information obtained from educational research to teachers and administrators, and spelled out in some detail the responsibilities of the state educational agencies and the Commissioner of Education.

ANALYSIS OF TITLE I The administration considered Title I the most important part of ESEA: five-sixths of the $1,345,000,000 requested—totaling over 1 billion dollars—was for Title I programs. Among the most significant strategic decisions and compromises made in Title I, the following are most significant:

1. The bill was written as an amendment to the highly popular impacted areas legislation; this deliberate effort to "pour new wine into old bottles" was done to grease the legislative skids.
2. An effort was made to channel money to meet the needs of educationally deprived children, not to schools. This distinction without a difference was adopted to allay fears of federal control of local schools and of public contributions to parochial schools.
3. Title I funds were to be used for programs to aid the children of low-income families, not the educational needs of all school children aged five through seventeen. This particular approach to federal aid to education was chosen, at least in part, to give Title I more political appeal.
4. The aid formula was set up to ensure that all states would be included; thus, no congressman could feel that his constituency was excluded from the benefits provided by Title I.
5. Under the formula, local school districts were entitled to specific sums of money. The money would flow from the federal government to the state educational agency for distribution to the local school districts, but the state agency would have limited discretion. This provision was designed to satisfy local school administrators and their congressional supporters, although it clearly would not please state educational administrators. On the other hand, no money would go directly from the federal government to local school districts.
6. State educational agencies were given the right to approve or disapprove program proposals submitted by local school districts. This idea was included to balance off point 5 above; it was thought that local school boards would not like the constraints imposed by state program control and supervision but that such control would be appreciated by state educational agencies.
7. Local school districts were given authority to dream up their own program proposals. The federal government was not given the right to approve programs, in order to forestall political controversy over the issue of federal control. Further-

more, a deliberate decision was made not to spell out particular programs in Title I but to leave the question of what actually could be done with Title I money vague. Ostensibly, this approach was followed in order to allow flexibility at the local level; underneath the surface, however, was the thought that political opposition in Congress would be weaker if there were no specific programs to oppose.

8. According to the formula chosen by the Office of Education, a large share of Title I money would go to major urban areas where large numbers of low-income families live and to poor rural areas. Thus, the formula was appealing to the old Roosevelt coalition of Northern and Southern Democrats; it was less appealing to representatives of many suburbs, smaller cities, and agricultural communities of the Midwest and elsewhere where poverty is not a widespread phenomenon.

9. Finally, local public school districts were to make arrangements to include in their projects services for parochial school students from low-income families. The nature of these services was deliberately left vague to forestall political controversy. On the other hand, parochial school students were not to be excluded from the calculations which would determine how much money local school districts were eligible to receive. No private school was to receive money directly from the federal government; instead, control over funds and property was to remain in the hands of local public school districts. Thus, parochial school administrators won part of what they wanted, but not all: the right of their students to benefit from federal aid was clearly established, but they were not to have full discretion over the availability and use of public funds. Such was the price of their support for ESEA.

TITLE II—SCHOOL LIBRARY RESOURCES, TEXTBOOKS, AND OTHER INSTRUCTIONAL MATERIALS

Title II ordered the Commissioner of Education to make grants for the acquisition of school library resources, textbooks, and other printed and published instructional materials for the use of children and teachers in public and private schools for a period of five years. During the first year, 100 million dollars was authorized for these grants, and the sum to be spent in the succeeding four years was to be authorized annually by Congress. The money was to be divided among the states on the basis of each state's proportional share of the total number of students enrolled in public and private schools in the entire country.

In order to receive its share of Title II funds, a state had to designate an agency responsible for administering its program and had to submit to the Commissioner a plan for spending the funds. Plans were to be approved if they spelled out the criteria to be used for allocating Title II funds among the children and teachers of the state, if they set forth the criteria to be used for selecting materials to be purchased, if they included policies designed to assure that the federal money would, "to the extent practical," be used to supplement and increase rather than replace money that would otherwise be spent on library resources and textbooks. The criteria to be used for allocating funds had to take into account the relative need of the children and teachers of the state and had to ensure that Title II money was distributed equitably to private school children and teachers. Ownership, control, and administration of materials purchased with Title II funds was to be vested in a public agency. Finally, only materials which had been approved by a state or local educational agency or which were actually used in a public school could be purchased with federal money.

ANALYSIS OF TITLE II   Like Title I, Title II reflects an earnest effort to balance off competing interests. Parochial school supporters believed Title II was extremely important, since the language used indicated clearly that parochial school children and teachers had as much right to assistance as their public school counterparts; on the other hand, the administration requested only a modest sum for Title II, less than 10 percent of the amount sought for Title I. Nevertheless, parochial school interests were somewhat satisfied since Title II would stand as a precedent for greater support in the future.

An attempt was made to defuse the constitutional issue of federal contributions to parochial schools by legislating aid to children and teachers rather than aid to institutions. This effort was aided further by a legislative exhortation that "to the extent possible" federal aid should not be used to replace existing expenditures for library resources, textbooks, and other instructional materials.

In addition, parochial schools were denied the right to receive money directly for use as they saw fit. Instead, ownership of library resources and textbooks was to remain in the hands of a public agency, and parochial schools were constrained further by the fact that only materials which had been approved for use by a state or local public agency or were being used in the public schools of the state could be supplied under Title II.

Finally, primary authority for administering Title II grants was vested at the state rather than the local level. Each state was to develop a state plan and designate an agency responsible for administering the plan. This particular approach to Title II was deliberately chosen in order to reduce criticism by state education officers of their limited role in Title I programs.

TITLE III—SUPPLEMENTARY EDUCATIONAL CENTERS AND SERVICES

Title III authorized the Commissioner of Education to make grants for supplementary educational centers and services designed to make up for inadequate educational services and to develop exemplary educational programs. Grants were to be used for planning purposes, for leasing or construction of facilities, or for the operation of programs. Supplementary educational services were defined to include such services as guidance and counseling; remedial instruction; school health; physical education; vocational guidance; exemplary educational programs including programs enrolling both public and private school students; specialized instruction and equipment for science, foreign languages, and subjects not ordinarily offered in schools; programs for making equipment and personnel available to public and private schools on a temporary basis; and efforts to stimulate use of educational radio and television.

While Title III funds were to be divided among the states by formula, programs were to be approved by the Commissioner of Education rather than by state or local educational agencies. As in Title II, federal funds were to be used primarily to supplement existing expenditures, and ownership of all materials and facilities was to remain in the hands of a public agency. Applications for grants were not to be approved unless representative groups of individuals were to participate in planning and carrying out proposed programs and unless adequate provision was made for participation by private school children.

ANALYSIS OF TITLE III   Title III was designed to stimulate educational innovation and experimentation. Local public school administrators found it attractive, since it offered them a source of money for educational centers and services which they could not provide out of existing resources. Further, local administrators would not be limited by tradition-oriented state educational agencies, since the final decision on which proposals would be funded was to be made by the Office of Education in Washington.

State educational agencies, on the other hand, were unhappy with Title III, since it limited what they considered to be their own supervisory responsibilities; their displeasure was softened, to some extent at least, by knowledge that only a relatively small amount of money would be available for each state unless Title III appropriations were expanded greatly in future years and awareness that no proposals would be approved without an opportunity for review and analysis by state educational authorities.

Finally, parochial school interests supported Title III, since it required local educational agencies to consult private school administrators during both the planning and implementation stages of Title III projects and to provide for equitable participation by parochial school students in any supplementary educational centers and services established with federal funds.

TITLES IV, V, AND VI OF THE ELEMENTARY AND SECONDARY EDUCATION ACT

The remaining titles of the act attempted to support educational research, to strengthen state departments of education, and to ward off fears of federal control of education as well as concern that the federal government might finance religious instruction. Title IV placed emphasis on establishing research organizations throughout the nation; on training of researchers; on helping state agencies, local school districts, and supplementary education centers carry out demonstration projects; and on dissemination of research results.

Title V focused on grants to improve state education departments. Commissioner Keppel worked hard for this title in the belief that state agencies in the field of education needed substantial assistance; other officials in the Office of Education were less sanguine about the possibility of meaningful self-improvement and reform. As a result, Title V funds were limited to 25 million dollars for the fiscal year ending June 30, 1966, and program approval was vested in the hands of the Commissioner of Education. The Commissioner's discretion was not left unlimited, however. He was not allowed to disapprove any request for assistance without first holding a hearing; furthermore, states were given the right to appeal adverse decisions of the Commissioner in the federal courts. Title V was designed, at least in part, to act as a counterweight to other titles of the act which cramped the traditional power of state departments of education.

The crucial provisions of Title VI were sections 604 and 605. The first of these stated that nothing contained in the act authorized the United States or any of its employees to exercise control over the curriculum, program, administration, or personnel of any school or school system. Since the Elementary and Secondary Education Act would increase substantially the power of the federal government in the field of education, the authors of the bill felt it was politically astute to reassure congressmen who feared federal control of education. Section 605 stated bluntly that nothing in the act authorized the expenditure of federal money for religious worship or instruction. It too was designed primarily to alleviate the fears of congressmen who might otherwise oppose those provisions of the bill which called for the inclusion of parochial school students in federally funded programs. Furthermore, of course, it was hoped that this section might help ESEA to withstand the test of constitutionality if and when it was challenged in the courts.

CONGRESSIONAL ACTION ON ESEA

On January 12, 1965, President Johnson sent his education message to Congress and the proposed Elementary and Secondary Education Act of 1965 was introduced by Senator Morse and Representative Perkins. Less than three months later the President signed into law a bill which, with the exception of several relatively minor amendments, embodied all the administration's proposals.

Viewing what happened in Congress from a distance, it looks to the observer as if the proposed act swept through the legislative body without significant challenge. Closer analysis suggests, however, that speedy passage of ESEA was not due to congressional consensus but to effective legislative leadership, strategy, and pressure from the administration.

So many compromises were built into the bill that the administration and key congressmen like Morse and Perkins felt the coalition of supporters could become unbalanced at any moment. They felt that unless the bill were swallowed whole, it would be chewed apart piece by piece until nothing was left. Thus, it was decided to rush the bill through Congress in the hope that quick action would prevent opponents of particular provisions from rallying together. This same strategy led to a decision to seek House passage first, since the House had always been the major stumbling block to federal aid to education, and then to try to get Senate approval of the House-passed bill; if the Senate could be persuaded to adopt the language of the House bill without amendment, the risks of delay, unacceptable compromises, and possible defeat inherent in sending any bill to a conference committee could be avoided. Of course, it was realized that this strategy could backfire if Congress reacted adversely to pressure for rapid passage.

That the administration and its legislative strategists were right in their assessment of the desirability of speedy consideration was immediately demonstrated: many Democrats who supported in principle the concept of federal aid objected to various provisions of ESEA. A counteroffensive was quickly started in order to retain the initiative and keep the opposition off balance.

An air of crisis and emergency was generated; administration spokesmen indicated their belief that federal aid was a now-or-never proposition. From the White House came the message that all loyal Democrats should swallow their objections to particular provisions of the bill in order to get the principle of massive federal aid established. President Johnson stated at a White House "summit" meeting that he was aware the bill could be improved, but he held out for passage without such improvement on the ground that ESEA was like the Model T Ford, which had been improved over the years. The same stance was taken during the House hearings on ESEA when Representative Perkins, the chairman of the education subcommittee of the Education and Labor Committee, indicated "Let me state immediately after we dispose of this bill, I have been instructed to open up some hearings; and I intend to . . . see if we cannot come up with some good answers."[16]

The message was plain, and it was effective. Witness, for example, the comments of one Democrat who ultimately voted for ESEA:

> The 1965 bill, in all candor, does not make much sense educationally; but it makes a hell of a lot of sense legally, politically, and constitutionally. This was a battle of principle, not substance, and that is the main reason I voted for it. If I could have written a bill that would have included provisions to meet the national interest in the education field, it would not have been 89–10 [ESEA].[17]

Hearings began in the House on January 22 and lasted for twelve days. It was clear from the outset that the major professional and interest groups were not going

---

[16] *Hearings on H.R. 2362 Before the General Subcommittee on Education of the House Committee on Education and Labor*, 89th Cong., 1st Sess., at 953 (1965).

[17] As quoted in Eidenberg and Morey, *op. cit.*, p. 93. (Brackets added.)

to back away from their announced support for the administration's bill. Minor amendments were adopted, but there was little support within the General Education Subcommittee of the Committee on Labor and Education for major changes in the proposed legislation. Only one of the subcommittee Democrats—but an important one—Representative Edith Green of Oregon, expressed serious misgivings about certain aspects of the bill. Mrs. Green objected to (1) the aid formula, on the ground that it gave too much money to wealthier states that were already spending subsantial sums on their schools and not enough to poorer states, and (2) the absence of a provision allowing taxpayers to challenge the constitutionality of assistance to parochial schools in the courts. Mrs. Green believed a judicial review provision was essential, since the Supreme Court had held repeatedly over a period of more than forty years that no individual taxpayer has a sufficient monetary interest in a federal appropriation to justify allowing him to bring suit in a federal court. Thus, in the absence of such a provision, it was questionable whether the parochial aid provisions of ESEA could even be challenged on constitutional grounds in the courts.

Mrs. Green's defection was considered dangerous because she was a liberal Democrat who had supported federal aid to education in the past; thus, other liberal Democrats might be persuaded to join her. The delicate balance of interests could easily fall apart on a judicial review amendment, since such an amendment would definitely be opposed by parochial school interests. Republicans on the subcommittee lined up in support of Mrs. Green's proposals, which only helped confirm the administration's view that she was a "spoiler," out to subvert ESEA.

On the Republican side, there was a good deal of anger over how the bill was handled in the subcommittee. Republican members wished to call twenty-eight witnesses to testify on the legislation, but they were allotted only one day, the final day of the hearings, to present their witnesses. They blamed the administration as much as Subcommittee Chairman Perkins for this high-handed treatment. Shortly, some of the Republicans began referring to ESEA as "the railroad act of 1965." Thus provoked, and clearly powerless to alter the onrush of events, the Republican subcommittee members boycotted the markup sessions on the bill.

On February 5, the subcommittee reported the bill to the full Education and Labor Committee. As has already been mentioned, this committee was strongly liberal and strongly in favor of federal aid to education as a result of shifts in membership following the decisive 1964 elections. The "no amendment" strategy of the leadership was now in operation, and Chairman Adam Clayton Powell prevented Mrs. Green's views from getting lengthy consideration. Several relatively minor changes were made in the bill, but only after the administration and its supporters determined that the changes would not undermine the principles on which the bill had been built. In early March the full committee reported the bill out by a twenty-three to eight vote.

The power of the House Rules Committee to delay or block legislation from reaching the floor of the House had gradually been curtailed during the Kennedy-Johnson presidencies, first by the addition of three members in 1961 and then by adoption of the twenty-one-day rule in January 1965. Under this latter provision, any legislation could be brought to the floor by the Speaker of the House after it had been considered by the Rules Committee for twenty-one days. Thus, even if the Rules Committee had wished to pigeonhole ESEA, it no longer had the power to do so. As it was, Representative Delaney of New York, whose vote in the committee had killed the Kennedy aid to education bill, announced that he would support ESEA. On March 22 the rule for debate was issued, and two days later floor action commenced.

The Democratic leadership in the House planned their strategy several days before the bill reached the floor. The whips polled the Democrats in the House and reported that final passage was virtually assured if the bill remained intact on the floor. It was decided to push the bill through quickly and to make sure that sufficient supporters were on the floor at all times to defeat any crippling amendments. Telephone calls would be made and letters and telegrams sent by the private interest groups, the White House, the Office of Education, and the Democratic leadership to Democrats who were still undecided.

Finally, since the amendments supported by Mrs. Green were the most threatening, decisions were made on how to handle them. A call was put in to Emanuel Celler, the senior member of the House of Representatives, chairman of the House Judiciary Committee, and an influential liberal, to request him to argue against the judicial review amendment. Since Jews throughout the nation had generally opposed federal aid to private schools in the past, it was felt that a statement by Celler in favor of ESEA would rally any wavering liberals; furthermore, Celler's position on the Judiciary Committee would allow him to speak persuasively on the judicial review question.

In the House, debate and voting on the bill took three days. Attempts to amend the aid formula were defeated, as were nearly fifty other amendments. Toward the end, the galleries were packed as Congressman Celler and Judge Howard Smith of Virginia squared off to debate the need for an explicit provision for judicial review; Celler insisted that the provision was unnecessary, since the courts would be able to test the constitutionality of ESEA. This was a bold argument, given existing Supreme Court precedents on taxpayers' standing to sue. Tempers were heated by this time, as the bill's floor manager, Congressman Powell, had allowed only five minutes' debate on each amendment before calling for a vote. When the vote on the judicial review amendment was called, it was defeated 204 to 154.

With the end now in sight, Powell relented and accepted a noncontroversial amendment to create an advisory council to advise the Commissioner of Education in carrying out his functions. Ultimately, this was the only change made by the House in the bill reported out of the Education and Labor Committee. The final vote on passage was 263 to 153, with seventeen members not voting. Of the Northern Democrats, 187 supported the bill, as did forty-one Southern Democrats and thirty-five Republicans. The opposition consisted of ninety-six Republicans and fifty-seven Democrats, all but three of whom came from the South.

Following House passage on March 26, attention shifted to the Education Subcommittee of the Senate Labor and Public Welfare Committee, where Senator Wayne Morse, the Senate's leading proponent of federal aid to education, attempted to persuade his colleagues to report the House bill to the Senate without changing as much as a comma. On the basis of past experience, Morse knew there were enough supporters of federal aid in the Senate to pass a bill; what he did not know was whether the House would balk at a conference committee if the Senate passed its own bill. Thus, Senator Morse and the administration wanted to avoid the risk of defeat when they were on the verge of victory.

Morse's subcommittee agreed with this strategy, as did the full committee: in less than a week's time, the Labor and Public Welfare Committee reported the House bill to the floor by unanimous vote. The five Republican members of the committee submitted minority views, which helped to put a bipartisan imprint on the proposed legislation.

By April 9, the House bill was passed intact. Senate support for the bill was so strong that opponents recognized they had little chance of affecting the outcome. One potential source of trouble was the unhappiness of many senators at the prospect of seeing the Senate's prerogative to write its own bill curtailed; the floor managers of the bill, led by Senator Morse, countered this charge by asserting that the legislation was extremely significant, that the strategy being followed in no way limited the powers of the Senate, that the bill was not being forced upon the Senate by excessive presidential influence.

Eleven amendments were proposed but none accepted. The two most significant proposals should be mentioned: (1) an amendment to change the allocation formula, and (2) an amendment by Senator Sam Ervin, Jr., of North Carolina, one of the Senate's most knowledgeable constitutionalists, to add a judicial review section to the bill. Senator Morse spoke against the Ervin amendment but acknowledged that doubts about whether the bill could be tested in the courts in the absence of such a provision were indeed justified. He promised to introduce and support a separate judicial review bill later in the session.[18] Morse's strategy, of course, was to undercut support for changing the House bill in any way. In the end, the Ervin amendment was defeated fifty-three to thirty-two.

Bipartisan support for the Elementary and Secondary Education Act is demonstrated by the vote on final passage: seventy-three to eighteen. Supporting the act were fifty-five Democrats and eighteen Republicans; ultimately, only fourteen Republicans and four Southern Democrats voted against it.

President Johnson signed the bill on April 11, outside the one-room schoolhouse in rural Texas where he first attended school. Administration supporters and editorial writers called it Johnson's greatest legislative victory. The President himself declared that ESEA was the cornerstone of his legislative program. In the short space of three months Congress had reacted to the President's dream of a major federal commitment to increased educational opportunity for the nation's young, had put aside decades of divisive quarreling which had killed earlier legislative efforts, and had enacted a new and potentially far-reaching program.

THE STRUGGLE SHIFTS TO THE COURTS

Opponents of aid to religious schools admitted they had lost a battle but refused to concede that they had lost the war; instead, they licked their wounds for a year and planned a strategic retreat to their next line of defense, the courts. They hoped the courts would do the job of "defeating" the act for them by ruling that certain of its provisions violated the First Amendment prohibition of establishment of religion.

Major attacks on Titles I and II of ESEA were brought in state and federal courts in Ohio, Pennsylvania, and New York. While individuals brought the lawsuits, the attacks were launched, coordinated, and pressed by various interest groups, including Protestants and Other Americans United for Separation of Church and State, the American Jewish Congress, the New York Civil Liberties Union, the United Parents Association, and the United Federation of Teachers of New York City. Thus, as is frequently the case in modern constitutional law, the interest group struggle was simply transferred from the legislature to the judiciary; passage of the law did not mean the group struggle had ended but did mean that Congress was no longer the relevant forum.

Opponents of the new law recognized that it would not be easy to win in the courts, but they knew they had no other option. They knew that their lawsuit would be extremely complex, would probably take from three to five years, and would be very costly. They knew that the suit would have to be taken through the lower courts to the Supreme Court not once but twice: first for a ruling on the jurisdictional question of whether the courts would even accept a lawsuit brought against the federal government by an ordinary taxpayer, and second for a ruling on the

---

[18] Several months after passage of ESEA, Senators Morse, Clark, and Yarborough did introduce a bill to provide judicial review of all federal grant programs challenged on the ground they violated the First Amendment. The bill was passed by the Senate but died in the House.

merits of their constitutional claim. If the Supreme Court adhered to precedent and refused to vary its historic doctrine that a taxpayer has no "standing to sue," the opponents of ESEA would never be able to get a ruling on the merits.

Furthermore, opponents of public aid to parochial schools began to realize that they would not be able to concentrate their efforts and resources on a legal battle against the federal statute. Pressure for state aid to parochial schools had been increasing rapidly during the early 1960s in states with large Catholic populations. At the same time, non-Catholic attitudes toward aid to religious schools were shifting. Further, many citizens began to realize the impact that parochial school closings would have on the public schools and property-tax rates. Legislators perceived this change in public outlook and began to respond. New York, for example, passed a "textbook loan" statute in 1965 obligating the state to supply $15 worth of textbooks each year to *every* pupil in grades seven through twelve.

Since it would do the opponents of public aid to parochial schools little good to win a suit against federal aid if the same purposes could be achieved through state aid, it was necessary to challenge the New York statute—and other comparable legislation which might be passed by various states—as well. Thus, a lawsuit testing the New York textbook loan statute was brought in the state courts.

Initially, both lawsuits went against the opponents of public aid to parochial schools. The suit against ESEA was dismissed by the federal district court on the basis of the historic doctrine that taxpayers lacked legal standing to contest the expenditure of federal funds.[19] An appeal to the Supreme Court was immediately made. In the meantime, the New York textbook loan act was upheld by the highest court of New York, the Court of Appeals.[20]

The Supreme Court set both cases down for argument in the 1967 to 1968 term of Court. Briefs were filed, oral arguments held, and, in due course, the decisions were handed down; both decisions were announced the same day—June 10, 1968.[21] The New York law was upheld, by a six to three vote, with Justices Black, Douglas, and Fortas dissenting. Speaking for the majority, Justice White ruled that the lending of textbooks to children benefits the children and not the schools they attend. Thus, the New York textbook loan law did not constitute state support of religion in violation of the establishment clause of the First Amendment. The decision was a clear victory for proponents of public aid to parochial education.

On the other hand, the victory was marred by the Court's eight to one ruling in *Flast v. Cohen* that the Elementary and Secondary Education Act could be challenged by individual taxpayers. The Court ruled that (1) the establishment clause specifically limits the power to tax and spend conferred on Congress by Article 1, section 8 of the Constitution, and that (2) whenever such specific limitations on Congress's power exist, a taxpayer will have standing to sue.

Admittedly, the two decisions seemed somewhat mystifying. Was the Court granting opponents of federal aid to parochial education the right to sue at the same

---

[19] *Flast v. Cohen*, 271 F. Supp. 1 (S.D.N.Y. 1967).

[20] *Board of Education v. Allen*, 20 N.Y.2d 109 (1967).

[21] *Flast v. Cohen*, 392 U.S. 83 (1968); *Board of Education v. Allen*, 392 U.S. 236 (1968). It is noteworthy that the New York case, no less than the federal lawsuit, involved a conflict between opposing pressure groups, each seeking a preferred policy choice. Appellants in the *Allen* case were aided by briefs submitted by Protestants and Other Americans United for Separation of Church and State and by nine different Jewish organizations. Amicus curiae briefs in support of the state law were filed by the United States, the attorneys general of five states, the National Association of Independent Schools, the New York State AFL-CIO, the National Catholic Education Association, two Lutheran organizations, two Jewish organizations, two organizations of parochial school administrators, and Citizens for Educational Freedom.

time as it was saying they had little hope of winning? While the interest groups opposed to public aid to parochial schools were trying to decipher the two decisions, state legislatures did not stand still. In 1968 Pennsylvania passed a statute authorizing the state to reimburse parochial schools for salaries paid to teachers of secular subjects. Rhode Island passed a salary supplement act the following year. By 1970, six states had enacted comparable legislation. Confronted with the prospect that what was starting as salary supplements might end as state-financed private school systems, the leaders of the anti-aid groups decided to defer further action against ESEA and to seek clarification of the constitutionality of the new salary supplement laws instead. After all, if the courts did not throw out the salary supplements, there would not be much sense challenging the federal legislation.

The Pennsylvania and Rhode Island cases were decided in contradictory fashion by the lower courts, were combined for argument before the Supreme Court, and decided on June 27, 1971. Given precedents on the use of public funds for textbooks and auxiliary services like busing, the decision in *Lemon v. Kurtzman*, 403 U.S. 602 (1971), that public purchase of secular educational services violated the establishment clause came as a surprise to most observers. The Court ruled, by an eight to nothing vote, that salary supplements constituted excessive entanglement between church and state since state surveillance would have to be continuous to ensure that teachers of secular subjects hired by religious authorities and under their control avoided religious topics, and since the programs in question had tremendous potential for political divisiveness.

If the constitutionality of public aid to parochial schools was confused prior to *Lemon v. Kurtzman*, it is now in a state of complete flux. State officials confounded by the decision are already searching for new ways of shoring up parochial school systems, ways which might avoid constitutional infirmities. Advocates of separation of church and state, having defeated salary supplements, are preparing legal challenges to ESEA and organizing to prevent the passage of new aid legislation.

. . . .

II. Hypothetical Case: Flast v. Secretary of HEW*

BRIEF FOR APPELLANTS   *BRIEF FOR APPELLEE*

1. *Does the Elementary and Secondary Education Act of 1965 violate the establishment clause of the First Amendment?*

For the first time in American history, the federal government has enacted legislation providing for massive public aid to public and private schools. To the extent that such aid supports sectarian schools, we believe that the government has violated the command of the First Amendment that "Congress shall make

All citizens of the United States have a vital interest in the outcome of this case, since the future of the country depends in large part on the quality of education offered to today's youth. Given the crucial role of education and the accelerating financial difficulties facing our educational institutions, it is not at all surpris-

* Author's note: As of this writing, a case on the merits of ESEA has not been argued before the Supreme Court. Thus, the case presented below is hypothetical in nature; among the sources used by the author are decisions of both federal and state courts in numerous establishment clause cases.

no law respecting an establishment of religion. . . ."

The proponents of federal aid to religious schools argued before Congress that the courts would not hold such aid unconstitutional if the legislation were written to provide aid to children attending parochial schools rather than directly to the schools themselves. We do not believe that this Court will submit supinely to this devious attempt to accomplish indirectly what cannot be accomplished directly. Since the Elementary and Secondary Education Act provides federal aid to parochial schools, it is the duty of this Court to rule that the act is unconstitutional.

As counsel for the appellants, we do not disagree with appellee's initial point, that Congress has a legitimate interest in the quality of education received by the nation's youth. It is, of course, true that education is a critical factor in the life of an individual and in the future of a nation.

From this premise, however, appellee draws an invalid conclusion: that efforts by Congress to improve education are inherently constitutional. It is our contention that the First Amendment prohibits certain aid to education, regardless of the national interest in improving the education offered by the nation's schools. Aid which violates the Constitution cannot be justified on the grounds that it serves the national interest, is socially wise, or is politically expedient.

Under Title I of the Elementary and Secondary Education Act of 1965, local public school officials are authorized to use federal funds to meet the special needs of educationally deprived children coming from areas where many low-income families live. Section 205 (a) (2) provides that:

> . . . [T]o the extent consistent with the number of educationally deprived children in the school district of the local educational agency who are enrolled in private elementary and secondary schools, such agency has made provision for including special educational services and arrangements (such as dual enrollment, educational radio and television, and mobile educational services and equipment) in which such children can participate.[1]

[1] 79 Stat. 30–31.

ing that Congress focused on the growing crisis in education and passed the Elementary and Secondary Education Act of 1965.

Appellants claim that this act violates the clause of the Constitution prohibiting government establishment of religion because Title I of the act provides guidance services and remedial instruction in secular subjects to students from low-income families attending private parochial schools and Title II supplies such schools with textbooks, reference books, library materials, and other instructional materials.

We believe the Court should and will reject the contention that Congress is without power to upgrade the quality of education in secular subjects now offered in parochial schools. To accept such a contention would be paramount to saying that the public has no interest in the education received by the millions of young citizens enrolled in nonpublic elementary and secondary schools.

It is clear, however, that Congress has a legitimate interest in the education in secular subjects received by all students, not just those attending public schools. Decisions of this Court, as well as presidential messages, reinforce this conclusion.

For example, in *Brown v. Board of Education*, 347 U.S. 483, at 493 (1954), the critical decision outlawing segregation in public education, the members of this Court ruled unanimously that:

> Today, education is perhaps the most important function of the state and local governments. Compulsory school attendance laws and the great expenditures for education both demonstrate our recognition of the importance of education to our democratic society. It is required in the performance of our most basic public responsibilities, even service in the armed forces. It is the very foundation of good citizenship. Today it is the principal instrument in awakening the child to cultural values, in preparing him for later professional training, and in helping him to adjust normally to his environment. In these days, it is doubtful that any child may reasonably be expected to succeed in life if he is denied the opportunity of an education. Such an opportunity, where the state has undertaken to provide it, is a right which must be made available to all on equal terms.

Other subsections require that funds remain under the control of the local educational agency and that title to all property purchased shall be held in a public agency. In addition, the local agencies are responsible for developing procedures for measuring the effectiveness of Title I programs and for making annual reports to state educational authorities.

In order to carry out the provisions of Title I, public school authorities and parochial school administrators meet together to determine what programs will be made available to parochial school students. Most of the programs which have been established to date provide for remedial classes in basic subjects like English, mathematics, and reading and for guidance services. While some of the programs are conducted on public school grounds, most are held within the sectarian schools themselves. Thus, publicly paid teachers are being sent into religious schools to give instruction in certain subjects and publicly purchased educational equipment is being "loaned" to such schools.

Title II provides for the ". . . [A]cquisition of school library resources, textbooks, and other printed and published instructional materials for the use of children and teachers in public and private elementary and secondary schools."[2] Title to all books loaned to private schools is to be vested in a public agency. In addition, the act requires that Title II funds be used to supplement and, "to the extent practical," increase the amount of money that would otherwise be available for similar purposes.

Section 205 (b) of Title II restricts the resources that may be purchased to those which have been approved by state or local educational agencies for use in the public schools. Finally, we should note section 605 of Title VI, which states, "Nothing contained in this Act shall be construed to authorize the making of any payment . . . for religious worship or instruction."[3]

At the outset, we should like to establish clearly that the aid provided under the Ele-

President Kennedy focused on federal aid to education on numerous occasions. To illustrate his interest in educational opportunity, we need only select a quotation from his speeches and messages on this subject:

Education is the keystone in the arch of freedom and progress. . . . [I]ncreasing the quality and availability of education is vital to both our national security and our domestic well-being. . . . Today we need a new standard of excellence in education, matched by the fullest possible access to educational opportunities, enabling each citizen to develop his talents to the maximum possible extent.[1]

President Johnson said in his 1965 State of the Union Address that "Every child must have the best education that this Nation can provide."[2] The following week, in his special message to Congress on education, the President emphasized that:

Nothing matters more to the future of our country; not our military preparedness, for armed might is worthless if we lack the brainpower to build a world of peace; not our productive economy, for we cannot sustain growth without trained manpower; not our democratic system of government, for freedom is fragile if citizens are ignorant. . . .

One hundred years ago, a man with 6 or 7 years of schooling stood well above the average. His chances to get ahead were as good as the next man's. But today, lack of formal education is likely to mean low wages, frequent unemployment, and a home in an urban or rural slum. . . .

Nearly half the youths rejected by Selective Service for educational deficiency have fathers who are unemployed or else work in unskilled and low-income jobs. . . .

The burden on the Nation's schools is not evenly distributed. Low-income families are heavily concentrated in particular urban neighborhoods or rural areas. Faced with the largest

[2] *Id.*, at 36; library resources are defined as books, periodicals, documents, audiovisual materials, and other related library materials.

[3] *Id.*, at 58.

[1] Message to Congress preceding introduction of the 1963 Federal Aid to Education Bill, 109 CONG. REC. 1247–48.

[2] 111 CONG. REC. 30.

mentary and Secondary Education Act of 1965 is aid to sectarian schools, not simply aid to children attending such schools. Up to now, no one has suggested that the decision of public school authorities to offer certain courses within public schools represents anything other than an institutional decision. Yet, appellee is now suggesting that the same decision, when arrived at by parochial school administrators and public authorities, acting together, represents "assistance to educationally deprived children."

Up to now, no one has suggested that the hiring of teachers by public schools constitutes "aid to children" as distinguished from financing the operations of the schools. Yet, according to appellee, publicly paid teachers can conduct courses within sectarian schools without aiding the operation of such schools, since children receive the benefits of the education offered. Surely, the English language cannot be twisted to an extent which does violence to the common meaning of ordinary words.

Public financing of educational equipment such as chairs, desks, blackboards, chalk, erasers, etc., has always been regarded as an integral part of financing the operations of the public schools, not as "aid to children." Now, however, we are told that financing of major educational equipment under Title I and purchase of library resources, textbooks, and other printed educational materials under Title II does not benefit parochial schools but merely the children attending such schools. Should this Court hold that Title I and Title II programs do not constitute forbidden aid to sectarian institutions but are instead a constitutionally permissible aid to children, would it not then have to conclude that any future public financing of all facilities of parochial schools which are not directly related to religious instruction or practices is equally permissible? What then would be left of the "wall of separation between church and state" supposedly erected by the establishment clause of the First Amendment? What then would be left of government neutrality toward religion?

But, argues counsel for the appellee, public financing of educational equipment, of library resources, of textbooks, and of educational materials is not aid to sectarian institutions, since the act provides for the retention of

educational needs, many of these school districts have inadequate financial resources.[3]

Commissioner of Education Francis Keppel testified in support of the proposed Elementary and Secondary Education Act that:

When we turn to survey the needs of our schools for modern textbooks, we find that all too often our children must use textbooks which are out of date and grossly inadequate for this era of expanding educational horizons. It is a sad fact that "modern history" books often have nothing to teach our children about events after World War I and that physics texts frequently deal with the state of our knowledge in the 1940's and 1950's—ignoring, for example, the atomic revolution. . . .

For many families the purchase of a child's textbook is a luxury they can ill afford. A 1964 study shows that one-fourth of the school systems in 128 of our largest cities do not provide free textbooks at the high school level. Nonpublic schools rarely provide free textbooks. A poor family with children in high school may be required to spend $15 to $20 or more per child for up-to-date textbooks—a prohibitive sum when money doesn't exist for many of the barest necessities of life. In 1961, parents spent over $90 million for textbooks—approximately 40 percent of that year's total expenditures for textbooks. Children in families unable to support this extra burden are often turned from the halls of the schools to the alleys of the slums.[4]

In passing the Elementary and Secondary Education Act of 1965, Congress recognized that adequate education is an important aspect of public welfare: it recognized that children from poor families living in economically disadvantaged areas had suffered and would continue to suffer from inadequate educational opportunities regardless of whether they attended public or private schools; it recognized that exclusion of students attending sectarian schools from a program of federal aid would weaken both the students themselves and the

[3] Id. at 499, 500.

[4] Hearings on H.R. 2361 and H.R. 2362 Before the General Subcommittee on Education of the House Committee on Education and Labor, 89th Cong., 1st Sess., pt. 1, at 93 (1965).

public ownership. It is clear to us that Congress inserted the provision for "loan" of publicly purchased equipment and books in order to get around the constitutional conflict that would arise if such materials were given directly to nonpublic schools. Common knowledge, however, suggests that the "loan" is merely a subterfuge.

A loan implies use by the borrower for a specific period of time and the return of the item loaned within a reasonable period. But there is nothing in the Elementary and Secondary Education Act which implies that the materials "loaned" will be returned to the public educational authority making the so-called "loan." The implication of the act is that publicly financed materials will be "loaned" to sectarian schools and retained by the schools for an indefinite period of time. Anyone who has attended an elementary or secondary school knows that textbooks, reference books and other library resources, and teaching equipment receive hard use and wear out within a relatively short period of time. Materials which do not wear out become outdated and need to be replaced with up-to-date editions. Thus, the loan concept is a convenient fiction; legal title may remain with the public educational authorities, but beneficial ownership is clearly in the hands of the sectarian schools. Can the First Amendment's barrier to public financing of sectarian schools be evaded simply by labeling the permanent and exclusive use of public property a loan rather than a gift?

It is true that in *Board of Education v. Allen*, 392 U.S. 236 (1968), this Court upheld a New York statute requiring the loan of textbooks to private as well as public school students. But the Court made much of the fact that the law required the students themselves to request books and the related fact that no funds or books were furnished to parochial schools.

The Elementary and Secondary Education Act of 1965 is far broader than the New York textbook loan statute, since it includes provisions that can hardly be construed as aid to individual students at their request. Title I programs do provide aid to parochial schools. The purchase of library resources, including reference works, and "loan" of the materials

nation as a whole.[5] It expressed the belief that sectarian schools are significant units in the national educational system.

Congress concluded that a government program to provide secular educational services and materials to all school-age children, regardless of the school they attend, was a constitutional exercise of the power to make expenditures for the general welfare contained in Article 1, section 8 of the Constitution. This conclusion that the legislation in question had a legitimate secular purpose and was not an unconstitutional aid to religion should not be treated lightly by this Court.

There is no litmus paper test for determining whether a statute violates the command of the First Amendment that "Congress shall make no law respecting an establishment of religion...." Because the clause is not self-explanatory, it is difficult to apply it to specific state or federal statutes. In numerous past cases, this Court has allowed legislatures a certain measure of discretion where statutes did not clearly violate the establishment clause. We do not believe the act in question here transgresses the limits of that discretion.

In order to prove that the Elementary and Secondary Education Act does not violate the establishment clause, it is necessary to look first at the origin of the First Amendment and at early instances of government aid to religion and then at postwar standards adopted by the Supreme Court. We will attempt to prove that the act falls within the tests followed by the Court in recent litigation on the meaning of the constitutional prohibition of an establishment of religion.

The Supreme Court has had numerous opportunities to study the original meaning of the First Amendment. For example, in *Everson v. Board of Education*, 330 U.S. 1 (1947), the case which made the establishment clause applicable to the states through the Fourteenth Amendment, the goals of the men who drafted the amendment were analyzed in depth.

[5] To put the point clearly, it should be noted that over 5 million students attend nonpublic schools throughout the nation. In 1970, more than 4.5 million children were enrolled in over 11,000 Catholic educational institutions. Nearly 10 percent of all elementary and secondary school pupils attended Catholic schools.

purchased, also can be defined only as institutional support. Even the textbooks supplied under the act differ from those supplied by New York State: there is no requirement that individual students request the textbooks; instead, the textbooks are to be chosen by agreement between parochial school administrators and public authorities.

In *Board of Education v. Allen*, the majority predicated its opinion in part on the ground that parents rather than parochial schools had purchased textbooks for students prior to passage of the New York statute. Thus, the Court held that the textbook assistance did not constitute aid to the school. Would the Court have come to the same conclusion if New York had tried to "loan" chairs, desks, bookcases, blackboards, erasers, or any of the other pieces of educational equipment without which a parochial school cannot function? We think not.

Yet, is this not exactly what the Elementary and Secondary Education Act of 1965 does? Teachers are normally hired by the parochial schools; the equipment used in classrooms is normally purchased by the schools; reference books and other library resources are part of the accepted burden of running a school. In effect, Congress has declared in the challenged act, for the first time in American history, that the federal government will hereafter finance a certain portion of the cost of running a religious school. Assuming for a moment that the assistance provided is solely for secular education and that a valid distinction can be made between secular and religious education within the context of a parochial school, what are the constitutional limits on such assistance? Can the government, for example, buy land, build a science building, equip it, and then turn the keys over to parochial school administrators along with enough cash to hire teachers and maintain the building?

Textbook loans may not constitute an invalid grant of public property to sectarian institutions, as the Court ruled in *Allen*, since the schools themselves never provided books previously. Here, however, Congress has set out to provide funds for functions normally financed by the institutions themselves. And logically, if government can provide limited assistance to secular programs offered by

As stated in the *Everson* case, the early settlers brought with them many of the religious differences and hatreds which marked European society at that time. Many of them had fled religious persecution, conducted in the name of religions which had been established and supported by various European nations. Despite this fact, a number of colonies followed similar practices. Thus, at the time of the signing of the Constitution and the Bill of Rights, there were established churches in more than half of the original thirteen colonies and nearly every colony exacted taxes for support of churches. According to the opinion of the Court:

> These practices became so commonplace as to shock the freedom-loving colonials into a feeling of abhorrence. The imposition of taxes to pay ministers' salaries and to build and maintain churches and church property aroused their indignation. It was these feelings which found expression in the First Amendment.
>
> 330 U.S. 1, 11 (1947).

Thus, it is evident that the original purpose of the amendment was to prohibit the direct establishment of a national church and, further, to prohibit the direct support of any single religion or of all religions. Yet, additional evidence indicates that the first generation of American citizens did not wish the government to be hostile to organized religion.

James Madison, the man who was primarily responsible for the wording of the First Amendment, stated in the First Congress that the meaning of the amendment was that "Congress should not establish a religion, and enforce the legal observation of it by Law, nor compel men to worship God in any manner contrary to their conscience."[6] In that same session, Congress established the chaplain service for the Army and the Navy, for which federal funds are still being used today; federal funds for missionaries to the Indians in order to christianize and civilize them were first voted under President Washington and were appropriated for over a century, until 1900. Madison himself was President for eight years, yet at no time did he criticize the ex-

---

[6] 1 *Annals of Cong.* 729–31 (Benton ed. 1858).

parochial schools without breaching the strict command of the First Amendment, it can, using the same constitutional justification, finance the entire cost of sectarian schooling other than the cost of missals and prayer books, of buildings used for religious purposes, and of money spent on religious instruction.

Counsel for appellee claim, nevertheless, that the Elementary and Secondary Education Act does not allow public subsidy of functions normally conducted by sectarian schools. They cite section 203 (a) (5) of Title II which reads:

> . . . [F]ederal funds made available under this title for any fiscal year will be so used as to supplement and, to the extent practical, increase the level of . . . private school funds that would in the absence of such Federal funds be made available . . . and in no case supplant such . . . private school funds.[4]

First, we believe that the quoted words actually prove our point rather than the opposite. According to section 203 (a) (5) of Title II, the federal government intends to supply additional funds above and beyond funds already being spent by sectarian schools, but the existing funds and the additional money are to be spent primarily for educational purposes normally financed by the schools themselves. The only exception, of course, is money for the purchase and loan of textbooks.

Secondly, there is no comparable requirement in Title I. Thus, Title I programs may or may not supplement existing private school expenditures. Even if we assume that local public school authorities will not wish to establish programs supplanting existing expenditures, there may be pressures on them to do so.

Furthermore, local authorities who hold to a firm policy of supplementary assistance only will still be faced with serious problems: for example, does a parochial school which has emphasized religious education at the expense of remedial secular programs qualify for Title I aid, while a similar school which has sacrificed religious training in order to spend

penditure of federal funds for either of these purposes.

Along with Madison, Thomas Jefferson was a leading spokesman for the antiestablishment cause. It was Jefferson who first used the phrase that the First Amendment created "a wall of separation between church and state." Yet, Jefferson clearly did not consider that this "wall" barred all relations between government and religion. Like Madison, Jefferson never criticized the use of federal funds to support military chaplains and Indian missionaries during his eight years as President.

In addition, throughout American history, Congress has supported chaplains in both the House of Representatives and the Senate as well as in federal hospitals and correctional institutions. Religious services have always been held at the United States military academies. Property owned by churches is tax exempt, as is church income. Contributors to churches are allowed to reduce their taxable income accordingly. Clergy and divinity students are exempt from the draft. Religious organizations receive special postal privileges.

Furthermore, the pledge of allegiance includes reference to God, as do coins issued by the United States Treasury. The Bible is used for swearing oaths, including the oath of office taken by newly elected Presidents. And, finally, daily sessions of the houses of Congress begin with prayers.

More directly to the point, a number of postwar statutes provide for federal aid to *all* students, including those attending sectarian institutions. Among these are scholarships under the GI Bill of Rights and the National Defense Education Act of 1958; free lunches and milk under the National School Lunch Act and the Agriculture Act of 1949; dormitories, classrooms, and other facilities under the College Housing Act of 1950, the Higher Education Facilities Act, the Higher Education Act, and the Surplus Property Act. It would be excessive to go into detail to explain what has been done under each of these acts, but perhaps one illustration would be helpful: under the last act cited, 488 grants of land and buildings had been given to schools of thirty-five different religious denominations between passage of the act in 1944 and 1961.

From the above listing, it is impossible to

[4] *Id.*, at 38.

available funds on remedial education courses and guidance services not qualify? Such a result would be absurd. Yet what other result could follow if the guiding principle was "supplementary assistance only"?

Thirdly, what, exactly, is meant by the qualifying phrase that "to the extent practical" federal funds shall be used to increase the level of private school spending? Who is to determine whether it is "practical" for a particular parochial school to devote a specific dollar amount of its resources to programs which the federal government appears willing to finance? Who is to determine whether any particular school is maximizing its resources, avoiding waste, and making a legitimate effort to finance, out of its own income, programs which are important from the viewpoint of secular education but perhaps less so from the viewpoint of religious education? Certainly, the judgment cannot be left solely to parochial school administrators. On the other hand, as the Court ruled in *Lemon v. Kurtzman*, 403 U.S. 602 (1971), governmental inquiry into revenues, expenses, programs offered, etc. would represent excessive entanglement of church and state.

Thus, we believe that the phrase "to the extent practical" is at best an overly vague and permissive generalization which severely limits the possibility that section 203 (a) (5) will in fact restrict what is done with public funds. At worst, the phrase constitutes an open invitation to local public school authorities to make in-depth inquiries into the financial practices and educational programs of parochial schools requesting assistance. In either case, the decisions of local authorities charged with administering the act would be unconstitutional.

The point we are trying to make is simply that regardless of whether public funds supplant or supplement existing expenditures, the aid is to sectarian institutions, not to children. Any statutory language or legal arguments to the contrary should be recognized for what they are: attempts to get around the First Amendment's prohibition of state aid to religious institutions.

If, as we have demonstrated, the Elementary and Secondary Education Act provides aid to schools, it can and should be dis-conclude otherwise than that the Elementary and Secondary Education Act of 1965 is but the latest in a long line of federal statutes providing public assistance to students attending parochial schools. If the statute challenged today is unconstitutional, does that mean that all the above acts violate the prohibition against establishment of religion? Certainly, this Court should be extremely cautious about overthrowing so much legislation in a field as vital to the national interest as the education of young Americans.

In the postwar period, the members of this Court have had many opportunities to examine the meaning of the establishment clause. The line between neutrality toward religion and state support of religion has been difficult to locate. As the Supreme Court said in *Zorach v. Clauson*, 343 U.S. 306, 314 (1952), "The constitutional standard is the separation of Church and State. The problem, like many problems in constitutional law, is one of degree."

Gradually, however, a definition of the limits of the establishment clause has been developed. In order to demonstrate that the challenged act does not violate these limits, we plan, first, to examine the important precedents and, second, to analyze the act itself.

The starting point in any examination of Supreme Court precedents involving the establishment clause is clearly *Everson v. Board of Education*. In *Everson*, plaintiffs claimed that a New Jersey statute providing bus transportation for children attending public and parochial schools violated the clause. The Court ruled against this contention by a five to four vote.

In a frequently quoted attempt to define the meaning of the clause, Justice Black, the author of the majority opinion, stated:

> The "establishment of religion" clause of the First Amendment means at least this: Neither a state nor the Federal government can set up a church. Neither can pass laws which aid one religion, aid all religions, or prefer one religion over another. Neither can force nor influence a person to go to or to remain away from church against his will or force him to profess a belief or disbelief in any religion. No person can be punished for entertaining or professing religious beliefs or disbeliefs, for church at-

tinguished from the New York textbook loan act upheld in *Board of Education v. Allen.* In *Allen,* the Court held that the aid was to children and only indirectly to schools. The majority leaned heavily on the seminal case in this field, *Everson v. Board of Education,* 330 U.S. 1 (1947), which upheld by a five to four vote the power of New Jersey to offer public transportation to parochial school students. The *Everson* decision was based on the belief that the statute in question was a public welfare measure which conferred a public benefit on children as such and conferred no more than an incidental benefit on the schools they attended. The opposite is the case here. The benefits conferred by the challenged act can in no sense be considered "incidental" aid to sectarian schools. Instead, the public is being asked to finance part of the operation of such schools.

Appellee argues that even if this Court should find that the aid provided by the government is aid to religious schools rather than aid to children, the Court need not find such aid unconstitutional, since no federal funds will be used for religious training. In contesting this argument, we would like to point out that the Court has only recently ruled, in *Lemon v. Kurtzman,* that states could not pay any part of the salaries of parochial school teachers who teach nonreligious subjects without running afoul of the establishment clause.

The question at issue here is an important one, for if government can finance educational equipment, pay the salaries of certain teachers, and purchase library books, it can do a great deal to underwrite the operation of religious schools. Elementary and Secondary Education Act programs may represent only a slight breach in the wall of separation between church and state, but, in the words of Justice Clark, "The breach of neutrality that is today a trickling stream may all too soon become a raging torrent, and, in the words of Madison, 'It is proper to take alarm at the first experiment on our liberties.' "[5]

We do not argue, as appellant did in *Allen,* that there is no such thing as secular education in sectarian schools; we accept the decision of the Court that secular education is offered in

[5] *School District of Abington Township v. Schempp,* 374 U.S. 203, at 225 (1963).

tendance or non-attendance. No tax in any amount, large or small, can be levied to support any religious activities or institutions, whatever they may be called, or whatever form they may adopt to teach or practice religion. Neither a state nor the Federal Government can, openly or secretly, participate in the affairs of any religious organizations or groups and vice versa. In the words of Jefferson, the clause against establishment of religion by law was intended to erect "a wall of separation between church and state."

> 330 U.S. 1, 15–16 (1947).

The Court went on to rule that the bus transportation statute was not designed to support institutions which teach religion. As Justice Black said,

> The State contributes no money to the schools. It does not support them. Its legislation, as applied, does no more than provide a general program to help parents get their children, regardless of their religion, safely and expeditiously to and from accredited schools.
>
> 330 U.S. 1, 18 (1947).

The Court did not deny that the transportation statute might make it easier for parents to send their children to parochial schools. However, it held that any benefit to schools was a collateral effect of the statute and, therefore, the challenged legislation did not violate the prohibition against establishment of religion.

Accompanying the Court's ruling that the transportation statute aided children rather than religious schools was a second corollary, that the legislation served a legitimate public purpose. After stating that "Changing local conditions create new local problems which may lead a state's people . . . to believe that laws authorizing new types of public services are necessary to promote the general wellbeing of the people . . ." the opinion of the Court continued, as follows:

> It is much too late to argue that legislation intended to facilitate the opportunity of children to get a secular education serves no public purpose. . . . The same thing is no less true of legislation to reimburse needy parents, or all parents, for payment of the fares of their chil-

such schools, although we agree with the dissenters in that case that the fine line between secular and religious education may be extremely hard to locate within the context of a school run by members of a particular sect for the purpose of inculcating in the young certain specific religious beliefs and values.

Nevertheless, as the Supreme Court said with approval in *Lemon v. Kurtzman*, 403 U.S. 602, at 615, "The District Court made extensive findings on the grave potential for excessive entanglement that inheres in the religious character and purpose of the Roman Catholic elementary schools...."

It is quite clear that the primary purpose of sectarian schools is to further particular religious tenets. For example, the Catholic parochial school system is founded on certain provisions of the Canon Law, as quoted by Justice Jackson in his dissent in *Everson*:

> 1215. Catholic children are to be educated in schools where not only nothing contrary to Catholic faith and morals is taught, but rather in schools where religious and moral training occupy the first place.... (Canon 1372.)
>
> 1216. In every elementary school the children must, according to their age, be instructed in Christian doctrine.
>
> The young people who attend the higher schools are to receive a deeper religious knowledge, and the bishops shall appoint priests qualified for such work by their learning and piety. (Canon 1373.)
>
> 1217. Catholic children shall not attend non-Catholic, indifferent schools that are mixed, that is to say, schools open to Catholics and non-Catholics alike. The bishop of the diocese only has the right, in harmony with the instructions of the Holy See, to decide under what circumstances, and with what safeguards to prevent loss of faith, it may be tolerated that Catholic children go to such schools. (Canon 1374.)
>
> 1224. The religious teaching of youth in any schools is subject to the authority and inspection of the Church.
>
> The local Ordinaries have the right and duty to watch that nothing is taught contrary to faith or good morals, in any of the schools of their territory.
>
> They, moreover, have the right to approve the books of Christian doctrine and the teachers of religion, and to demand, for the sake of safeguarding religion and morals, the removal

dren so that they can ride in public buses to and from schools rather than run the risk of traffic and other hazards incident to walking or "hitchhiking."

330 U.S. 1, 6–7 (1947).

Thus, the critical factors in the Court's conclusion that the bus statute was constitutional were that the legislation did not attempt to aid religion as such, that the bus program aided all children, regardless of religious faith rather than because of it, that a program designed to achieve a legitimate, secular purpose was not impermissible merely because it incidentally or collaterally aided adherents of particular religions.

This latter point was made even more strongly in a subsequent decision, *McGowan v. Maryland*, 366 U.S. 420 (1961), which upheld the validity of laws making Sunday a universal day of rest, even though such laws were originally passed for religious purposes and even though they continue to benefit churches which hold services on Sunday. The Court believed that "... [T]he 'Establishment' Clause does not ban Federal or state regulation of conduct whose reason or effect merely happens to coincide or harmonize with the tenets of some or all religions."[7]

Justice Frankfurter, in a concurring opinion, stated that the purpose of the establishment clause was to ensure that religion, as such, was not made the object of legislation. He continued:

> To ask what interest, what objective, legislation serves, of course, is not to psychoanalyze its legislators, but to examine the necessary effects of what they have enacted. If the primary end achieved by a form of regulation is the affirmation or promotion of religious doctrine—primary, in the sense that all secular ends which it purportedly serves are derivative from, not wholly independent of, the advancement of religion—the regulation is beyond the power of the state.... Or if a statute furthers both secular and religious ends by means unnecessary to the effectuation of the secular ends alone—where the same secular ends could equally be attained by means which do not

---

[7] 366 U.S. 420, 442 (1961).

of teachers and books. (Canon 1381.) (Woywod, Rev. Stanislaus, *The New Canon Law*, under imprimatur of Most Rev. Francis J. Spellman, Archbishop of New York and others, 1940.)[6]

Pope Pius XI stated, in his encyclical *On the Christian Education of Youth* that the ". . . only school approved by the Church is one where . . . the Catholic religion permeates the entire atmosphere [and where] all teaching and the whole organization of the school and its teachers, syllabus and textbooks in every branch [is] by the Christian spirit."[7]

Protestant and Jewish parochial schools have the same purpose and perform a similar function for members of their faith. Thus, to quote one Protestant theologian:

> Policywise, these schools fall into three general groups. The first maintains schools because it feels that the necessity for doing so is implied in its theological point of view. The second appears to maintain its schools because of the close relationship between its doctrine, its religious practices, and the total culture in which it feels its children and youth must be nurtured. The third group maintains its schools because of the conviction that an education that is not permeated with religious values of a specific Christian sort tends to promote secularism and gives the pupil the idea that religion is a thing apart from the rest of his major concerns.[8]

Similarly, a noted authority on Jewish schools observes:

> Integration is incorporated into the subject matter as well. In the expressional arts, general and Jewish arts are combined and taught as one. Jewish history will encompass the history of the many people with whom the Jews came into contact. General geography will include the geography of Israel. The important events studied in the Bible, such as the Exodus from Egypt and the Revelation at Sinai, are

have consequences for promotion of religion—the statute cannot stand. A State may not endow a church although that church might inculcate in its parishioners moral concepts deemed to make them better citizens, because the very *raison d'être* of a church, as opposed to any other school of civilly serviceable morals, is the predication of religious doctrine. However, inasmuch as individuals are free, if they will, to build their own churches and worship in them, the State may guard its people's safety by extending fire and police protection to the churches so built.

366 U.S. 420, at 466–67 (1961).

In *School District of Abington Township v. Schempp*, 374 U.S. 203, at 222 (1963), the Court drew together the principles of state neutrality toward religion which it had evolved in *Everson*, *McGowan*, and other cases and enunciated the following standard:

> The test may be stated as follows: what are the purpose and the primary effect of the enactment? If either is the advancement or inhibition of religion then the enactment exceeds the scope of legislative power as circumscribed by the Constitution. That is to say that to withstand the strictures of the Establishment Clause there must be a secular legislative purpose and a primary effect that neither advances nor inhibits religion.

Applying this test to the statute before the Court in *Schempp*—a statute requiring public school students to read from the Bible and to recite the Lord's Prayer at the beginning of each school day—the Court found the statute unconstitutional. The legislative purpose behind the statute was clearly religious, not secular. The effect of the statute was not government neutrality toward religion but government aid to religion. And, given the purpose of the legislation, such aid could not be defended on the ground it was merely an incidental consequence of the administration of an otherwise valid, secular act.

Finally, we would like to review *Board of Education v. Allen*, 392 U.S. 236 (1968). *Board of Education v. Allen* is extremely significant because the statute in question in that case did not differ in any substantial way from the Elementary and Secondary Education Act of 1965.

---

[6] 330 U.S. 1, 22–23 (1947).

[7] Redden and Ryan, *A Catholic Philosophy of Education*, pp. 107 and 118, 1942. (Brackets added.)

[8] Wyckoff, "The Protestant Day School," *School and Society*, vol. 82, pp. 98 and 99, 1955.

associated with the emancipation of other peoples, and especially with the independence won by America, as well as with the doctrines of liberty and democracy that are universal in character and biblical in origin. In the domestic science laboratory nutrition and homemaking are taught along with the laws of Kashruth and Dietary observances.[9]

Given these facts about the atmosphere, environment, and educational purpose of sectarian schools, how can it be said that government financing of any part of the operations of such schools does not amount to government aid to religion, in violation of the establishment clause? How can it be said that a distinction of constitutional dimensions can be drawn on whether or not the aid provided is limited to secular programs? Given the context in which sectarian education occurs, it is our contention that government financing of any part of the operations of religious schools is tantamount to government establishment of religion. Attempts to evade this reality—by labeling government aid to secular aspects of a parochial school's budget "aid to children" or "aid to education" rather than aid to the operation of an institution whose primary purpose is the teaching of religion—are merely efforts to play with words in order to achieve by indirection what cannot be done directly without violating the Constitution.

Furthermore, even if public money is in fact used solely for secular education, religious education still benefits indirectly. One need not be an economist to recognize that all costs in America have gone up in the past, are going up now, and will continue to go up in the future. The cost of financing private education is no exception. Now Congress has declared that the government will pay that part of the increasing expenditures of parochial schools which results from Title I and Title II programs. Even if the parochial schools were to continue to spend the same dollar amount on

[9] Goodside, "Religious and Secular Studies in the Day School," *Jewish Education*, vol. 24, pp. 55 and 56, 1953; see also symposium, "The Jewish Day School in America: Its Theory and Practice," *Jewish Education*, vol. 20, no. 1, 1948, and Kaminetsky, "The Hebrew Day School Movement," *School and Society*, vol. 82, p. 105, 1955.

We believe that the present litigation should be decided on the same basis, with the same logic, and the same outcome, as the *Allen* case.

First of all, what was at issue in *Allen?* Section 701 of the New York Education Law required local public school boards to lend without charge textbooks which had been approved for use in public schools or were approved by a local board of education to all children enrolled in grades seven to twelve in any school which complied with all the requirements of the state's compulsory education law. Parochial school students were to request such books through their schools, which would compile lists of requested books, pick up the books, distribute them, collect them, store them, etc. Ownership of the books was to remain in the hands of the local public school board.

Six members of the Court applied the *Schempp* test to the New York statute. Justice White, speaking for the Court, stated:

This test is not easy to apply, but the citation of *Everson* by the *Schempp* Court to support its general standard made clear how the *Schempp* rule would be applied to the facts of *Everson*. The statute upheld in *Everson* would be considered a law having "a secular legislative purpose and a primary effect that neither advances nor inhibits religion." We reach the same result with respect to the New York law. . . . The express purpose of § 701 was stated by the New York legislature to be furtherance of the educational opportunities available to the young. Appellants have shown us nothing about the necessary effects of the statute that is contrary to its stated purpose. The law merely makes available to all children the benefits of a general program to lend school books free of charge. Books are furnished at the request of the pupil and ownership remains, at least technically, in the State. Thus no funds or books are furnished to parochial schools, and the financial benefit is to parents and children, not to schools. Perhaps free books make it more likely that some children choose to attend a sectarian school, but that was true of the state-paid bus fares in *Everson*. . . .

392 U.S. 236, 243–44 (1967).

The majority rejected the argument that secular textbooks should be distinguished from

secular programs, they would be contributing a smaller and smaller percentage of the cost of such programs as time went on due to the increasing cost of education and the devaluation of the dollar through inflation.

If the government assumes any part of the increasing expenses of parochial schools, money is saved which might otherwise have been spent on secular programs. Or, assuming that the dollar income of parochial schools does not remain constant as time passes but increases to reflect the gradually declining value of the dollar, contribution to secular programs based on constant dollars also saves money which might otherwise be spent on such educational activities.

In either instance, the parochial schools save money, which, given their primary purpose, they can devote to strengthening religious education. Such indirect government financing of religious education would be no less unconstitutional than direct and unrestricted gifts of public money to sectarian institutions. As this Court stated in *McCollum v. Board of Education,* 333 U.S. 203 (1948), *Engel v. Vitale,* 370 U.S. 421 (1962), and *School District of Abington Township v. Schempp,* 374 U.S. 203 (1963), it is no part of the business of government to further the teaching of religion. The federal government must remain neutral if it is to avoid breaching the wall of separation between church and state.

Unlike appellee, we do not believe that the precedents of this Court provide a simple answer to the question of whether the challenged act violates the establishment clause. Several early precedents suggest that the act is unconstitutional. *School District of Abington Township v. Schempp* clouds the issue considerably, but the eight to nothing decision in *Lemon v. Kurtzman* suggests that this Court will not approve of attempts to aid parochial schools which cause excessive entanglement of church and state.

In *Everson v. Board of Education,* the Court ruled by a five to four vote that New Jersey could constitutionally finance bus transportation of parochial school as well as public school children. All the members of the Court agreed with the following definition of the meaning of the establishment clause, although

buses because bus transportation is clearly secular in nature, while all teaching in sectarian schools is inherently oriented toward the religious beliefs of the particular sect. Instead, the Court ruled that religious schools pursue two goals, religious instruction and secular education.

To prove the above point, Justice White cited cases upholding the right of parents to send their children to sectarian schools and the right of the state to regulate hours of instruction, attendance, teacher certification, and curriculum at such schools. Thus, while the state may not compel public school attendance, it may insist that sectarian schools offer secular education and that such education be substantially equivalent to that offered by public schools. In the absence of proof that textbooks in subjects such as mathematics, physics, foreign languages, history, or literature are used by parochial schools for the teaching of religion, the Court refused to hold ". . . [T]hat all teaching in a sectarian school is religious or that the processes of secular and religious training are so intertwined that secular textbooks furnished to students by the public are in fact instrumental in the teaching of religion."[8]

The appellants in *Allen* argued, further, that even if the state expenditures were not directly unconstitutional, they achieved an unconstitutional effect, since funds which would otherwise have been used for the purchase of secular texts were thereby freed for religious purposes. Noting that prior to passage of the legislation parents of parochial school students purchased books for their children, the Court ruled that parents rather than schools benefited from the textbook loan program and that, therefore, the legislation did not aid parochial schools in achieving their religious goals either directly or indirectly, through a "substitution effect."

Now, let us apply the logic of *Everson, McGowan, Schempp,* and *Allen* to the Elementary and Secondary Education Act of 1965. First, what is the purpose and primary effect of the legislation?

We have already demonstrated that the federal government and the nation as a whole

[8] 392 U.S. 236, 248 (1967).

the dissenters disagreed with the manner in which the majority applied the definition to the facts of the specific case:

> The "establishment of religion" clause of the First Amendment means at least this: Neither a state nor the Federal Government can set up a church. Neither can pass laws which aid one religion, aid all religions, or prefer one religion over another. Neither can force nor influence a person to go to or to remain away from church against his will or force him to profess a belief or disbelief in any religion. No person can be punished for entertaining or professing religious beliefs or disbeliefs, for church attendance or non-attendance. *No tax in any amount, large or small, can be levied to support any religious activities or institutions, whatever they may be called, or whatever form they may adopt to teach or practice religion.* Neither a state nor the Federal Government can, openly or secretly, participate in the affairs of any religious organizations or groups and vice versa. In the words of Jefferson, the clause against establishment of religion by law was intended to erect "a wall of separation between church and State."
>
> 330 U.S. 1, 15–16 (1947).
(Emphasis added.)

Next, Justice Black, speaking for the majority, applied this definition to the New Jersey statute. Stating that the Court must not strike down any state statute which was within the constitutional power of the state, even if it approached the verge of that power, Justice Black reiterated that a state could not contribute tax-raised funds "... [T]o the support of an institution which teaches the tenets and faith of any church."[10]

But, said Black, providing transportation was like state provision of police and fire protection. States could not interfere with the free exercise of religion by excluding members of any particular faith, because of their faith, from the benefits of public welfare legislation. The opinion concluded:

> The State contributes no money to the schools. It does not support them. Its legislation, as applied, does no more than provide a general program to help parents get their children, re-

have a substantial interest in the secular education received by students attending sectarian institutions. There is no doubt that the Elementary and Secondary Education Act was intended by Congress to improve the quality of education in secular subjects received by both public and parochial students rather than to aid sectarian schools in carrying out their religious functions. Witness, for example, the Declaration of Policy accompanying Title I of the act:

> In recognition of the special educational needs of children of low-income families and the impact that concentrations of low-income families have on the ability of local educational agencies to support adequate educational programs, the Congress hereby declares it to be the policy of the United States to provide financial assistance (as set forth in this title) to local educational agencies serving areas with concentrations of children from low-income families to expand and improve their educational programs by various means (including preschool programs) which contribute particularly to meeting the special educational needs of educationally deprived children.[9]

In order to carry out the above Declaration of Policy, Congress provided for grants to local public school districts. These districts were required to make arrangements for special educational services, dual enrollment programs, educational radio and television, and mobile educational services and equipment for private school students, to the extent consistent with the number of educationally deprived children in the school district attending such schools. Furthermore, the act prohibited the expenditure of public funds for religious training or instruction. Thus, Title I made federally supported programs of both enrichment and remedial training in secular subjects available to all educationally deprived students, not just students from low-income families enrolled in public schools.

Similarly, the purpose of Title II was to improve educational quality and opportunities, although, unlike Title I, Title II assistance was not limited to children from low-income families. Under Title II, public agencies were

---

[10] 330 U.S. 1, 16 (1947).

[9] 79 Stat. 27.

gardless of their religion, safely and expeditiously to and from accredited schools.

330 U.S. 1, 18 (1947).

The four dissenters disagreed with the conclusion that the busing law provided no aid to parochial schools. They believed that the primary purpose of sectarian schools was religious training, and that the statute aided parents in achieving this objective; thus, the provision of transportation to parochial schools violated the establishment clause.

It is important to point out that *Everson* does not stand for the concept that aid to parochial schools is constitutional if the aid is limited to financing secular activities within such schools. It does not stand for the proposition that public money can be used to pay teachers or guidance counselors in sectarian schools, to finance library acquisitions, to purchase educational equipment or textbooks for use in religious schools. All of these things would, according to the definition of the establishment clause given in *Everson*, constitute forbidden aid to religious institutions; all would constitute public contributions to schools, which would clearly violate the *Everson* definition of the scope of the establishment clause.

In subsequent cases, the Court refined and developed its *Everson* doctrine. *McCullum v. Board of Education*, 333 U.S. 203 (1948), outlawed released time programs in which public facilities were used for sectarian teaching; thus, the Court indicated that the First Amendment prohibited impartial government assistance to all religions. In *Zorach v. Clauson*, 343 U.S. 306 (1952), the Court upheld a released time program in which children were released from public school for religious instruction on private property. No expenditure of public funds and no use of public facilities was involved. The majority opinions in both *McCullum* and *Zorach* reiterated the *Everson* principle that government cannot finance religious groups.

In *Engel v. Vitale*, 370 U.S. 421 (1962), the Court struck down the reading of a nondenominational prayer in the New York public schools on the ground that the First Amendment was violated when "the power, prestige,

to acquire library resources—including books, periodicals, documents, audiovisual materials, and other related library materials—textbooks and other printed and published instructional materials for the use of children and teachers in public and private schools. The agencies concerned were to assure that private school children and teachers received equitable treatment in the acquisition of library materials and textbooks. The purchase of sectarian library resources or textbooks was forbidden by a requirement that the public agencies concerned purchase only materials which had been approved by public authorities for use in the public schools.

Thus, the purpose of Titles I and II was not to aid religion or religious institutions, but the education of children attending all schools which meet the requirements of state compulsory attendance laws. The act clearly meets the "secular legislative purpose" requirement of the *Schempp* test. But, what about the effect of the act? Is the primary effect an aid to religion forbidden by the establishment clause?

The Elementary and Secondary Education Act of 1965 does not provide funds for religious instruction or sectarian books and library materials. If it did so, there would be no question but that the act violated the establishment clause. Unlike the Bible-reading requirement judged unconstitutional in the *Schempp* case, the act does not have an effect which is primarily religious in nature.

The effect of Title II does not appear to us to be different in any significant way from the secular effect of the New York textbook loan act upheld in *Board of Education v. Allen*. Admittedly, the New York statute did not provide for the loan of library resources as well as textbooks. Yet, it is hard to support the contention that library resources differ from textbooks. If textbooks are for the benefit of students and teachers rather than for the benefit of a church-related school, can reference materials be any different? Clearly, as in the New York instance, any benefit to sectarian schools from the loan of library resources and textbooks is incidental and no more violates the establishment clause than the provision of bus transportation upheld in *Everson v. Board of Education*.

Furthermore, the effect of Title II can be

and financial support of government is placed behind a particular religious belief."[11] Again, the Court referred to the *Everson* interpretation of the establishment clause.

Then, in *School District of Abington Township v. Schempp*, 374 U.S. 203 (1963), the Court had to construe a law which required public school children to recite the Lord's Prayer and to participate in a Bible reading exercise at the beginning of each school day. With this particular ceremony in mind, the majority fashioned the following test:

> The test may be stated as follows: what are the purpose and the primary effect of the enactment? If either is the advancement or inhibition of religion then the enactment exceeds the scope of legislative power as circumscribed by the Constitution. That is to say that to withstand the strictures of the Establishment Clause there must be a secular legislative purpose and a primary effect that neither advances or inhibits religion.
>
> 374 U.S. 203, 222 (1963).

Appellee asks the Court to disregard its decisions prior to *Schempp*, to ignore its holding in *Lemon v. Kurtzman*, and to base its ruling in this case on the *Schempp* test. His view that the test justifies government aid to parochial schools as long as the public is not called upon to support the actual teaching of religion is hardly credible. To suggest that the federal and state governments can now, under the *Schempp* test, finance all the secular educational activities of sectarian schools, *or any part of such activities*, is to ignore obvious realities: no matter how words are twisted, such aid will help parochial schools to achieve their primary purpose, the teaching of religion.

Nor does the Court's recent decision in *Board of Education v. Allen*, 391 U.S. 236 (1968), support the appellee's contention. It is true that the majority upheld the New York textbook loan statute on the basis of the *Schempp* test; however, one cannot ignore the Court's explicit statement that the books were given to children, at their request, and that no aid was given to parochial schools as such. In

judged, in part, from the restrictions imposed on federal assistance. As in *Allen*, title to all materials purchased is to remain in the hands of a public agency. And, as has already been indicated, no materials can be obtained for use in parochial schools which are not approved for use in the public schools.

The only major difference between the New York statute and the textbook loan provision of Title II lies in the New York requirement that individual students request the particular texts they wish to borrow. It is our contention that the absence of this particular procedure from the requirements for receiving Title II loans does not alter the secular effect of Title II.

The New York requirement was inserted into the statute merely to emphasize the belief of the New York Legislature that it was aiding students and not sectarian schools. This is the only logical interpretation of the requirement of individual requests for textbooks, since no student could or would order a text other than the one used by the rest of his classmates. Thus, the request had more form than substance, since, ultimately, the teacher of the particular class determined what book his class would use. Given the somewhat artificial nature of the student request procedure, this Court should not hold that the absence of such a form from the Elementary and Secondary Education Act of 1965 indicates that the primary effect of the federal act is aid to religious institutions rather than to individual students. Such a distinction would indeed be artificial.

Finally, there is no validity to appellants' claim that the purchase of textbooks and library resources with public money and the loan of such materials to parochial school students and teachers allows parochial schools to shift funds which would otherwise have been spent on their secular education programs to expenses for religious instruction. Congress was aware of the possibility of a "substitution effect" at the time it considered the Elementary and Secondary Education Act of 1965 and it acted to prevent such a subversion of its goals by including an explicit requirement that the books and other materials loaned shall not supplant but must supplement existing resources and expenditures.

In sum, Title II aid to parochial school children and teachers is in accord with the

---

[11] 370 U.S. 421, 431 (1962).

the *Allen* case the majority believed that any aid to schools was remote and incidental, since the schools had not provided textbooks prior to passage of the statute. In the present case, however, one can hardly argue persuasively that the benefits conferred on parochial schools themselves are remote and incidental.

We do not deny that a primary effect of public financing of the secular aspects of parochial education is to improve and enrich secular education in such schools. But, it would be extraordinarily naive to suggest that that is the only primary effect of such aid and that all other "effects" are incidental and remote. No student of public policy would agree with what appears to be appellee's belief that policies, like coins, have only two sides.

The facts are plain: the primary purpose of parochial schools—their raison d'être—is the teaching of religion. Sectarian schools are eager to receive any and all aid, in an era of increasing costs, because such aid will help them to achieve their primary purpose. The public has traditionally provided fire and police protection for parochial schools because such assistance amounts at most to an incidental benefit to the schools; bus transportation and textbooks provided directly to students are equally incidental, since in neither instance do the schools themselves receive the benefit in anything more than an oblique fashion.

But public financing of any part of the educational budget of parochial schools does not provide an "incidental" benefit to such schools. The benefit is direct: it serves the purposes of the sectarian schools. Whether the aid is limited to secular programs or not, it advances religion since it advances parochial schools. Thus, even if the Court chooses to apply the *Schempp* test to the facts of this particular case, we believe it should rule that a primary effect of the aid provided by the Elementary and Secondary Education Act is advancement of religion, in violation of the establishment clause of the First Amendment.

However, given the Court's 1971 decision invalidating state payment of the salaries of parochial school teachers of nonreligious subjects, there is no need for the court to apply the *Schempp* test. In *Lemon v. Kurtzman* the appellants argued that state purchase of

Court's six to three decision in *Board of Education v. Allen*, has a secular legislative purpose and no primary effect which can be construed as aid to religion, provides for nondiscriminatory aid to all children regardless of religion, and confers benefits on sectarian schools which are no less indirect and incidental than the benefits conferred on such schools by the statutes contested in the *Everson* and *Allen* cases.

Appellants' objections to Title I of the act are even stronger than his objections to Title II. Let us be sure we know exactly what the source of these objections is: Title I provides for "dual enrollment" programs, in which parochial school students take certain of their courses in public schools, and "mobile educational services," which are defined as remedial programs not ordinarily offered in the curriculum of the parochial schools. Where possible such programs are held on public property; in some instances, however, remedial services are provided within the sectarian school itself.[10] In New York City, for example, the Board of Education has endorsed Title I proposals for remedial reading, remedial arithmetic, speech therapy, and guidance services to be offered in nonpublic schools.

As counsel for the appellee, we believe that everything we have said about the validity of textbook loans applies to supplementary services for remedial education. Of course, we do not mean that textbooks and supplementary services are the same in substance. What we do mean is that the same test should be applied to determine whether Title II textbook loans and Title I expenditures violate the establishment clause, and that application of the *Schempp* standard leads to the conclusion that the federal government may purchase textbooks and finance supplementary educational services for parochial school students without breaching the First Amendment.

First of all, it is clear that the legislative purpose behind Title I is secular in nature:

[10] For remarks that publicly paid teachers could be sent to parochial schools only for remedial programs which go beyond existing curricular offerings and only when the local public school agency deems it advisable, see the statements of Congressman Carl Perkins, manager of the bill, and of other congressmen, 111 CONG. REC. 5743–5748, 6096–6097, 6099–6100 (1965).

secular educational services was valid under the test, but the majority refused to determine the primary effect of the statutes since it concluded that their cumulative impact involved excessive entanglement between church and state.

The Court's finding of "excessive entanglement" was grounded on not one but a number of factors, including 1) the potential for entanglement inherent in the religious character and purpose of the Roman Catholic elementary schools, 2) the danger that teachers under religious control and direction would find it hard to maintain total separation of secular education and religious doctrine, 3) the necessity of continuous state surveillance to ensure that the separation is in fact maintained, 4) the divisive political potential that would result from lobbying and other efforts to obtain aid, aggravated by the need for annual appropriations, the likelihood that demands for aid would grow, and the fact that the aid benefits relatively few religious groups. It is our belief that the challenged provisions of the federal act involve at least as much entanglement of government and religion.

The constitutional guarantee of free exercise of religion and the prohibition against religious establishment were included in the First Amendment as a result of the unhappy experiences of the founding fathers with the divisive and embittering consequences of state involvement with religion. The authors of the amendment saw clearly that religious hatred and strife were the inevitable outcome of state attempts to dominate religion or religious attempts to use the agencies of the state to achieve sectarian purposes.

For nearly two hundred years the First Amendment has stood as a barrier to legislation which creates hatred, disharmony, and discord among the American people. Now, due to the active political involvement and pressure of certain religious groups, Congress has passed a law which involves the state so significantly and directly in the realm of the sectarian as to generate the very divisiveness feared by the authors of the establishment clause. Involvement of religious groups in government decisions for the purpose of furthering the advancement of particular religious sects is the very essence of establishment of

secular educational benefits are to be given to most children from low-income families regardless of religion. There is no primary effect which aids religion or religious institutions: no public money is to be spent to teach religion; only subjects which meet the special educational needs of educationally deprived students —including therapeutic, remedial, and welfare services—are to be supported; no substitution effect will be possible, since support will be limited to services which do not duplicate programs already offered by sectarian schools. And, as the act specifically states: "Nothing contained in this Act shall be construed to authorize the making of any payment . . . for religious worship or instruction."[11]

It is far too late to argue that Titles I and II are invalid because there is no such thing as secular education in a parochial school. That argument is foreclosed by the clear-cut ruling of six members of the Court in *Board of Education v. Allen* that sectarian schools perform a dual function. As Justice White stated for the Court, ". . . [A] wide segment of informed opinion, legislative and otherwise, has found that those [parochial] schools do an acceptable job of providing secular education to their students."[12] Only Justices Black, Douglas, and Fortas insisted that New York State could not provide secular textbooks since such books inevitably would be used in such a way as to propagate the religious views of the particular parochial school. Nothing has happened in the interim since the *Allen* decision to suggest that the majority was wrong or that its 1968 judgment should be reversed. If anything, the opposite is the case, since the trend toward ecumenicism and toward increasing employment of lay teachers in Catholic parochial schools has continued unabated. A study done in 1963 showed that the proportion of lay teachers in elementary schools had grown from 8 percent to over 30 percent in little more than a decade.[13]

Appellants argue, however, that the Elementary and Secondary Education Act should not be judged by the *Schempp* test, nor by

[11] 79 Stat. 58.

[12] 392 U.S. 236, 248 (1968). (Brackets added.)

[13] William D. Pflaum, "Lay Teachers: How Many in Elementary Schools?" *National Catholic Education Association Bulletin*, November 1963, pp. 17–23.

religion. Nor can it be argued that the challenged legislation amounts to such limited state involvement with religious organizations that it does not violate the First Amendment; small and insidious attacks on constitutional liberties are no more justifiable than large and obvious ones.

First, the act requires that taxpayers contribute to the support of religious schools whose teachings many taxpayers oppose. Nothing can result from such coerced support of religious schools but disharmony and animosity.

Second, the act requires local public school authorities to consult with parochial school authorities in devising programs, spending money, accounting for expenditures, and testing the results of the programs. In order to comply with the establishment clause the act includes mechanisms and procedures designed to ensure that (1) teachers hired with public funds maintain total separation between secular education and religious doctrine, and (2) equipment and library resources are used solely for secular purposes. While mobile TV units, movie projectors, and other equipment are themselves neutral, it is obvious they can be used for sectarian purposes. Thus, the act creates the comprehensive and continuous state surveillance necessary to ensure that the First Amendment is respected. As the Court concluded in Lemon v. Kurtzman, such policing involves constitutional entanglement.

Third, it is quite clear that only a limited amount is available for special educational programs, library resources, textbooks, and other educational materials and equipment. Thus, inevitably, the act encourages religious school interests and public authorities and parents to engage in a political struggle to see who can get the most benefit from the public expenditures. Parochial school parents will be encouraged to elect public officials who sympathize with the educational needs of their children; thus religious animosity may increase and local communities become polarized.

If local school boards submit to pressures from sectarian interests, state and church will no longer be separate; if school boards resist such pressures, the battle lines will be drawn and the political conflict for domination and control of the public purse strings will rage.

the *Allen* precedent, but by the ruling of the Court in *Lemon v. Kurtzman*, 403 U.S. 602 (1971), that states cannot pay the salaries of parochial school teachers of secular subjects without violating the establishment clause. We do not believe the Court will agree with this argument, since the *Lemon* decision made it quite clear that the justices did not mean to overrule their decision in *Board of Education v. Allen*. Chief Justice Burger's opinion held that:

> Our decisions from *Everson* to *Allen* have permitted the States to provide church-related schools with secular, neutral, or nonideological services, facilities, or materials. Bus transportation, school lunches, public health services, and secular textbooks supplied in common to all students were not thought to offend the Establishment Clause.... We cannot, however, refuse here to recognize that teachers have a substantially different ideological character from books. In terms of potential for involving some aspect of faith or morals in secular subjects, a textbook's content is ascertainable, but a teacher's handling of a subject is not. We cannot ignore the danger that a teacher under religious control and discipline poses to the separation of the religious from the purely secular aspects of precollege education.
>
> 403 U.S. 602, 616–17 (1971).

Thus, the crucial fact in *Lemon* was that the aid in question went to teachers under the control and direction of religious authorities. Furthermore, the salary supplements were not general in nature, but went only to parochial school teachers. Since the *Lemon* decision did not challenge earlier rulings regarding the provision of non-ideological textbooks to schools in general, it is not a useful precedent for a ruling on Title II programs.

Furthermore, Title I programs of supplementary educational services do not fall under the *Lemon* ban, since control and administration of Title I programs rest in the hands of the local educational agency establishing the particular program, not in the hands of the administration of the recipient school.

And, finally, we come to appellants' most sweeping and hortatory contention: that the act will lead to open conflict between church and state, that sect will be pitted against sect

Fourth, the powerful religious groups that were able to write their own preferences into the Elementary and Secondary Education Act will not cease their activity as a result of passage of the act. They will, inevitably, come back to Congress, seeking additional funds for the parochial schools. They will, inevitably, seek further federal legislation, legislation which will provide for taxpayer support of more and more of the "secular" aspects of sectarian education. Already, one hears arguments that parochial school students have a constitutional "right" to public support of their education.

We mention these political realities only to suggest that the Elementary and Secondary Education Act of 1965 is a creature of church-state involvement and will, in turn, be the cause of future bitterness, hostility, and religious antagonism unless this Court announces firmly that government cannot support sectarian institutions without violating the constitutional prohibition against establishment of religion.

Appellee dismisses our concern over government participation in and stimulation of religious divisiveness by stating that the church-state conflicts which will occur will be insignificant. While it is correct that the majority rejected this argument in *Board of Education v. Allen*, it is important to note, however, that the New York statute allowed *all* seventh- to twelfth-grade students attending schools which met the requirements of the state's compulsory education law to borrow up to $15 worth of textbooks from local public school authorities.

Thus, under the New York statute, parochial and public school interests did not have to compete for limited funds; the same benefits were available to all students. The benefit to the schools themselves was minimal, since, as has been said, parents normally purchased the textbooks used by parochial school students; thus, the schools had no comparable interest in competing with one another in the political arena for public benefits.

None of these points is applicable to the challenged act: instead, schools benefit directly; parochial school interests must compete for limited funds both among themselves and with the public schools; the benefits are varied and

in the competition for limited public benefits, that church groups will struggle for control over local public school agencies—that, in sum, the act constitutes a forbidden establishment of religion because it will create the religious hatred and strife that the authors of the First Amendment feared.

This argument is purely speculative. It assumes that certain events are inevitable, in the absence of any evidence or proof whatsoever that such events are in fact likely to happen. Should a law which has been passed by two-thirds of both houses of Congress and viewed by the President as one of the most important acts passed under his administration be thrown out by this Court on an argument so ephemeral in nature?

While it is true that the *Lemon* opinion includes expressions of concern about the divisive political potential of state payment of the salaries of teachers of secular subjects in parochial schools, we believe that the Court's concern did not constitute an independent basis for judgment that the salary subsidies were unconstitutional. Instead, it is our opinion that the Court's remarks on this subject merely added to its fundamental view that government cannot support teachers of secular subjects who are subject to the direction and discipline of religious authorities.

Furthermore, the same argument about divisiveness was used only three years earlier by the opponents of the New York textbook loan statute and it received short shrift from the Court majority. Justice White stated, for the Court:

Absent evidence, we cannot assume that school authorities, who constantly face the same problem in selecting textbooks for use in the public schools, are unable to distinguish between secular and religious books or that they will not honestly discharge their duties under the law.

392 U.S. 236, 245 (1968).

This statement is equally applicable to Titles I and II of the Elementary and Secondary Education Act of 1965. Certainly, it would be inappropriate for the Court to assume that local authorities would abuse their responsibilities

unequal in value; they are not equally available to all students, since some students will get certain ones and others may not get any, depending on the persuasiveness of their school administrators and the receptivity of local public school officials. The New York act was written in such a way as to avoid political conflict; the federal act, in contrast, invites sectarian divisiveness. Under the circumstances, *Lemon v. Kurtzman* appears to be the relevant precedent. Thus, we ask the Court to hold that the Elementary and Secondary Education Act of 1965 involves the government so significantly in the realm of the sectarian as to violate the First Amendment.

in administering the law, or that state educational agencies and the United States Commissioner of Education would fail to fulfill their obligation to correct any such abuse. It will be time enough for the courts to act if and when such a remote and unlikely series of events actually occurs.

2. *Does the Elementary and Secondary Education Act of 1965 violate the free-exercise clause of the First Amendment?*

While we believe that the Elementary and Secondary Education Act violates the establishment clause of the First Amendment because it supplements the budgets of parochial schools, we also believe that it restricts the free exercise of religion guaranteed American citizens by the amendment. Two factors lead us to this conclusion: first, the law compels taxpayers to contribute to the support and propagation of beliefs which they do not share and, second, the law creates a substantial danger of state control over religious education.

The history of the First Amendment shows clearly that the founding fathers believed it was destructive of religious freedom to compel any man to pay taxes for religious purposes. As the majority of this Court stated in *Everson v. Board of Education:*

These practices became so commonplace as to shock the freedom-loving colonials into a feeling of abhorrence. The imposition of taxes to pay ministers' salaries and to build and maintain churches and church property aroused their indignation. . . . The people . . . reached the conviction that individual religious liberty could be achieved best under a government which was stripped of all power to tax, to support, or otherwise to assist any or all re-

Appellants claim that the Elementary and Secondary Education Act of 1965 violates their free exercise of religion because it compels them as taxpayers to contribute to the propagation of religious opinions which they do not share. Thus, they insinuate that the act amounts to a tax to support religion, comparable to the religious assessments which James Madison and Thomas Jefferson opposed in the years just prior to the adoption of the First Amendment.

Yet what is this argument other than a clever reiteration of the establishment clause arguments the appellants have already made? If, in fact, the act does not violate the establishment clause because the public money involved is spent for legitimate secular purposes and not for spreading religious beliefs or aiding sectarian institutions, then how can it lead to the propagation of religious beliefs in violation of the free exercise clause of the Constitution?

No public money is being spent under the act for religious instruction or for unconstitutional aid to religious institutions. Appellants' religious beliefs or nonbeliefs are not coerced in any way whatsoever by the expenditure of public funds for Title I and Title II programs. Furthermore, this same argument was made in *Board of Education v. Allen* and rejected by the Court.

ligions, or to interfere with the beliefs of any religious individual or group.

330 U.S. 1, 11 (1947).

James Madison's famous "Memorial and Remonstrance Against Religious Assessments" —one of the high points in the early struggle for religious liberty—was provoked by demands in the Virginia legislature for a tax to continue support of the Christian religion and Christian worship. Madison argued that religion was properly a private affair, not an object of state support or regulation.

Shortly after the defeat of the tax bill, Thomas Jefferson introduced his monumental "Bill for the Establishment of Religious Freedom," which was passed by the Virginia Legislature in 1786. Following a preamble which stated that "to compel a man to furnish contributions of money for the propagation of opinions which he disbelieves is sinful and tyrannical," the Bill itself provided that "no man shall be compelled to frequent or support any religious worship, place, or ministry whatsoever. . . ."[12]

Jefferson, Madison, and other supporters of the First Amendment recognized that forced support was no different from coerced attendance at religious exercises; in either instance, the state was not only establishing one or more religions, it was also violating the free exercise of religion and denying equality under the law. Thus, the founding fathers conceived of the establishment clause and the free exercise clause as two related parts of a single fundamental freedom encompassed in the First Amendment.

The Elementary and Secondary Education Act violates this historic tradition because it compels men to support private sectarian institutions whose primary purpose is the teaching of beliefs they do not share.

Furthermore, government aid to sectarian schools threatens the religious liberty of recipient schools, since such aid necessitates government controls and regulations. As Justice Jackson said in *Everson*, 330 U.S. 1, at 27,

[12] References to the history of the First Amendment's religion clauses are taken from the Appendix to Justice Rutledge's dissent in *Everson v. Board of Education*, 33 U.S. 1, 63–74 (1947).

Appellants also argue that the act endangers the free exercise of religion by the recipients of federal aid. They suggest that religious liberty will be restricted by the political controls which will accompany Title I and Title II programs.

This argument ignores the fact that parochial schools are already highly regulated by the states in order to ensure that they offer secular educational programs comparable to those being offered in local public schools. These regulations have been upheld in many cases, and there is no doubt as to their constitutionality. Certainly, they restrict the freedom of the parochial schools, but they do not, as a necessary and inevitable consequence, restrict religious liberty in violation of the command of the First Amendment.

Moreover, in their rush to protect the religious freedom of parochial school students, appellants fail to explain how schools and pupils are compelled to accept the government's offer of special educational services, secular textbooks, and other printed materials, or why no recipients of the aid offered by the act have rushed to the courts to defend their religious freedom from government suppression.

On the other hand, we believe that the exclusion of pupils from the benefits of a public aid program, solely because of their religion, *would* violate their religious freedom. As this Court unanimously established in *Pierce v. Society of Sisters*, 268 U.S. 510 (1925), the state cannot compel parents to send their children to public schools. Thus, children have a right to attend sectarian schools. As Justice Black said in *Everson v. Board of Education:*

New Jersey cannot consistently with the "establishment of religion" clause of the First Amendment contribute tax-raised funds to the support of an institution which teaches the tenets and faith of any church. *On the other hand, other language of the Amendment commands that New Jersey cannot hamper its citizens in the free exercise of their own religion. Consequently, it cannot exclude individual Catholics, Lutherans, Mohammedans, Baptists, Jews, Methodists, Nonbelievers, Presbyterians, or the members of any other faith, because of their faith or lack of it, from receiving the benefits of public welfare legisla-*

"Many persons have sought aid from tax funds only to find that it carried political controls with it."

Appellee derides this argument, saying that the challenged act precludes the possibility of limitation of the religious freedom of sectarian schools since it expressly includes a provision forbidding federal control of education.[13] One would be naïve, however, to assume that public funds can be given, or should be given, to any individual or institution without concern for just how that money is spent. The act in question, for example, provides for an elaborate system of reporting and accounting simply to ensure that the government and the public know exactly how sectarian schools and public educational authorities are spending the sums they receive from the Treasury.

No one who has witnessed the long fight between the Southern school districts and the federal government over segregation in the public schools would state cavalierly that federal sums do not lead to a certain measure of control. For example, recipients of federal funds are forbidden to discriminate on the basis of race as a result of Title VI of the Civil Rights Act of 1964.[14] Private sectarian schools have historically controlled their own admissions, and many of them have refused to admit students of other faiths. Discrimination in admissions is a deliberate policy, based on the desire of school authorities to create an atmosphere, environment, and student body which will encourage teaching and learning of particular sectarian values and beliefs. In most instances, discrimination leads, whether consciously or not, to racial exclusion. Our point is simply that federal aid is incompatible with the free exercise clause of the First Amendment, since it creates the opportunity for the government to control the aid recipients.

Finally, we wish to reply to appellee's argument that a decision of this Court excluding parochial schools from the assistance offered by the Elementary and Secondary Education Act would deny the religious freedom of students attending such schools. In recent years, the Court has heard many convoluted arguments, but this must be the strangest of all.

[13] 79 Stat. 57.
[14] 78 Stat. 252.

tion. While we do not mean to intimate that a state could not provide transportation only to children attending public schools, we must be careful, in protecting the citizens of New Jersey against State established churches, to be sure that we do not inadvertently prohibit New Jersey from extending its general state law benefits to all citizens without regard to their religious belief.

> 330 U.S. 1, 16 (1947).
> (Emphasis added.)

If appellants' claim that the contested provisions of the Elementary and Secondary Education Act are unconstitutional were to be sustained, the religious affiliation of a child or of the school he attended would thus become the test of whether he was eligible for secular benefits designed for all school children. This Court only recently emphasized, in *Sherbert v. Verner*, 374 U.S. 398 (1963), that public benefits cannot be denied individuals because of their religion without violating the free exercise clause. In that case, South Carolina had denied unemployment benefits to a Seventh Day Adventist who refused to take a job which required work on Saturday, in violation of her religious beliefs. The Court held:

We turn first to the question whether the disqualification for benefits imposes any burden on the free exercise of appellant's religion. We think it is clear that it does. In a sense the consequences of such a disqualification to religious principles and practices may be only an indirect result of welfare legislation within the State's general competence to enact; it is true that no criminal sanctions directly compel appellant to work a six-day week. But this is only the beginning, not the end, of our inquiry. For "(i)f the purpose or effect of a law is to impede the observance of one or all religions or is to discriminate invidiously between religions, that law is constitutionally invalid even though the burden may be characterized as being only indirect." *Braunfeld v. Brown, supra,* at 607. Here not only is it apparent that appellant's declared ineligibility for benefits derives solely from the practice of her religion, but the pressure upon her to forego that practice is unmistakable. The ruling forces her to choose between following the precepts of her religion and forfeiting benefits, on the one hand, and abandoning one of the precepts of

In effect, appellee is urging that regardless of the unconstitutionality of aid to parochial schools, this Court must uphold the act.

Let us turn the question around. Do parochial schools have a right to share in public aid on the ground that the refusal of a state legislature or Congress to include sectarian schools in aid to education measures denies the freedom of religion of parochial school students? The Constitution certainly does not require the federal or state governments to treat sectarian schools the same as public schools.

It is inconceivable to us that failure to include parochial schools in an aid program interferes with free exercise of religion when no religious practices are compelled or forbidden in any way whatever by such legislation. Using appellee's logic, however, one could easily argue that the failure of the federal government to assist churches in every way possible makes the free exercise of religion harder and thereby violates the First Amendment. In *McCullum v. Board of Education*, 333 U.S. 203 (1948), this Court rejected a "released time" program under which public school facilities were turned over to religious teachers for religious instruction. The majority refused to accept the argument that a decision against the released time program would be a manifestation of government hostility to religion, in violation of the free exercise clause.

Even if the aid provided by the Elementary and Secondary Education Act is construed to be general welfare aid to students rather than aid to religious schools, there is absolutely nothing in the First Amendment which requires government to provide such assistance. According to the majority in *Everson*, states can provide general welfare services to students attending parochial schools if they choose to do so; on the other hand, they have no obligation to do so.[15] The only obligation actually imposed by the First Amendment's free exercise clause is that the state cannot discriminate against individuals because of their religious beliefs.

In the present instance, a holding by the Court that the challenged provisions of the Elementary and Secondary Education Act of

[15] 330 U.S. 1, 16 (1947).

her religion in order to accept work, on the other hand. Governmental imposition of such a choice puts the same kind of burden upon the free exercise of religion as would a fine imposed against appellant for her Saturday worship.

Nor may the South Carolina court's construction of the statute be saved from constitutional infirmity on the ground that unemployment compensation benefits are not appellant's "right" but merely a "privilege." It is too late in the day to doubt that the liberties of religion and expression may be infringed by the denial of or placing of conditions upon a benefit or privilege.

374 U.S. 398, 403–04 (1963).

Similarly, it is our belief that no child whose religious beliefs impel him to attend a parochial school should be compelled to choose between following the precepts of his religion and thereby forfeiting public benefits or abandoning one of the precepts of his religion in order to secure those benefits. Such a choice would be forced on all parochial school children if appellants' contentions are sustained by this Court.

Congress was faced with a difficult task when it considered the Elementary and Secondary Education Act of 1965. It wished to raise the level of secular education offered American schoolchildren, and in particular, it recognized the need to increase the educational opportunities available to children from low-income families. Yet, given the large number of students enrolled in private schools, it could not achieve its legitimate secular purpose by passing a bill to aid public school students.

Congress recognized that a bill to provide remedial training, textbooks, and library resources for all children, regardless of religion, would raise delicate questions about government aid to religion and to religious institutions. On the other hand, it also knew that exclusion of sectarian-school pupils would defeat the purposes of the act and would raise equally sensitive questions about discriminating against children because of their religion.

Given these complex constitutional alternatives, we cannot believe other than that Congress acted wisely and circumspectly in passing the act in question. Congress tailored the act carefully to maintain government neutrality

1965 violate the establishment clause, the free exercise clause, or both would not be indicative of government hostility to religion and would not deny the religious freedom of students attending sectarian schools. As has already been said, the denial of aid would in no shape, manner, or form compel or forbid any religious practices. Students attending parochial schools would not receive the benefit of aid to their schools, but the benefits would not be withheld because of the religious faith of such students, since students of the same religion attending public schools would obtain publicly financed remedial help, library resources, etc. Aid would be withheld not because of the religious beliefs of individuals but because they chose, voluntarily, to reject public education in favor of a religiously oriented education.

Parents are free to send children to parochial schools, but if they do so, they must bear the burden of financing parochial education. The government cannot, without violating the First Amendment, pass legislation compelling the public to share this burden.

toward religion as well as to achieve a legitimate secular purpose. Viewed in this light, the Elementary and Secondary Education Act of 1965 is wholly compatible with the objectives of the First Amendment.

. . . .

III   Politics, Pressures, and Constitutional Interpretation

Until the passage of the Elementary and Secondary Education Act of 1965, parochial schools received no more than a trickle of public financial support. ESEA burst the dam, and in the following years millions of dollars flowed into parochial schools from both federal and state sources. Federal assistance alone totaled 250 million dollars between 1965 and 1970.

ESEA also had a tremendous impact in states with large parochial school enrollments: supporters of state aid programs could and did use the federal act to illustrate both the need for aid, and the legitimacy of such assistance. ESEA was a precedent for aid to private schools, and supporters of state aid could argue that Congress would not have enacted a federal program if there had been much doubt as to its constitutionality.

Within the short space of a few years, opponents of public support for sectarian schools found their political position undermined: thirty-six of the fifty states passed some form of aid legislation. By 1970, twenty-three states were providing bus transportation, nine were providing textbooks, eight general health services, and six were paying salary supplements to parochial school teachers. In general, statutes providing bus services or school lunch programs went unchallenged in the courts. Legislation which went beyond such nominal assistance invariably became the focal point of litigation. By the end of 1970, at least thirty cases had been filed in various courts around the country.[1]

---

[1] *The New York Times*, Oct. 20, 1970, p. 23.

Opponents of public aid to religious schools had been triumphant for decades; now they were in total disarray. Pessimism permeated their ranks, particularly because the change had taken place so fast that it was hard to comprehend. For example, the Civil Liberties Union of Massachusetts stated in its Annual Report for 1970, ". . . [W]e sometimes feel as if we were approaching the status and stance of a Don Quixote, struggling in favor of principles and values that in wide circles are apparently less esteemed today than formerly."[2] The Massachusetts state affiliate of the ACLU went on to question whether it should give up futilely protesting church-state aid issues and devote its energies to more promising policy areas.

What had happened? Why were the opponents of aid to parochial schools reduced to feelings of impotence? Let us attempt to draw together points which have already been mentioned as well as several additional reasons for the new state of affairs.

1. The primary reason for the growing strength of parochial school supporters was clearly their ability to persuade federal and state legislators that financial insolvency would cause mass closing of parochial schools, which in turn would overburden public education and require vast new expenditures to accommodate former parochial school students. Legislators who were neutral or were nominally opposed to public support could and did see the logic of this argument, since it took the issue of aid out of a religious context and put it into a simple, practical one.

2. The ecumenical movement, fostered by Pope John XXIII, weakened opposition to aid for Catholic schools. Many Protestant clergymen, for example, became less and less willing to oppose such aid publicly because of the new spirit of ecumenicism. This subtle shift made Catholic pleas for "justice" seem more and more reasonable and made opposition sound more and more like anti-Catholicism. Thus, the legitimacy of the anti-aid position was undercut by changing public attitudes.

3. As public attitudes changed, more and more legislators and governors concluded that it would not be politically dangerous to address themselves to what had once been an extremely touchy subject. Discussions which had once been taboo became commonplace, providing further legitimacy for the pro-public aid position. Indeed, even the church itself decided that it no longer had to treat the issue with kid gloves because of fear of a negative public response.

4. To a certain extent, the opponents of aid to religious schools were responsible for their own downfall. By compromising on ESEA they sold out a historic principle in favor of a short-term practical solution to the question of federal aid to education. While one can argue over the wisdom of this decision, the simple fact that opponents of aid acted on pragmatic rather than philosophical grounds had unfortunate consequences. For one thing, the decision to act on political grounds rather than on principle helped to make the principle seem somewhat fraudulent. After the passage of ESEA, how could National Education Association officials, for example, present a convincing case against state aid proposals on grounds they violated the principle of separation of church and state?

5. Moreover, the decision to support ESEA had disastrous consequences for the interest groups which had led the fight against public aid to parochial schools. For example, the NEA was split wide open and it has not recovered. The NEA prides itself on being more democratic than other interest groups; major policies are adopted at annual meetings of representatives from every state. When the

---

[2] Civil Liberties Union of Massachusetts, *Civil Liberties in the Bay State*, Summer, 1970, p. 4.

Washington leadership decided to support ESEA, they compromised one of the existing policies, and they did so without consulting the annual meeting or the membership in general. Inevitably, many members and state leaders reacted angrily to what they regarded as a betrayal of trust. At every annual meeting since that time resolutions condemning the new policy and resolutions supporting it have been offered, debated heatedly, rejected, and occasionally passed. One faction has had the upper hand from time to time, but neither seems to predominate. Internal feuding has paralyzed the NEA and destroyed its unity and effectiveness on the church-state issue.

6. Finally, the ground was cut out from under the anti-aid position by decisions of the Supreme Court. Through the 1940s and 1950s, the Court seemed to be a bulwark against public aid to parochial schools; the *Everson* doctrine that no public money could be used to support a religious institution was the prevailing interpretation of the establishment clause, and interest groups opposed to parochial school aid could wrap themselves in a cloak of loyalty to the dictates of the Constitution. It was widely assumed that the Court would strike down any program that provided funds for use within the doors of parochial schools. Under the circumstances, it was no wonder that parochial school supporters were reluctant to invest much energy in efforts to woo state legislators.

Then, in a series of cases dealing with prayer in public schools, rather than the use of public funds, the members of the Court attempted to define the limits of the establishment clause more precisely. Even innocuous prayers were thrown out, on the theory that the establishment clause was violated whenever the "legislative purpose and primary effect" of a statute was aid to religion. Thus, the Court took a very narrow view of what was permissible in a policy area of limited significance. While the school prayer decisions were highly controversial, it is true nevertheless that prayers in school are not a major source of a child's religious development, nor do they involve expenditures of vast sums of money, nor do they threaten the whole complex of policies which shape elementary and secondary education in the United States.

Ironically, the "legislative purpose and primary effect" test, originally designed to prohibit state-imposed prayers, became the vehicle of state support for nonsectarian activities within parochial schools. At the same time as the Court was developing the test, politicians started to think in terms of aid to pupils rather than aid to religious institutions. Clearly, the line of demarcation between so-called "child benefit" aid and aid to the parochial school which the child attended was, and would be, murky; but as long as the aid in question could be reasonably justified on the child benefit theory, it might conceivably withstand the "legislative purpose and primary effect" test.

Proponents of public aid to parochial schools won a tremendous victory when the Supreme Court upheld the New York textbook loan act under this theory in *Board of Education v. Allen*, 392 U.S. 236 (1968). The Supreme Court had come a long way from the very tentative step it took in *Everson v. New Jersey*, 330 U.S. 1 (1947), where it upheld the right of a state to provide bus service for parochial school students at public expense. The only members of the Court which decided *Everson* still on the bench, Justices Black and Douglas, both dissented in the Allen case.

With the wall of separation between church and state thus breached, and with no indication of whether there were any limits to the child benefit theory, opponents of aid to sectarian schools no longer had the Supreme Court or constitutional doctrine on their side. Under the circumstances, it is no wonder they were disheartened.

New life was breathed into the anti-aid position by the decision of the Supreme Court in *Lemon v. Kurtzman,* 403 U.S. 602 (1971). Just when they were about to decide that the game was not worth the candle, opponents of public aid to parochial schools were presented with an unexpected eight to nothing ruling that state purchase of secular educational services violated the First Amendment. The refusal of the Court to hold that state payment of some proportion of the salaries of teachers of secular subjects constituted merely an attempt to improve the education offered parochial school children meant that there was some limit to the "child benefit" theory after all. It meant that the Court would not continue to judge establishment clause cases solely by the arbitrary formula that as long as the "legislative purpose and primary effect" of a statute were secular, public aid was constitutional.

A Supreme Court decision upholding salary supplements would have meant, in political terms, that the members of the Court believed the question of whether states should finance two parallel school systems, one public and the other private and sectarian, was a political question, to be resolved through the channels of the political system and not through the judicial process. On the other hand, the corruption of the "legislative purpose and primary effect" test and the development of the concept of "excessive entanglement" constituted an open invitation to further litigation and to further judicial determination of the limits of allowable aid to parochial schools.

But what is "excessive entanglement"? Is it a return to a position like that held by the dissenters in *Everson* that any aid and comfort, direct or indirect, violates the First Amendment? Is it a momentary lapse in a stream of decisions allowing more and more public aid to parochial schools? Is it an objective standard, capable of being understood and applied by law-makers considering proposed statutes, or is it merely a conscious rationalization of the policy preferences of particular justices?

To the extent that "excessive entanglement" appears to be a subjective response to circumstances, it is a standard which will encourage interest groups, executives, and legislators to seek new and different means of channeling funds to parochial schools. If the Court upholds the Elementary and Secondary Education Act, the *Lemon* decision may prove, in the long run, to have been no more significant than a warning by the Court that legislators must be more careful when they enact public aid programs.

President Nixon has stated plainly that he is committed to helping the parochial schools survive. Legislators are already considering such options as tax deductions for parents of private school children, direct grants to parents in the form of educational vouchers which would be valid in any school, public scholarships, dual enrollment programs which would bring parochial school students to public schools for instruction in secular subjects, and programs which would send public school teachers into parochial schools to teach nonreligious subjects. If the Court interprets its new concept of "excessive entanglement" narrowly, it may well be that any or all of these programs will be held constitutional. And, if they are constitutional, what then will be left of the *Everson* view that financial assistance to religious institutions breaches the wall of separation between church and state?

DE FACTO SEGREGATION AND THE FOURTEENTH AMENDMENT:

Do Communities Have an Obligation to Eliminate Racial Imbalance in the Schools?

ISSUES RAISED   Equal Protection of the Laws / Local Control of Education / The Scope of State Action / The Constitutionality of Racial Classifications

I. The Background of the Racial Imbalance Conflict

Ten or twenty years from now, if present trends continue unchecked, all but a small minority of the Negro and white children who live in the major cities and suburbs of urban America will attend separate schools. The contemporary European caricature of the United States as a country in which self-satisfied white people live prosperously in suburban sanctuaries which surround our large cities or in high-rent urban residential areas and black citizens live in decaying central city slums will be caricature no longer.

Of course, as middle-class white people flee urban deterioration or withdraw their children from urban public schools and send them to private schools, the pace of decay will speed up; as the cities are taken over by the poor, crime rates, welfare rolls, unemployment, and exploitation will soar. Even more meaningful, perhaps, than cold statistics will be the personal cost to individuals and families destroyed or corrupted by the harsh everyday events of life in our urban slums and the moral cost to the nation as a whole which will follow hard on the heels of widespread cynicism about the historic American ideals of democracy, equality, and opportunity.

If the above picture appears overdrawn, consider the following disturbing statistics on population trends in the twenty-four metropolitan areas in the country which contained more than 1 million people as of 1960. Between 1950 and 1960 the twenty-four central cities in these areas lost nearly 1½ million white residents and gained more than 2 million black inhabitants. For example, the Baltimore suburbs gained 324,000 whites and 7,000 blacks; Baltimore itself lost 113,000 whites and gained 100,000 blacks. Similarly, the Cleveland suburbs gained 367,000 whites and 2,000 blacks, while the city lost 142,000 whites and gained 103,000 blacks. New York City gained 727,000 blacks and Puerto Ricans and lost 837,000 non-Puerto Rican whites.

In the decade from 1960 to 1970, 14 million white Americans moved to suburban homes and apartments. Over 3 million black Americans moved to the cities in the first seven or eight years of the decade, and approximately 400,000 moved to suburbs. Late in the decade, the mobility of black people improved somewhat, and the ratio declined from 8 to 1 to roughly 3 to 1. It is important, however, not to misunderstand this change: most of the black families who moved to the suburbs in this period did not move to integrated middle-class communities but to the aging, inner suburbs just over city lines from urban poverty areas. As the National Advisory Commission on Civil Disorders concluded in its final report, released in 1968, America is moving toward two separate and unequal societies, one black and one white.

Between 1950 and 1960 the school-age population of the twenty-four metropolitan areas mentioned above increased by 5 million, but 80 percent of the white increase was in the suburbs and nearly 90 percent of the nonwhite increase in the central cities; by 1960, four out of every five black metropolitan children lived in central cities, and nearly three out of every five of the white children lived in the suburbs. Studies since 1960 indicate that the trend toward increasing separation of the races in the public schools has been continuing.[1] The following table suggests the dimensions of the problem:

GROWTH OF NONWHITE ENROLLMENT IN PUBLIC ELEMENTARY SCHOOLS IN SELECTED CITIES*

City	Time Period	Percentage Growth
Washington, D.C.	1950–1965	52–91
Wilmington, Del.	1950–1965	29–69
Newark, N.J.	1961–1965	58–69
Baltimore, Md.	1954–1965	42–64
East St. Louis, Ill.	1954–1965	50–63
Philadelphia, Pa.	1950–1965	34–59
Detroit, Mich.	1960–1965	46–55
Cleveland, Ohio	1952–1962	31–54
Oakland, Cal.	1949–1965	14–52
New Haven, Conn.	1963–1965	40–46
Kansas City, Mo.	1950–1965	17–42
Cincinnati, Ohio	1950–1965	23–40
Pittsburgh, Pa.	1950–1965	25–39

*Source: U.S. Commission on Civil Rights, "Growth of Segregation in 40 School Systems in Southern, Border, and Northern States, Elementary Schools," *Racial Isolation in the Public Schools,* vol. 2, appendix A, table 3, U.S. Government Printing Office, 1967, pp. 12–19. In New York City, the percentage of Negroes and Puerto Ricans in both elementary and secondary schools grew from 32 to 48 in the period from 1957 to 1965; Negro and Puerto Rican students constituted 53 percent of all elementary school pupils in 1965. *The New York Times,* June 7, 1966, p. 36.

The handwriting is on the wall for all those who care to read it. Fortunately, there are many people, both in and out of government, who are unwilling to sit back and bemoan the deterioration of urban America. At all levels of government, federal, state, and local, attention is being focused on the growing problems of urban life, and efforts are being made to rehabilitate slums, to improve the quality of education, and to provide job training and opportunities. The crucial debates of domestic politics in the coming decades will undoubtedly focus on the success or failure of these efforts.

[1] U.S. Commission on Civil Rights, *Racial Isolation in the Public Schools,* vol. 1, U.S. Government Printing Office, 1967, pp. 11–12.

Critics of government involvement in the affairs of the individual see these attempts to deal with urban problems as new illustrations of the proclivity of the welfare state to regulate and regiment the lives of the people. Opponents of this view are so shaken by the growth of urban problems and their vision of what metropolitan life will be like two or three decades from now that they consider such polemics merely irrelevant vestiges of the New Deal era. Many observers are so impatient with what they consider our indolent approach to problems of ever-increasing magnitude that they are quick to indict the American people and their elected leaders for negligent lack of concern for the urban poor and the quality of life in the United States in the future.

It is commonplace to observe that the problems of slum housing, of discrimination in the sale or rental of housing, of inadequate education, of racial concentration in the schools, of unemployment, of broken families, welfare, and delinquency are both interconnected and intransigent. Obviously, none of these problems can be isolated and handled in a vacuum; nor can it be argued that any single agency of government is responsible for solving them or failing to solve them.

In many ways, however, public education is at the center of the dilemmas described above, possibly because government has traditionally been responsible for education and not for housing and employment, possibly because the schools played such an important role in assimilating immigrant minorities into the mainstream of American cultural and economic life in the past, and possibly simply because the urban poor, including Negroes and members of other minority groups, tend to share the belief of middle-class citizens that the future of one's children will be determined in some measure by the educational opportunities they receive.

Racial separation is and has been the pattern rather than the exception in American public schools. In the post-Civil War South, separation resulted from laws requiring segregation of the races; in the North and West, however, separation most frequently was the result of the tendency of black families—because of discrimination and poverty—to live together in the oldest and most dilapidated quarters of our cities. Residential separation led to educational separation, since school authorities followed attendance policies designed to send children to the schools nearest their homes. Unlike Southern segregation, separation in the North and West was only infrequently based on discriminatory laws and was rarely total separation, since Negroes who were able to obtain housing in white residential areas sent their children to the local, predominantly white public school. Of course, the educational consequences of segregation by law and separation via geographic attendance zones were similar.

Although separation of the races in public schools outside the South was an established fact for many years, it was not a political problem and did not become one until the early 1960s. Political scientists often puzzle over—and frequently are unable to determine—how, when, and why long-existing social or economic problems enter the political arena and become major political issues; however, the problem of racial concentration in the urban public schools is different from many other issues, since it is possible to pinpoint its development into one of the most significant issues of contemporary American politics.

Prior to 1954, it was not unconstitutional to segregate blacks and whites by law. Since school authorities could require blacks to attend all-black schools, there was no sense devoting any attention to separation which resulted from geographic attendance zones. Segregation by law was a more blatant problem and could be more easily challenged as a violation of the command of the Fourteenth Amendment that no state shall deny the equal protection of the laws.

In addition, civil rights activists concentrated their efforts on Southern segregation because of the widespread denial of other constitutional rights—including the right to vote and to a fair trial—in the South. Many Northerners sympathized with these efforts, primarily because of moral indignation at Southern treatment of black citizens but also because they were unaware that the overthrow of state-imposed discrimination would have any real impact on their own lives.

Thus, it is possible to conclude that as long as segregation by law was a major issue, racial concentration could not become a significant political problem. One could argue further that the overthrow of legally imposed discrimination could not help but stimulate the efforts—and strength—of civil rights activists and the concern of all three branches of the federal government with the need to make the Fourteenth Amendment effective and to erase the moral burden of centuries of discrimination against blacks. Given the similar educational effects of segregation and racial concentration, it was inevitable that overthrow of state-imposed discrimination would lead to consideration of the question of what, if anything, should be done about what has become known as "racial imbalance" in the public schools.

SCHOOL SEGREGATION: THE EARLY YEARS

In order to understand fully the contemporary conflict over balancing the public schools, it is necessary to be familiar with the history of school segregation in the United States, the litigation which has taken place, the constitutional provisions which have been argued in the courts, and the activities of private pressure groups and government agencies. At the outset it is important to note the complex and frequent interrelations among government institutions throughout the history of the public education conflict. The Supreme Court has acted as final arbiter in a limited sense only; instead, decisions by one public body have been appealed to other institutions of government at the state and federal levels to overthrow earlier decisions, to frustrate them, to demand new decisions, or simply to gain more effective enforcement of existing policies.

National concern with civil rights questions is basically a post-World War II phenomenon. The major political controversies of the preceding decades revolved around economic questions—the rights of organized labor, regulation of business, social welfare legislation, federal power to fight the Depression. Education was considered primarily a responsibility of local government; besides, individuals who might have fought to eliminate discrimination in public education already had their hands full.

While the conflict over public intervention in the economy may at first hand seem unrelated to the struggle for full enjoyment of civil rights by all citizens, postwar efforts to achieve civil rights have grown out of the earlier struggle: federal activism today has its roots in the growth of federal power and federal institutions during the Depression and in widespread public acceptance of the New Deal philosophy of government responsibility for the welfare of society.

During the period of federal unconcern, the rule of *Plessy v. Ferguson*, 163 U.S. 537 (1896), encouraged segregation in public facilities, including schools. In the *Plessy* case, the Supreme Court construed the requirement of the Fourteenth Amendment that no state shall deny the equal protection of the laws to mean that segregation could be maintained as long as equal facilities were provided. In a classic statement which qualified its author for a high place in history among the ranks of the politically naïve, Justice Henry Brown wrote:

We consider the underlying fallacy of the plaintiff's argument to consist in the assumption that the enforced separation of the two races stamps the colored race with a badge of inferiority. If this be so, it is not by reason of anything found in the act [which required separation of the races on Louisiana trains] but solely because the colored race chooses to put that construction on it.

163 U.S. 537, at 551. (Brackets added.)

Given the absence of pressure groups devoted to seeking integrated education, of public commitment to equality, of presidential and congressional initiative, the Supreme Court was, in fact, only reflecting contemporary American social values. Subsequent Courts accepted the *Plessy* doctrine almost as if it were a literal reading of the Fourteenth Amendment. It was not until 1938 that the Court was no longer dominated by men who were philosophically opposed to social and economic innovation generally and to innovation by the federal government specifically. Starting in the late 1930s and throughout the 1940s, the majority cautiously narrowed the scope of the *Plessy* doctrine by insisting more strongly that separate facilities must be equal in quality; the doctrine itself, however, remained in force.

Meanwhile, changes were taking place in American society which threatened the civil rights status quo. As has already been indicated, the political battles of the 1930s ended with victory going to the proponents of the new philosophy of federal activism. Nearly a million blacks served in the Armed Forces during the Second World War and endured discrimination, humiliation, and other hardships which made many of them reluctant to resume placidly their prewar status in American society. Millions of others left the rural South to work in the war plants of the industrial centers of the North. Pressure groups like the National Association for the Advancement of Colored People gathered strength and asserted the rights and demands of black citizens more forcefully.

President Truman became the first President to speak out strongly in favor of full constitutional rights for blacks; his efforts to get Congress to include a nondiscrimination provision in the Selective Service Act of 1948 failed, but they set the stage for future presidential initiatives. Truman subsequently issued an executive order banning segregation in the Armed Forces and an order requiring business firms holding federal contracts to follow fair employment practices.

Finally, the composition of the Supreme Court had changed; by 1950 the Court was dominated by judges who were less committed to the philosophy of states rights expressed in the Tenth Amendment than to their obligation to protect the constitutional rights of the individual against infringement by state governments.

Shortly after Earl Warren was appointed Chief Justice in 1953, the Court accepted five cases which directly challenged the "separate but equal" doctrine. The Court reviewed the half-century old *Plessy* precedent and held unanimously, in a decision which has probably had a greater impact on American social and political life than any other single act in the postwar period, that separate education was inherently unequal and, therefore, violated the command of the Fourteenth Amendment.[2]

The decision of the Supreme Court in *Brown v. Board of Education* touched off a display of fireworks which shows little sign of coming to an end, despite the passage of time. The first explosions took place in Congress and certain state capitols; nearly a hundred congressmen signed a "Southern Manifesto" challenging the constitutionality of the Court's decision. State governors moved to interpose the power of the state between the federal courts and the public schools.

The most dramatic cases of interposition occurred in 1957 in Little Rock, Arkansas, and in 1962 in Oxford, Mississippi. In the first of these confrontations, Governor Orval Faubus called out the National Guard to prevent the desegregation

[2] *Brown v. Board of Education*, 347 U.S. 483 (1954). Since the *Brown* decision has been treated fully in numerous studies, no attempt to analyze it will be made here; see, for example, Daniel M. Berman, *It Is So Ordered*, Norton, New York, 1966.

ordered by the federal court from taking place. Ultimately, President Eisenhower had to federalize the guard and use units of the regular army to ensure that the orders of the court were carried out. Five years later, President Kennedy had to use 25,000 United States troops to integrate the University of Mississippi over the adamant opposition of Governor Ross Barnett.

Following the *Brown v. Board of Education* decision, pressure groups sprang up to defend segregated education. Gradually, efforts to overthrow the integration decision were defeated, but they were replaced frequently by policies of sullen noncompliance. Tokenism, strategic retreats, and endless litigation achieved what outright opposition could not: by 1963, nearly a decade after the decision, the percentage of black children attending integrated schools in the Deep South had climbed to only 1.17 percent; in seven states, less than 1 percent of black pupils attended integrated schools.[3]

Secondary explosions were caused by those who were dissatisfied with the pace of integration—by pressure groups like the NAACP, by certain segments of the press, by Presidents Eisenhower, Kennedy, and Johnson, by certain congressmen from the Northern and Western states, by the Office of Education of the Department of Health, Education, and Welfare. The efforts of these private individuals, organs of mass communication, government agencies, and elected leaders were directed primarily at obtaining federal legislation which would make it easier to defeat resistance to integration and ease the transition from segregated to integrated school systems.

Gradually, attention began to focus on public education outside the South. It was natural for those groups and individuals who had led the fight against segregation imposed by law to inquire into the state of education in Northern cities. What they found disturbed them greatly: most black pupils attended schools which were 90 percent or more black; these schools were almost invariably the oldest, most dilapidated, and most overcrowded schools in each urban area; the achievement levels of students attending these schools usually lagged behind those of students attending white or integrated schools; and the trend was not toward integration, but toward increased separation of the races due to the movement of large numbers of black families to urban centers and white families to the suburbs. By the early 1960s, Atlanta, Baltimore, Chicago, Cleveland, Detroit, Newark, Philadelphia, St. Louis, and Washington, D.C., had already passed the point of 50 percent black enrollment in the elementary schools; in these cities, meaningful integration was no longer possible within the boundaries of the city school district.

Perusal of the index of *The New York Times* from 1954 onward reveals that the problem of separation of the races in Northern public schools first gained widespread public attention in the years 1961 to 1963. During this period, isolated and infrequent requests for action by school authorities gradually were replaced by continuous and increasingly vocal demands by parents, the NAACP, and other organizations for integration of the schools. Lawsuits, boycotts, and demonstrations slowly replaced earlier, more restrained methods of inducing school boards to act. Because of the complex nature of the problem of racial separation in Northern schools, let us look first at the part played by the legal system in the conflict and then at presidential, congressional, and state attempts to speed the process of integration.

JUDICIAL DECISIONS AFFECTING SEGREGATION IN NORTHERN SCHOOLS

Where black parents could prove to the satisfaction of a court that a Northern school board was deliberately following a discriminatory policy in its pupil assign-

---

[3] *Statistical Summary of School Segregation-Desegregation in the Southern and Border States,* Southern Education Reporting Service, Nashville, 1964.

ments, judicial enforcement of integration was possible. For example, parents in New Rochelle, New York, brought a suit in the Federal District Court for the Southern District of New York to force integration of the Lincoln Elementary School, which was 94 percent black. The parents were able to show that the school board had altered district lines in 1930 to allow white students living in an irregular corridor within the Lincoln School attendance zone to attend an all-white school; as the black population expanded in the ensuing years, the Lincoln lines had repeatedly been extended to include the black residents. The school board did not refute the plaintiffs' evidence of gerrymandering but countered that the case did not fall within the *Brown* precedent since New Rochelle did not maintain a dual system and the school was 94 percent rather than 100 percent black.

The district court ruled that while the *Brown* decision had dealt with a state-maintained dual system of education, it ". . . [W]as premised on the factual conclusion that a segregated education created and maintained by official acts had a detrimental and deleterious effect on the educational and mental development of the minority group children."[4] The court went on to conclude that there was no difference between segregation established by a formalized dual system of education and that achieved by gerrymandering of school district lines. Subsequently, the decision of the district court was upheld by the Second Circuit Court of Appeals, and the Supreme Court allowed the decision to stand by refusing to hear the school board's appeal.[5]

The New Rochelle case was unusual, however, because the plaintiffs were able to demonstrate convincingly that the school board intended to discriminate, notwithstanding the absence of any law requiring or permitting segregation. In most Northern school systems, no such evidence has been obtainable. School boards make so many complex decisions that parents have found it next to impossible to prove to the satisfaction of a court that the real motive of the school board in question is to discriminate against black pupils.

The problem of proving purposeful discrimination has been compounded by the virtually nationwide practice of assigning pupils to schools nearest their homes. Because discrimination in the rental or sale of housing has forced the preponderant majority of blacks to live in highly segregated areas within the cities, adherence to the concept of "neighborhood" schools has meant that most black pupils attend schools which are all black or virtually all black. Although some school boards have undoubtedly used residential segregation to achieve surreptitiously an otherwise unconstitutional purpose, many others have claimed, without obvious hypocrisy, that any separation which results from an honestly conceived and fairly administered neighborhood school attendance plan is purely adventitious and does not constitute segregation since it is not imposed by discriminatory laws or administrative decisions.

Brown v. Board of Education specifically held segregation by law unconstitutional but was silent on the question of separation which results from residential patterns rather than overt discrimination by public officials. As a result, parents protesting de facto segregation have not had a controlling Supreme Court precedent on which to base their demands for integration. A number of de facto segregation cases have been appealed to the Supreme Court, but each time the Court has used its power to determine what cases it will hear to refuse the appeal; thus, as of the date of publication of this book, the constitutionality of de facto segregation, or "racial imbalance," as it has frequently been called, is still an open question.

As would be expected in the absence of a controlling precedent, lower-court deci-

[4] *Taylor v. Board of Education*, 191 F. Supp. 181 (S.D.N.Y. 1961).
[5] 294 F.2d 36 (2d Cir.), *cert. denied*, 368 U.S. 940 (1961).

sions have occasionally been contradictory. Most lower courts, both state and federal, have taken the conservative position that the Fourteenth Amendment requires school boards not to discriminate on the basis of race but does not require school boards to take positive action to integrate the schools.

Four of the ten United States circuit courts of appeals have held that the equal protection clause of the Constitution does not require school boards to abandon neighborhood attendance plans, even though they result in racial imbalance, as long as they have been honestly and conscientiously constructed with no intention of creating or maintaining segregated schools; thus, the clause does not command integration in the schools and black children have no constitutional right to attend school with white children.[6]

Two other circuit courts of appeals have implied by way of dictum that the Constitution does not require school authorities to integrate the schools.[7] Another circuit court bypassed the basic question of whether the Fourteenth Amendment imposes an affirmative duty on school boards and ruled that even if such a duty exists, it is a limited one and requires only that officials take integration into account along with other educationally relevant factors in making administrative decisions.[8]

No court of appeals has squarely held that a school system has an affirmative duty to end adventitious segregation. On the other hand, three circuit courts of appeals have suggested in various dicta that the view that the Constitution forbids segregation but does not require integration should be laid to rest as inconsistent with the *Brown* decision and statutory law in the civil rights field which has been passed in recent years.[9]

At least four federal district court opinions hold that the Constitution does impose a duty to relieve racial imbalance. However, several of these decisions are, at the least, ambiguous, since they attempt to draw a distinction between "mere" racial imbalance and imbalance which is tantamount to segregation; thus school authorities do not have an unqualified obligation to integrate public education regardless of circumstances, but they do have an obligation to take positive action in instances where separation of the races is extreme and virtually complete.[10]

In two cases, district courts have ruled explicitly and forcefully that de facto segregation violates the constitutional guarantee of equal protection of the laws.[11] The more important of these decisions is *Hobson v. Hansen*, in which racial imbalance in the public schools of Washington, D.C., resulting from neighborhood population patterns, was declared as unconstitutional as segregation imposed by law. Judge J. Skelly Wright ruled on June 19, 1967, that:

> Racially and socially homogeneous schools damage the minds and spirit of all children who attend them—the Negro, the white, the poor and the affluent—and block the at-

[6] *Bell v. School City of Gary*, 324 F.2d 209 (7th Cir. 1963), *cert. denied*, 377 U.S. 924 (1964); *Downs v. Board of Education*, 336 F.2d 988 (10th Cir. 1964), *cert. denied*, 380 U.S. 914 (1965); *Deal v. Cincinnati Board of Education*, 369 F.2d 55 (6th Cir. 1966), *cert. denied*, 389 U.S. 847 (1967); *Swann v. Charlotte-Mecklenburg Board of Education*, 369 F.2d 29 (4th Cir. 1966).

[7] *Sealy v. Department of Public Instruction*, 252 F.2d 898 (3d Cir.), *cert. denied*, 356 U.S. 975 (1958); *Avery v. Wichita Falls Independent School District*, 241 F.2d 230 (5th Cir.), *cert. denied*, 353 U.S. 938 (1957).

[8] *Barksdale v. Springfield School Committee*, 348 F.2d 261 (1st Cir. 1965).

[9] *Singleton v. Jackson Municipal Separate School District*, 348 F.2d 729 (5th Cir. 1965); *Evans v. Ennis*, 281 F.2d 385 (3d Cir. 1960), *cert. denied*, 364 U.S. 802 (1961); *Kemp v. Beasley*, 352 F.2d 14 (8th Cir. 1965).

[10] *Branche v. Board of Education*, 204 F. Supp. 150 (E.D.N.Y. 1962); *Blocker v. Board of Education*, 226 F. Supp. 208 (E.D.N.Y. 1964).

[11] *Barksdale v. Springfield School Committee*, 237 F. Supp. 543 (D. Mass.), *vacated*, 348 F.2d 261 (1st Cir. 1965); *Hobson v. Hansen*, 269 F. Supp. 401 (D.C.D.C. 1967).

tainment of the broader goals of democratic education, whether the segregation occurs by law or by fact.

269 F. Supp. 401, at 406.

Because of the clear-cut determination by Judge Wright that unintentional separation is unconstitutional, civil rights leaders viewed his decision as a tremendous victory. However, the opinion failed to order the enforced merger of the Washington school system with those of the predominantly white suburbs of neighboring Maryland and Virginia, despite the fact that meaningful integration within the boundaries of the District of Columbia was impossible, since 93 percent of the 180,000 pupils attending the schools of the nation's capital in 1966 and 1967 were black. Judge Wright held that the court had no authority to create an areawide school system, but he criticized Washington school officials for failing to explore the possibility of voluntary cooperation to promote integration between the District and suburban communities.

Although the court's opinion fell short of the remedy sought by counsel for the plaintiff, it did order busing of black pupils to predominantly white schools within the District, mandatory reassignment of teachers to integrate all school faculties, and elimination of Washington's "track system" of assigning pupils to classes according to ability. The district court's opinion was appealed, but the court of appeals affirmed Judge Wright's findings.[12]

PRESIDENTIAL AND CONGRESSIONAL EFFORTS

Although no President has taken an unequivocal stand against de facto segregation, President Johnson laid the groundwork for a federal policy. Earlier Presidents had to face up to the complex political problems of Southern desegregation and federal aid to public education and were spared the necessity of taking a position on the de facto segregation controversy. Through a combination of political skill, timing, commitment, and luck, President Johnson was able to bridge the conflicts over the church-state issue and over fear of federal domination which had paralyzed aid-to-education efforts during the Eisenhower and Kennedy eras. His success in persuading Congress to pass legislation withholding federal aid from school systems which discriminate on the basis of race indicated to advocates of integration that a new source of leverage against local officials would be available in the coming decades: executive and legislative action at the federal level.

The chronology of federal activity is as follows: the Civil Rights Act of 1964 included several provisions for speeding the process of desegregation. For the first time, school systems which discriminated were prohibited from receiving federal funds; in addition, the act authorized the Attorney General to bring suits against segregated schools and empowered the Office of Education of the Department of Health, Education, and Welfare to give technical and financial assistance to school systems which were attempting to desegregate.

---

[12] 408 F.2d 175 (D.C. Cir. 1969). Like the federal courts, state courts have occasionally expressed the view that de facto segregation is inconsistent with the federal Constitution. For example, the California Supreme Court announced in a dictum in *Jackson v. Pasadena School District* that:

Even in the absence of gerrymandering or other affirmative discriminatory conduct by a school board, a student under some circumstances would be entitled to relief where, by reason of residential segregation, substantial racial imbalance exists. . . . Where such segregation exists, it is not enough for a school board to refrain from affirmative discriminatory conduct. The right to an equal opportunity for education and the harmful consequences of segregation require that school boards take steps, insofar as reasonably feasible, to alleviate racial imbalance in schools regardless of its cause. 31 Cal. Rptr. 606, at 609–10 (1963).

The 1964 act was aimed at segregation by law and not at adventitious separation of the races; in fact, the act specifically provided that "nothing herein shall empower any official or court of the United States to issue any order seeking to achieve a racial balance in any school by requiring the transportation of pupils or students from one school to another or one school district to another in order to achieve such racial balance...."[13] While this provision prohibited attempts to compel racial balancing, it did not prevent the Commissioner of Education from authorizing grants for training of teachers and employment of specialists to school systems which voluntarily undertook to minimize or eliminate racial imbalance, i.e., to systems which were "in the process of desegregating."

The Elementary and Secondary Education Act of 1965 provided 1 billion dollars of financial assistance through the states to school districts in order to help meet the needs of educationally deprived students and school systems which were responsible for educating large numbers of financially impoverished pupils. The act represented the culmination of President Johnson's efforts to improve the nation's schools by supplying them with a massive infusion of federal money. While the act did not allow the Commissioner of Education to require school authorities to correct racial imbalance, it did not prevent school systems from using funds provided under the act for the transportation of educationally deprived students to less crowded or better schools. Thus, Berkeley, California, for example, has used federal money to transport black children from overcrowded, predominantly black schools to under-utilized white schools. Similarly, the METCO program in Boston has used funds granted under the Elementary and Secondary Education Act to pay the transportation and tuition costs of black children from Roxbury enrolled in schools in a number of suburban communities.

Three months after he signed the Elementary and Secondary Education Act into law, President Johnson convened a 650-delegate White House Conference on Education. The Conference was called to provide the President with information and ideas for the evolution of fresh programs and new legislative proposals and to draw public attention to the major problems confronting the schools. The participants focused on a number of problems, but particular emphasis was placed on the failure of the schools to provide leadership in racial integration, on the problem of de facto segregation, on schools in the inner-city ghettos, on the need for new techniques for educating the educationally deprived.

Later in 1965, President Johnson's concern with segregation in Northern cities became public again when he requested the United States Commission on Civil Rights to gather information on the extent and consequences of de facto segregation and to make these data available to the nation as soon as possible. The commission's report, issued in the spring of 1967, concluded with an impassioned plea for Congress to pass—under its power to enforce the provisions of the Fourteenth Amendment—a law requiring the correction of adventitious racial isolation in the schools.[14] The President did not, however, throw his weight behind the commission's proposal, and it failed to make much headway in Congress.

If the President had backed the commission, he probably would not have had much success, since the tenor of Congress in the last years of the Johnson administration was to move backward rather than forward on the school segregation issue. In fact, the administration spent a great deal of time fighting off Southern efforts to pass legislation preventing the Department of Health, Education, and Welfare from withholding federal school-aid funds in order to compel desegregation. The House of Representatives repeatedly passed restrictive amendments only to find them

---

13 78 Stat. 247 (1964).

14 U.S. Commission on Civil Rights, *op. cit.*, vol. 1, pp. 209–12 and 239–63.

rejected or amended by the Senate and/or deleted in conference committee. For example, the House several times passed an amendment to the annual HEW appropriations bill prohibiting the department from threatening to withhold funds in order to force school districts to bus students or to assign students to particular schools against their parents' wishes; the Senate then amended the restrictions to limit them to instances where federal officials were trying to overcome de facto segregation. The narrower Senate version, which protected HEW's efforts to fight de jure segregation in the South but did prohibit federal efforts to compel busing in the North, ultimately became law.

The election of Richard M. Nixon to the Presidency put an end, at least temporarily, to the possibility that the federal government would act more strongly against de facto segregation. During the election campaign, Nixon had opposed busing as a means of achieving integration and had expressed admiration for the neighborhood school concept. As President, Nixon not only urged Congress to continue to appropriate money to help school officials desegregate their schools, but asked for a specific prohibition on the use of federal funds for busing.

STATE ATTEMPTS TO RELIEVE RACIAL IMBALANCE

A few states have concluded that racial imbalance, regardless of its origin, has a damaging effect on the educational opportunities of black students. In 1960, the New York Board of Regents, the New York Commissioner of Education, and the New Jersey Commissioner of Education stated publicly that attendance at an all-black or virtually all-black school has an undesirable effect on educational achievement. The Massachusetts State Board of Education, the Wisconsin State Superintendent of Education, and the Connecticut Board of Education adopted roughly equivalent policy statements in 1965 and 1966.

Several states have gone beyond policy statements and have passed laws or administrative regulations requiring school boards to correct or alleviate racial imbalance in the schools. Massachusetts passed a Racial Imbalance Act in August 1965 which requires school committees to eliminate all schools in which the percentage of nonwhites exceeds 50 percent of the total enrollment; if a school committee does not show progress within a reasonable time, the Commissioner of Education must withhold all state financial aid from the recalcitrant school system.[15] While Massachusetts is the only state which requires that state aid be withheld from systems which have failed to eliminate imbalanced schools, the effectiveness of its statute is questionable. In Boston, for example, a running battle has been waged ever since the statute was passed; in the first five years of the new law, observers were hard pressed to find any perceptible change in the racial composition of the schools.

Illinois passed a statute designed to alleviate racial imbalance in 1963. The Armstrong Act, as the statute is known, requires school boards (1) not to erect, purchase, or build schools in such a manner as to promote segregation and separation of children in schools because of race, color, or nationality, and (2) to revise attendance zones in order to attempt to eliminate separation of the races in the schools. The act does not define racial imbalance and leaves enforcement of its provisions to the state courts.[16]

In 1968 the Illinois Supreme Court held that the Armstrong Act did not violate either the state or federal constitutions.[17] The defendant school board had argued

---

[15] Mass. Gen. Laws, ch. 15, § 1 (I) and ch. 71, § 37D (1965).

[16] Ill. Rev. Stat. 1967, ch. 122, par. 10–21.3.

[17] *Tometz v. Board of Education*, 237 N.E.2d 498 (1968).

that no statute could require that race be taken into consideration in setting up school zones, since such a racial classification would violate the equal protection clause. The Illinois Supreme Court rejected this conception of state neutrality and insisted that the test of any legislative classification was one of reasonableness; using this test the Court ruled that taking race into account in order to avoid separation was not like taking it into account in order to segregate black students. The Constitution did not prohibit voluntary state action to reduce de facto segregation.

It should be noted that the verdict of the Illinois Supreme Court agreed with a substantial number of earlier decisions by federal courts and the highest courts of Pennsylvania, New Jersey, New York, Massachusetts, and California. Where state authorities or local school boards have acted to alleviate racial imbalance, the courts have consistently refused to accept the argument that school officials are constitutionally prohibited from taking race into account in drawing or redrawing school attendance lines to reduce de facto segregation. This ruling has been based on the proposition that the purpose of a racial classification is determinative of its constitutionality; thus, the Fourteenth Amendment, according to this view, prohibits invidious discrimination but does not bar cognizance of race in a proper effort to eliminate or minimize racial separation.[18]

New York, New Jersey, and California have used administrative regulations, rulings of the state commissioner of education, and judicial decisions to attack the problem of racial imbalance. Both New York and New Jersey guarantee equal educational opportunity by state law and authorize their respective commissioners of education to withhold state funds if a school district fails to comply with regulations designed to provide equal opportunity. In addition, the New York Commissioner of Education has authority to remove school board members for failure to comply with his determinations.[19]

On the other hand, New York passed an antibusing statute in 1969, at least in part because of white reaction to racial balancing efforts. The law was subsequently held unconstitutional on the ground that it encouraged segregation, limited affirmative efforts to reduce imbalance, and constituted state involvement in invidious racial discrimination. Newspaper reports of the political infighting over the antibusing law indicate clearly that most efforts to achieve racial balance in New York State have not been successful.

The California State Board of Education has adopted a policy against attendance practices which establish or maintain racial separation and has issued regulations requiring special attention to ethnic factors in site selection and organization of new school districts. The state board does not, however, have any sanctions comparable to those available in New York and New Jersey to enforce its decisions. Finally, four other states—Indiana, Michigan, Wisconsin, and Washington—have encouraged local authorities to take action to alleviate racial imbalance but have hesitated to go beyond encouragement to actual enforcement.

THE STATUS OF DE FACTO SEGREGATION TODAY

Brown v. Board of Education expressly invalidated segregation imposed by law; subsequent cases have applied this ruling to segregation resulting from the deliberate acts of school authorities regardless of the presence or absence of a discriminatory law.

[18] See, e.g., *Fuller v. Volk*, 230 F. Supp. 25 (D.N.J. 1964); *Morean v. Board of Education*, 42 N.J. 237 (1964); *Balaban v. Rubin*, 20 App. Div.2d 438, aff'd 14 N.Y.2d 193, cert. denied, 379 U.S. 881 (1964); *Katalinic v. City of Syracuse*, 44 Misc.2d 734 (1964); *Springfield School Committee v. Barksdale*, 348 F.2d 261 (1st Cir. 1965).

[19] See N.Y. Ed. Code, title 1, art. 7, § 306 (1957) and N.J. Stat. Ann. 18:10–29.44 (1954).

Although adventitious segregation has not yet been considered by the Supreme Court, lawsuits challenging segregation which results from residential patterns have been brought in many lower courts. Most courts have refused to hold that such de facto segregation is unconstitutional, but there are several important judicial decisions to the contrary. Few states have taken meaningful steps to require local school officials to eliminate or minimize racial imbalance; on the other hand, corrective action, when taken, has almost always been upheld by the courts against challenges by white parents that such measures violate their constitutional rights.

Finally, the executive branch of the federal government has taken some hesitant steps in the direction of remedial action. With the help of presidential persuasion, Congress passed legislation designed to (1) speed the process of desegregation, and (2) provide large amounts of federal money to school districts responsible for educating disadvantaged pupils. In both instances, however, Congress refused to give the U.S. Office of Education authority to use sanctions to overcome de facto segregation. Despite the absence of authority to require local school officials to take corrective measures, the Office of Education has acted under the legislation to assist schools which have voluntarily chosen to reduce racial imbalance. On balance, one can conclude that the executive and legislative branches of the federal government have been no more eager to grapple with the complex and politically dangerous question of segregation in the important population centers of the North than have the states themselves.

Is de facto segregation unconstitutional? Do cities, states, and the federal government have a legal obligation to combat it? Why is the Supreme Court reluctant to face up to these questions? And, further, why are the justices dodging this issue when they have demonstrated repeatedly in the past decade that they are willing to risk public criticism and political counterattacks in order to fight against racial discrimination? These questions are faced in Part II of this chapter, which employs a hypothetical case to explore the legal arguments for and against the constitutionality of de facto segregation, and Part III, which analyzes the Supreme Court's evasion and its political consequences.

. . . .

II. Hypothetical Case: Jackson v. Board of Education of Middlefield*

STATEMENT OF THE CASE:

Harold Jackson and other parents of black children attending the public schools of Middlefield brought an action on behalf of their minor children alleging that blacks were being assigned to certain schools for the purpose of segregating them from white pupils and that the unusually high concentration of black children in certain of Middlefield's schools constituted segregation in violation of the guarantee of equal protection of the laws of the Fourteenth Amendment of the Constitution.

The lawsuit split the black community, many of whose members are disinterested in integration of the public schools. While the local chapter of the NAACP supports the suit, a number of parents, political leaders, and militant blacks have attempted to persuade the plaintiffs to drop the case on the grounds that the posture of the plaintiffs is demeaning, that integration is impossible, that integration of the black minority will not improve the education offered black children, that what is needed is not integration but black control of the predominantly black schools so

*Author's note: The hypothetical case and briefs presented below are original; arguments used in the briefs were drawn primarily from decisions of lower state and federal courts in de facto segregation cases.

that students can learn about black culture and black values rather than white culture and white values. Despite the split, the plaintiffs have refused to drop the litigation.

Middlefield itself is an aging industrial city of approximately 200,000 inhabitants surrounded by one affluent bedroom community and several more typical suburbs. Few black families live in these neighboring towns. The white residents of the central city are mainly first-generation Americans of Polish and German background; most of these people have lived in Middlefield all their lives. On the other hand, few of the black residents, who now make up more than one-third of the inhabitants, have lived in Middlefield for more than twenty years.

At present, the economy of Middlefield is in rough shape, due to overdependence in earlier years on the meat-packing industry. Unemployment tends to run consistently over the national average. Little new industry has been brought to the town to replace the jobs lost as a result of the closing of several large packing plants; for that matter, the skills possessed by former employees of these plants are not readily transferable to other industrial jobs. Thus, an air of futility permeates the city, adding in some unknown measure to black-white tensions.

Racial tensions have also been heightened by the fact that black residents feel excluded from the important economic and political decisions made in the city. The city government is firmly in the hands of long-term residents, although a number of blacks work for the city in jobs below the policymaking level. Thus, there are some black policemen and teachers as well as black civil servants. Even though one member of the five-man school board is black, the board as a whole is responsive primarily to the needs of the majority which elected it.

The facts regarding pupil assignments in the Middlefield schools are not in dispute. Of the 60,000 students currently attending the public schools, 20,000 are black and 40,000 are white. The school board operates sixty schools and has traditionally assigned students to the schools nearest their places of residence. This neighborhood school assignment plan has had the following results: 7,000 black students attend six schools having a nonwhite enrollment of 91 to 100 percent; 3,000 attend four schools with a nonwhite enrollment of 81 to 90 percent; 7,500 attend fourteen schools with 51 to 80 percent nonwhite enrollment; and, finally, 2,500 attend twelve schools in which they are in the minority. On the other end of the scale, white students constitute from 91 to 100 percent in the remaining twenty-four schools. Requests by black parents that the school board change its pupil assignment practices have repeatedly been rejected by the board.

The district court refused to issue a declaratory judgment that the defendant school board, by assigning plaintiffs to racially concentrated schools, had violated the Fourteenth Amendment; an injunction barring the defendant from continuing its pupil assignment practices was also denied. On appeal, the circuit court upheld the verdict of the trial court. The plaintiffs below now ask the Supreme Court to reverse the decision of the lower courts and to remand the case with orders to issue the requested injunction.

BRIEF FOR APPELLANTS	*BRIEF FOR APPELLEES*

1. *Does Middlefield's neighborhood pupil assignment plan constitute state action forbidden by the Fourteenth Amendment?*

The Fourteenth Amendment requires that "No State shall . . . deny to any person within its jurisdiction the equal protection of the laws." Ever since the decision of this Court in *Brown*	Despite their desire to prove that black children in Middlefield are being deprived of their constitutional rights, the appellants have been unable to cite any state law, city ordinance, or

v. Board of Education, 347 U.S. 483 (1954), segregation in public education has been unconstitutional. In that case, the Court faced the question whether segregation by law on the basis of race deprived blacks of equal educational opportunities, regardless of efforts to provide equal facilities for the segregated children. Chief Justice Warren, speaking for an undivided Court, quoted with approval from the opinion of the lower court:

> Segregation of white and colored children in public schools has a detrimental effect upon the colored children. The impact is greater when it has the sanction of the law; for the policy of separating the races is usually interpreted as denoting the inferiority of the Negro group. A sense of inferiority affects the motivation of a child to learn. Segregation with the sanction of law, therefore, has a tendency to retard the educational and mental development of Negro children and to deprive them of some of the benefits they would receive in a racially integrated school system.
>
> 347 U.S. 483, at 494.

The Chief Justice concluded that "... [I]n the field of public education the doctrine of separate but equal has no place. Separate educational facilities are inherently unequal."[1]

If the present litigation involved a state law or school board regulation requiring strict separation of the races in public schools, the case could be disposed of easily, since it would fall squarely within the *Brown* precedent. In this instance, however, no such law or regulation exists; the appellants have been segregated, just as the black students in *Brown v. Board of Education* were segregated, but the segregation complained of here is not total and does not result from an express public policy of separation of the races. Respondents contend that the concentration of black students in certain of Middlefield's schools results from the fact that black families in Middlefield tend to reside in several definite geographic areas within the city and not from a deliberate policy of the school board. They argue that since the neighborhood school plan followed by the board is not based on race, there has been no

school board regulation requiring separation of the races in the public schools. The simple fact is that no such discriminatory laws or policies exist. Pupils in Middlefield are assigned to schools on the basis of residence, without regard to race.

It should be made abundantly clear at the outset, then, that this is not a case involving discrimination by law or by public policy. The school board has not manipulated school districts, built new schools, or followed other devious plans for the purpose of segregating black students. Present school district lines were drawn up long before the influx of black families to certain well-defined areas of Middlefield in recent years, on the basis of pupil safety, ease of transportation, lines of existing neighborhoods, administrative efficiency, and pupil accommodations. The board has refused to change school district lines solely because it believes that these criteria are as valid today as they were when first adopted.

Thus, the facts of this case clearly distinguish it from the historic case of *Brown v. Board of Education*, 347 U.S. 483 (1954), in which this Court ruled unanimously that segregation of public schools by law violated the Fourteenth Amendment requirement that "No State shall ... deny ... the equal protection of the laws." Despite the differences between *Brown v. Board of Education* and the case at bar, appellants claim that the *Brown* precedent should be applied and should be broadened to require the Middlefield School Board to abandon its traditional policy of neighborhood schools.

We believe that this Court should reject appellants' argument, since separation of the races in Middlefield does not result from any discriminatory act of the state or of public officials subject to the authority of the state and does not, therefore, constitute a denial of equal protection of the laws. This Court has never held that nondiscriminatory state action based on a rational and responsible public policy violates the federal Constitution and it should not do so now.

Stripped to its bare fundamentals, appellants' argument, in reality, comes down to a request that the Supreme Court use the Fourteenth Amendment prohibition against discriminatory state action as an excuse to

[1] 347 U.S. 483, at 495

discriminatory state action in violation of the command of the Fourteenth Amendment.

We believe, however, that there has been sufficient state action to bring the case within the *Brown* precedent. Public schools in Middlefield are compulsory and are supported by public funds. Compulsory enrollment of black students in schools which are predominantly black as a result of the choice of geographic boundaries by school authorities represents state action, regardless of how those boundaries have been determined. The crucial fact in this case is that the establishment and maintenance of school district lines have created segregated schools. Whatever the intention of the school board, it has administered the compulsory school attendance law in such a way as to maintain a large number of almost exclusively white schools and a substantial number of predominantly black schools.

This Court should not give credence to respondents' argument that a constitutional distinction should be made between racial imbalance that results from the deliberate decision of school authorities to assign black children to separate schools and imbalance that results from adherence to a neighborhood school assignment plan. While we do not contend that the trial court erred in finding that there was no deliberate intent on the part of the school board to segregate pupils, we do submit that the board was well aware of the consequences of its pupil assignment practices. Racially imbalanced schools are not the automatic consequence of a neighborhood school policy, even given the existence of racial ghettos. Whether racially imbalanced schools result will depend largely on how the neighborhood or district which each school serves is defined. Our contention is that the school board used the neighborhood school plan to maintain the status quo; with the movement of black ·families into Middlefield in recent years, this policy became the justification for maintaining schools which were increasingly imbalanced.

An objective assessment of the actions of the Middlefield School Board reveals that it was aware of the racial effects of its policies and that it continued these policies in the face of evidence that they helped to create segre-

legislate a new pupil assignment policy which overturns the considered judgment of professional educators and requires them to eliminate racial concentration in Middlefield's schools, regardless of the cost in terms of established educational values. The Court has stated frequently in the past that it is not a legislature and that it will not make legislative judgments. We believe that this position is sound, and that the Court should be doubly cautious when it is asked to substitute its own conception of desirable social policy for that of men whose entire careers have been dedicated to making professional judgments in an extremely complex and difficult field. Clearly, the Court should, in the present case, limit itself to determining whether the Middlefield school authorities have acted in a discriminatory fashion.

The district court found that there was no deliberate intent on the part of the school board to segregate pupils on the basis of race. While the appellants claim that they accept that finding, they in fact attempt to discredit it by implication. They suggest that the school board's awareness of the racial effects of its pupil assignment practices and decision to continue those practices prove that the board deliberately chose to segregate black students. This argument simply ignores the fact that the neighborhood school plan followed by the board is based on a rational, objective, and long-established evaluation of educational needs in Middlefield. Thus, the appellants' "proof" seems extremely dubious and far-fetched.

Furthermore, entirely apart from the question of whether the board's failure to act constitutes proof of discriminatory state action, the Supreme Court should not attempt to reevaluate the district court's finding that the school board was not guilty of deliberately segregating black students. In many past cases, the Court has insisted that the only questions it would decide on review were questions of law and not questions of fact. Admittedly, there are exceptions to this general rule, but they are limited to cases in which the appellant claims that the lower court's determination of the facts is arbitrary and irrational. Appellants make no such claim here.

gated schools. Thus, while the school board did not overtly adhere to a regulation requiring segregation in the schools, it followed policies which achieved roughly the same results, in violation of the Fourteenth Amendment's guarantee of equal protection of the laws.

Respondents argue that the Fourteenth Amendment is inapplicable because no evidence has been introduced to show that they intended to follow a policy of separating black and white students; appellants ask whether the applicability of the Fourteenth Amendment should be determined by an attempt to determine the subjective intent of the school authorities. Where a neighborhood school plan has substantially the same effects as a statutory requirement of discrimination, the Fourteenth Amendment should not be rendered inapplicable simply because the school authorities have not deliberately, expressly, and maliciously designed to keep white and black children separate.

Appellants have been unable to find any Supreme Court decision in which a distinction is drawn between intentional and unintentional violation of the Fourteenth Amendment. Indeed, this Court has always focused on whether the official action violated the constitutional guarantee and not on the intention or motivation of the officials involved.

For example, in *Wesberry v. Sanders*, 376 U.S. 1 (1964), this Court upheld the appellants' contention that the failure of the state legislature to reapportion congressional districts to eliminate underrepresentation of their vote violated the Constitution, even though no specific legislative intent to cause the underrepresentation of voters of some districts and the overrepresentation of voters of other districts had been established. Thus, the absence of an intent on the part of the school board to maintain a racially segregated school system should not foreclose a claim based on the constitutional rights of the appellants.

Furthermore, the question of intent to violate the appellants' rights should not be dispositive where, as here, the school board was aware of the racial effects of its policies and chose to maintain them without change. To create a constitutional difference, where racial

In the absence of either discriminatory laws or any showing of deliberate intention to discriminate, it is hard to understand how respondents could be held to have violated the command of the Fourteenth Amendment. The *Brown* case and other precedents forbid discrimination; they do not forbid separation which results from the maintenance of nondiscriminatory public policies.

Since the appellants are unable to prove that the Middlefield School Board intended to discriminate against them, they insist that the intent of the school board is not really relevant, especially where the effect of the board's policies is essentially the same as a statutory requirement of segregation. Their assumption is that since segregation is unconstitutional, the assignment of a pupil to a racially imbalanced school is equally unconstitutional, even if the assignment is based on objective, nondiscriminatory policies. Yet there is a world of difference between these two situations.

We believe that the reason segregation is unconstitutional is not because it results in separation of the races but because it is based on state action which treats whites and blacks differently and, therefore, stamps black pupils with a state-imposed badge of inferiority. Thus, the fact that the educational effects of official segregation and adventitious separation may be similar is not constitutionally relevant. The Constitution says the state may not discriminate; it does not say the state must integrate. The appellants do have a constitutional right to an impartial and nondiscriminatory school system; they do not have a constitutional right to attend racially balanced schools.

Appellants further argue that even if the Court rejects their claim that the Middlefield School Board overtly discriminates against black pupils by assigning them to neighborhood schools, it should not allow the board to discriminate *sub silentio* by taking advantage of patterns of residential segregation. This is no more than another attempt to persuade the Court that the school board deliberately intends to discriminate on a racial basis. It is a particularly vicious attempt, since it is based solely on inference and not on any evidence whatsoever. If the school board had no legiti-

imbalance exists, between a school board openly taking advantage of patterns of residential segregation and one doing so *sub silentio* could make the work of the courts more difficult by encouraging evasion in the form of unspoken policies and "gentlemen's agreements." The crucial question should be, simply, whether the student assigned to a racially imbalanced school created and maintained by the districting policies of school authorities has been deprived of his constitutional rights.

Where school authorities elect to make school assignments on a geographic basis and where such assignments lead to racial concentration, the authorities should not be allowed to escape responsibility for what they have wrought. The fact that they claim to have had only the purest motives for their decision to follow the neighborhood school concept may seem reasonable but should not be held to relieve them of responsibility where the effect of the otherwise reasonable decision is to deprive certain persons of their constitutional rights.

Finally, respondents argue that even if this Court should find that the establishment and maintenance of Middlefield's neighborhood school plan constitutes state action in violation of the equal protection clause since it results in racial concentration tantamount to legally enforced segregation, and even if it should find that the intent of the school board is constitutionally irrelevant when the effects of its policies are to create and maintain racially concentrated schools, it should not look beyond the fact that the neighborhood school plan is rationally related to the purpose of education. But rational relationship is not an appropriate test for the legality of state action where that action results in racial segregation.

Middlefield's school board has exercised state power so as to violate the constitutional prohibition against official discrimination on the basis of race. Such state action even though "pursuant to a valid state interest, bears a heavy burden of justification . . . and will be upheld only if it is necessary, and not merely rationally related to, the accomplishment of a permissible state policy."[2] Where

[2] *McLaughlin v. Florida*, 379 U.S. 184, 196 (1964).

mate basis for its pupil assignment rules at all, such an inference might be worthy of consideration; as it is, however, since the neighborhood school concept is historic, is used by school systems throughout the United States, and is highly preferred by professional educators, the inference should not be accepted by a court of law.

Since the school board's motives and actions have been above reproach, we believe—as we have said—that the board is under no constitutional duty to abandon its present pupil assignment plan. However, even if this Court should find that the Fourteenth Amendment has been violated by Middlefield's neighborhood school policy, it should not order the school authorities to eliminate racial imbalance in the public schools.

The Middlefield School Board is responsible for ensuring that all the children of Middlefield, regardless of race, receive the best education possible within the limited resources available to the school system. The board is not an integration agency, nor is it set up for the purpose of sociological experimentation; its purpose is education. The members of the school board have determined in an objective and nondiscriminatory manner that the values of neighborhood school attendance outweigh whatever advantages might conceivably be gained from busing children throughout the city in order to achieve racial balance.

Further, the board has assessed the disadvantages to both white and black students of its present plan and has concluded that they are far less serious than the disadvantages which would accompany any plan to achieve racial balance in Middlefield's schools. In particular, the board hopes to prevent (1) a repetition in Middlefield of the flight by white families to the suburbs and to private schools which has taken place in those cities where large numbers of nonwhite students have enrolled in formerly all-white schools without a sufficient transition period, and (2) segregation by ability level within integrated schools which has frequently resulted from the addition of children from culturally, educationally, and economically deprived backgrounds to schools whose students come primarily from middle-class families.

racial segregation results from state action, the responsible officials must show not only that the policies followed are rationally related to a valid state purpose but that there is no way to accomplish that purpose without racial segregation. In this instance, respondents have made no effort to eliminate or reduce racial concentration in the schools under their administration. The record does not show that the respondents considered any of the alternative corrective measures open to them, much less that none of these alternatives was possible.

The board believes that the only way to prevent these tragedies from occurring is to concentrate its efforts now on the educational problems of the underprivileged and to integrate the schools gradually as the housing barriers which have caused residential segregation erode in coming years. Respondents hope that the Court will appreciate the complexity of the problem facing the school board, will accept the determination of the district court that the board has acted in a nondiscriminatory and objective fashion, and will refrain from ordering the board to abandon policies which it believes are in the interest of all of the parents and students of Middlefield.

2.   Is there an affirmative constitutional duty to eliminate racial imbalance in public schools?

Even if this Court concludes that the state action complained of in this case does not fall within the limits of its decision in *Brown v. Board of Education*, it should find for the appellants on the ground that the Constitution requires public school authorities to provide equal educational opportunities for all children. Racial imbalance resulting from residential segregation deprives black children of equal educational opportunities to the same extent as legally compelled segregation and should therefore be eliminated to the fullest extent possible. In *Brown v. Board of Education*, this Court ruled that:

> Today, education is perhaps the most important function of state and local governments. Compulsory school attendance laws and the great expenditures for education both demonstrate our recognition of the importance of education to our democratic society. In these days, it is doubtful that any child may reasonably be expected to succeed in life if he is denied the opportunity of an education. Such an opportunity, where the state has undertaken to provide it, *is a right which must be made available to all on equal terms.*
>
> 347 U.S. 483, at 493
> (Emphasis added.)

The Court went on to conclude that racial separation deprived the child of the minority

Appellants argue that the school board is under an affirmative constitutional duty to recast innocently arrived at school boundaries and to bus children throughout the city in order to balance the schools. Respondents believe that this view is incorrect, and that the Fourteenth Amendment requires only that the school board not discriminate against pupils on the basis of race. Further, respondents hope the Court will recognize that appellants are arguing that the Fourteenth Amendment requires positive action by the state because they know they have not been able to prove that the school board has discriminated against black students.

What is the source of the obligation asserted by our opponents? Certainly, an obligation to take affirmative action to balance the public schools cannot be found in the negative wording of the amendment itself. Appellants rely on certain statements in *Brown v. Board of Education* that state-provided educational opportunities must be available to all on equal terms, without regard to race; they conclude, therefore, that *Brown* stands for the proposition that the state must balance the schools. They have developed a three-word formula, "equal educational opportunities," which they repeat over and over. But since they define equal educational opportunities to mean the right to attend racially balanced schools, they are in fact doing no more than redefining in

group of equal educational opportunities because it impregnated his heart and mind with a feeling of inferiority and made it impossible for him to learn or achieve to the same extent as he would were his educational experience free of restrictions based on race. Thus, the *Brown* decision adds weight to the argument that the constitutional standard required by the Fourteenth Amendment is the provision of equal educational opportunity. *Brown* should not be read so narrowly as to limit the requirement of the Fourteenth Amendment solely to a prohibition against de jure segregation in the schools. Since the basic purpose of the Fourteenth Amendment was to guarantee equality to Negroes, the critical question should not be the form of the restriction but whether in its operation equality is denied.

There is little need to belabor the point that racially imbalanced schools deny black pupils equal educational opportunity to the same extent as racially segregated schools. The harmful effects of segregation of the races on black children found in the *Brown* decision are the same whether the separation results from de facto or de jure segregation. Evidence gathered since the *Brown* decision supports the conclusion reached there that separate education is inherently unequal education.

For example, the Advisory Committee of the Massachusetts State Board of Education, in its July 1964 report, concluded that racial imbalance damages the self-confidence and motivation of black children, reinforces the prejudice of children regardless of their color, and does not prepare the child for life in an integrated, multiracial community, nation, and world.

These findings correspond with those of the Board of Regents of the University of the State of New York in a statement issued at its meeting of January 27 to 28, 1960, and quoted with approval in *Blocker v. Board of Education of Manhasset*, 226 F. Supp. 208, 209 (E.D.N.Y. 1964). New York, New Jersey, and California have concluded that imbalanced schools are inadequate educationally and have ordered that corrective action be taken. Illinois and Massachusetts have taken action to correct racial imbalance by statute.[3]

[3] See Fiss, "Racial Imbalance in the Public Schools: The Constitutional Concepts," 78 *Harv. L.R.* 564, 567–70 (1965).

attractive-sounding words what they are actually trying to prove. Arguments in semantics do not prove the existence of constitutional obligations.

We believe that the conclusions appellants draw from the *Brown* decision are unwarranted and based on a deliberate desire to ignore the circumstances of the case. In *Brown v. Board of Education* the Supreme Court faced the question of whether a state could, within the guarantee of the Fourteenth Amendment, require students to attend schools segregated by law. The Court ruled specifically that state-imposed segregation violated the equal protection clause of the Constitution; it did not rule *at all* on (1) the question of whether separation of blacks and whites which results from nondiscriminatory policies also violates the Constitution, and (2) whether school boards must abandon nondiscriminatory policies in order to eliminate racial imbalance. Thus, respondents are convinced that appellants' "constitutional obligation" cannot be found in this Court's decision in *Brown v. Board of Education*.

Appellants make a great deal of the fact that adventitious separation of black and white children has the same deleterious consequences as deliberate segregation imposed by law. As we have already said, we believe that this argument entirely misses the point. This Court was not established in order to cure the social ills of our society; it is a court of law, not a legislative body. As the late Justice Frankfurter said: ". . . [T]here is not under our Constitution a judicial remedy for every political mischief, for every undesirable exercise of legislative power. The Framers carefully and with deliberate forethought refused so to enthrone the Judiciary."[1]

Since the Supreme Court has refused in the past to rule on the question of whether there is a constitutional mandate to remedy racial imbalance in the schools, there is no Supreme Court precedent which establishes the appellants' "constitutional obligation." *Jackson v. Board of Education of Middlefield* is thus a case of tremendous constitutional significance.

A number of lower courts, including the United States Courts of Appeals for the First, Seventh, and Tenth Circuits, have ruled that

[1] *Baker v. Carr*, 369 U.S. 186, at 270 (1962).

It is clear that by failing to take any steps to eliminate or reduce racial concentration in its schools, the Middlefield School Board has failed to meet the constitutional requirement of equal educational opportunity. The board has attempted to insulate itself from the reach of the Fourteenth Amendment by claiming that the amendment only forbids segregation and does not require integration. This Court has not ruled on the question of "... [H]ow far a public body may save itself from constitutional constraint by mere inaction," but there are precedents on both sides in the lower courts.[4]

Respondents rely on *Bell v. School City of Gary*, 324 F.2d 209 (7th Cir.), *cert. denied* 377 U.S. 924 (1964), and *Downs v. Board of Education of Kansas City*, 336 F.2d 988 (10th Cir. 1964), *cert. denied* 380 U.S. 914 (1965), both of which hold that the Fourteenth Amendment forbids segregation but does not require integration. In *Bell* and *Downs* the courts did not discuss the question of deprivation of equal educational opportunity and the resultant harm to black students.

Respondents also cite a dictum in a First Circuit case, *Springfield School Committee v. Barksdale*, 348 F.2d 261, at 264 (1st Cir. 1965), in which the court rejected any intimation in the decision of the district court that the plaintiffs in a de facto segregation suit possessed "... [A]n absolute right ... to have what the court found to be 'tantamount to segregation' removed at all costs."

But the *Springfield* decision hardly lends strength to respondents' case, since the court went on to accept the view of the district court that racial imbalance impaired the educational opportunities of black students in Springfield to such a degree that they had a right to insist that the school committee consider their special problems along with all other relevant factors when making administrative decisions. The court refused to determine whether the right discussed was a constitutional right, since the school committee had recognized the existence of such an obligation prior to the commencement of the suit.

We believe that *Bell* and *Downs* err in placing emphasis on the form of the racial restriction rather than on its educational effect. In the Constitution does not require integration of a school system in which no deliberate segregation is practiced. The statement of the district court in *Bell v. School City of Gary*, 213 F. Supp. 819, at 829 (N.D. Ind.), *affirmed* 324 F.2d 209 (7th Cir.), *cert. denied* 377 U.S. 924 (1964), best reflects our view that racial imbalance, in the absence of any showing of contrivance, raises no Fourteenth Amendment question:

> The neighborhood school which serves the students within a prescribed district is a long and well established institution in American public school education. It is almost universally used. ... It has many social, cultural and administrative advantages. ... I have seen nothing in the many cases dealing with the segregation problem which leads me to believe that the law requires that a school system developed on the neighborhood school plan, honestly and conscientiously constructed with no intention or purpose to segregate the races, must be destroyed or abandoned because the resultant effect is to have a racial imbalance in certain schools where the district is populated almost entirely by Negroes or whites.[2]

In setting up guidelines for desegregation in the *Brown* case, the Supreme Court ruled that lower courts:

> ... [M]ay consider problems relating to administration, arising from the physical condition of the school plant, the school transportation system, personnel, revision of school districts and attendance areas into compact units to achieve a system of determining admission to the public schools on a non-racial basis. ...
>
> 349 U.S. 294, at 300–01 (1955).

Thus, the Court squarely approved of non-racial geographic districting, regardless of any resulting racial imbalance. Numerous lower courts have interpreted the guidelines to mean

---

[4] *Taylor v. Board of Education*, 294 F.2d 36, at 39 (2d Cir. 1961).

[2] See also *Downs v. Board of Education of Kansas City*, 336 F.2d 988 (10th Cir. 1964), *cert. denied* 380 U.S. 914 (1965), and *Springfield School Committee v. Barksdale*, 348 F.2d 261 (1st Cir. 1965). In the Springfield case, the court rejected any suggestion in the opinion of the district court that plaintiffs in a de facto segregation suit possess an absolute right to racial balancing of the schools.

both instances, the courts construed equal protection in the narrowest and most restricted terms possible consistent with the *Brown* decision. We believe that inaction by school authorities is not beyond the reach of the Fourteenth Amendment if equal education is denied.

This is the position that was taken by the district court in *Branche v. Board of Education,* 204 F. Supp. 150, at 153 (E.D.N.Y. 1962), where the court ruled that public educational systems must deal with inadequacies resulting from adventitious segregation and cannot accept segregation on the ground that it was not deliberate or planned.

In *Blocker v. Board of Education,* 226 F. Supp. 208 (E.D.N.Y. 1964), another district court in the same circuit held that the neighborhood school plan followed by Manhasset authorities involved enforced segregation within the scope of the *Brown* decision; in this case, all the black children in the community attended one school and 99 percent of the white students attended other schools. No changes in school district lines had been made for a long time and the black school had, when originally zoned, been predominantly white. Thus, the intent of the authorities was not held to be decisive. The crucial factor, according to the court, was that no decision had been taken to alter the district lines even though the school board was aware that its inaction resulted in the maintenance of a segregated school.

The California Supreme Court has stated in a dictum that school boards are required to eliminate racial imbalance without regard to how it was produced:

> ... [A] student under some circumstances would be entitled to relief where, by reason of residential segregation, substantial racial imbalance exists in his school.... Where such segregation exists, it is not enough for a school board to refrain from affirmative discriminatory conduct.... The right to an equal opportunity for education and the harmful consequences of segregation require that school boards take steps, insofar as reasonably feasible, to alleviate racial imbalance in schools regardless of its cause....
>
> *Jackson v. Pasadena City School District,*
> 382 P.2d 878, 879 (Cal. Sup. Ct. 1963).

that students could not be prevented from attending school together because of race, but not that desegregation required racial balancing.[3]

While the Supreme Court has not ruled on the question of racial imbalance in the schools, it has held unanimously that racial imbalance in election districts does not violate any constitutional right, even though the "Negro vote" may be diluted by the concentration of blacks in one or more districts due to residential patterns, provided that the districts are drawn on the basis of nondiscriminatory geographical standards.[4] Although Justices Douglas and Goldberg dissented on the ground that there was sufficient evidence to prove intentional segregation, they agreed with the majority that racial imbalance raised no constitutional problem. Justice Douglas said:

> Of course neighborhoods in our larger cities often contain members of one race; and those who draw the lines of Congressional Districts cannot be expected to disregard neighborhoods by drawing zigzag tortuous lines so as to make each district a multiracial one.
>
> 376 U.S. 52, at 59.

We submit that the right to vote is as fundamental as the right to go to school; since the Court approves of nondiscriminatory geographic districting in cases involving the right to vote, it should similarly approve of Middlefield's neighborhood school policy.

While appellants argue that several lower court decisions run counter to the great majority of holdings discussed above, none of these precedents actually support the proposition that school boards must take affirmative action to eliminate racial imbalance.

In *Blocker v. Board of Education of Manhasset,* 226 F. Supp. 208, at 230 (E.D.N.Y. 1964), the district court stated that "The Court does not hold that the Constitution re-

---

[3] See, for example, *Brown v. Board of Education,* 139 F. Supp. 468 (D.Kan. 1955), *Craggett v. Board of Education of Cleveland,* 234 F. Supp. 381 (N.D. Ohio 1964), *Henry v. Godsell,* 165 F. Supp. 87 (E.D. Mich. 1958), *Evans v. Buchanan,* 207 F. 820 (D.C. Del.), *aff'd* 256 F.2d 688 (3rd Cir. 1962).

[4] *Wright v. Rockefeller,* 376 U.S. 52 (1964).

Appellants firmly believe that the precedents cited above are more in keeping with the spirit of the equal protection clause of the Fourteenth Amendment than decisions based on a narrow version of the responsibilities of public school authorities. Events in the last decade suggest that America is at a turning point in race relations. Today, this Court must decide whether it will add its voice once again to the drive for equality and full enjoyment of constitutional rights which have been delayed or denied for more than a century, or whether it will slam the doors of the urban ghetto on those whose opportunities to participate fully in American life have been circumscribed solely because of race.

quires a compulsive distribution of school children on the basis of race in order to achieve a proper representation of white and Negro children in each elementary school within a school district." In this case, the school district consisted of only three schools, two of which were entirely white. The court concluded that the facts of the case presented a situation that went far beyond adventitious racial imbalance.

In *Branche v. Board of Education*, 204 F. Supp. 150 (E.D.N.Y. 1962), the court refused to grant a motion for summary judgment made by the defendants on the issue of whether they were operating the schools in good faith rather than with an intent to segregate. Since the case was later discontinued, any statements made by the court at the time it rejected the defendants' motion can hardly be used to support a rule of constitutional law.

Jackson v. Pasadena School District, 382 P.2d 878 (Cal. Sup. Ct. 1963), did not involve adventitious separation but a claim that the school district lines had been gerrymandered to discriminate against the plaintiff. Thus, any statements by the court about the constitutional obligation of school boards to eliminate racial imbalance are not related to the holding in the case and are mere dicta.

3. *Would pupil assignments based on race violate the Fourteenth Amendment guarantee of equal protection of the laws?*

Respondents argue in their brief that the Fourteenth Amendment certainly cannot be held to require affirmative action on the part of the Middlefield School Board to eliminate racial imbalance since such action would necessitate racial quotas and racial assignments in violation of the equal protection of the laws.

The proposition that the Constitution is color-blind, that public authorities cannot take race into consideration in passing or enforcing laws, cannot be viewed out of the context in which it was developed. From 1896 to 1954, the Supreme Court upheld state acts requiring segregation of the races, despite repeated challenges, on the ground that the Fourteenth Amendment did not require more than

Since any educational system based on racial quotas would be repugnant to the Constitution, the Fourteenth Amendment should not be construed to read that school boards have a constitutional duty to establish racially balanced schools.

Coerced attendance of black and white students at schools outside their residential areas in order to eliminate racial imbalance would be segregation at its worst, since the affected pupils would be required by public authorities to attend certain schools because of race. This Court has repeatedly declared that state and local authorities cannot accord differential treatment to American citizens on the basis of race, ancestry, color, or religion. To recognize

"equality" of treatment. When the Court finally rejected the concept that separate facilities could be "equal" facilities, it put an end to the long period of discriminatory public policies; given the history of the segregation problem to that time, it was natural for the Court to rule that public officials could not take race into consideration in passing legislation.

Now, the respondents urge on the Court that the spirit and purpose of this rule should be perverted to prevent officials from eliminating segregation. To argue that school boards must ignore known patterns of residential segregation in formulating policies for the continuance and improvement of public education is to argue in favor of an abstract legalism which would effectively gut the life and substance of the guarantee of equal protection of the laws.

Respondents raise the evil of "racial quotas" and "racial assignments" to strengthen their argument that race cannot be taken into account in the formulation of school board policies. Racial quotas are not the only alternative, however; a school board could reject the idea of quotas in favor of revision of district lines, appropriate location of new schools, campus-style neighborhood schools serving wider areas, or combination of two schools with all the pupils in certain grades attending one of the paired schools. If respondents' argument were accepted, *none* of these alternatives would be constitutionally permissible as long as the school board's decision was based on a desire to eliminate racial imbalance.

We ask the Court to reject the argument that classification by race is unconstitutional, regardless of the objective. Admittedly, classifications based on race bear a heavier burden of justification than nonracial classifications; admittedly, such classifications should be examined with care to ensure that their motive is not discrimination. However, where the classification has been made solely pursuant to an attempt to alleviate racially related deprivation of equal educational opportunities, it should not be held invalid as a violation of the Fourteenth Amendment.

the constitutionality of racial quotas, for whatever purpose, would be to take the first step toward the creation of a planned society, a society contrary to the intentions of the authors of the Constitution, odious to the beliefs of a free people, and alien to the basic American concept of equality before the law.

A decision that the Middlefield School Board is not prohibited from taking race into account in its pupil assignment practices will open a Pandora's box whose ultimate consequences are indeed disturbing. Either the Court will have to limit the right thereby created to blacks, or it will have to grant the same privilege to every other racial, ethnic, and religious group. Parents opposed to the quotas will be unable to prevent their children from being assigned to public schools outside their residential areas. It is no answer to say that such parents may send their children to private schools.

Appellants' argument that there are alternative means of achieving racial balance besides racial quotas does not meet the constitutional objection to classifications based on race. While we believe that the factual premise on which the appellants make this assertion is seriously open to question, we prefer to rest our objection on the ground that all deliberate attempts to balance individual schools—and not just the imposition of racial quotas—are constitutionally invalid since they necessitate pupil assignments based on race.

Finally, regardless of constitutional objections to decisions of school administrators based on race, it should be noted that racial quotas are no panacea for the problems faced by black students as a result of residential segregation. If it is true that racial imbalance is harmful to both black and white students, it is equally true that pupil assignments based on race, regardless of their motive, stimulate the feeling among black students that they are different, that this difference is the result of the color of their skin, and that this difference requires that special consideration be given to them as it is given to the physically and mentally retarded child now. Thus, a system of racial quotas may in fact be just as harmful to the black child as a neighborhood school system which results in racial imbalance.

III. Anatomy of a Nondecision

WHY HAS THE SUPREME COURT REFUSED TO RULE ON RACIAL IMBALANCE?

Certiorari denied . . . certiorari denied . . . certiorari denied. Repeatedly, appellants who have attempted to obtain a judicial decision on the constitutionality of de facto segregation have been met with these stony words from the Supreme Court. Repeatedly, the members of the Court have refused to accept a petition to review an adverse decision by one of the circuit courts of appeals. Since the sole requirement for a petition to send the complete record of lower court action to the Supreme Court for a final decision is that four members of the Court wish to hear the case, it is quite clear that the Supreme Court has no desire to rule on racial imbalance in the schools.

Unfortunately, the Court does not make public its reasons for turning down appeals. Thus, any analysis of why the members of the Court decide to avoid an important constitutional issue must be exceedingly speculative. All the analyst can do is cite the wide range of possible alternative reasons for inaction and then hint at what appear to be the more plausible explanations.

Let us assume at the outset that every member of the Court has more than a vague impression of how his fellow justices will react to innovative questions in general and innovative questions in the civil rights field in particular. Each knows that some of his brethren on the Court already lean to the view that de facto segregation is constitutional, some to the opinion that it is unconstitutional, and that some do not wish to make up their minds, for varying reasons. Obviously, there must be an element of uncertainty in each justice's estimation of how certain members of the Court would decide a racial imbalance case.

Given this ambiguous situation, and the impossibility of finding out anything more specific without actually accepting and deciding a case, those justices who wish to avoid the issue clearly have the upper hand, even if they are in the minority. In the private meetings of the Court to decide what appeals to accept, the "avoiders" can play on the fears of those who lean to one side or the other on the substantive issue itself. Justices who prefer either of these sides could easily decide that the best strategy for any given moment is to join the "avoiders" and postpone the issue to a more propitious time rather than risk defeat by forcing the constitutional question on the Court. Of course, if six or more members of the Court actually wish to avoid the racial imbalance question, there is no question of strategy confronting those justices who prefer to decide the issue.

In sum, then, the decision to grant or not to grant *certiorari*, when viewed from the inside, is a strategic decision of great importance. It would be a serious analytical mistake to assume that this decision is made in a simple, naïve fashion, with no thought given to the possible outcome if a case is accepted.

Ultimately, of course, one must assess why those justices who wish to avoid the issue of racial imbalance have been able to convince their colleagues of the rectitude of their position. For ease of analysis, the various rationalizations for the "avoidance" stance have been categorized below as "legal" and "sociopolitical"; it should be noted, however, that these categories are somewhat crude and are by no means mutually exclusive.

THE CONSTITUTIONAL EXPLANATION FOR JUDICIAL RELUCTANCE

First, the literal wording of the Fourteenth Amendment establishes a prohibition on discriminatory state action, not a positive command that the states must take affirmative action.

Second, the history of the Fourteenth Amendment does not suggest that the authors of the amendment meant to require the states to take affirmative action to achieve "equal protection of the laws." At any rate, the authors of the amendment never considered the question of de facto segregation, since public school education was in its infancy at the time the amendment was passed and even legally separate education was virtually nonexistent for black children.

Third, there is no direct precedent in constitutional law for a ruling that the equal protection clause requires affirmative state action and a great deal of precedent, direct and by analogy from other fields, to support the opposite conclusion.

Fourth, the Supreme Court has an obligation to exercise judicial restraint and to avoid judicial lawmaking. The American political system is weakened every time the Supreme Court usurps the responsibilities of Congress and the state legislatures. Furthermore, legislatures are better equipped than courts to handle complex social problems, since they can issue flexible rules to deal with individual situations rather than general standards to be applied in uniform fashion to the nation as a whole. Whether or not this conclusion is accepted, Congress and the states should be given more time to come to grips with the extremely complex problem of racial imbalance in the schools.

Fifth, and of major importance, is the problem of legal standards. The Court should not decide issues which are not susceptible of definition in simple, unambiguous terms. Unless school administrators, city officials, parents, and other interested parties know what the Constitution requires, a holding that racial imbalance violates the Fourteenth Amendment will lead to endless litigation and bickering; in the absence of meaningful standards, the courts will be unable to handle these controversies. Given the endless variety of de facto segregation situations—in cities and towns where meaningful integration is actually possible within existing school district boundaries; in large cities where black students are in the majority and integration seems impossible; in cities where integration can be achieved only by absorbing neighboring school districts; in cities where such neighboring school districts are across state lines; in Washington, D.C., where large-scale integration could be achieved only by amalgamating the public schools of the federal capital and schools in the Maryland and Virginia suburbs—simple, generally applicable standards seem totally out of the question. Certainly, no ruling is appropriate until the range of potential de facto segregation situations has been clarified and until lawyers and other specialists have had more opportunity to think about and try to work out judicially enforceable standards.

Sixth, a rule that the Fourteenth Amendment requires states to take positive action to achieve equal protection might open a Pandora's box. Would such a rule apply to employment, to housing, to family income, and to innumerable other social and economic questions? What would be its limits? How would it be applied? Would equality be defined as racial quotas, or would equality mean that the state would have to do more for blacks than for whites in order to rectify centuries of inequality? Should the Supreme Court force its definition of equality on the American people? None of these questions can be answered easily. None should be answered hastily.

Seventh, if there is a chance that the majority will rule that adventitious racial imbalance is constitutional, it might be advisable not to rule at all. No one would claim that segregation by law has been fully eliminated. If the Court acted now to legitimize separation of the races in the public schools, such a rule would undercut existing constitutional doctrine, and make the problems of enforcing that doctrine far more severe than they are even at present.

SOCIOPOLITICAL REASONS FOR JUDICIAL RELUCTANCE

First, the members of the Supreme Court—and Americans in general—have learned a great deal from the bad experience of Southern integration. If anyone was naïve about the capacity of white majorities, backed up by local officials, to resist court-ordered integration, they are so no longer. If anyone was naïve about the limited capacity of the Supreme Court to bring about a social change which strikes at the root of historic, widely accepted behavior, they are so no longer. The endless litigation, evasions, and frustrations which have characterized the process of desegregation of Southern public schools demonstrate clearly that under certain sociopolitical conditions the Supreme Court can play the music but cannot call the tune.

Opponents of judicial intervention to eliminate racial imbalance in the North can easily point to data which suggest that the goal of integrated education will be just as hard or harder to reach than it has been in the South. They can argue persuasively that the cliché "one thing at a time" makes profound sense.

Second, the avoiders can argue that the Supreme Court cannot afford to get too far in front of the rest of society or, to put it more precisely, in front of the popularly elected institutions of government, without facing a real threat of having its wings clipped. Past experience has shown that the effectiveness of the Supreme Court, its power to bring about changes in popular norms, varies with the degree of support it gets from the President and Congress. If either the President or Congress is actively hostile, the Court has difficulty implementing many of its constitutional policies. The appointments process can be used to reshape the Court, as has frequently happened in the past, or, if the hostility is extreme, the Court can be hamstrung by statutes limiting its jurisdiction or constitutional amendments changing its judicial interpretations.

A judicial decision that de facto segregation violates the Constitution could be extremely threatening to Northern urban and suburban congressmen, many of whom have supported the Court's attempts to eliminate segregation by law in the South. The Court has sufficient enemies at present, as a result of its innovative decisions in many fields, and it may be extremely dangerous to augment their numbers further.

Third, changes in residential patterns in many Northern cities suggest that a ruling against de facto segregation would be an exercise in futility unless the Court were willing and able to go far beyond such a ruling. The experience of most cities has been that school integration is ephemeral: when black families first move into a particular neighborhood, the local schools become integrated, but the new pattern is transitional rather than stable. The acute shortage of housing for urban black families leads more and more families to move to the newly integrated area; at the same time, and for whatever reasons, white families move to the suburbs or elsewhere within the city. Within a remarkably short time, the transition is completed and the schools are resegregated.

A judicial ruling against racial imbalance would not affect the attitudes of white families who fear the encroachment of black neighbors. To the extent that such a ruling brought more and more black students to formerly white schools, it might actually speed the white flight to the suburbs and the resegregation of the schools. Efforts to prevent resegregation could be made, but the experience of most communities which have attempted to preserve integrated schools by voluntary action has not been promising. In some communities, the only possible path to integration would be court-ordered amalgamation of school districts or some other more drastic limitation on the freedom of white families to live where they wish and to send their children to local schools. Such a radical break with the American political tradition would lead to explosive racial situations, a reactionary backlash, and, ultimately, overthrow of the policies which caused the furor.

Fourth, the relationship between integration and quality education for black students is an extremely subtle and convoluted one. Even if integrated education is defined as one of the requisites for quality education in the next decades, is it therefore true that all black students must be in integrated schools and classrooms all of the time? Might not some students, some of the time, benefit from separate education? The question of what constitutes equal educational opportunity should be left to the professionals in the field and should not be approached cavalierly by nine justices who have no expertise in the psychology and sociology of education. Since these questions are the subject of heated disagreement among experts on education, a judicial pronouncement would be extremely premature and might well be wrong educationally. Thus, the Court would be wise to await further development and clarification of the educational issues before attempting to resolve the dilemma of adventitious racial separation in the schools.

THE CONSEQUENCES OF LEGAL AND POLITICAL INACTION

For more than a decade the Supreme Court has refused to rule on the constitutionality of de facto segregation. Congress has refused to pass a statute requiring the elimination of racial imbalance and, in fact, has made it explicitly clear that laws such as the Civil Rights Act of 1964 do not authorize federal officials and federal courts to seek to correct de facto segregation.

Legal and political inaction at the federal level has meant, essentially, that the problem of racial separation has been left in the hands of the cities themselves. Cities which have black majorities cannot, by definition, solve the problem; cities with white majorities will not solve it, since these majorities tend to be opposed to major integration efforts and city officials tend to be responsive, in democratic fashion, to the majorities which elect them. Suburban communities which surround cities with racial imbalance problems are able, ostrichlike, to avoid the entire unpalatable question, since they administer and finance their own school districts; thus, the suburbs have little stake in what happens in nearby municipal schools. Without outside intervention by the federal or state government, there is no meaningful impetus for changing the status quo.

Under the circumstances, it is no wonder that advocates of integrated education have become disheartened. For all their efforts, relatively little has been accomplished. Inevitably, they face moments of doubt when they are forced to ask themselves whether the game is worth the candle. Inevitably, they must ask themselves whether the struggle for integration is not really the cause of the middle-class white liberal and the middle-class black, rather than the struggle of the vast majority of urban blacks.

For many thoughtful black citizens, the effort to achieve integration in the schools has turned sour. Integration appears more and more to be merely another of the long list of promises on which the white man failed to deliver. With disenchantment has come an increasing turning inward, less willingness to play the white man's game by the white man's rules, and growing militancy. Of course, the failure of integration efforts is only one of various causes of increased militancy; slum housing, unemployment, poverty, and inadequate delivery of city services have all been at least as important in fanning the flames of racial animosity in most large cities.

Inevitably, as black citizens have grown increasingly aware that significant integration is not about to occur in Northern cities and that representative and legal institutions are not going to press the issue, the value of integration has been thrown into question. To a certain extent, the view that integration is not an advantage for black children is simply a normal psychological reaction to the facts of contemporary life; after all, it is far healthier to rationalize one's inability to obtain a desired goal by concluding that the goal is not really desirable than it is to go on pining away indefinitely.

But there is more than rationalization to the view that integration is of questionable value. Integration may well mean the submergence of a black minority in a white school and possibly their segregation within the school. Taught by white teachers, surrounded by white students, led by white administrators, black students will be encouraged to learn and assimilate the values of the majority; the successful black student will be the one who becomes, in a figurative sense, as white as most of his classmates. Anti-integrationists contend, however, that most students will be unsuccessful. Overwhelmed by the dominance of whites in the school, constantly reminded that white values are the preferred ones, unable to identify with successful black adults in the school environment, torn by the desire to assimilate and the fear of rejection, the majority of black students will fail to develop the psychological strength necessary for them to become effective adults.

Having come to the conclusions expressed above, the anti-integrationists have developed an educational philosophy based on black awareness and black pride. Students should go to black schools where they will be taught by black teachers and led by black principals. The curriculum and the entire school environment should emphasize blackness: black music, black art, black literature, black history. The goal of the schools should be to develop strong, self-aware, and secure adults who will have the capacity and desire to make their own way in the world, to serve the needs of the black community, and to fight white racism.

The political consequences of the black consciousness educational philosophy have been marked. Since the philosophy cannot be implemented without control of ghetto schools, bitter political battles have occurred and are occurring throughout the country. While militant blacks have disagreed with other blacks who believe that the schools should concentrate on academic education and not on racial awareness, the main antagonists have been the militants and white school boards, administrators, and teachers. Teachers and administrators, in particular, feel threatened by the militants, since their jobs as well as their freedom to teach are at stake. No teacher wants to have his every word scrutinized by parents, particularly if the parents themselves are not college graduates, and by "outside agitators" who, in the view of many teachers, are merely using the schools for their own political purposes.

The shape of the political and legal conflicts of urban school systems in the 1970s has already emerged: the fight against de facto segregation has assumed a secondary role, and the fight for community control of education has become the central conflict. State legislatures and city councils will have to decide how much local control is politically feasible. Courts will have to evaluate and rule on the contractual rights of tenured teachers fired by community school boards dominated by black militants as well as on the legal significance of regulations for hiring and promotion which these boards may choose to ignore. Political and legal battles for control of school finances and curricula are inevitable.

Black parents have already brought a number of lawsuits in order to test the historic method of financing public school education in the United States. Under this method, public education is not financed by the state, but by each city or town. Affluent communities have high tax bases, because of the value of the property in the community, and are able to raise far more money for public education than poorer areas. Thus, suburban communities, with lower population densities, tend to spend more for the education of each student than cities with large ghetto populations. From the viewpoint of public policy rather than the viewpoint of private self-interest, this arrangement makes little sense, since students from poor families need enriched education, smaller classes, individual attention, etc., in order to receive educational opportunities comparable to those of middle-class suburban students. It may well be necessary to spend more per capita on students from urban poverty areas than on students from affluent communities if equality of opportunity is to be achieved. At any rate, even equality of expenditure would be far more in keeping with the goal of equal educational opportunity than the present method of financing public school systems.

Using the above logic, parents of seven black students attending Chicago public schools brought a suit against Illinois on the ground that the state was denying the equal protection of the laws by failing to allocate available funds in such a way as to equalize the quality of education in the slums and suburbs. Despite compensatory state aid, the city spent only 75 percent as much per student as the suburbs.

A three-judge federal district court ruled that the state had no constitutional duty to equalize either expenditures or the quality of education offered students in various communities. The court held that the questions involved were questions of public policy, to be decided by the legislature, not the courts.[1] The Supreme Court affirmed the lower court's judgment summarily, without oral argument or written opinion.[2] In a similar suit brought by eleven poor families in Bath County, Virginia, the Court again affirmed without opinion a three-judge district court holding that the state had no constitutional obligation to spend as much in poor districts as in wealthy districts.[3]

The California Supreme Court ignored the Illinois and Virginia precedents and ruled in a case brought by parents of children attending Los Angeles schools that California's system of financing education made the quality of education received by each child dependent on the wealth of his parents and neighbors. The court concluded that the property tax system for financing public education violated the Fourteenth Amendment.[4] Whether or not the California decision is appealed to the United States Supreme Court, it is clear that pressures for more equitable financing are mounting and that the nation's highest tribunal will have to explore the constitutional question in depth.

The country is going through a crisis of political philosophy caused in large part by increasing dissatisfaction with traditional definitions of equality and justice. In the past, equality has ordinarily been interpreted as the absence of discriminatory laws. Thus, the historic method of financing public education appears to be consistent with the accepted equality norm, since it is based on the value of local control of education, not on an antipoor or antiblack philosophy. Similarly, de facto segregation has not been considered discriminatory, since it is not imposed by law.

Demands for a new definition of equality, a definition based on a positive obligation of the state to deliver equality in a concrete, meaningful sense, have been articulated and will increase in frequency in coming years. Ultimately, resolution of the philosophical conflict, and of individual political and legal crises which pose the conflict in narrow, highly specific terms, is inevitable. Voters, elected officials, and judges will have no choice but to face squarely the difficult questions of how best to educate white and black students for life in a multiracial society.

[1] *McInnis v. Shapiro*, 293 F. Supp. 327 (D.C. N.Ill. 1968).
[2] *McInnis v. Ogilvie*, 394 U.S. 322 (1969).
[3] *Burress v. Wilkerson*, 397 U.S. 44 (1970).
[4] *Serrano v. Priest*, 96 Cal. Rptr. 601 (1971).

THE CONSTITUTION

PREAMBLE

We, the people of the United States, in order to form a more perfect Union, establish justice, insure domestic tranquillity, provide for the common defence, promote the general welfare, and secure the blessings of liberty to ourselves and our posterity, do ordain and establish this Constitution for the United States of America.

ARTICLE I

Section 1. All legislative powers herein granted shall be vested in a Congress of the United States, which shall consist of a Senate and House of Representatives.

Section 2. (1) The House of Representatives shall be composed of members chosen every second year by the people of the several States, and the electors in each State shall have the qualifications requisite for electors of the most numerous branch of the State Legislature.

(2) No person shall be a Representative who shall not have attained to the age of twenty-five years and been seven years a citizen of the United States, and who shall not, when elected, be an inhabitant of that State in which he shall be chosen.

(3) Representatives and direct taxes[1] shall be apportioned among the several States which may be included within this Union according to their respective numbers, which shall be determined by adding to the whole number of free persons, including those bound to service for a term of years, and excluding Indians not taxed, three-fifths of all other persons.[2] The actual enumeration shall be made within three years after the first meeting of the Congress of the United States, and within every subsequent term of ten years, in such manner as they shall by law direct. The number of Representatives shall not exceed one for every thirty thousand, but each State shall have at least one Representative; and until such enumeration shall be made, the State of New Hampshire shall be entitled to choose 3; Massachusetts, 8; Rhode Island and Providence Plantations, 1; Connecticut, 5; New York, 6; New Jersey, 4; Pennsylvania, 8; Delaware, 1; Maryland, 6; Virginia, 10; North Carolina, 5; South Carolina, 5, and Georgia, 3.

(4) When vacancies happen in the representation from any State, the Executive Authority thereof shall issue writs of election to fill such vacancies.

(5) The House of Representatives shall choose their Speaker and other officers, and shall have the sole power of impeachment.

Section 3. (1) The Senate of the United States shall be composed of two Senators from each State, chosen by the Legislature thereof,[3] for six years and each Senator shall have one vote.

(2) Immediately after they shall be assembled in consequence of the first election, they shall be divided as equally as may be into three classes. The seats of the Senators of the first class shall be vacated at the expiration of the second year, of the second class at the expiration of the fourth year, and of the third class at the expiration of the sixth year, so that one-third may be chosen every second year; and if vacancies happen by resignation or otherwise, during the recess of the Legislature of any State, the Executive thereof may make temporary appointment until the next meeting of the Legislature, which shall then fill such vacancies.[3]

(3) No person shall be a Senator who shall not have attained to the age of thirty years, and been nine years a citizen of the United States, and who shall not, when elected; be an inhabitant of that State for which he shall be chosen.

(4) The Vice President of the United States shall be President of the Senate, but shall have no vote unless they be equally divided.

(5) The Senate shall choose their other officers, and also a President pro tempore, in the absence of the Vice President, or when he shall exercise the office of the President of the United States.

(6) The Senate shall have the sole power to try all impeachments. When sitting for that purpose, they shall be on oath or affirmation. When the President of the United States is tried, the Chief Justice shall preside; and no person shall be convicted without the concurrence of two-thirds of the members present.

(7) Judgment in cases of impeachment shall not extend further than to removal from office,

---

[1] Changed by 16th amendment.

[2] "Other persons" meant slaves. This was changed by the 14th amendment.

[3] Changed by 17th amendment.

and disqualification to hold and enjoy any office of honor, trust, or profit under the United States; but the party convicted shall nevertheless be liable and subject to indictment, trial, judgment, and punishment, according to law.

Section 4. (1) The times, places and manner of holding elections for Senators and Representatives shall be prescribed in each State by the Legislature thereof; but the Congress may at any time make or alter such regulations, except as to places of choosing Senators.

(2) The Congress shall assemble at least once in every year, and such meeting shall be on the first Monday in December, unless they shall by law appoint a different day.[4]

Section 5. (1) Each House shall be the judge of the elections, returns, and qualifications of its own members, and a majority of each shall constitute a quorum to do business; but a smaller number may adjourn from day to day, and may be authorized to compel the attendance of absent members in such manner and under such penalties as each House may provide.

(2) Each House may determine the rules of its proceedings, punish its members for disorderly behavior, and with the concurrence of two-thirds expel a member.

(3) Each House shall keep a journal of its proceedings, and from time to time may publish the same, excepting such parts as may in their judgment require secrecy; and the yeas and nays of the members of either House on any question shall, at the desire of one-fifth of those present, be entered on the journal.

(4) Neither House, during the session of Congress shall, without the consent of the other, adjourn for more than three days, nor to any other place than that in which the two Houses shall be sitting.

Section 6. (1) The Senators and Representatives shall receive a compensation for their services to be ascertained by law, and paid out of the Treasury of the United States. They shall in all cases, except treason, felony, and breach of the peace, be privileged from arrest during their attendance at the session of their respective Houses, and in going to and returning from the same; and for any speech or debate in either House they shall not be questioned in any other place.

(2) No Senator or Representative shall, during the time for which he was elected, be appointed to any civil office under the authority of the United States which shall have been created, or the emoluments whereof shall have been increased during such time; and no person holding any

office under the United States shall be a member of either House during his continuance in office.

Section 7. (1) All bills for raising revenue shall originate in the House of Representatives, but the Senate may propose or concur with amendments, as on other bills.

(2) Every bill which shall have passed the House of Representatives and the Senate shall, before it becomes a law, be presented to the President of the United States; if he approve, he shall sign it, but if not, he shall return it, with his objections, to that House in which it shall have originated, who shall proceed to reconsider it. If after such reconsideration two-thirds of that House shall agree to pass the bill it shall be sent, together with the objections, to the other House, by which it shall likewise be reconsidered; and if approved by two-thirds of that House it shall become a law. But in all such cases the votes of both Houses shall be determined by yeas and nays, and the names of the persons voting for and against the bill shall be entered on the journal of each House respectively. If any bill shall not be returned by the President within ten days (Sundays excepted) after it shall have been presented to him, the same shall be a law in like manner as if he had signed it, unless the Congress by their adjournment prevent its return; in which case it shall not be a law.

(3) Every order, resolution, or vote to which the concurrence of the Senate and House of Representatives may be necessary (except on a question of adjournment) shall be presented to the President of the United States, and before the same shall take effect shall be approved by him, or being disapproved by him, shall be repassed by two-thirds of the Senate and the House of Representatives, according to the rules and limitations prescribed in the case of a bill.

Section 8. (1) The Congress shall have power:

To lay and collect taxes, duties, imposts, and excises to pay the debts and provide for the common defense and general welfare of the United States; but all duties, imposts, and excises shall be uniform throughout the United States.

(2) To borrow money on the credit of the United States.

(3) To regulate commerce with foreign nations, and among the several States and with the Indian tribes.

(4) To establish a uniform rule of naturalization and uniform laws on the subject of bankruptcies throughout the United States.

(5) To coin money, regulate the value thereof, and of foreign coin, and fix the standard of weights and measures.

(6) To provide for the punishment of counter-

---

[4] Modified by 20th amendment.

feiting the securities and current coin of the United States.

(7) To establish post-offices and post-roads.

(8) To promote the progress of science and useful arts by securing for limited times to authors and inventors the exclusive rights to their respective writing and discoveries.

(9) To constitute tribunals inferior to the Supreme Court.

(10) To define and punish piracies and felonies committed on the high seas, and offences against the law of nations.

(11) To declare war, grant letters of marque and reprisal and make rules concerning captures on land and water.

(12) To raise and support armies, but no appropriation of money to that use shall be for a longer term than two years.

(13) To provide and maintain a navy.

(14) To make rules for the government and regulation of the land and naval forces.

(15) To provide for calling forth the militia to execute the laws of the Union, suppress insurrections, and repel invasions.

(16) To provide for organizing, arming, and disciplining the militia, and for governing such part of them as may be employed in the service of the United States, reserving to the States respectively the appointment of the officers, and the authority of training the militia according to the discipline prescribed by Congress.

(17) To exercise exclusive legislation in all cases whatsoever over such district (not exceeding ten miles square) as may, by cession of particular States and the acceptance of Congress, become the seat of Government of the United States, and to exercise like authority over all places purchased by the consent of the Legislature of the State in which the same shall be, for the erection of forts, magazines, arsenals, drydocks, and other needful buildings.

(18) To make all laws which shall be necessary and proper for carrying into execution the foregoing powers and all other powers vested by this Constitution in the Government of the United States, or in any department or officer thereof.

Section 9. (1) The migration or importation of such persons as any of the States now existing shall think proper to admit shall not be prohibited by the Congress prior to the year one thousand eight hundred and eight, but a tax or duty may be imposed on such importation, not exceeding ten dollars for each person.

(2) The privilege of the writ of habeas corpus shall not be suspended, unless when in cases of rebellion or invasion the public safety may require it.

(3) No bill of attainder or ex post facto law shall be passed.

(4) No capitation or other direct tax shall be laid, unless in proportion to the census or enumeration hereinbefore directed to be taken.[5]

(5) No tax or duty shall be laid on articles exported from any State.

(6) No preference shall be given by any regulation of commerce or revenue to the ports of one State over those of another, nor shall vessels bound to or from one State be obliged to enter, clear, or pay duties to another.

(7) No money shall be drawn from the Treasury but in consequence of appropriations made by law; and a regular statement and account of the receipts and expenditures of all public money shall be published from time to time.

(8) No title of nobility shall be granted by the United States. And no person holding any office of profit or trust under them shall, without the consent of the Congress, accept of any present, emolument, office, or title of any kind whatever from any king, prince, or foreign state.

Section 10. (1) No State shall enter into any treaty, alliance, or confederation, grant letters of marque and reprisal, coin money, emit bills of credit, make anything but gold and silver coin a tender in payment of debts, pass any bill of attainder, ex post facto law, or law impairing the obligation of contracts, or grant any title of nobility.

(2) No State shall, without the consent of the Congress, lay any impost or duties on imports or exports, except what may be absolutely necessary for executing its inspection laws, and the net produce of all duties and imposts, laid by any State on imports or exports, shall be for the use of the Treasury of the United States; and all such laws shall be subject to the revision and control of the Congress.

(3) No State shall, without the consent of Congress, lay any duty of tonnage, keep troops or ships of war in time of peace, enter into agreement or compact with another State, or with a foreign power, or engage in war unless actually invaded, or in such imminent danger as will not admit of delay.

ARTICLE II

Section 1. (1) The Executive power shall be vested in a President of the United States of America. He shall hold his office during the term of four years[6] and together with the Vice-President, chosen for the same term, be elected as follows:

---

[5] Modified by 16th amendment.

[6] The 22nd amendment limited President to two terms.

(2) Each State shall appoint, in such manner as the Legislature thereof may direct, a number of electors equal to the whole number of Senators and Representatives to which the State may be entitled in the Congress; but no Senator or Representative or person holding an office of trust or profit under the United States shall be appointed an elector.

The electors shall meet in their respective States and vote by ballot for two persons, of whom one at least shall not be an inhabitant of the same State with themselves. And they shall make a list of all the persons voted for, and of the number of votes for each, which list they shall sign and certify and transmit, sealed, to the seat of the Government of the United States, directed to the President of the Senate. The President of the Senate shall, in the presence of the Senate and House of Representatives, open all the certificates, and the votes shall then be counted. The person having the greatest number of votes shall be the President, if such number be a majority of the whole number of electors appointed, and if there be more than one who have such a majority, and have an equal number of votes, then the House of Representatives shall immediately choose by ballot one of them for President; and if no person have a majority, then from the five highest on the list the said House shall in like manner choose the President. But in choosing the President, the vote shall be taken by States, the representation from each State having one vote. A quorum, for this purpose, shall consist of a member or members from two-thirds of the States, and a majority of all the States shall be necessary to a choice. In every case, after the choice of the President, the person having the greatest number of votes of the electors shall be the Vice-President.[7] But if there should remain two or more who have equal votes, the Senate shall choose from them by ballot the Vice-President.

(3) The Congress may determine the time of choosing the electors and the day on which they shall give their votes, which day shall be the same throughout the United States.

(4) No person except a natural born citizen, or a citizen of the United States at the time of the adoption of the Constitution, shall be eligible to the office of President, neither shall any person be eligible to that office who shall not have attained to the age of thirty-five years and been fourteen years a resident within the United States.

(5) In case of the removal of the President from office, or of his death, resignation, or inability to discharge the powers and duties of the

said office, the same shall devolve on the Vice-President, and the Congress may by law provide for the case of removal, death, resignation, or inability, both of the President and Vice-President, declaring what officer shall then act as President, and such officer shall act accordingly until the disability be removed or a President shall be elected.

(6) The President shall, at stated times, receive for his services a compensation which shall neither be increased nor diminished during the period for which he shall have been elected, and he shall not receive within that period any other emolument from the United States or any of them.

(7) Before he enter on the execution of his office he shall take the following oath or affirmation:

"I do solemnly swear (or affirm) that I will faithfully execute the office of President of the United States, and will, to the best of my ability, preserve, protect, and defend the Constitution of the United States."

Section 2. (1) The President shall be Commander-in-Chief of the Army and Navy of the United States, and of the militia of the several States when called into the actual service of the United States; he may require the opinion, in writing, of the principal officer in each of the executive departments upon any subject relating to the duties of their respective offices, and he shall have power to grant reprieves and pardons for offences against the United States except in cases of impeachment.

(2) He shall have power by and with the advice and consent of the Senate to make treaties, provided two-thirds of the Senators present concur: and he shall nominate and by and with the advice and consent of the Senate shall appoint ambassadors, other public minister and consuls, judges of the Supreme Court, and all other officers of the United States whose appointments are not herein otherwise provided for, and which shall be established by law; but the Congress may by law vest the appointment of such inferior officers as they think proper in the President alone, in the courts of law, or in the heads of departments.

(3) The President shall have power to fill up all vacancies that may happen during the recess of the Senate by granting commissions, which shall expire at the end of their next session.

Section 3. He shall from time to time give to the Congress information of the state of the Union, and recommend to their consideration such measures as he shall judge necessary and expedient; he may, on extraordinary occasions, convene both Houses, or either of them, and in case of disagreement between them with respect to the time of adjournment, he may adjourn them to

---

[7] Changed by 12th amendment.

such time as he shall think proper; he shall receive ambassadors and other public ministers; he shall take care that the laws be faithfully executed, and shall commission all the officers of the United States.

Section 4. The President, Vice-President, and all civil officers of the United States shall be removed from office on impeachment for and conviction of treason, bribery or other high crimes and misdemeanors.

ARTICLE III

Section 1. The judicial power of the United States shall be vested in one Supreme Court, and in such inferior courts as the Congress may from time to time ordain and establish. The judges, both of the Supreme and inferior courts, shall hold their offices during good behavior, and shall at stated times receive for their services a compensation which shall not be diminished during their continuance in office.

Section 2. (1) The judicial power shall extend to all cases in law and equity arising under this Constitution, the laws of the United States, and treaties made, or which shall be made, under their authority; to all cases affecting ambassadors, other public ministers and consuls; to all cases of admiralty and maritime jurisdiction; to controversies to which the United States shall be a party;[8] to controversies between two or more States, between a State and citizens of another State, between citizens of different States, between citizens of the same State claiming lands under grants of different States, and between a State, or the citizens thereof, and foreign states, citizens, or subjects.

(2) In all cases affecting ambassadors, other public ministers, and consuls, and those in which a State shall be a party, the Supreme Court shall have original jurisdiction. In all the other cases before mentioned the Supreme Court shall have appellate jurisdiction both as to law and fact, with such exceptions and under such regulations as the Congress shall make.

(3) The trial of all crimes, except in cases of impeachment, shall be by jury, and such trial shall be held in the State where the said crimes shall have been committed; but when not committed within any State the trial shall be at such place or places as the Congress may by law have directed.

Section 3. (1) Treason against the United States shall consist only in levying war against them, or in adhering to their enemies, giving them aid and comfort. No person shall be convicted of treason unless on the testimony of two witnesses to the same overt act, or on confession in open court.

(2) The Congress shall have power to declare the punishment of treason, but no attainder of treason shall work corruption of blood or forfeiture except during the life of the person attainted.

ARTICLE IV

Section 1. Full faith and credit shall be given in each State to the public acts, records, and judicial proceedings of every other State. And the Congress may by general laws prescribe the manner in which such acts, records, and proceedings shall be proved, and the effect thereof.

Section 2. (1) The citizens of each State shall be entitled to all privileges and immunities of citizens in the several States.

(2) A person charged in any State with treason, felony, or other crime, who shall flee from justice, and be found in another State, shall, on demand of the Executive authority of the State from which he fled, be delivered up, to be removed to the State having jurisdiction of the crime.

(3) No person held to service or labor in one State, under the laws thereof, escaping into another shall in consequence of any law or regulation therein, be discharged from such service or labor, but shall be delivered up on claim of the party to whom such service or labor may be due.[9]

Section 3. (1) New States may be admitted by the Congress into this Union; but no new State shall be formed or erected within the jurisdiction of any other State, nor any State be formed by the junction of two or more States, or parts of States, without the consent of the Legislatures of the States concerned, as well as of the Congress.

(2) The Congress shall have power to dispose of and make all needful rules and regulations respecting the territory or other property belonging to the United States; and nothing in this Constitution shall be so construed as to prejudice any claims of the United States, or of any particular State.

Section 4. The United States shall guarantee to every State in this Union a Republican form of government, and shall protect each of them against invasion, and, on application of the Legislature, or of the Executive (when the Legislature cannot be convened) against domestic violence.

ARTICLE V

The Congress, whenever two-thirds of both Houses shall deem it necessary, shall propose amendments to this Constitution, or, on the application of the Legislatures of two-thirds of the

---

[8] Changed by 11th amendment.

[9] Became irrelevant after passage of 13th amendment abolishing slavery.

several States, shall call a convention for proposing amendments, which in either case, shall be valid to all intents and purposes, as part of this Constitution, when ratified by the Legislatures of three-fourths of the several States, or by conventions in three-fourths thereof, as the one or the other mode of ratification may be proposed by the Congress, provided that no amendment which may be made prior to the year one thousand eight hundred and eight shall in any manner affect the first and fourth clauses in the Ninth Section of the First Article; and that no State, without its consent, shall be deprived of its equal suffrage in the Senate.

ARTICLE VI

(1) All debts contracted and engagements entered into before the adoption of this Constitution shall be as valid against the United States under this Constitution as under the Confederation.

(2) This Constitution and the laws of the United States which shall be made in pursuance thereof and all treaties made, or which shall be made, under the authority of the United States, shall be the supreme law of the land, and the judges in every State shall be bound thereby, anything in the Constitution or laws of any State to the contrary notwithstanding.

(3) The Senators and Representatives before mentioned and the members of the several State Legislatures, and all executives and judicial officers, both of the United States and of the several States, shall be bound by oath or affirmation to support this Constitution; but no religious test shall ever be required as a qualification to any office or public trust under the United States.

ARTICLE VII

The ratification of the Conventions of nine States shall be sufficient for the establishment of this Constitution between the States so ratifying the same.

THE AMENDMENTS TO THE CONSTITUTION

AMENDMENT I

Congress shall make no law respecting an establishment of religion, or prohibiting the free exercise thereof; or abridging the freedom of speech or of the press; or the right of the people peaceably to assemble and to petition the Government for a redress of grievances.

AMENDMENT II

A well-regulated militia being necessary to the security of a free State, the right of the people to keep and bear arms shall not be infringed.

AMENDMENT III

No soldier shall, in time of peace, be quartered in any house without the consent of the owner, nor in time of war but in a manner to be prescribed by law.

AMENDMENT IV

The right of the people to be secure in their persons, houses, papers, and effects, against unreasonable searches and seizures, shall not be violated, and no warrants shall issue but upon probable cause, supported by oath or affirmation, and particularly describing the place to be searched, and the persons or things to be seized.

AMENDMENT V

No person shall be held to answer for a capital or other infamous crime unless on a presentment or indictment of a Grand Jury, except in cases arising in the land or naval forces, or in the militia, when in actual service, in time of war or public danger; nor shall any person be subject for the same offence to be twice put in jeopardy of life or limb; nor shall be compelled in any criminal case to be a witness against himself, nor be deprived of life, liberty or property, without due process of law; nor shall private property be taken for public use without just compensation.

AMENDMENT VI

In all criminal prosecutions, the accused shall enjoy the right to a speedy and public trial, by an impartial jury of the State and district wherein the crime shall have been committed, which districts shall have been previously ascertained by law, and to be informed of the nature and cause of the accusation; to be confronted with the witnesses against him; to have compulsory process for obtaining witnesses in his favor, and to have the assistance of counsel for his defence.

AMENDMENT VII

In suits at common law, where the value in controversy shall exceed twenty dollars, the right of trial by jury shall be preserved, and no fact tried by a jury shall be otherwise reexamined in any court of the United States than according to the rules of the common law.

AMENDMENT VIII

Excessive bail shall not be required, nor excessive fines imposed, nor cruel and unusual punishments inflicted.

AMENDMENT IX

The enumeration in the Constitution of certain rights shall not be construed to deny or disparage others retained by the people.

AMENDMENT X

The powers not delegated to the United States by the Constitution, nor prohibited by it to the States, are reserved to the States respectively, or to the people.[10]

AMENDMENT XI

The judicial power of the United States shall not be construed to extend to any suit in law or equity, commenced or prosecuted against one of the United States, by citizens of another State, or by citizens or subjects of any foreign state.[11]

AMENDMENT XII

The Electors shall meet in their respective States and vote by ballot for President and Vice-President, one of whom at least shall not be an inhabitant of the same State with themselves; they shall name in their ballots the person voted for as President, and in distinct ballots the person voted for as Vice-President; and they shall make distinct lists of all persons voted for as President, and of all persons voted for as Vice-President, and of the number of votes for each, which list they shall sign and certify, and transmit, sealed, to the seat of the Government of the United States, directed to the President of the Senate; the President of the Senate shall, in the presence of the Senate and House of Representatives, open all the certificates and the votes shall then be counted;

the person having the greatest number of votes for President shall be the President, if such number be a majority of the whole number of Electors appointed; and if no person have such majority, then from the persons having the highest number, not exceeding three, on the list of those voted for as President, the House of Representatives shall choose immediately, by ballot, the President. But in choosing the President, the votes shall be taken by States, the representation from each State having one vote; a quorum for this purpose shall consist of a member or members from two-thirds of the States, and a majority of all the States shall be necessary to a choice. And if the House of Representatives shall not choose a President, whenever the right of choice shall devolve upon them, before the fourth day of March next following, then the Vice-President shall act as President, as in the case of the death or other constitutional disability of the President. The person having the greatest number of votes as Vice-President shall be the Vice-President if such number be a majority of the whole number of Electors appointed, and if no person have a majority, then, from the two highest numbers on the list the Senate shall choose the Vice-President; a quorum for the purpose shall consist of two-thirds of the whole number of Senators, and a majority of the whole number shall be necessary to a choice. But no person constitutionally ineligible to the office of President shall be eligible to that of Vice-President of the United States.[12]

AMENDMENT XIII

Section 1. Neither slavery nor involuntary servitude, except as a punishment for crime whereof the party shall have been duly convicted, shall exist within the United States, or any place subject to their jurisdiction.
Section 2. Congress shall have power to enforce this article by appropriate legislation.[13]

AMENDMENT XIV

Section 1. All persons born or naturalized in the United States, and subject to the jurisdiction thereof are citizens of the United States and of the State wherein they reside. No State shall make or enforce any law which shall abridge the privileges or immunities of citizens of the United States, nor shall any State deprive any person of life, liberty, or property, without due process of law; nor deny to any person within its jurisdiction the equal protection of the laws.

---

[10] The first 10 amendments were ratified in 1791.
[11] Ratified January 8, 1798.

[12] Ratified September 25, 1804.
[13] Ratified December 18, 1864.

Section 2. Representatives shall be apportioned among the several States according to their respective numbers, counting the whole number of persons in each State, excluding Indians not taxed. But when the right to vote at any election for the choice of Electors for President and Vice-President of the United States, Representatives in Congress, the executive and judicial officers of a State, or the members of the Legislature thereof, is denied to any of the male inhabitants of such State, being twenty-one years of age and citizens of the United States, or in any way abridged, except for participation in rebellion or other crime, the basis of representation therein shall be reduced in the proportion which the number of such male citizens shall bear to the whole number of male citizens twenty-one years of age in such State.

Section 3. No person shall be a Senator or Representative in Congress, or Elector of President and Vice-President, or hold any office, civil or military, under the United States, or under any State, who, having previously taken an oath, as a member of Congress, or as an officer of the United States, or as a member of any State Legislature, or as an executive or judicial officer of any State, to support the Constitution of the United States, shall have engaged in insurrection or rebellion against the same, or given aid or comfort to the enemies thereof. But Congress may, by a vote of two-thirds of each House, remove such disability.

Section 4. The validity of the public debt of the United States, authorized by law, including debts incurred for payment of pensions and bounties for services in suppressing insurrection or rebellion, shall not be questioned. But neither the United States, nor any State shall assume or pay any debt or obligation incurred in aid of insurrection or rebellion against the United States, or any claim for the loss or emancipation of any slave; but all such debts, obligations, and claims shall be held illegal and void.

Section 5. The Congress shall have power to enforce, by appropriate legislation, the provisions of this article.[14]

AMENDMENT XV

Section 1. The right of the citizens of the United States to vote shall not be denied or abridged by the United States or by any State on account of race, color, or previous condition of servitude.

Section 2. The Congress shall have power to enforce the provisions of this article by appropriate legislation.[15]

[14] Ratified July 28, 1868.
[15] Ratified March 30, 1870.

AMENDMENT XVI

The Congress shall have power to lay and collect taxes on incomes, from whatever sources derived, without apportionment among the several States, and without regard to any census or enumeration.[16]

AMENDMENT XVII

The Senate of the United States shall be composed of two Senators from each State, elected by the people thereof, for six years; and each Senator shall have one vote. The Electors in each State shall have the qualifications requisite for Electors of the most numerous branch of the State legislatures.

When vacancies happen in the representation of any State in the Senate, the executive authority of such State shall issue writs of election to fill such vacancies: Provided, That the legislature of any State may empower the executive thereof to make temporary appointments until the people fill the vacancies by election as the legislature may direct.

This amendment shall not be construed as to affect the election or term of any Senator chosen before it became valid as part of the Constitution.[17]

AMENDMENT XVIII

Section 1. After one year from the ratification of this article the manufacture, sale or transportation of intoxicating liquors within, the importation thereof into, or the exportation thereof from the United States and all territories subject to the jurisdiction thereof for beverage purposes is hereby prohibited.

Section 2. The Congress and the several States shall have concurrent power to enforce this article by appropriate legislation.

Section 3. This article shall be inoperative unless it shall have been ratified as an amendment to the Constitution by the legislatures of the several States, as provided in the Constitution, within seven years from the date of the submission hereof to the States by Congress.[18]

AMENDMENT XIX

Section 1. The right of citizens of the United States to vote shall not be denied or abridged by the United States or by any State on account of sex.

[16] Ratified February 25, 1913.
[17] Ratified May 31, 1913.
[18] Ratified January 29, 1919. Repealed by the 21st amendment.

Section 2. Congress shall have power, by appropriate legislation, to enforce the provisions of this article.[19]

AMENDMENT XX

Section 1. The terms of the President and Vice-President shall end at noon on the 20th day of January, and the terms of Senators and Representatives at noon on the 3rd day of January, of the years in which such terms would have ended if this article had not been ratified; and the terms of their successors shall then begin.

Section 2. The Congress shall assemble at least once in every year, and such meeting shall begin at noon on the 3rd day of January, unless they shall by law appoint a different day.

Section 3. If, at the time fixed for the beginning of the term of the President, the President elect shall have died, the Vice-President elect shall become President. If a President shall not have been chosen before the time fixed for the beginning of his term, or if the President elect shall have failed to qualify, then the Vice-President elect shall act as President until a President shall have qualified; and the Congress may by law provide for the case wherein neither a President elect nor a Vice-President elect shall have qualified, declaring who shall then act as President or the manner in which one who is to act shall be selected, and such person shall act accordingly until a President or Vice-President shall have qualified.

Section 4. The Congress may by law provide for the case of the death of any of the persons from whom the House of Representatives may choose a President whenever the right of choice shall have devolved upon them, and for the case of the death of any of the persons from whom the Senate may choose a Vice-President whenever the right of choice shall have devolved upon them.

Section 5. Sections 1 and 2 shall take effect on the 15th day of October following the ratification of this article (Oct., 1933).

Section 6. This article shall be inoperative unless it shall have been ratified as an amendment to the Constitution by the legislatures of three-fourths of the several States within seven years from the date of its submission.[20]

AMENDMENT XXI

Section 1. The eighteenth article of amendment to the Constitution of the United States is hereby repealed.

Section 2. The transportation or importation into any State, Territory, or Possession of the United States for delivery or use therein of intoxicating liquors, in violation of the laws thereof, is hereby prohibited.

Section 3. This article shall be inoperative unless it shall have been ratified as an amendment to the Constitution by convention in the several States, as provided in the Constitution, within seven years from the date of the submission hereof to the States by the Congress.[21]

AMENDMENT XXII

Section 1. No person shall be elected to the office of the President more than twice, and no person who has held the office of President, or acted as President, for more than two years of a term to which some other person was elected President shall be elected to the office of the President more than once. But this Article shall not apply to any person holding the office of President when this Article was proposed by the Congress, and shall not prevent any person who may be holding the office of President, or acting as President, during the term within which this Article becomes operative from holding the office of President or acting as President during the remainder of such term.

Section 2. This article shall be inoperative unless it shall have been ratified as an amendment to the Constitution by the legislatures of three-fourths of the several States within seven years from the date of its submission to the States by the Congress.[22]

AMENDMENT XXIII

Section 1. The District constituting the seat of Government of the United States shall appoint in such manner as the Congress may direct:

A number of electors of President and Vice President equal to the whole number of Senators and Representatives in Congress to which the District would be entitled if it were a State, but in no event more than the least populous State; they shall be in addition to those appointed by the States, but they shall be considered, for the purposes of the election of President and Vice President, to be electors appointed by a State; and they shall meet in the District and perform such duties as provided by the twelfth article of amendment.

Section 2. The Congress shall have power to enforce this article by appropriate legislation.[23]

AMENDMENT XXIV

Section 1. The right of citizens of the United States to vote in any primary or other election for

[19] Ratified August 26, 1920.

[20] Ratified January 23, 1933.

[21] Ratified December 5, 1933.

[22] Ratified March 1, 1951.

[23] Ratified April 3, 1961.

President or Vice President, for electors for President or Vice President, or for Senator or Representative in Congress, shall not be denied or abridged by the United States or any State by reason of failure to pay any poll tax or other tax.
Section 2. The Congress shall have power to enforce this article by appropriate legislation.[24]

AMENDMENT XXV

Section 1. In case of removal of the President from office or of his death or resignation, the Vice President shall become President.

Section 2. Whenever there is a vacancy in the office of the Vice President, the President shall nominate a Vice President who shall take office upon confirmation by a majority vote of both Houses of Congress.

Section 3. Whenever the President transmits to the President pro tempore of the Senate and the Speaker of the House of Representatives his written declaration that he is unable to discharge the powers and duties of his office, and until he transmits to them a written declaration to the contrary, such powers and duties shall be discharged by the Vice President as Acting President.

Section 4. Whenever the Vice President and a majority of either the principal officers of the executive departments or of such other body as Congress may by law provide, transmit to the President pro tempore of the Senate and the Speaker of the House of Representatives their written declaration that the President is unable to discharge the powers and duties of his office, the Vice President shall immediately assume the powers and duties of the office as Acting President.

Thereafter, when the President transmits to the President pro tempore of the Senate and the Speaker of the House of Representatives his written declaration that no inability exists, he shall resume the powers and duties of his office unless the Vice President and a majority of either the principal officers of the executive department or of such other body as Congress may by law provide, transmit within four days to the President pro tempore of the Senate and the Speaker of the House of Representatives their written declaration that the President is unable to discharge the powers and duties of his office. Thereupon Congress shall decide the issue, assembling within forty-eight hours for that purpose if not in session. If the Congress, within twenty-one days after receipt of the latter written declaration, or, if Congress is not in session, within twenty-one days after Congress is required to assemble, determines by two-thirds vote of both Houses that the President is unable to discharge the powers and duties of his office, the Vice President shall continue to discharge the same as Acting President; otherwise, the President shall resume the powers and duties of his office.[25]

AMENDMENT XXVI

Section 1. The right of citizens of the United States, who are eighteen years of age or older, to vote shall not be denied or abridged by the United States or by any state on account of age.

Section 2. The Congress shall have power to enforce this article by appropriate legislation.[26]

[24] Ratified February 4, 1964.

[25] Ratified February 23, 1967.

[26] Ratified July 1, 1971.

BIBLIOGRAPHY

General

Abraham, Henry J.: *Freedom and the Court: Civil Rights and Liberties in the United States*, Oxford University Press, New York, 1967.

Considers the fundamental problem of reconciling freedom and order in a democratic society and the role played by the judiciary in the evolution and implementation of individual rights and liberties. The author analyzes the Bill of Rights and its application to the states, due process of law, freedom of expression, freedom of religion and separation of church and state, and constitutional aspects of race relations. Includes an excellent annotated bibliography.

———: *The Judicial Process*, 2d rev. ed., Oxford University Press, New York, 1968.

A thorough and painstaking study of the judicial process in the United States, England, France, and the Soviet Union. Compares legal philosophies, methods of selecting judges, and the administration of justice in both inferior and superior courts. Includes four extensive bibliographies, containing more than three thousand works, on American constitutional law, judicial biography and autobiography, comparative constitutional law, and civil liberties.

Barker, Lucius J., and Twiley W. Barker, Jr.: *Freedoms, Courts, Politics: Studies in Civil Liberties*, 2d rev. ed., Prentice-Hall, Englewood Cliffs, New Jersey, 1972.

Six case studies of conflicts involving civil liberties, including the school prayer issue, free speech for unpopular speakers, obscenity and free expression, internal security, school segregation, and illegal search and seizure. The authors focus on the dynamics of civil liberties rather than on decisions of the Supreme Court.

Civil Rights: Progress Report 1970, Congressional Quarterly, Washington, D.C., 1971.

A comprehensive review of developments in the field of civil rights from 1968 to 1970. This volume supplements an earlier Congressional Quarterly publication, *Revolution in Civil Rights*, which covers the postwar period up to 1968. Between them, these two short volumes contain a wealth of information on presidential, congressional, and judicial activities, and on important trends in employment, education, housing, elections, racial violence, etc.

Cox, Archibald: *The Warren Court: Constitutional Decision as an Instrument of Reform*, Harvard, Cambridge, 1968.

A lucid description by the former Solicitor General of the United States of the development of constitutional doctrine by the Warren Court. The author concentrates on race relations, administration of criminal justice, and the operation of the political process.

Emerson, Thomas I., David Haber, and Norman Dorsen: *Political and Civil Rights in the United States,* 3d rev. ed., 2 Vols., Little, Brown, Boston, 1967.

An excellent casebook designed primarily for law students but extremely useful for anyone interested in the rights of the individual in American society. Extensive notes and references to nonlegal sources supplement the legal materials contained in the text.

Friedman Leon (ed.): *Southern Justice,* World Publishing, Cleveland, 1967.

A hard-hitting account written by nineteen lawyers who have handled civil rights cases in the South. The authors relate their experiences with local police and sheriffs, prosecuting attorneys, trial courts, juries, state courts of appeal, the FBI, and federal courts.

Gunther, Gerald, and Noel T. Dowling: *Individual Rights in Constitutional Law,* Foundation Press, Mineola, 1970.

One of the two or three best casebooks in the field of individual rights.

Lewis, Anthony: *Portrait of a Decade,* Random House, New York, 1964.

A readable description of the civil rights revolution and of the role of the courts in it from the school segregation decisions of 1954 to the historic Civil Rights Act of 1964.

Lockard, Duane: *Toward Equal Opportunity: A Study of State and Local Antidiscrimination Laws,* Macmillan, New York, 1968.

This brief but useful paperback focuses on the politics and enforcement of antidiscrimination laws in the fields of employment, housing, and public accommodations.

Lockhart, William B., Yale Kamisar, and Jesse Choper: *Constitutional Rights and Liberties,* 3d rev. ed., West, St. Paul, 1970.

One of the two or three leading casebooks in the field of individual rights.

Miller, Loren: *The Petitioners,* World Publishing, Cleveland, 1967.

A fascinating history of the Supreme Court's decisions on the constitutional rights of Negroes from 1789 to 1965 written by the son of a man born into slavery. Loren Miller practiced law in California for twenty-five years, argued numerous discrimination cases before the Supreme Court, was a newspaper publisher and vice-president of the NAACP, and was a judge on the Los Angeles Municipal Court at the time this book was published.

Mitau, G. Theodore: *Decade of Decision: The Supreme Court and the Constitutional Revolution 1954–1964,* Scribner, New York, 1967.

An analysis of political and judicial responses to the complex problems of internal subversion, desegregation, reapportionment, school prayers, procedural rights, and demonstrations during the first decade of the Warren Court.

Myrdahl, Gunnar: *An American Dilemma: The Negro Problem and Modern Democracy,* rev. ed., Harper & Row, New York, 1962.

Gunnar Myrdahl's classic study of the Negro in the United States, first published in 1944, is still essential reading for students of race relations.

North, Arthur A., S. J.: *The Supreme Court: Judicial Process and Judicial Politics,* Appleton Century Crofts, New York, 1966.

Includes a useful analysis of the conflict over the meaning of the due process clause of the Fourteenth Amendment. The author's chapters on the nature of judicial review and the Warren Court's use of this power to reinterpret the equal protection and due process clauses amply demonstrate why the Court became the center of political controversy in the last two decades.

Spicer, George W.: *The Supreme Court and Fundamental Freedoms,* 2d rev. ed., Appleton Century Crofts, New York, 1967.

An analysis of the role of the Supreme Court in the protection of individual liberties. The author concentrates on the absorption of the First Amendment and of procedural rights into the Fourteenth Amendment, on the substantive guarantees of the First Amendment, on equal protection and voting rights, and on constitutional problems arising out of loyalty-security programs.

U.S. Commission on Civil Rights: *The Federal Civil Rights Enforcement Effort,* Washington, D.C., 1971.

A comprehensive analysis of the federal government's activities in the field of civil rights during the past three decades. Discusses the five civil rights laws passed by Congress between 1957 and 1968, executive orders and other actions of the executive branch, and judicial decisions by the Supreme Court and lower courts. This detailed treatment of federal efforts to lessen discrimination in education, employment, housing, voting, administration of justice, access to public accommodations, and participation in federally assisted programs concludes that federal departments and agencies have failed to carry out their responsibilities adequately.

Chapter 1: Literacy Tests and the Right to Vote

Aikin, Charles (ed.): *The Negro Votes,* Chandler, San Francisco, 1962.

A sourcebook of materials on discrimination in voting. Contains a general introduction to the subject, plus Supreme Court decisions on grandfather clauses, white primaries, and discriminatory gerrymanders.

Avins, Alfred: "Fifteenth Amendment and Literacy Tests: The Original Intent," 18 *Stan. L. Rev.* 808 (1966).

An analysis of the legislative history of the Fifteenth Amendment by a leading proponent of local control of voting requirements. Argues that the framers of the amendment contemplated use of literacy tests despite their possible discriminatory effects and that federal legislation suspending such tests is not a legitimate exercise of congressional power. See also Avins: "Literacy Tests and the Fourteenth Amendment: The Contemporary Understanding," 30 *Albany L. Rev.* 229 (1966).

Berman, Daniel M.: *A Bill Becomes a Law: the Civil Rights Act of 1960,* Macmillan, New York, 1962.

A brief, highly readable account of the political struggles over passage of the Civil Rights Act of 1960. Berman's book is a useful introduction for readers unfamiliar with the legislative process.

Bernhard, Berl I.: "The Federal Fact-Finding Experience—A Guide to Negro Enfranchisement," 27 *Law and Contemp. Prob.* 468 (1962).

This report by a former staff director of the U.S. Commission on Civil Rights contains an appraisal of experience under the Civil Rights Act of 1957 and a brief discussion of the 1960 Act.

Christopher, Warren M.: "The Constitutionality of the Voting Rights Act of 1965," 18 *Stan. L. Rev.* 1 (1965).

Detailed and highly informative discussion of the Voting Rights Act of 1965, focusing in particular on the suspension of literacy tests. Concludes that the act is not only constitutional but long overdue.

Ervin, Sam, Jr.: "Literacy Tests for Voters: A Case Study in Federalism," 27 *Law and Contemp. Prob.* 481 (1962).

Senator Sam Ervin of North Carolina, the Chairman of the Subcommittee on Constitutional Rights of the Senate Committee on the Judiciary, presents a cogent argument for the view that abolition of literacy tests threatens state control of the electoral process.

Havens, Charles W.: "Federal Legislation to Safeguard Voting Rights: The Civil Rights Act of 1960," 46 *Va. L. Rev.* 945 (1960).

Useful discussion of the legislative and legal history of the 1960 act. Includes material on the history of voting discrimination since the Civil War and on methods of voting discrimination during the 1950s.

Hearings Before the Senate Committee on the Judiciary on Voting Rights, 89th Cong., 1st Sess., 1965.

Testimony on the merits of the proposed Voting Rights Act of 1965. Includes a statement by Attorney General Katzenbach on the inadequacies of the 1957, 1960, and 1964 acts. See also the wealth of material contained in hearings held between 1955 and 1970 by the House Committee on the Judiciary and its subcommittees, the House Committee on Rules; the Senate Committee on the Judiciary, its Subcommittee on Constitutional Rights and Subcommittee on Constitutional Amendments, and the Senate Committee on Rules and Administration.

Key, V. O., Jr.: *Southern Politics*, Knopf, New York, 1949.

Although dated, Key's classic study of politics in the Southern states remains an excellent starting point for obtaining an understanding of the politics of racial conflict in the South.

Lewinson, Paul: *Race, Class, and Party: A History of Negro Suffrage and White Politics in the South*, Grosset & Dunlap, New York, 1964.

This study of suffrage discrimination focuses on the impact of white politics and class struggles on the political rights of black citizens.

Marshall, Burke: "Federal Protection of Negro Voting Rights," 27 *Law and Contemp. Prob.* 455 (1962).

In this article, President Kennedy's Assistant Attorney General in charge of the Civil Rights Division of the Department of Justice discusses the techniques of discrimination and intimidation used to deny the right to vote and the efforts of the Department of Justice to lessen voting discrimination.

Matthews, Donald R., and James W. Prothro: *Negroes and the New Southern Politics*, Harcourt, Brace & World, New York, 1966.

A careful, detailed analysis of the growing influence of Negro voters in Southern politics.

Price, H. Douglas: *The Negro and Southern Politics*, New York University Press, New York, 1957.

A useful study of the suffrage problem in Florida. Price examines the history of Negro voting, changes in registration, and the impact of such changes on campaigns and politics in general.

Tuttle, Elbert P.: "Equality and the Vote," 41 *N.Y.U. L. Rev.* 245 (1966).

The author, chief judge of the U.S. Court of Appeals for the Fifth Circuit, discusses the voting rights guarantee of the Constitution and many of the enforcement problems faced by the courts.

U.S. Commission on Civil Rights: *Political Participation*, Washington, D.C., 1968.

A detailed and lucid study of participation by blacks in Southern politics and elections during the years from 1965 to 1968. Stresses the great upsurge in voter registration, voting, and other forms of participation brought about as a result of the Voting Rights Act of 1965, but the report indicates that new barriers to full and equal political participation have been created to replace earlier discriminatory practices. See also the large amount of material on voting discrimination contained in other reports of the Commission on Civil Rights, notably its 1961 study entitled *Voting*.

Chapter 2: Free Speech in the Vietnam War

Alfange, Dean, Jr.: "Free Speech and Symbolic Conduct: The Draft Card Burning Case," 1968 *Sup. Ct. Rev.* 1.

Detailed analysis and criticism of the Supreme Court's decision in *United States v. O'Brien*. Alfange attempts to show that both the effect of the law and the intent of its framers was to limit free expression. The author concludes that the test employed by the Court in upholding the card-burning statute is inadequate since it does not distinguish clearly between expressive conduct entitled to First Amendment protection and conduct subject to regulation.

Chaffee, Zechariah, Jr.: *Free Speech in the United States*, Atheneum, New York, 1969.

The classic study of freedom of expression, first published by Harvard University Press in 1941. While Chaffee's book does not focus on the contemporary problem of the constitutionality of symbolic forms of expression, it does provide excellent background for understanding the history of the conflict between public order and freedom of speech as well as the development of First Amendment legal doctrine.

"Constitutional Law—Freedom of Speech—Desecration of National Symbols as Protected Political Expression," 66 *Mich. L. Rev.* 1040 (1968).

Discusses the extent to which the First Amendment protects individuals who desecrate the flag in order to protest particular public policies. Analysis of lower court decisions in *New York v. Radich* and *New York v. Street*.

Cord, Robert L.: *Protest, Dissent and the Supreme Court*, Winthrop Publishers, Cambridge, 1971.

Introductory essays and Supreme Court opinions on 1) war protests, 2) political association, participation, and free expression, 3) political expression in the courtroom and, 4) protests on both public and private property.

Denno, Theodore F.: "Mary Beth Tinker Takes the Constitution to School," 38 *Ford. L. Rev.* 35 (1968).

Discussion of a wide range of First Amendment questions related to expressive conduct in the context of the Supreme Court decision upholding the right of students to wear black armbands to school as a form of antiwar protest.

Douglas, William O.: *Points of Rebellion*, Random House, New York, 1970.

This brief book by Supreme Court Justice Douglas argues that American society has not been responsive to the need to eradicate poverty, segregation, inequitable laws, pollution, etc., and that civil disobedience may well be the only effective means of causing change. Douglas adopts the rhetoric of the New Left and condemns an undefined "Establishment" for the polarization which exists in contemporary America. Worthwhile reading because of the prominence of the author.

Emerson, Thomas I.: "Freedom of Expression in Wartime," 116 *U. Pa. L. Rev.* 975 (1968).

Discussion of draft card burning, flag desecration, and other forms of dissent by a leading authority on constitutional law. The author concludes that a strict distinction must be made between expression and action if the right of free expression is to be preserved. For a more detailed discussion of Professor Emerson's criticisms of First Amendment legal doctrine as well as an analysis of his own view of the meaning of the amendment, see his *Toward a General Theory of the First Amendment*, Random House, New York, 1966.

Fortas, Abe: *Concerning Dissent and Civil Disobedience*, New American Library, New York, 1968.

A general statement by former Supreme Court Justice Fortas of the fundamental conflict between freedom of speech and the necessity for public order. Fortas defends the rule of law and argues that significant changes have and will take place without resort to violence. He concludes that civil disobedience is justified only when it is nonviolent, when the law itself is the target of the protest, only if other laws are not broken, and only if the protesters are prepared to accept the judgment of the courts; any other protest attacks the rule of law itself and threatens to undermine the freedoms of all, including the dissenters themselves.

Gurr, Ted Robert: *Why Men Rebel,* Princeton, Princeton, N.J., 1970.

An outstanding study of civil violence emphasizing the psychological factors underlying civil unrest. Summarizes and synthesizes a wealth of materials on revolution and attempts to arrive at a general explanation of political violence. Includes a lengthy bibliography of experimental studies, case studies, and theoretical analyses of group conflict and resolution within societies. While not on the subject of symbolic expression, this book is a useful complement to knowledge of the law and politics of antiwar protests.

Henkin, Louis: "On Drawing Lines," 82 *Harv. L. Rev.* 63 (1968).

Attempts to outline criteria for expressive conduct that should receive First Amendment protection. The author, a professor at Columbia Law School, argues that if the conduct is intended as expression, if it communicates, and especially if the conduct is a commonly understood form of communication, it should be covered by the constitutional guarantee of free speech.

Puner, Nicholas W.: "Civil Disobedience: An Analysis and Rationale," 43 *N.Y.U. L. Rev.* 651 (1968).

Significant cases growing out of the civil rights movement are compared with cases stemming from antiwar protests. Includes a discussion of draft card burning and refusal to submit to induction into the armed services as forms of civil disobedience.

Summers, Marvin (ed.): *Free Speech and Political Protest,* Heath, Boston, 1967.

Presents a wide range of opinions on the conflict between freedom of expression and the need for public order. Includes case studies of antiwar protests.

Velvel, Lawrence R.: "Freedom of Speech and the Draft Card Burning Cases," 16 *Kan. L. Rev.* 149 (1968).

A good critique of the Supreme Court's reasoning in *United States v. O'Brien.* The author argues that burning a draft card is just as much the common man's way of getting his views across to citizens at large as participating in a civil rights demonstration. He concludes that a rule that such expressive acts lie beyond the First Amendment restricts the full value of free speech to those who are rich enough or famous enough to have access to the media.

Walzer, Michael: *Essays on Disobedience, War, and Citizenship,* Harvard, Cambridge, 1970.

A philosophical study of the nature of obligation to government and of the abandonment of such obligation under certain circumstances. This collection of essays on civil disobedience, conscientious objection, dissent, war, and revolution places some of the most perplexing issues of contemporary American life in a theoretical perspective.

Zinn, Howard: *Disobedience and Democracy: Nine Fallacies on Law and Order,* Random House, New York, 1968.

A response to Justice Fortas' *Concerning Dissent and Civil Disobedience,* which Zinn views as exemplary of the standard "liberal" view of civil disobedience. The author is an advocate of disobedience and believes that personal moral codes are more important than the rule of law. Professor Zinn has been a leading spokesman for the New Left position that meaningful change cannot take place without disobedience to law.

Chapter 3: Confessions, Self-Incrimination, and the Right to Counsel

Bator, Paul M., and James Vorenberg: "Arrest, Detention, Interrogation and the Right to Counsel: Basic Problems and Possible Legislative Solutions," 66 *Col. L. Rev.* 62 (1966).

Two leading authorities on criminal law analyze various aspects of the administration of justice and suggest ways in which certain procedural problems can be resolved.

Beaney, William M.: *The Right to Counsel in American Courts,* University of Michigan Press, Ann Arbor, 1955.

Although dated, Beaney's book is a useful starting place for information on the history of the right to counsel in federal and state courts and on the evolution of constitutional doctrine prior to the Warren Court.

Blumberg, Abraham S.: *Criminal Justice,* Quadrangle, Chicago, 1967.

A significant study of the organization and structure of American criminal courts by a Yale Law School professor. Focuses on the emergence and operation of a system in which due process has given way to efficiency and results.

Challenge of Crime in a Free Society, Washington, D.C., 1967.

The monumental report of the President's Commission on Law Enforcement and the Administration of Justice contains an enormous amount of information on crime, delinquency, drug abuse, the police, the courts, and correctional institutions. Includes more than 200 recommendations for combatting crime.

Crime and Justice in America, 2d rev. ed., Congressional Quarterly, Washington, D.C., 1968.

An extremely useful background report on many aspects of law enforcement. Although short, this report is filled with detailed information on violence in America, federal activities in 1967 and 1968, the important Omnibus Crime Control and Safe Streets Act of 1968, wiretapping, delinquency, gun controls, relevant Supreme Court decisions, and recommendations for improving the administration of justice.

Cray, Edward: *Big Blue Line: Police Power vs. Human Rights,* Coward-McCann, New York, 1967.

A writer for the American Civil Liberties Union of Southern California discusses more than 200 instances of police malpractice including cases involving coerced confessions. The author supports the decisions of the Warren Court restraining the power of the police.

Dowling, Donald C.: "Escobedo and Beyond: The Need for a Fourteenth Amendment Code of Criminal Procedure," 56 *J. Crim. L. C. & P. S.* 143 (1965).

Discusses the evolution of the *Escobedo* doctrine, the differing viewpoints on the Court, the issues left unresolved by the *Escobedo* decision, and suggests that Congress become involved in state criminal procedure by using its powers under the Fourteenth Amendment to define the requirements of due process of law.

English, Robert E.: "Lawyers in the Station House?" 57 *J. Crim. L. C. & P. S.* 283 (1966).

A state court judge expresses deep concern about the possible consequences of an extension of the *Escobedo* rule to require the presence of counsel at every interrogation.

Fellman, David: *The Defendant's Rights,* Rinehart, New York, 1958.

Although Fellman's book is dated, given the numerous developments in the field of criminal procedure during the 1960s, it is still an excellent reference work.

Griswold, Erwin N.: *The Fifth Amendment Today,* Harvard, Cambridge, 1955.

A strong defense of Fifth Amendment guarantees against arbitrary government by the former Dean of Harvard Law School.

Inbau, Fred E., and John E. Reid: *Criminal Interrogation and Confessions*, 2d rev. ed., Williams & Wilkins, Baltimore, 1967.

An important work on the law in regard to police interrogations and on techniques for successful interrogation. Inbau and Reid is used by many police departments, prosecuting attorneys, and teachers of criminology.

Kamisar, Yale: "Equal Justice in the Gatehouses and Mansions of American Criminal Procedure," in A. E. Dick Howard (ed.): *Criminal Justice in Our Time*, University of Virginia Press, Charlottesville, 1965.

An excellent statement of the argument for expanding the rights of suspects during interrogation by one of the leading authorities in the field. See also Professor Kamisar's other works on the subject of confessions, many of which are critical of the interrogation methods supported by Inbau and Reid.

Karlen, Delmar: *Anglo-American Criminal Justice*, Oxford University Press, New York, 1967.

Extremely useful comparison of the rights of individuals accused of crime and of the administration of justice in Great Britain and the United States.

Levy, Leonard Williams: *Origins of the Fifth Amendment: The Right Against Self-Incrimination*, Oxford University Press, New York, 1968.

A thorough investigation of the history of the protection against self-incrimination beginning with its origins in the thirteenth century.

Lewis, Anthony: *Gideon's Trumpet*, Random House, New York, 1964.

Dramatic, award-winning account of the case in which the Warren Court reversed an earlier decision and established the right to counsel in all felony prosecutions. This book is also an outstanding introduction to the legal process.

Poverty and the Administration of Federal Criminal Justice, Washington, D.C., 1963.

The comprehensive report of the Attorney General's Committee on Poverty and the Administration of Criminal Justice.

Skolnick, Jerome H.: *Justice Without Trial: Law Enforcement in Democratic Society*, Wiley, New York, 1966.

This empirical study examines the day-to-day thoughts and actions of policemen in order to get at the reality underlying the structure of constitutional rights and judicial decisions. Skolnick's book provides many insights into the dynamics of law enforcement.

Sutherland, Arthur E., Jr.: "Crime and Confession," 79 *Harv. L. Rev.* 21 (1965).

Harvard Law Professor Sutherland defends decisions of the Supreme Court against attacks from law officers and others who believe the balance has been tipped against law enforcement agencies.

Tompkins, Dorothy C. (comp.): *The Confession Issue: From McNabb to Miranda: A Bibliography*, University of California Institute of Governmental Studies, Berkeley, 1968.

Trebach, Arnold S.: *The Rationing of Justice: Constitutional Rights and the Criminal Process*, Rutgers, New Brunswick, 1964.

A critique of the American system of criminal justice, especially useful for material on problems faced by indigents accused of crimes.

U.S. Commission on Civil Rights: *Justice*, Washington, D.C., 1961.

This book, volume five of the comprehensive *1961 Report of the U.S. Commission on Civil Rights*, provides an excellent overview of problems in the administration of justice.

Chapter 4: Federal Open Housing Legislation

Abrams, Charles: *Forbidden Neighbors: A Study of Prejudice in Housing*, Harper, New York, 1955.

A classic study of discrimination in housing by one of the leading authorities in the field, a former administrator of the U.S. Housing Authority. Contains historical background, case studies, and suggestions for individual and government action. See also other publications by the same author.

Casstevens, Thomas W.: *Politics, Housing and Race Relations: California's Rumford Act and Proposition 14*, University of California Institute of Governmental Studies, Berkeley, 1967.

A detailed case study of the politics of open housing in California.

————: *Politics, Housing and Race Relations: The Defeat of Berkeley's Fair Housing Ordinance*, University of California Institute of Governmental Studies, Berkeley, 1965.

Factual study of the background of the 1963 ordinance, the part it played in local politics, and an analysis of voting on the ordinance.

Commission on Race and Housing: *Where Shall We Live? Report of the Commission on Race and Housing*, University of California Press, Berkeley, 1958.

Conclusions of a three-year study made by an independent citizens' group formed to inquire into problems of housing discrimination.

Housing a Nation, Congressional Quarterly, Washington, D.C., 1966.

A detailed study of housing in the United States. Includes material on quality and availability of housing, urban renewal, public housing, discrimination, and federal statutes and agencies.

Eley, Lynn W., and Thomas W. Casstevens (eds.): *The Politics of Fair-Housing Legislation: State and Local Case Studies*, Chandler, San Francisco, 1968.

Eight case studies of attempts to combat housing discrimination in five states and cities. Contains an analysis of the history, politics, and future of open housing legislation.

Glazer, Nathan, and Davis McEntire (eds.): *Studies in Housing and Minority Groups*, University of California Press, Berkeley, 1961.

Presents the findings of seven studies of housing discrimination prepared for the Commission on Race and Housing.

Grier, George, and Eunice Grier: *Equality and Beyond: Housing Segregation and the Goals of the Great Society*, Quadrangle, Chicago, 1966.

The authors examine the development of segregated housing, its impact on other areas of urban life and offer suggestions for improving the situation. A compact, readable summary of the problem of discrimination in housing.

————: *Privately Developed Interracial Housing: An Analysis of Experience*, University of California Press, Berkeley, 1960.

A study of the fifty known integrated developments constructed between 1946 and 1955. Presents practical reasons for interracial housing.

Hahn, Harlan: "Northern Referenda on Fair Housing: The Response of White Voters," 21 *Western Pol. Q.* 483 (1968).

Summation and analysis of data on the public response to open housing measures. Disturbing data for proponents of housing integration.

Housing and Home Finance Agency: *Equal Opportunity in Housing: A Series of Case Studies*, Washington, D.C., 1964.

————: *Fair Housing Laws . . . Summaries and Text of State and Municipal Laws*, Washington, D.C., 1964.

————: *Housing of the Non-White Population, 1940 to 1950,* Washington, D.C., 1952.

This volume and its successor, *Non-White Population and Its Housing: The Changes Between 1950 and 1960,* provide detailed data on the kind and quality of housing occupied by nonwhites and on changes in minority-occupied housing between 1940 and 1960.

McEntire, Davis: *Residence and Race: Final and Comprehensive Report to the Commission on Race and Housing,* University of California Press, Berkeley, 1961.

A thoroughly researched report on where members of minority groups live, on minorities in the housing market, and on the relationship between government and housing discrimination.

Messner, Stephen D. (ed.): *Minority Groups and Housing: A Selected Bibliography, 1950–1967,* Center for Real Estate and Urban Economic Studies, University of Connecticut, Hartford, 1967.

Pearl, Lawrence, and Benjamin B. Terner: "Survey: Fair Housing Laws—Design for Equal Opportunity," 16 *Stan. L. Rev.* 849 (1964).

Reviews the scope of eighteen state open housing laws and relevant judicial decisions. The authors suggest ways in which most antidiscrimination laws can be strengthened.

Taeuber, Karl E., and Alma F. Taeuber: *Negroes in Cities,* Aldine, Chicago, 1965.

A carefully researched study of urban residential segregation. Contains a great deal of valuable statistical data.

U.S. Commission on Civil Rights, *Housing,* Washington, D.C., 1961.

Volume four of the comprehensive *1961 Report of the U.S. Commission on Civil Rights.* See also other materials published by the Commission on the subject of discrimination in housing.

Vose, Clement E.: *Caucasians Only: The Supreme Court, the NAACP, and the Restrictive Covenant Cases,* University of California Press, Berkeley, 1959.

Focuses on the fight between white property owners, associations, and real estate boards and the NAACP over the legality of restrictive covenants. A useful study of the origins of the doctrine that judicial enforcement of discrimination is state action forbidden by the Fourteenth Amendment.

Weaver, Robert C.: *The Negro Ghetto,* Harcourt, Brace, New York, 1948.

A seminal study of housing discrimination by the former secretary of the Department of Housing and Urban Development. This book is still an excellent introduction to the subject.

Chapter 5: Federal Aid to Parochial Education

Bailey, Stephen K., and Edith K. Mosher: *ESEA: The Office of Education Administers A Law,* Syracuse University Press, Syracuse, 1968.

An outstanding analysis of the politics of the Elementary and Secondary Education Act of 1965 and of the efforts of the Office of Education to implement the law. Detailed study of bureaucratic decision making.

Blanshard, Paul: *Religion and the Schools: The Great Controversy,* Beacon Press, Boston, 1963.

Written from the viewpoint of a Protestant who believes in strict separation of church and state, this book discusses many important issues including public aid to parochial schools and their students in the form of free bus transportation, free textbooks, and payment of teachers' salaries.

Callahan, Daniel J. (ed.): *Federal Aid and Catholic Schools,* Helicon Press, Baltimore, 1964.

A compilation of ten articles on the issue of federal aid to parochial schools. The editor has attempted to produce a balanced rather than one-sided volume.

Choper, Jesse H.: "Establishment Clause and Aid to Parochial Schools," 56 *Calif. L. Rev.* 260 (1968).

Thorough consideration of the question of public aid to parochial schools by a professor of constitutional law at the University of California at Berkeley.

Drinan, Robert F.: *Religion, the Courts, and Public Policy*, McGraw-Hill, New York, 1963.

A strong presentation of the views of Father Drinan on the issues involved in the controversy over aid to parochial schools. The author was professor of law and dean of the law school at Boston College and is now a member of the House of Representatives.

Eidenberg, Eugene, and Roy D. Morey: *An Act of Congress*, Norton, New York, 1969.

A lucid description and analysis of the politics of federal aid to parochial education focusing on the controversy over the Elementary and Secondary Education Act of 1965.

Howe, Mark DeWolfe: *The Garden and the Wilderness: Religion and Government in American Constitutional History*, University of Chicago Press, Chicago, 1965.

An excellent sourcebook on the origins of the religion clauses of the First Amendment. Challenges many commonly accepted generalizations about the meaning of the establishment clause.

Kauper, Paul G.: "Church, State and Freedom: A Review," 52 *Mich. L. Rev.* 829 (1954).

An extensive, analytical review of Leo Pfeffer's *Church, State and Freedom*.

Kerwin, Jerome G.: *Catholic Viewpoint on Church and State*, Hanover House, Garden City, New York, 1960.

Clear presentation of the stance taken by many Catholics on the issue of aid to parochial schools.

Kurland, Philip B.: *Religion and the Law: Of Church and State and the Supreme Court*, Aldine, Chicago, 1962.

Brief analytical study of the meaning and application of the religion clauses of the Constitution by a noted constitutional law scholar. Includes thought-provoking criticism of relevant Supreme Court decisions.

Oaks, Dallin H. (ed.): *The Wall Between Church and State*, University of Chicago Press, Chicago, 1963.

An excellent collection of essays on the pros and cons of critical church-state issues, including public aid to sectarian schools.

Pfeffer, Leo: *Church, State and Freedom*, rev. enl. ed., Beacon Press, Boston, 1967.

Professor Pfeffer, one of the country's leading authorities on church-state issues and a strong advocate of strict separation, focuses on the historical and constitutional dimensions of the freedom of religion and establishment clauses and discusses questions raised by Supreme Court decisions and federal programs.

Powell, Theodore: *The School Bus Law: A Case Study in Education, Religion, and Politics*, Wesleyan, Middletown, Conn., 1960.

Thorough analysis of the 1957 Connecticut law authorizing bus transportation for private school students at public expense.

Stokes, Anson Phelps: *Church and State in the United States*, 3 vols., Harper, New York, 1950.

A monumental collection of data on church-state relations throughout American history and a detailed analysis of their meaning from the perspective of a leading proponent of strict separation. Contains an extensive bibliography. For easier reference, see the one volume condensation of this classic study edited by Leo Pfeffer and published under the same name by Harper and Row in 1964.

Tussman, Joseph: *The Supreme Court on Church and State*, Oxford University Press, New York, 1962.

Includes an introductory essay and major Supreme Court decisions on the freedom of religion and establishment clauses.

Van Alstyne, William W.: "Constitutional Separation of Church and State: The Quest for a Coherent Position," 57 *Am. Pol. Sci. Rev.* 865 (1963).

This useful article describes the standards applied by the Supreme Court as of 1963, discusses questions left unresolved by Court decisions, and suggests possible answers to these questions.

Ward, Leo R.: *Federal Aid to Private Schools*, Christian Classics, Westminster, Md., 1964.

A documented analysis and defense of Federal aid to parochial and other private schools.

Chapter 6: De Facto Segregation and the Fourteenth Amendment

"Affirmative Integration: Studies of Efforts to Overcome De Facto Segregation in the Public Schools—A Symposium," 2 *Law and Soc. Rev.* 11 (1967).

Contains individual articles on de facto segregation in Evanston, Berkeley, New Haven, Pasadena, St. Louis, Albany, San Francisco, and Chicago as well as a comparative analysis of integration activities in the eight cities.

Crain, Robert L.: *The Politics of School Desegregation: Comparative Case Studies of Community Structure and Policy-Making*, Aldine, Chicago, 1968.

Comparative analysis of the desegregation process in St. Louis, Newark, Buffalo, Baltimore, San Francisco, Pittsburgh, and other cities. The author attempts to identify the reasons some of the cities reduced de facto segregation with minimal friction while others became virtual battlegrounds.

Dentler, Robert A., Bernard Mackler, and Mary Ellen Warshauer (eds.): *The Urban R's: Race Relations as the Problem in Urban Education*, Praeger, New York, 1967.

Eighteen essays by educators, sociologists, and psychologists on urban education, intergroup relations, programs for minorities, achievement differences, and black children in northern cities. Contains statistical data on resistance to integration, on attitudes and school performance, on integration and achievement, etc. Although this book does not focus on the law and politics of de facto segregation, it does contain valuable material on the changing nature of urban education.

Edwards, Thomas Bentley, and Frederick M. Wirt (eds.): *School Desegregation in the North: The Challenge and the Experience*, Chandler, San Francisco, 1967.

Detailed examination of the response of ten communities to the challenge of de facto segregation. Focuses on New York City and three suburbs, Manhasset, Teaneck, and Englewood, and on six California communities, Sacramento, Berkeley, Riverside, San Bernardino, Mill Valley, Sausalito. Includes analytical chapters on the politics of desegregation and the social and psychological consequences of segregation based on race and social class.

Fiss, Owen M.: "Racial Imbalance in the Public Schools: The Constitutional Concepts," 78 *Harv. L. Rev.* 564 (1965).

An excellent article on the constitutional aspects of de facto segregation. Includes a discussion of the remedies available to school officials seeking to integrate schools. The author argues that school boards are constitutionally permitted to correct racial imbalance and that in some circumstances the equal protection clause may in fact require them to take corrective action.

Fuchs, Estelle: *Pickets at the Gates: The Challenge of Civil Rights in Urban Schools*, Free Press, New York, 1966.

Two separate studies to acquaint teachers, administrators, and others with some of the problems that arise in racially imbalanced schools. Part I is a case study of a confrontation between an inner city school principal and a black community. In Part II the author examines the 1965 New York City school boycott "Operation Shutdown" and reports on interviews with some of the black teenagers who participated in the boycott.

Harvard Educational Review: *Equal Educational Opportunity*, Harvard, Cambridge, 1969.

An examination of the American commitment to equal educational opportunity in the light of the record of educational failure revealed by the Coleman Report, *Equal Educational Opportunity*, and other social science research. Includes significant articles on the educational impact of school segregation as well as a summary of the Coleman Report itself.

Kaplan, John: "Segregation Litigation and the Schools—Part II: The General Northern Problem," 58 *Nw. U. L. Rev.* 157 (1963).

A useful analysis of the constitutionality of de facto segregation. In Part I of this two part article, published earlier in 1963, the author dissects the school segregation controversy in New Rochelle.

Mack, Raymond W. (ed.): *Our Children's Burden: Studies of Desegregation in Nine American Communities*, Random House, 1968.

Designed to supplement the statistical data contained in the Coleman Report, these studies focus on desegregation in large, medium, and small communities in the Northeast, Midwest, Southwest, and South.

"Racial Imbalance in the Public Schools—Legislative Motive and the Constitution," 50 *Va. L. Rev.* 465 (1964).

An extensive research note on the legal questions presented by the attack on de facto segregation. Discusses relevant constitutional principles, problems associated with developing adequate remedies for de facto segregation, the growing body of state law on the subject, and the possible constitutional limitations of the policies adopted by the courts or school officials in their efforts to promote integration.

"Symposium: De Facto School Segregation," 16 *Western Res. L. Rev.* 475 (1965).

An excellent collection of articles on the question of de facto segregation. Includes pieces by Federal Judge J. Skelly Wright, NAACP General Counsel Robert L. Carter, *Georgia Bar Journal* editor Charles J. Bloch, and others.

U.S. Commission on Civil Rights: *Civil Rights U.S.A.: Public Schools, Cities in the North and West, 1962, Staff Reports*, Washington, D.C., 1962.

This volume of reports submitted to the U.S. Commission on Civil Rights provides detailed data on public school segregation and the dynamics of efforts to integrate the schools of Philadelphia, Chicago, St. Louis, Highland Park, Michigan, and New Rochelle, New York.

———: *Education*, Washington, D.C., 1961.

Volume two of the comprehensive *1961 Report of the U.S. Commission on Civil Rights*. Includes material on the law of desegregation, on public school segregation in the North and West as well as in the South, and on the role of the Executive Branch in specific controversies. Also contains numerous recommendations of the Commission for encouraging desegregation.

———: *Racial Isolation in the Public Schools*, 2 vols., Washington, D.C., 1967.

A thorough and detailed study of racial imbalance. These volumes contain a wealth of information on the extent and causes of de facto segregation, on the impact of racial isolation on education, and on various means for alleviating the problem. Volume two consists primarily of working papers and statistical appendices.

Vieira, Norman: "Racial Imbalance, Black Separatism, and Permissible Classification by Race, 67 *Mich. L. Rev.* 1553 (1969).

A detailed analysis of the constitutional problem of classification by race, with particular reference to de facto segregation. The author criticizes judicial opinions supporting racial classifications for the purpose of correcting racial imbalance because of the failure of the courts to develop rules of law that would not only sustain corrective action but would differentiate it from invidious use of racial criteria.

Wright, J. Skelly: "Public School Desegregation: Legal Remedies for De Facto Segregation," 40 *N.Y.U. L. Rev.* 285 (1965).

An important article by Federal Judge J. Skelly Wright on the problem of de facto segregation in the schools. The author urges courts to rule that the Fourteenth Amendment covers de facto as well as de jure segregation, since children are compelled by statute to attend school.

INDEX